POLITICAL WRITINGS

Simone de Beauvoir

POLITICAL WRITINGS

Edited by Margaret A. Simons
and Marybeth Timmermann

Foreword by Sylvie Le Bon de Beauvoir

University of Illinois Press

Urbana, Chicago, and Springfield

Library of Congress Cataloging-in-Publication Data
Beauvoir, Simone de, 1908–1986
[Selections. English. 2012]
Political writings / Simone de Beauvoir; edited by Margaret A. Simons
and Marybeth Timmermann; foreword by Sylvie Le Bon de Beauvoir.
p. cm. — (The Beauvoir series)
Includes bibliographical references and index.
ISBN 978-0-252-03694-1 (cloth : acid-free paper)
I. Simons, Margaret A. II. Timmermann, Marybeth. III. Title.
PQ2603.E362A2   2012
844'.914—dc23   2011052712

The editors gratefully acknowledge the support of a grant from the
National Endowment for the Humanities, an independent federal
agency, and a Matching Funds grant from the Illinois Board of
Higher Education. The volume also received a translation grant from
the French Ministry of Culture.

IN MEMORY OF
VÉRONIQUE ZAYTZEFF AND
FREDERICK M. MORRISON

Contents

Foreword to the Beauvoir Series

Sylvie Le Bon de Beauvoir

TRANSLATED BY MARYBETH TIMMERMANN

It is my pleasure to take this opportunity to honor the monumental work of research and publication that the Beauvoir Series represents, which was undertaken and brought to fruition by Margaret A. Simons and the ensemble of her team. These volumes of Simone de Beauvoir's writings, concerning literature as well as philosophy and feminism, stretch from 1926 to 1979, that is to say throughout almost her entire life. Some of them have been published before, and are known, but remain dispersed throughout time and space, in diverse editions, diverse newspapers or reviews. Others were read during conferences or radio programs and then lost from view. Some had been left completely unpublished. What gives them force and meaning is precisely having them gathered together, closely, as a whole. Nothing of the sort has yet been realized, except, on a much smaller scale, *Les écrits de Simone de Beauvoir* (The Writings of Simone de Beauvoir), published in France in 1979. Here, the aim is an exhaustive corpus, as much as that is possible.

Because they cover more than 50 years, these volumes faithfully reflect the thoughts of their author, the early manifestation and permanence of certain of her preoccupations as a writer and philosopher, as a woman and feminist. What will be immediately striking, I think, is their extraordinary *coherence.* Obviously, from this point of view, *Les cahiers de jeunesse* (*The Student Diaries*), previously unpublished, constitute the star document. The very young 18-, 19-, 20-year-old Simone de Beauvoir who writes them is clearly already the future great Simone de Beauvoir, author of *L'invitée,* (*She Came to Stay*), *Pour une morale de l'ambiguïté* (*The Ethics of Ambiguity*), *Le deuxième sexe* (*The Second Sex*), *Les Mandarins* (*The Mandarins*), and *Mémoires* (*Memoirs*). Not only is her vocation as a writer energetically affirmed in these diaries, but one also discovers in them the roots of her later reflections. It is particularly touching to see the birth, often with hesitations, doubt, and anguish, of the fundamental choices of thought and existence that would have such an impact on so many future readers, women and men. Torments, doubt, and anguish are expressed, but also exultation and confidence in her strength and in the future—the foresight of certain passages is impressive. Take the one from June 25, 1929, for example: "Strange certitude that these riches will be welcomed, that some words will be said and heard, that this life will be a fountain-head from which many others will draw. Certitude of a vocation."

These precious *Cahiers* will cut short the unproductive and recurrent debate about the "influence" that Sartre supposedly had on Simone de Beauvoir, since they incontestably reveal to us Simone de Beauvoir *before* Sartre. Thus, their relationship will take on its true sense, and one will understand to what point Simone de Beauvoir was even more herself when she agreed with some of Sartre's themes, because all those lonely years of apprenticeship and training were leading her to a definite path and not just any path. Therefore, it is not a matter of influence, but an encounter in the strong sense of the term. They each *recognized themselves* in the other because each one already existed independently and intensely. One can all the better discern the originality of Simone de Beauvoir in her ethical preoccupations, her own conception of concrete freedom, and her dramatic consciousness of the essential role of the Other, for example, because they are prefigured in the feverish meditations, pen in hand, which occupied her youth. *Les cahiers* constitute a priceless testimony.

I conclude by thanking Margaret A. Simons and her team again for their magnificent series, which constitutes an irreplaceable contribution to the study and the true understanding of the thoughts and works of Simone de Beauvoir.

Acknowledgments

Simone de Beauvoir's *Political Writings* is dedicated to the memory of Véronique Zaytzeff and Frederick M. Morrison, who have made such important contributions in translating Beauvoir's works. This volume would not have been possible without the generous support of a Collaborative Research Grant from the National Endowment for the Humanities (NEH), an independent federal agency; a Matching Funds grant from the Illinois Board of Higher Education allocated by the Graduate School of Southern Illinois University Edwardsville (SIUE); and a translation grant from the French Ministry of Culture. We are very grateful to Nicole Garner for her assistance with the annotations to "Must We Burn Sade?"; to Kasia Leousis, reference librarian at the Washington University Library, for her help locating the publication information for "Right-Wing Thought Today"; and to Marianne Ahrne for the permission to publish the transcription of her documentary film *A Walk through the Land of Old Age.* We would like to extend warm thanks to Sylvie Le Bon de Beauvoir, coeditor of the Beauvoir Series, for her continuing support and encouragement; and a very special thanks to our longtime editor, Joan Catapano, who has been a constant champion of the Beauvoir Series.

INTRODUCTION

Margaret A. Simons

A volume chronicling almost three decades of Simone de Beauvoir's leftist political engagement may come as a surprise to readers more familiar with her multivolume autobiography, her writings in existentialist ethics, or her classic feminist essay, *The Second Sex*. But the texts collected here complement and enrich our understanding of Beauvoir's better known works, providing a new interpretive context for her autobiographical writing, prefiguring her later feminist activism (the subject of a forthcoming volume in the Beauvoir Series), and shedding new light on French intellectual history during the turbulent era of decolonization.

Among the many surprises in this volume are two newly discovered texts, translated here for the first time. "Poetry and Truth of the Far West" is a 1947 article written for the American francophone newspaper, *France-Amérique*, during Beauvoir's lecture tour of the States. Referring to Charlie Chaplin's film, "The Gold Rush," Beauvoir reflects on the French fascination with the Far West—both the historic lure of the gold fields and the glittering "modern reincarnation of these hopes, Hollywood." But, as Eleanore Holveck points out, Beauvoir's article, far from an apolitical travelogue, is a critique of the "illusion of abundance and free choice" presented in films and adver-

1

tisements by which "the dominant economic class in the United States has convinced its poorer citizens that they, too, can strike it rich."

The second forgotten text may be even more of a surprise. *A Walk through the Land of Old Age*, the transcription of a 1974 documentary film directed by the Swedish filmmaker Marianne Ahrne for Swedish television and written by Ahrne with Simone de Beauvoir and others, is one of Beauvoir's few collaborative works. The film draws on Beauvoir's analysis of the situation of the elderly in postwar France from her 1970 essay, *Old Age* (euphemistically titled *The Coming of Age* in the 1972 American edition).[1] Beauvoir, who appears throughout the film, was closely involved in the production of the film, which, as Oliver Davis explains "revisits many of the key locations of Beauvoir's treatise" and offers a critique of the state-run "nursing home as institution by drawing attention to the way in which 'care' is bound up with repressive treatment." The film continues Beauvoir's critical reflections on the ways in which apparently biological differences of gender, race, and, in this case age, are shaped by one's socioeconomic situation. But here, unlike *The Second Sex*,[2] Beauvoir herself is presented as an example of socioeconomic privilege, with her fluent narrative and scenes of her souvenir-filled apartment intercut with the barely articulate ramblings of people scarcely older than herself and confined to impersonal institutions.

Beauvoir's essay, "Must We Burn Sade?" first published in 1951–52, reprinted in her 1955 volume, *Privilèges* (Privileges), and presented here in a new, philosophically accurate translation, is widely known. But her defense of the Marquis de Sade, a misogynist eighteenth-century pornographer, as a "great moralist" can still be a surprise. Beauvoir hails Sade as a precursor of psychoanalysis and admires the defiant authenticity of his defense of an eroticism that proved irreconcilable with "his social existence," but—making a point that his thought was shaped by his privileged situation—she argues that Sade's claim of universality for his libertine ethics fails to recognize the extent to which his ethics reflects his situation as an aristocrat: "He was socially on the side of the privileged, and he did not understand that social inequality affects the individual even in his ethical possibilities." Yet Beauvoir shares some of Sade's metaphysical assumptions and in this study returns to her prewar interest in the problem of solipsism. Debra Bergoffen describes Sade as "Beauvoir's Janus-faced ally" who, like Beauvoir, "begins with the fact of our basic separateness and confronts the realities of our selfishness and injustice." But, Bergoffen explains, Beauvoir rejects Sade's conclusions, arguing that he "mistook power for freedom and misunderstood the meanings of the erotic desires of the flesh."

The biggest surprise of this volume of political writings for fans of Beauvoir's prewar texts might be that it exists at all—given her defiant rejection of politics in the May 24, 1927, entry in her student diary: "[W]hat value could I put on the search for humanity's happiness when the much more serious problem of its reason for being haunts me? I will not make one move for this earthly kingdom; only the inner world counts."[3] Beauvoir's leftist political sympathies in the late 1930s are apparent in her attack on bourgeois society in her 1937–39 short story cycle, *When Things of the Spirit Come First*. But the depth of her postwar political engagement might still come as a surprise to fans of her egoistic 1939–41 novel, *She Came to Stay*, the story of an unconventional solipsist who resorts to murder as a solution to the problem of the Other.

The key to Beauvoir's post–World War II political engagement is, of course, her experience of the war itself, an experience recounted in her *Wartime Diary* and in *The Blood of Others*, a novel set in the French Resistance and written during the Nazi Occupation.[4] Although Beauvoir escaped the worst horrors of the war—on the front lines or in the concentration camps—she lost friends murdered by the Nazis and found her own life profoundly changed. The Occupation that began in June 1940 confronted her with the realization that freedom, which she had assumed to be a metaphysical given, was contingent upon an economic and political situation that she had previously ignored. In her *Wartime Diary*, Beauvoir writes of joining the flood of refugees fleeing Paris and the invading army, with Sartre a prisoner or dead, and losing any sense of her self as author of her life story. Immersing herself in Hegel's *Phenomenology*, she tried to reconcile herself to being a passive witness to History. But her anguished concern for Sartre undermined her attempts to evade the realities of the war. Her life, she writes in a September 20, 1940, diary entry, was "nothing but a series of insomnia, nightmares, tears and headaches. [. . .] I vaguely see a map of Germany with a heavy barbed wire border [. . .], and then phrases I have heard, such as 'they are starving to death.'"[5] A turning point comes six months into the Occupation while Sartre (whom she describes as "absent, gagged") was still a prisoner.

Beauvoir's diary entry dated January 9, 1941, records her disgust at the growing evidence of French intellectual collaboration with the Nazis, evidence that initiates the transformation in her thought grounding her postwar political engagement:

"One idea that struck me so strongly in Hegel is the exigency of mutual *recognition* of consciousnesses—it can serve as a foundation for a social view of the world—the only absolute being this human consciousness, exigency of *freedom* of each consciousness in order for the recognition to be valid and free: recognition in love, artistic expression, action, etc. And at the same time, the existential idea that human reality *is* nothing other than what it *makes itself* be, that toward which it transcends itself. [. . .] And according to the other idea of Heidegger that the human species and I are the same thing, it's really *I* that am at stake. After reading a ridiculous and despicable issue of the *NRF*, I experienced this to the extent of feeling anguished. I am far from the Hegelian point of view that was so helpful to me in August. I have become conscious again of my individuality and of the metaphysical being that is opposed to this historical infinity where Hegel optimistically dilutes all things. Anguish. [. . .] To make oneself an ant among ants, or a free consciousness facing other consciousnesses. *Metaphysical solidarity* that I newly discovered, I, who was a solipsist. I cannot be consciousness, spirit, among ants. I understand what was wanting in our anti-humanism" (319–20).

The wartime transformation in Beauvoir's thought is evident in the two articles in this volume from 1945 reporting on conditions in Spain and Portugal, "Four Days in Madrid" and "Portugal under the Salazar Regime." Published in the Resistance newspaper, *Combat*, edited by Albert Camus, the articles reflect Beauvoir's political alignment with the postwar leftist coalition government of France—the Communists benefiting from having led the Resistance while the political right was discredited by their collaboration with the Nazis. In these two articles Beauvoir alludes to her experience of the near-starvation conditions of occupied France and exposes the "oppression and injustice" suffered by impoverished working people under fascist right-wing dictatorships in Spain and Portugal, surrounded by a wealth of food and luxury goods that they cannot afford. Eleanore Holveck writes that Beauvoir re-created the trip to Portugal in her 1954 novel, *The Mandarins*, through the eyes of her character Henri Perron. "Henri acknowledges that he had seen similar squalor before in his travels, but now it haunts him, and he can no longer ignore poverty." He promises himself to wage a campaign in the press to expose the political and economic exploitation, the terror, and the complicity of the clergy. "Like Perron," Holveck writes, "never again would Beauvoir devote herself to pure literature and ignore the misery of the majority of the human race."

During the 1950s, when the fighting in Korea signaled the beginning of the Cold War and a resurgent political right led France in futile battles to retain control of its colonies, Beauvoir produced a series of articles analyzing conservative thought (the essay on Sade is one of them). The title of the 1955 volume in which they were reprinted, *Privilèges*, highlights Beauvoir's focus on the ways in which conservative thought is shaped by the socioeconomic privilege of its thinkers. "Right-Wing Thought Today" (1955), the second of the three articles included in *Privilèges*, is an extension of Beauvoir's analysis in *The Second Sex* of the ways in which sexist thought is shaped by men trying—in bad faith—to justify their privileges in male-dominated societies. But her analysis here also surprisingly anticipates the three volumes of her autobiography published between 1958 and 1963 where she explores the ways in which her own thought was shaped by her privileged upbringing, perhaps explaining the harshness of her attacks in this article on thinkers whose penchant for idealism, justification of ethical egoism, and preoccupation with death characterize her own early work. Sonia Kruks points out that the article's "methodologically troubling" political "manichaeism," which "cuts uncomfortably across the grain of Beauvoir's less polemical essays on politics," also reflects the "increasingly polarized world of the Cold War" when Beauvoir became a "staunch fellow traveler" of the French Communist Party. But Kruks finds that the essay offers prescient insight into "the Eurocentric and masculinist tones of Western elite thought" with Beauvoir's "critique of meritocracy as a ruse that justifies privilege" and her critique of "the elitism of the cult of 'elegance'" that are still relevant today.

Readers may be surprised to find Beauvoir's 1955 defense of Sartre's philosophy, "Merleau-Ponty and Pseudo-Sartreanism," which is presented here in a revised translation, included in a volume of her political writings. But Beauvoir saw Maurice Merleau-Ponty's attack on Sartre's philosophy, to which her article is a response, as fundamentally political, a "bad faith" defense of bourgeois interests, as she explains in the foreword to *Privilèges* where this article was reprinted. As William Wilkerson explains in his introduction, Beauvoir's polemical article was written in response to a political confrontation between Sartre and Merleau-Ponty. In 1952 Sartre published "a strident defense of both communism and the party's role in creating the society of the future" while Merleau-Ponty retreated from Marxism, resigned as political editor of *Les temps modernes*, and in 1955 published an article arguing that Sartre's ontology in *Being and Nothingness* is irreconcilable with communism. In her article, as Wilkerson explains, Beauvoir comes to Sartre's defense, arguing, with some justification, that Merleau-Ponty misreads Sartre and ignores his postwar development as a thinker. But Wilkerson calls our attention to the final pages of the essay, where he observes that Beauvoir drops the defense of Sartre and engages Merleau-Ponty's political thinking directly: "here we find a truly provocative dialogue, one that reveals Beauvoir's own political thinking at this critical moment in history."

In 1960 Beauvoir emerged on the political stage for the first time as a public figure in the struggle against French colonialism, as recounted in her 1962 preface to *Djamila Boupacha*. Coauthored by Beauvoir and Gisèle Halimi, *Djamila Boupacha* recounts the defense of a young, female Algerian freedom fighter imprisoned and tortured during the 1954–62 war of independence fought by Algeria. As Julien Murphy points out, Beauvoir, who "led the charge of marshalling public opinion" in support of Djamila Boupacha's case in 1960, "became a prominent force against the use of torture in the French internment camps in Algeria." Murphy reports that Beauvoir's active involvement in the case brought a dramatic change in Beauvoir's life, although one that, Murphy notes with surprise, is barely mentioned in her autobiography. Taking on a public role despite its dangers broke down Beauvoir's "rage and disillusionment" over the war, fueled by her shameful sense of unjustifiable privilege, and replaced them with a warmth of shared efforts and hopes that she found in the growing antiwar movement. Beauvoir's public involvement in the Boupacha case might thus be seen as laying the groundwork for her active political engagement in the women's movement in the 1970s.

Another surprise in this volume might be the wide range of political issues in which Beauvoir was engaged, as in her 1971 article, "In France Today, Killing Goes Unpunished," which exposes the injustice of a suspended sentence for a factory owner whose flagrant disregard for safety regulations led to the death and disfigurement of fifty-seven of his female workers in a factory fire. As Karen Shelby notes, when Beauvoir asserts of the factory inspectors that "[t]*hey look the other way*," "she is implicitly asking her readers if they too will look the other way" in such cases. The article ends with a militant call to workers to make their owners comply with safety measures: "do not let your exploiters play with your health and your life." Beauvoir's political focus on women in her defense of Djamila Boupacha and in her article calling for justice for the female factory workers is also evident in "Syria and Its Prisoners," her 1973 *Le monde* article calling on Syria to release the names of Israeli prisoners of war and agree to a prisoner exchange following the Yom Kippur War—an appeal addressed in part to the mothers of Syrian soldiers.

As a leftist Beauvoir's defense of Israel might be surprising, but arising from her memories of the Holocaust, her support was steadfast, if not uncritical, as evidenced by the four short texts in this volume. Susan Suleiman writes that these four texts, written over a twenty-year period, together "offer an excellent glimpse into the evolution of French public discourse about the Holocaust and about Israel." After the war, Suleiman explains, France "made no special effort to recognize the specific experience of Jewish deportees." Jean-François Steiner's 1966 "non-fiction novel," *Treblinka*, for which Beauvoir wrote the preface, included here, was "one of the first attempts, in France, to give a literary representation of Jewish suffering—as well as of Jewish heroism—during the Holocaust." Ten years later, in "Solidarity with Israel: A Critical Support," Beauvoir's May 1975 speech to a left-wing Jewish group, she takes what Suleiman describes as a courageous position at odds with the leftist orthodoxy. Arguing for what is now called the two-state solution, Beauvoir, according to Suleiman, provides insights into "the negative effects of isolation and fear of insecurity on Israeli politics" that may "prevent Israel from attending to social problems that demand attention," and "offers an extremely nuanced and still timely analysis" of the Left's "vehement condemnation of Israel and its unconditional sympathy for the Palestinians." Finally, in 1985, at a time, as Suleiman explains, when "Jewish memory" had become an established concept in French public discourse, Beauvoir wrote the preface to the transcription of Claude Lanzmann's film *Shoah*, lauding as a major artistic achievement this effort to "make the Holocaust *present* to its viewers." Written only months before her death in 1986, the preface is also evidence of Beauvoir's own enduring political engagement.

NOTES

1. Simone de Beauvoir, *La vieillesse* (Paris: Gallimard, 1970); trans. Patrick O'Brian, *The Coming of Age* (New York: G. P. Putnam, 1972).

2. Simone de Beauvoir, *Le deuxième sexe* (Paris: Gallimard, 1949); trans. Constance Borde and Sheila Malovany-Chevalier, *The Second Sex* (New York: Knopf, 2010).

3. Simone de Beauvoir, *Diary of a Philosophy Student: Volume 1, 1926–27*, ed. Barbara Klaw et. al., trans. Barbara Klaw (Urbana: University of Illinois Press, 2006), 264.

4. See my introduction to Simone de Beauvoir's *Wartime Diary* (Urbana: University of Illinois Press, 2009), 1–33.

5. Simone de Beauvoir, *Wartime Diary*, trans. Anne Deing Cordero, ed. Margaret A. Simons and Sylvie Le Bon de Beauvoir (Urbana: University of Illinois Press, 2009), 316.

Political Reporting from Spain, Portugal, and the United States

INTRODUCTION

by Eleanore Holveck

These reports from Spain, Portugal, and the United States from 1945 to 1947 reflect a change in Simone de Beauvoir's view of her own role as a writer and intellectual in relation to politics. Beauvoir often described herself up to the 1930s as an apolitical, idealistic Kantian, a solitary individual content to exercise her own petty bourgeois freedom as a teacher and writer and eager to take her place among the great writers of her culture. For example, Françoise and Pierre in Beauvoir's *She Came to Stay* (1943) are devoted to an ahistorical ideal, timeless Art and Beauty even as they present the play "Julius Caesar." But World War II completely changed Beauvoir's point of view, forcing her to take into account the concrete experience of actual human beings struggling to act freely in situations of oppression.

Beauvoir's writings from 1945 to 1947 reflect this turn to the concrete political. *The Blood of Others* (1945) is a novel concerned with the French labor movement up to the time of the Resistance; her essay, *Pyrrhus and Cineas* (1944), the play, *Les bouches inutiles* (The Useless Mouths), and her novel, *All Men Are Mortal* (1946) reflect Beauvoir's historical, political interest back to the medieval period. Working on the political and literary journal she helped to establish, *Les temps modernes*, Beauvoir wrote political essays such as "Moral Idealism and Political Realism" and "An Eye for an Eye." The political reports we have here not only echo these interests; they show a development toward her theory of free choice in *The Ethics of Ambiguity* (1947), an early use of the method she uses in *The Second Sex* (1949), and her turn to the use of writing as an act of collective responsibility, as testimony, in *The Mandarins* (1954).

In the fall of 1944, Albert Camus, who had worked with a Resistance cell, asked Sartre to write an eyewitness account of the Liberation of Paris for its newspaper, *Combat*. Deirdre Bair reports that Beauvoir explained that she actually wrote these accounts, because "Sartre was too busy."[1] In any case Beauvoir did write the reports in *Combat* from Spain and Portugal printed here using the pseudonym Daniel Secretan, because she did not want to harm her brother-in-law, Lionel de Roulet, who was working with the French Institute in Lisbon.

These reports from Spain and Portugal reveal Beauvoir's attempt to grapple with the problem of the place of the intellectual in a Marxist world characterized by class conflict. In his *Introduction to the Reading of Hegel*, Alexandre Kojève argues that consciousness as nothingness realizes itself, literally makes itself real, i.e., exists in time, through labor as action on material. Writers and artists, however, do not negate matter. In the fight to the death for recognition that characterizes the world of master and slave, the writer-intellectual is neither. The writer-intellectual can conceive of the time when there will be neither master nor slave, but her synthesis is an abstract conception; it is purely verbal, and, in effect, an empty, useless illusion.

Hence, in her political reports, Simone de Beauvoir seems to content herself with pointing out the intellectual's dilemma concerning the contradictions between the haves and have-nots by the use of striking images. In "Four Days in Madrid," as Beauvoir both enters and leaves the city, she notes the City University. It is bombed, almost destroyed, yet it may be rebuilt. Is this monument to human knowledge the ruin of the past or the way to a free future? Intellectual knowledge is at a crossroad. Her report emphasizes the contradictions in a capitalist country ruled by a right-wing dictatorship. On the wide boulevards there are stores filled with luxury goods that remind her of the prewar Faubourg St. Honoré in Paris. First, Beauvoir lists in great detail the luxury foods available. Then, however, she gives the actual cost of the foods, which she measures in the daily wages of laborers. She concludes that workers cannot afford eggs, milk, meat, vegetables, or fruit. She goes on to describe in painful detail the "Faubourgs de la misère," the poor outlying sections of Madrid such as Tetuan, which are the neighborhoods of those who live on the crumbs from the master's table. She focuses on children and women. Her procedure anticipates her Husserlian method in *The Second Sex* in that she outlines concepts such as abundance and neutrality and then traces the abstract meanings back to the evidence, the grounding actual experiences. In the language of American pragmatism, she takes an ideal term back to its cash value.

Finally, she ends with the thought that despite their lack of material necessities, poverty has not destroyed the Spanish people's love of life nor their desire for liberty, themes she will develop in *The Ethics of Ambiguity*. The concrete love of life and freedom, the joy of existence, underlies all human effort and should be the basis of all governments. Beauvoir emphasizes that even though all dissent is brutally punished, some men in Spain strive to exercise their freedom. To face death in order to live is a free, albeit heartbreaking, choice.

Beauvoir's report from Portugal is even more grim; the image that expresses the social situation is a cemetery where the extravagant tombs of distinguished, wealthy citizens contrast with the plain placards, bearing only numbers, which grace the bare plots of the poor. Here love of life and freedom are so impoverished that only tombs and numbers remain. Beauvoir's descriptions of the lives of children and her statistics are staggering, e.g., out of seven million people only seventy thousand have food. In her Prix Goncourt novel, *The Mandarins* (1956), Beauvoir re-created this trip to Portugal through the eyes of her characters Henri Perron and Nadine Dubreuilh. At first Perron is dazzled by the luxury goods available in the stores of Lisbon, but then, a group of government officials from pre-Salazar days arranges for Henri to see "a series of wretched hovels."[2] Henri acknowledges that he had seen similar squalor before in his travels, but now it haunts him, and he can no longer ignore poverty. "He promised that he would wage a campaign in the press in order to get the facts to the people. Political tyranny, economic exploitation, police terror, the systematic brutalization of the masses, the clergy's shameful complicity—he would tell everything."[3] Like Perron, never again would Beauvoir devote herself to pure literature and ignore the misery of the majority of the human race.

Many feminists have criticized Beauvoir for devoting so much time to Sartre's political travels and writings during the postwar period, claiming that this shows her feeling of intellectual inferiority or her emotional dependence on him. I would submit that these reports of actual people in pain reveal a true concern for political change, which her writings and activities with Sartre embody also. Without this political awareness we would not have *The Second Sex.*

One of the hot political debates in post–World War II France was whether to build political alliances with the Soviet Union's socialism or United States capitalism. In "Poetry and Truth of the Far West," we find Beauvoir's discussion of one of the fundamental cultural myths of the United States, a myth she finds in Charles Chaplin's "The Gold Rush." A silent version of this film appeared in 1925; an updated version with music and Chaplin's narration was produced in 1942. Beauvoir met Chaplin on her American tour in 1947.[4] The movie spins the tale of a poor, shy, "little man," who, after a series of amusing mishaps in the Klondike, eventually strikes gold, becomes a millionaire, and carries off the fetching heroine of the piece. To Beauvoir, shining Hollywood is the contemporary reincarnation of the dream of following the mirage of gold.

The reality is, however, artificial and dull. Hollywood films tend to be based on trite formulas. At the studio gates, striking carpenters and set decorators picket, warming their hands at wood fires in barrels, much like the vagrants in Paris. There is no nightlife in Hollywood, no conversation in cafés, no music, no dancing, no joy. The puritanism of Hollywood life is counteracted by Reno and Las Vegas. Nevada deals with its poverty by providing "services" like gambling, prostitution, and wedding chapels where one can obtain everything necessary for marriage, including divorce.

Many people in the United States can afford to travel, but this actually means mile after mile of bleak highways with cookie-cutter motels or trailer parks, hamburger stands, and Coca-Cola. By means of the myths of Hollywood and advertising, the dominant economic class in the United States has convinced its poorer citizens that they, too, can strike it rich; in the meantime they are pacified by the empty illusion of abundance and free choice.

Beauvoir ends her article by saying that readers should experience the Far West themselves and that it would take a book to describe more of what she saw; this book was of course *America Day by Day* (1948). In more detail, Beauvoir describes people she met and liked, numerous trips all over the United States, and both the good and the bad of American culture. But there is something haunting about the images she conjures up in the articles here. In the California mountains framed by the camera to look like India or Switzerland; in the desert that Von Stroheim used to exemplify death, the heart of solitude, in his film "Greed;" in Death Valley with its carcasses of wagon trains; and in ghost towns like Carson City, Beauvoir sees a world more distant than the Stone Age, an age where men followed the dream of gold. For her, obviously, the dream is over.

NOTES

1. Deirdre Bair, *Simone de Beauvoir: A Biography* (New York: Summit, 1990), 293. On the series of seven articles by Sartre on the Liberation of Paris, see also Michel Contat and Michel Rybalka, *The Writings of Jean-Paul Sartre, Vol. 1: A Bibliographical Life*, trans. Richard McCleary (Evanston, Ill: Northwestern University, 1974), 100: "Note that in spite of the opening sentence, 'I am only telling what I saw,' Simone de Beauvoir's collaboration gave Sartre a certain ubiquity."

2. Simone de Beauvoir, *Les Mandarins*, trans. Leonard M. Friedman as *The Mandarins* (Cleveland: World Publishing Co., 1956), 97.

3. Friedman, trans., *The Mandarins*, 98.

4. Simone de Beauvoir, *America Day by Day*, trans. Carol Cosman (Berkeley: University of California Press, 1999), 296.

FOUR DAYS IN MADRID

by Simone de Beauvoir

TRANSLATION AND NOTES BY MARYBETH TIMMERMANN

By ten o'clock in the morning, we have left the dark mass of the Escurial [*sic*] behind us and have crossed through Paravelo, which was devastated by the civil war, and where all the houses are still in ruins.[1] Now the train is crossing a rocky plateau covered with white frost. And suddenly, with no suburbs to announce it, Madrid surges up. Looking through the door, I see the sections of a large gutted building to the left above the train station; it is the outermost University residence hall.

"Taxi!" One single word, and instantly I've made a leap through time. I am transported into a large pre-war city: alongside the roadway filled with taxis and cars, masses of crowded pedestrians wait for the signal to rush across the street, and the sidewalks are dark with people. Lining the Alcalá and the Gran Via from top to bottom are dazzlingly luxurious shops: there are slippers, leather purses, silk stockings, dresses, ties, raincoats, watches, jewels, baskets of candied fruit, boxes of chocolate, cloth, suits, shirts, etc.[2] I don't remember the windows on the Faubourg-St-Honoré being more brilliant at the time of their splendor.[3] In the bars, cafés, and large pastry shops, coffee with cream

"Quatre jours à Madrid," *Combat*, April 14–15, 1945: 1–2, © Sylvie Le Bon de Beauvoir.

and chocolate flow freely. In theory, sugar and bread are rationed, but the famous phrase, "If they don't have bread, let them eat cake," applies exactly here. The rich upper-class easily do without bread; instead they eat little muffins made with milk that are called "Swissos," croissants, cream-filled cakes, and the cafés and pastry shops are allowed to supply sugar at their discretion. In theory, the restaurants are regulated, but in reality all the restaurants, in full view of everyone, serve every customer whatever he desires to order.

The New Neutrality

Dazed and dazzled, eyes blinking, I go up towards the Puerta del Sol.[4] On the way I notice a window devoted to German propaganda. Enormous photographs show a German woman at work and the Volksturm [sic], smiling widely, crowding into the draft offices.[5] Heroic phrases promise victory in big black letters. Not far from there, there is also an English propaganda office. Everyone knows that this symmetry is a lie and how much help Spain still provides to Germany. But what I learn here is how much the Gestapo has reigned here in Madrid as mistress. For example, it has demanded and obtained the expulsion of an 80 year old Polish bishop and several other leading Polish figures. On the other hand, their efforts to create a Spanish anti-Semitism, through press campaigns and every type of propaganda, have been in vain. There are no Jews in Spain since they were all expelled in the sixteenth century, and the colony created by the refugees in the East is seen by the people of this Peninsula as Spanish, not Jewish. A great tenderness is even felt for them because they have conserved the most ancient Spanish traditions intact. Now, the most stubborn German sympathizers cynically admit that the moment has come to "turn their coats" and newspapers that I have seen observe a strict neutrality.

The Apparent Abundance

I pass by the wooden palisades that do little to hide the debris of two large buildings pulverized during the civil war, and I leave Alcalá with relief. This morning it was very cold out, but now the sun beats down on the wide avenue that is thick with a luxury that makes me uneasy. By the Calle Mayor, I enter into the narrow and shadowy streets that are the densely populated heart of Madrid.[6] Here also, there is an amazing abundance. The streets are noisy with people. Clusters of young people and children are hanging on to the back and sides of jolting trams. The shops are overflowing with clothing and food:

fruit sellers with their enormous bunches of bananas and baskets of oranges and mandarins; fish shops where pink shrimp and bloody tuna are being cut up; pork butcher shops where hams, sausages, skinned mutton, and also little lambs with curly black wool are hanging up, and suckling pigs cut in half are displayed on large dishes; there are enormous round cheeses, eggs, marzipans, quince pasta, chocolates, and raisins. Under each archway of the Mayor Plaza and all around the Cascarro Plaza, there are street vendors offering the passersby olives, almonds, Swissos, candy, pink sugar scissors, red sugar canes, griddle cakes, doughnuts of all kinds: flat, puffed, round, twisted. They also walk around with baskets full of cigarettes and small loaves of bread. Bread and cigarettes are rationed, but they are sold illegally in full view, with no precautions taken. A little further down, at the end of the Cascarro Plaza and in the neighboring streets, a sort of flea market that sells everything is permanently set up: fabric, linen, phonographs, alarm clocks, frying pans, bullfighting vests, shawls, forks, and popular novels with vibrantly colored covers. And all around the square, all along the streets there are dark, cool taverns decorated with azulejo tiles open for business. Enormous barrels full of wine can be seen in the darkness, with others suspended from the ceiling, and on the counter there are plates of shrimp, prawn, chips, and olives.

Three Days of Work for a Meal

So one's first impression upon arriving in Madrid is a feeling of extraordinary abundance, a generous and easy life, but the perspective changes as soon as one looks at the price of things. An unskilled worker or a maid makes about 9 pesetas a day, and a skilled laborer makes 12 to 15 pesetas, but in the Alcalá region, a meager meal costs 15 pesetas, a decent meal costs 25 pesetas, and a good one costs 40 to 50 pesetas. A coffee with cream costs 1.5 pesetas, a Swisso is 1 peseta, and a piece of cake is 2 pesetas. Comparing these prices to those of the black market in France, one can see that the ratio of prices to working class salaries is about the same. In both cases, a good meal in a restaurant represents two to three days' work and a cream puff is a sixth of a worker's daily salary. The difference is that the meal will be better and more varied in Madrid, and the cakes easier to find. Luxury is not clandestine; it is shown off. But this is an advantage only for the rich.

What is still much more important to note is that not only the merchandise sold on the Gran Via, but even those in the Calle Mayor are practically inaccessible to the working class. The most necessary supplies are rationed. As for bread, 100, 150 or 200 grams per day are allowed, according to a higher or lower income. If a worker is allowed 200 grams per day, he must buy any additional bread at a higher price than that of the tax. Potatoes and chickpeas, which are the base of Spanish food, are distributed in ridiculously insufficient quantities. On the black market, a kilogram of chickpeas can reach 10 pesetas. As for the non-rationed foods, an egg costs 1 peseta, a kilogram of meat is 20, tomatoes and bananas are 1.6 pesetas. So the working class eats neither eggs, nor milk, nor meat, nor green vegetables, nor fruits. I asked a friend, "What do they eat?" And he responded, "They eat their fingers," adding, "Go take a walk through Tetuan and Vallecas. That will inform you better than any figure will."

Suburban Misery

I took the subway and went to Vallecas. The subway is about the only thing that is not expensive in Madrid. The price of a ticket varies between 0.10 and 0.20, so even for the poor, transportation is reasonably priced and convenient. The next day I went for a walk in the suburb of Tetuan, at the northernmost edge of Madrid. Tetuan is built on hills facing the snowy Sierra. To the southeast of town, Vallecas is more industrial, surrounded by a landscape of railroads and factories. But there are profound similarities between these two suburbs. Running through both is a long avenue, straight and wide, where stores, taverns, and cinemas can be found, with big new buildings painted in soft colors rising up here and there. But should one go but 20 meters to the right or the left, one finds oneself at the heart of a strange region that is no longer a town, but is not quite a zone, and where walking through it for only an instant is enough to understand that although the regime has forbidden begging in Madrid, it has not lessened the misery by doing so. There are no longer streets, but paths of beaten-down earth lined with houses with red tiled roofs. Not a single shop to be found. Children walk bare footed and they are often dressed in rags, bare backs showing. Men and women wear espadrilles or slippers, and never shoes. Parents, children, goats and chickens are crammed inside the minuscule shacks whose dark interiors can be seen through the open doors. On cold days and rainy days (and the winter is harsh in Madrid, and the rains are violent), it must be terrible to live in these houses and to walk through the soaked dirt. On sunny days, they live outside.

On the thresholds, women wash their children, scrub their laundry and do their mending. They do a tremendous amount of washing, and faded, patched up rags can be seen everywhere drying in the sun among the chickens and goats, for the least bit of fabric is terribly expensive. They must wear their clothing until it is falling into pieces. Life is very hard for the women. There is no water in the houses and very small girls can be seen bringing water back from the fountain in buckets that are too heavy for them. There is no fuel, and in order to have a bit of coal one must stand in a long line. So the women have a harassed air about them. They are dressed in black, prematurely old and ugly due to worry. The men seem less bleak; they feel the harshness of their condition but they are not crushed by it. Because of that, the misery in Madrid, as profound as it is, is not sordid. Children play, young girls laugh, men talk amongst themselves in cheerful voices. Poverty has not made them into resigned livestock; they remain living men, men who rebel and hope.

Dying to Live

Upon leaving Tetuan, I went through the place that used to be the University campus. In the center of the city, there are few remaining traces of the civil war: a destroyed building on the Alcalá, some rubble near the Royal Palace and the North train station. But the University campus, pulverized by bombs and shells, is still far from being reconstructed. On this immense wasteland—bare, cracked and uneven—one can see sections of houses, parts of walls, decapitated buildings, and vast ruins of dry bricks, seasoned like old roman thermal baths. New buildings are being built. Already there are big, brilliantly new buildings rising up along the campus. But the small villas north of the wastelands are gutted, nearly demolished. Even in the campus, they blow up the remains of the houses and ruined walls; the war is still very close.

Close in the past or close in the future? Two days before my arrival in Madrid, three bombs exploded at the headquarters of a Falange syndicate, and two Falangists were killed.[7] A crowd of workers, employees and students gathered at a grandiose demonstration at their funeral, which they were required to attend in order to avoid serious sanctions. Seventeen communists were officially shot in retaliation, and who knows how many in secret? They shoot a lot in Madrid. They torture. There are neighborhoods, like near Lauriston Street during the Gestapo's reign, where the cries of the victims during the night prevent people from sleeping. On the other hand, each week there are one or many bombings.

A brief walk through Madrid is enough to feel how unstable the current order and balance are. Without freedom, the least effort towards justice is not seen even here. And yet, the Spanish people have lost none of their life and their ardor. They feel the oppression and the injustice. They want to live; they love life. Must it be that, once again, in the name of this will and this love, they will be obligated to choose death?

NOTES

1. *El Escorial* is an imposing and lavish monastery built by Philip II located to the northeast of Madrid. The civil war referred to here is the Spanish Civil War (1936–39), which was a military revolt against the Republican government of Spain. The Republicans were supported by the Communist Party, anarchists, and socialists, who fought among themselves and were eventually defeated by the fascist General Francisco Franco, who was backed by Germany, Italy, Spanish nationalists, and some conservative elements in the Catholic clergy and the military.

2. Alcalá and Gran Via are major commercial avenues running through Madrid.

3. The Faubourg-St.-Honoré is one of the most luxurious shopping streets in Paris, located in the 8th arrondissement.

4. The Puerta del Sol is the old city gate at the heart of Madrid, considered the geographical center of Spain.

5. The *Volkssturm*, which means "people storm," was a German national militia during the last months of the Nazi regime, ordered by Adolf Hitler in October 1944. All German males between the ages of 16 and 60 who did not already serve in some military unit were required to join.

6. *Calle Mayor* means "main street," and many of Madrid's famous plazas can be found along this street.

7. The Falange is the fascist party led by General Franco that assumed power in Spain after the Spanish Civil War (1939) and was later abolished (1977).

PORTUGAL UNDER THE SALAZAR REGIME

by Simone de Beauvoir

TRANSLATION AND NOTES BY MARYBETH TIMMERMANN

Out of 7 Million Portuguese People, Only 70,000 of Them Eat

> Lisbon in April: *I have been told that "certainly the Salazar regime is an authoritarian regime, but it is a tempered and paternal authoritarianism that has been able to avoid the excesses of fascism, and the works that Salazar has accomplished justify his having taken power; what he has done for Portugal is immense." I have visited Portugal; I have looked to see what Mr. Salazar had done for his people. And I have seen.*

To the traveler who, arriving in Lisbon, would like to discover an obvious and immediate image of the social situation in Portugal, I would advise going up to the Lato Oriental cemetery, perched on a hill that dominates the [river] Tage.

Upon entering through the central gate, one finds oneself at the heart of a strange city. Not a tomb is tipped over, and all the sepulchres are stony chapels often with an extravagant architecture, decorated with allegoric sculptures

"Le Portugal sous le régime de Salazar," *Combat*, April 23, 1945: 1–2; and April 24, 1945: 1–2; "from our special correspondent Daniel Secretan"; in *Les écrits de Simone de Beauvoir*, ed. C. Francis and F. Gontier (Paris: Gallimard, 1979), 317–23, © Éditions Gallimard, 1979.

and busts of the deceased; inside in neat rows are the caskets covered with lace or brocades, and the engraved letters upon the walls display the cascade of sonorous names that constitute a distinguished Portuguese person's name.

After walking for a long time through the long, treeless and flowerless avenues of this vertical cemetery, one reaches a wasteland divided into thousands and thousands of narrow rectangles by slight depressions in the ground. Stuck in each rectangle is a stake with a numbered red or black sign on it; no tombstones, no crosses, no names; this is the poor people's turf.

The violent and brutal contrast between the superb mausoleums and the anonymous pits roughly, but very accurately, illustrates the division of the Portuguese people into two sorts of men; those who eat and are considered as men, and those who do not eat and are livestock.

Out of the 7 million inhabitants in this country, there are 70,000 who eat.

I can still hear the voices of the children in Braga, at the door of a confectionary where I was buying some marzipans, "*We* don't eat." In the North, in the South, in Lisbon, in Porto, in the country, and in the fishing ports I found the same starving children.

The Portuguese people have always been poor. But since 1939 the cost of living has increased 140% and in some cases even more, since a suit that cost 350 escudos before the war now costs between 1,200 and 1,500. The salaries, however, have only increased 35%, and as a result, as delegate Quirino Mealha said to the National Assembly, "Many can not go to work because they don't have anything to eat. . . . They are lacking supplies that are essential to their nutrition either because of the absence of these supplies or because they can't withstand the prices, which are incompatible with their salaries."

These words take on their full weight if one considers that the National Assembly includes no one from the opposition party since the delegates are elected from the unique list of the unique party. So it was a creature of the regime who was led to speak these words. The same goes for the indignant words of delegate Carlos Borges: "When the workers complain of not finding the necessary supplies, we advise them to go find them on the black market!"

Indeed the ration of bread is in principle 500 grams per day, but in many regions it is absolutely impossible to find bread. Each inhabitant is allowed at least 400 grams of rice, two kilograms of potatoes, and five deciliters of oil. For the worker who earns 35 escudos a day, and often only 20 or 25, buying meat, eggs, milk, or fresh vegetables is out of the question; besides, all those are very rare.

Except in the center of the city where a collection of opulent stores can be found, there are hardly any food shops in the streets of Lisbon or Porto, and those few are very miserable. Nothing can be really found in abundance except for oranges and fish, which are carried by the fish sellers in large flat baskets balanced on their heads. The people are nourished almost exclusively by these little fish, which they cook without grease on charcoal stoves. Nowhere in Portugal can one smell that odor of hot oil which used to be so characteristic, but only the odor of grilled fish.

There exist regions where peasants eat nothing but black bread and soup made from the hard leaves of cabbage whose tall stalks and white flowers can be seen all over the countryside. They lack vitamins to the point that they are afflicted with a kind of scurvy that makes their teeth fall out, along with parts of their gums, their ears, and their noses.

The men for whom the State is directly responsible are no better treated than the others, on the contrary. A garrison was sent to Açores in exchange for arms that the British provided to Salazar. The soldiers are dying over there like flies. For many weeks, the doctor responsible for filling out the death certificates left a blank for the reason of these deaths. Ordered by the military governor to fill them out, he from then on wrote, "starved to death, . . . starved to death." He was, of course, put into prison.

I will only cite one fact on this subject. In order to feed the workers in the factories of Barreira, pigs' heads had been bought, and once they were delivered, it was discovered that they were crawling with worms. Instead of being thrown out, they were resold at a low price to the troops, and the military quartermaster bought them.

Poorly nourished. Poorly dressed. A law forbids walking barefoot within Lisbon, but as soon as they are in the suburbs, the people remove their worn-out old shoes to prevent wearing them out, and in all the rest of the country only the bourgeoisie wears shoes.

It is true that the Portuguese people are so hardened to this regime that the traditional costume of certain peasant women is made up of sorts of woolen stockings that cover the thighs and legs and stop short at the ankle. All the same it is not unusual to see people with injured feet wrapped up in unclean bandages; insufficient protection is the rule in the rain, the cold, and even the snow.

As for the clothes themselves, they seem comfortable enough in the country. But in the cities they are patched up and miserable. The children especially are in rags; even in the winter—and the winters there are very harsh— the children wander the streets half naked. It will be a long time before I can forget the two children I saw one rainy morning in Porto; they were dressed in pieces of sackcloth and were searching through the garbage cans. . . .

The question of lodging is still more anguishing. In the country, the houses are small and impoverished; naturally they have no electricity (the average consumption of electricity for each inhabitant in Europe is 550 kw [kilowatts] per inhabitant per year; it reaches 200 kw in Spain and only 60 kw in Portugal).

Coal and even wood for heat are lacking, but at least the houses are built in open air [in the country]. One can see the sky from the window and breathe. In the cities, there are vast neighborhoods where the streets are but cesspools, and where the people live piled up in tall houses with no air and no light.

In Porto, what they call "the insalubrious blocks" rise up along the river. No streets cross them; there are only narrow, stooping passageways and courtyards where sunlight never penetrates. Porto is rainy and foggy, so the walls are damp with the humidity. Next to such hovels, the houses in Venice Street were palaces.

At the very heart of Lisbon, in the neighborhood around the embassies, I have seen houses where fish sellers live, obligated by their profession to stay not far from the port and the market. One enters through a stooping passageway where patched up laundry is drying and half naked children are playing in a sort of Miracle Courtyard.[1] One climbs a dark stairway and follows a hallway lined with rooms with windows opening out to the court-yard. They are minuscule rooms entirely filled up with beds where families are piled up—often families with eight or nine children—and no fireplace; the fish is cooked on a stove upon the floor itself and there is no way to keep warm in winter. The monthly rent however is as much as 150 escudos.

It is understandable that the poor people of Lisbon prefer to build wooden or zinc huts in this zone, even though they shiver there during the winter. All around Lisbon there is an immense zone in which the inhabitants basically live in the open air.

With such horrible misery, there is no avoiding the most horrible of con-sequences. As soon as she is a little bit older—14 years old, maybe 12 years old—the little girl that I saw rooting through the garbage cans of Porto will be searching for any way she can to earn a few escudos. Out of 194 prosti-tutes cared for in a certain clinic, 43% of them were minors. A professional permit is allowed to women starting at the age of 14. They do not need the authorization of their parents to obtain it, and the tax gathered from these permits constitutes a considerable source of revenue for the state.

One can imagine what the state of public health might be under such conditions. From 1939 to 1941 the birth rate was 2.5% and the death rate was

12.5%, which represents a decrease in population reaching 10%. The people are consumed by tuberculosis and syphilis; on every street corner and on the roads, one sees tabetics and cripples; children are frighteningly thin and pale; women are old at 25 years. Out of all the young people who show up to register for the draft, only 50% of them can be kept as fit enough for the service.

In Portugal, the Wealthy Fear the Hungry

Lisbon in April: *I have exposed what sort of misery is experienced by millions of Portuguese people under the authoritarian regime that Salazar has set up. Perhaps you will say, "Portugal has always been a poor country. One can not blame a regime for a misery whose causes are the very nature of the soil and the climate." But what is so heartbreaking when traveling through Portugal is not only the misery, but that for the most part, it is made not by nature but by men. Those who eat do not concern themselves with changing the fate of those who do not eat.*

Once, in a small village in the North, I happened to be eating lunch with a rich Portuguese man on the outdoor terrace of a restaurant. Right away a group of children with gleaming eyes crowded around us. At that moment I understood why in this country the restaurants and cafés almost never have outdoor terraces. Each mouthful that I swallowed was an insult to their misery.

After a while I handed a coin to one of the children, and the rich Portuguese man saw that it was a coin worth 5 escudos (which represents about 10 pre-war francs). He flushed red with anger, "How much did you give him?" And he got up to take the coin back. As I prevented him, he said sadly, "But he will take nothing back to his house; he will buy cigarettes and candy for himself!" while serving himself some prawn with mayonnaise.

The violence of such a reaction illustrates well the hatred that the rich over there have for the poor. They fear them, for they know very well that their fortune is the fruit of a shameful exploitation.

Even certain delegates of the National Assembly have admitted that the poor are exploited as consumers. For example, Antonio Christo stated, "The producer sells 10,000 kilograms of salt for 1,500 écus and the consumer pays for it starting at 5,400 écus and even as much as 26,000 écus on the black market in one district." And Duarte Marques said, "Rice goes through different *gremios*[2] and at each one something must be paid, so that the unlucky consumer makes up the cost, while the producer can not receive a fair price for his labor."

One year when the abundance of sardines risked causing a decrease in the price, proprietors in certain fisheries up North were known to have denatured the fish with petroleum and made fertilizer out of them. The outrage was so explosive that the government had to take the side against the criminals, but this was not a typical case; usually it closes its eyes. Duarte Marques again stated, "The traffickers on the black market have contacts with elements in corporate organizations that, at the very least, tolerate this kind of outrage."

This exploitation only reinforces the exploitation that the working class endures as laborers. There are 53,000 fishermen in Portugal. The official statistics show an annual revenue of 1,120 écus per person, or 3.10 écus each day for a numerous family. Yet the Portuguese Fishing Company, with assets of 10 million realized a liquid profit of 4,600,000 écus in one year. With 1,500,000 écus in assets, the fishing company in Viana de Castel had a liquid profit of 1,104,000 écus, and the one in Cap de Santa Marina, with assets of 275,000 écus, earned 5,542,000 écus in one year!

The government does nothing to limit these profits and put the brakes on capitalistic tyranny. Public opinion has forced it to impose a few restrictions upon the rich, as consumers. That is why restaurants are severely regulated; they serve strictly two dishes: fish or eggs and eggs or meat. Selling cream-filled cakes is forbidden, and selling meat is limited. Driving automobiles is authorized only three days of the week and they must consume only a small amount of gas.

As one might guess, these measures really only affect the middle classes, who have suffered greatly by the increase in the cost of living and to whom the black market is closed. The salaries of government workers as well as those of laborers have increased by only 35%. The average government worker earns from 1,200 to 2,000 écus per month; after twenty years, a high school teacher manages to earn 1,800 écus, which reduces them to one of the lowest standards of living the moment they have families to support.

However, the creatures of the regime make close to 25,000 escudos per month, without counting the profits they make as shareholders in different companies. The former Minister of Colonies Viena Machado headed up thirty two companies.

These scandals reach such proportions that last October 5, the Under-Secretary of War at a banquet for officers stated, in their name, that the army was outraged at the *Gremio* scandals and required a purging of those who profit from the regime.

The purge never happened. No measure has been taken against capitalism itself. Income tax is not progressive. In no case does the tax on using capital retain more than 14% of profits. On the other hand, one delegate indignantly brought to the attention of the National Assembly that in one year 40 million écus had been obtained from taxes on yearly incomes ranging from 100 to 5,000 escudos.

NOTES

1. *Cour des Miracles* was an area in Paris where vagrants had the right of sanctuary.
2. *Gremio* is a sort of guild of skilled professionals.

POETRY AND TRUTH OF THE FAR WEST

by Simone de Beauvoir

TRANSLATION AND NOTES BY VÉRONIQUE ZAYTZEFF

AND FREDERICK M. MORRISON

I think that for a Frenchman the Far West represents, after New York, the most fascinating area of North America. Thanks to the old Westerns many of us have discovered this art—the cinema—which has taken on such importance in today's civilization. The landscapes of *The Gold Rush* (1925), as immortalized by Chaplin, are as integral a part of our childhood memories as are Sleeping Beauty's castle or the Park of Versailles. The fabulous adventure that drove thousands of men across deserts of stone and salt was not solely an American adventure. Citizens of every nationality were violently caught up by the mirage of gold; and among others, many Frenchmen headed toward the gold fields, as if it were a promised land. They left because of the utter political confusion, after the financial disasters that left their mark in France in the middle of the last century. Among the French there were some whose amazing odyssey could be followed step by step from Le Havre to San Francisco. The modern reincarnation of these hopes, Hollywood, in the eyes of many ambitious young people, shines today with the glitter of an international paradise. Thus to see California is not only to

"Poésie et vérité du Far West" *France-Amérique*, May 11, 1947: 1–2, and May 18, 1947: 7, © Sylvie Le Bon de Beauvoir.

discover a part of America, it is to enter a land of legend that, as any land of legend, belongs to the past of all humanity and to its dreams.

However, there is nothing less legendary than Los Angeles. This first contact with the Far West would have been very disappointing to me had I not known that most happy experiences begin with similar disappointments. Furthermore, for a long time, French and American voices have been repeating that the glamour with which Hollywood adorns itself is a fake glamour, and that life there is very artificial and dull.

So, I was not too disappointed with this blue sky tainted with advertisements written in white letters by planes, these never-ending avenues where nobody ever strolls on foot, every avenue identical with every other one, running between identical houses, without any mystery, any longing, or any promise. But I did discover that, as a matter of fact, Hollywood was a sad place. At the doors of the studios, men in threadbare clothes stood guard: they were strikers: carpenters and set hands who had been waiting for months for a raise. On cold mornings they burnt hunks of wood by the sidewalks and stretched their hands toward the flames the same way Parisian tramps do.

In the studios, work was done without much joy. Perhaps, by dint of wanting to serve the public's taste too faithfully, Hollywood has lost the power to interest a public that certainly demands to be flattered, yet also wishes to be torn away from itself. French and English movies enjoy a success on Broadway that they have rarely known, while miles and miles of film in Los Angeles studios are waiting for the moment when they might hope for a favorable reception. Certainly, the American cinema is still very alive, but it is questioning itself, and seems confused. This is no time for great undertakings. The job has instead taken on the form of a routine. And when the day is finally over, Hollywood evenings are far from offering the gaiety and fever of New York evenings. Even Boston, renowned for its puritanical severity, seemed to me less austere. Few people are in the nightclubs, where the décor is cold and the music is ordinarily mediocre; at midnight they all close their doors. In this town that one readily imagines as a city of pleasure, there are immense areas where the sale of alcohol is forbidden. A law forbids children unaccompanied by their parents to be on the streets after 9:00 PM. And in the month of March, after midnight, the shadow of the "Black Dahlia" would roam the deserted streets.[1]

New York, as it is always said, is not America. And Los Angeles is not California. If one wishes to confront the truth with the legend, the naked face of the Far West with the poetic image given to us by cowboy movies and memories of Buffalo Bill, one should drive along the big smooth roads, the small bumpy roads, along the sea, in the hills planted with orange groves, in the snowy mountains, and through the deserts with their glaring colors. Besides the joy of gazing at landscapes of breathtaking and singular beauty, one will find still other points of interest during such a trip.

To begin with, there is a very precious fact for the tourist: the fact that in America, and particularly in the Far West, tourism does not conceal the truth of the country through which one travels. It is, to the contrary, a way of accessing it. When one travels in Italy, North Africa, Greece, or Spain, one finds himself without a truth due to one's condition as a traveler: the local people, except for a privileged few, do not travel. But Americans travel; all these roads, these gas pumps, these "motels"* where one can rent a whole small house with a garage for the night, are an integral part of American life. In certain corners of California, Nevada, and Arizona they are even the only manifestations of this life; without fields under cultivation and without industries, vast expanses exist only to be crossed and gazed at; it is the tourist who is its native inhabitant. And by the side of a brook, in the rare and precious shade of a cluster of trees, or in a cove protected from the wind, there are tables and chairs, swings, play-sets, and barbecue pits, all set up waiting for the campers. Here, on the edge of town, there is a great field reserved for "trailers."† Here, in the solitude of the forest, there is a village of white cabins where one can stop for days or weeks. In those deserts where not a single farm can be seen, the motorist can find everything he desires along the road: gas, restrooms,‡ hamburgers, Coca-Cola, records stacked in a magnificent neon-lit apparatus whose mechanism needs only a nickel§ to be activated. Nevertheless, since few people travel these far-off and difficult roads, each tourist might have the really flattering impression that all these preparations were especially meant for him. He is aware that he is participating in a collective phenomenon, but at the same time, he knows all the joys of solitude.

Moreover, for the one who liked and still likes American cinema, it is a moving experience to compare the landscapes of earth and sky, of stones, sand, and water with the black and white images that enchanted us. So, the camera and the screen did not deceive us: these abrupt footpaths on the edge of precipices, these giant cacti, these rocks, and these craters do exist. And therein lies the miracle: because they were so exactly true to themselves, they took on a fantastic aspect in my eyes, as if I had seen Van Eyck's paradise or a Hieronymus Bosch's hell come to life.[2]

---

* ["motels" is in English in the original.]
† ["trailers" is in English in the original.]
‡ ["restrooms" is in English in the original.]
§ ["nickel" is in English in the original.]

There is a site particularly dear to Hollywood directors because in some twenty square miles, they find assembled together the Alps and the plateaus of Tibet, the sands of Africa and the salty deserts of America itself. It is located four hours from Los Angeles in an area that spreads from Mount Whitney, the highest peak of the Rocky Mountains, to Death Valley whose floor is, in places, below sea level. This was where film director [George] Stevens filmed *Gunga Din* not long ago.[3] I had the opportunity to stroll in his company among these old yellow rocks that felicitously represented for him the worn mountains of Asia; these rocks rise at the foot of an elevated mountain range evoking the steep slopes of Switzerland. "You see here the youngest and the oldest mountains of earth brought together," he told me with as much pride as if he had created them himself. And he explained to me all the efforts it took to isolate the "old" mountains from their arrogant young sisters to evoke a picture of India. I expressed my surprise at not seeing anywhere that immense battlefield that triumphantly burst from the screen at the end of *Gunga Din*. "Here it is," he said to me, pointing to a small piece of land as big as a French vegetable garden. He explained to me that by perching the camera on a very isolated rock and by aiming it at a studied angle, he had transformed this pocket-handkerchief of land into an immense plain. Yet, that day, at the same site, they were in the process of getting ready to shoot a new movie. Some two weeks after that conversation, I recognized those chaotic yellow rocks in another Western that was a couple of years old.

About twenty miles from here Death Valley begins, where Von Stroheim filmed his great movie *Greed*.[4] Even more than at the foot of Mount Whitney, I was surprised by the fidelity of the tragic images: the scorched earth, the salty peaks burning under the sun. Nothing was missing, not even the heat exhaustion, so one was tempted to believe that those were true agonies, true deaths that Stroheim's camera had caught in the heart of this hopeless loneliness.*

It is difficult to distinguish between the poetry with which the cinema has imbued the Far West and the one its history has given it; for so many movies that moved us were based on this very history. Whatever its origin, one feels a strong emotion when one gazes at the most burning heart of this Death Valley (where, from time to time, some imprudent tourist is still assassinated by the sun), or at the same covered wagons or carts that the immigrants used to carry borax after the gold fever had passed. Many

* [The text from May 11, 1947, ends at this point, with the notice: (*to be continued*). The text that begins below, appeared in the issue dated May 18, 1947, with the notice (*Refer to our issue of May 11*).]

men who thought that they had found a shorter route to the coast, died in the same spot where nowadays rises a magnificent hotel. Their ghosts and also the shadows of those who, luckier than they were, discovered the first placers,[5] haunt all these roads winding through the mountains and deserts. Between Sacramento and Reno one can still see mile-posts with the inscription, "placer, one and a half miles." In the "ghost towns"* one can still see the rotten wooden shacks that remember having been theaters and inns: some illegible inscription remains, some strip of a poster. And the worm-eaten houses standing by are exactly similar to those that, a little bit further on, in the shade of the pine forests, shelter the lumberjacks of today.

I think that this is what gives my memories such a singular vividness. The age of gold seems as remote as the Stone Age. The world evoked by the old locomotive on exhibit in Carson City is almost foreign to ours, and yet it is only one hundred years old. Its remnants are still so fresh that we believe we are able to touch it; this past is worthy of the human immigration that makes us dream wildly, amidst inordinate hopes, of a world worthy of the human will.

This is at least the way that, at present, I explain to myself the naive joy I felt, when, at the place called Devil's Gate and exactly at the moment when we were asking ourselves "Will we see the Devil?" a man sprang out from among the solitary pines and demanded our papers, looking at us suspiciously. He wore a big cowboy hat and on his chest he had a star; he was the sheriff as immortalized in the Westerns. He had followed us by car, and he was flesh and bone; nevertheless, with his inexplicable appearance, fifty miles away from any dwellings, he seemed to escape the law of time as well as the law of space. It was one of those extreme points that Proust had experienced only in his own heart[6]—where past and present merge into one. No doubt the judge's house in Pecos, with its arsenal of rifles and the barrel on which he sat down to give out his arbitrary decisions, seems rather mummified; but it becomes singularly alive when one pushes open the door of the nearest restaurant and sits at the bar, in front of the coarse faces of cowboys wearing magnificent boots.

Even more than in California and Texas, it is perhaps in Nevada that the years intermingle in a most disquieting way. I was expecting to discover in Reno and Las Vegas a kind of Monte Carlo aimed at Hollywood stars yearning for divorce. And certainly, there are some elegant dance halls and bars in these cities where miles and miles of "motels," "courts,"

---

* ["ghost-towns" is in English in the original.]

"Court Houses"* are lined up, meant to shelter for a few weeks those men and women tired of conjugal bonds and eager to take on new chains. But, when one pushes the door to one of those immense bars located in the heart of the city, one is truly under the impression that time has begun to spin topsy-turvy. Through thick smoke and the heavy smell of cigars and alcohol, one makes out a confused bustling of checkered shirts and big grimy hats. These men seem as miserable as those who sleep standing up every Sunday on the sidewalks of New York's Bowery; however, they hold in their black hands big silver dollars they exchange for stacks of many-colored chips or warily put them on the green baize of the tables. All around them, the myth still so young and already so antiquated of the Gold Rush spreads all over the walls. For example, the Club's sign is a gleaming donkey, loaded down with neon gold ingots and trudging up a hill; inside there are wagon wheels hanging from the ceiling and black paintings representing the emigrants' wagons with their green tarpaulin and tired horses. And the gamblers gathered around the croupiers dressed in none too clean shirts would give the impression of participating in a historical reconstruction if it were not for such an air of truth in their destitution. There is no doubt that these are truly poor cowboys, men who struggle hard in the solitude of these ranches where the revolver is still an everyday utensil. When, by the sweat of their brows, they have gathered some of these handsome, round, and heavy dollars, they come here to live out feverishly a couple of hours or a couple of minutes of hope.

Nevada's strange fate is that it is such an impoverished state—the most impoverished in all of America, I was told—that one does not find any well-to-do class, capable of inspiring moral institutions. Clubs are open all night long; not only are alcohol and gambling allowed, but all around town there are flourishing houses of prostitution. And divorce requires but a few formalities. It is from this very destitution that Nevada draws its best resources. For its licentiousness attracts rich Californians, overcome by all those puritanical constraints that make Los Angeles so dreadfully bleak. And there is a strange contrast between these small, smoke-filled hells where every evening the desperate hopes of so many poor wretches are dashed, and the smiling "Star wedding chapels" (all wedding arrangements, divorces included), or the stores where wedding dresses, wedding rings, jewelry, and wedding gifts are on display.

---

* ["motels," "courts," and "Court Houses" are all in English in the original.]

California mistrusts Nevada; it mistrusts Mexico and Arizona. Crossing the state line* is far from a casual affair. Some kind of customs officer rummages through your luggage, turns your pockets inside out to make sure that you are not attempting to import any plants or grains. Several years ago, when a shipment of grain sent by the Emperor of Japan was not disinfected out of respect to the donor, terrible insect pests were introduced into the country, and now fortunes must be spent to exterminate them; therefore any importation of plants is rigorously forbidden. And when, in order to shorten the inspection, my friend objected by saying that we had spent only one night in Nevada, the employee winked knowingly: "So, one night was enough for you too!" he said, assuming that another divorce had been added to the list proudly published every day in Reno and Las Vegas newspapers.

The poetry of the Far West is not the result of art and history alone. It also emanates from this soil with its glaring colors, vast distances, and surprising contrasts. The landscape amazes European eyes. Going from Sacramento to Lake Tahoe, following a flat road crossing forests, I was suddenly surprised to see a sign that read: 6,000 feet. We didn't seem to have been climbing. But, further ahead, another sign announced: 7,000 feet. One had to recognize the obvious: the air had become colder, snow appeared, and skiers were going down white slopes. Compared to the convulsed Alps, the Rockies stretch out with such a peaceful majesty that their incline remains hidden. Around the lake, around Carson City, many roads were blocked by snow; yet, under the white powder, a soil reddened by the sun appeared: a desert that spoke of thirst and seemed already blazing. Man seems intimidated by these still new lands; the houses he builds are precarious; they do not take root in the ground and, by the same token, they do not humanize these vast stretches that retain the freshness of an uninhabited planet.

I would have also liked to talk about the farms of wild animals that entertain the tourist at the road junctions, and about those unexpected shops one finds in surrealistic disorder: stuffed animals, snakes, shells, roots, and fetuses in jars right next to the gas pumps. I would have liked to talk about villages and cities, of Monterey with its old Spanish houses, of abalone shells sold for five cents in the harbor of San Francisco, whose crisscrossed streets climb up the red brick hills with such a rational obstinacy. . . . It would be necessary to write an entire book. Yet, I would rather advise all

---

* ["State Line" is in English and capitalized in the original.]

35

those wishing to deepen the disconcerting miracle that is America, to go see the Far West with their own eyes.

NOTES

1. The "Black Dahlia" was really Elizabeth Short, who was a victim of a brutal murder committed in January 1947, in the South of Hollywood. Her body—bruised, beaten, and cut in half at the waist—was found in a vacant lot. She was an aspiring actress whose name evolved from her black hair and black attire. To date the case goes unsolved.

2. Jan Van Eyck (ca. 1395–1441) was the greatest artist of the early Netherlands school. He perfected the newly discovered technique of oil painting, using the oil medium to represent a variety of subjects with striking realism in microscopic details; Hieronymus, or Jerome, Bosch (ca. 1453–1516) was a Dutch painter. His obsessive and nightmarish vision has its antecedents in the Gothic twilight world of the late Middle Ages. At the time of his death, he was internationally celebrated as a painter of religious visions who dealt in particular with the torments of hell.

3. *Gunga Din* was a film made in 1939. The director was George Stevens (1904–57), and the actors included Cary Grant, Douglas Fairbanks Jr., and Victor McLaglen. It was filmed in the California desert at Lone Pine and based on Rudyard Kipling's *Barrack-Room Ballads*, first published in the *National Observer* in 1890. Among the films directed by George Stevens: *A Place in the Sun* (1951), *Shane* (1953), *Something to Live For* (1952), and *Giant* (1956). He won his first Oscar for best directing in 1951 for *A Place in the Sun* and a second Oscar in 1956 for *Giant*.

4. Erich Von Stroheim (1885–1957) was a silent-era film director/actor. *Greed* (1924) was a scenario by Von Stroheim and June Mathis of the novel *McTeague* by Frank Norris.

5. A *placer* is a surface deposit of minerals, such as gold, laid down by a river. The extraction of minerals from placers, as by panning, washing, or dredging, is called *placer mining*.

6. Marcel Proust (1871–1922) was a prolific French writer. Among his many works, the best known are *A la recherche du temps perdu* (*Remembrance of Things Past* or *In Search for Lost Time*) (1912), an autobiographical novel told mostly in a stream-of-consciousness style; and *Du côté de chez Swann* (*Swann's Way*) (1913).

2

Must We Burn Sade?

INTRODUCTION

by Debra Bergoffen

Published in 1951–52, five years after *The Ethics of Ambiguity*, and two years after *The Second Sex*, Simone de Beauvoir's essay "Must We Burn Sade?" may be read as a corrective sequel to *The Ethics of Ambiguity* and as an afterword to *The Second Sex*. As a corrective to *The Ethics of Ambiguity*, "Must We Burn Sade?" abandons the method of abstract analyses and imaginary examples for Beauvoir's now preferred concrete phenomenological-existential approach. Here, ethical principles as lived realities are elaborated through an in-depth analysis of a specifically situated singular human being who, in his particularity, exemplifies the ambiguities of the human condition in its existential and moral dilemmas. As an afterward to *The Second Sex*, "Must We Burn Sade?" directs us to *The Second Sex*'s discussions of the body, the flesh and the erotic. It draws our attention to the affinities between Beauvoir's phenomenology of our embodied ambiguity and Merleau-Ponty's phenomenology of the lived body and the wild flesh.[1]

More than a sequel to these earlier works, however, "Must We Burn Sade?" is an examination of the politics of writing. For if it is the case that what draws Beauvoir to consider the case of the Marquis de Sade is the fact that he identified his sexuality as an ethical choice and in this identification revealed the secrets of patriarchal politics, it is also the case that it is his other passion, the passion to write, that intrigues Beauvoir. For it is here, at the decision to write, that Sade joins the questions of ethics, politics, and aesthetics. As an author herself, Beauvoir's probing of Sade's decision to become a writer is neither abstract nor disinterested, for she, like Sade, often chose the route of the imaginary to expose the hypocrisies and injustices of the social order. When Beauvoir credits Sade with being aware of the ethics and politics of choosing to write; when she describes Sade's existential dilemmas and his attempts to negotiate them through the decision to write, Beauvoir may well be telling us much about herself.

"Must We Burn Sade?" examines the ethical position of the author. It interrogates Sade's writing style; it analyzes his perspective as an author; it explores the meaning of his choice to publish. It suggests that Sade's style, perspective, decision to write, and meaning as an author constitute an existential project. According to Beauvoir, the decision to write places Sade in the domain of the political; for in becoming an author, he transforms his ethical choices into a public act of rebellion. The state jails him for his private debaucheries. He responds with writings that critique and challenge the duplicities of the powers that refuse his desire. Sade's writings are not, however, merely critical. In uncovering the despotic secrets of the political machine, he issues a utopian appeal to freedom. Beauvoir grants the truth of the secrets Sade exposes. They anticipate many of her critiques of patriarchy. She does not, however, find his appeal to freedom legitimate. It perverts the meaning of our relationship to each other.

Beauvoir sees Sade as a great moralist who endorsed an unsatisfactory ethic. She criticizes his writings for being repetitive, cold, and mawkish, but praises their subtle irony. She says that he has the style of a great writer but that he lacked the perspective of an artist. He is, she concludes, neither the villain nor the hero of his age. As a man who confronted the plight of the individual caught in the crossfire between the demands of freedom and the desire for community, however, he is, according to Beauvoir, a man of/for all times. Not duped by the mystifications of his times, Sade was also a man ahead of his times. Beauvoir detects in his writings anticipations of Freud's insights regarding the powers and intentionalities of the erotic; foreshadowings of Heidegger's critique of the "one" (*das Man*); and signs of Marx's analysis of the material historical conditions that ground bourgeois ideology.

At the end of the Sade essay, Beauvoir joins those who identify their era with a single driving question. For W. E. B. DuBois it is the question of the color line, for Luce Irigaray it is the question of sexual difference, for Beauvoir it is the problem of "the true relation between man and man."[2] Sade, according to Beauvoir, understood this last problem (her problem) in all of its dimensions. He, like she, argued for neither an original human community nor an inherent species sympathy. He, like she, begins with the fact of our basic separateness and confronts the realities of our selfishness and injustice. He, like she, rejects the politics of the reign of terror. Unlike Beauvoir, however, Sade claims that the practices of cruelty solve the problem of the human relationships/relatedness. For Sade, the illusions of the ideal of fraternity justify torture. As he sees it, since it is the case that we are not inherently connected to each other, and since it is the case that we desire an existential relationship with each other, then, in the absence of any a priori moral laws prohibiting violence, the fact that cruelty indubitably connects us to each other allows us to conclude that the cuts of pain establish our bond to each other.

Beauvoir rejects Sade's solution to the problem of our age. She does, however, recommend him to us on two counts: One, that he chose cruelty rather than apathy, and two, that his testimonies unsettle us. As a man who refused pacifying illusions, his writings disturb our mystifications. Though we cannot say that Beauvoir was a woman duped by sanguine visions of "brotherly" love, we can say that Sade disturbed her. Beauvoir, like Sade, begins with the Cartesian premise of the solitary subject, and like Sade she refuses to accept a priori arguments for "fraternity." But where Beauvoir finds that the experiential confirmation of our relatedness to others entails a rejection of the justification of violence, Sade argues that experience of the other justifies violence.

Sade is Beauvoir's Janus-faced ally. Sharing his understanding of our age's problem and his orienting premises, she must confront his conclusions by establishing how, that, and why, torture is not the truth of our intersubjectivity. Beauvoir does not refute the claim that cruelty establishes a relationship between the self and the other. Sade is correct. Cruelty does bind us to each other. It reveals us to each other in our particularity and in the ambiguity of our conscious and fleshed existence. The tyrant and victim, Beauvoir tells us, are a genuine couple. They are united by the closest of bonds, the bonds of the flesh and freedom. Valuing the flesh, Sade exalted it by humiliating it. In subjecting others to these humiliations, he also subjected himself to them. Declaring that sensation was the only measure of reality, he found the sensations of torture and pain more powerful than others and concluded that only these sensations adequately validated our fleshed existence. Cruelty, Sade showed, breaks down the fleshed barriers that separate us. Valuing freedom, however, Sade reserved it for himself and his libertine elite. The point of torture is to assert the libertine's freedom and to bring the victim to the point of recognizing the libertine's freedom as his/her (the victim's) destiny. The equalities of the humiliated flesh are obliterated by libertine power structures.

Beauvoir does not dispute Sade's validations of the flesh and freedom. She does not quarrel with his descriptions of the powers of cruelty and the meaning of torture. She even goes so far as to call his ethics authentic, derived as it is from his own experiences rather than from abstract formulas or principles. She rejects his ethics, however, as being false, and criticizes his descriptions for being incomplete. As effective as Sade's ethics may be as a critique of current facades of justice, it fails to provide a solution to the problem of our age.

In the end, Sade was misled (which does not mean that he was innocent). He mistook power for freedom and misunderstood the meanings of the erotic desires of the flesh. In the end his Cartesian commitment to lucidity betrayed him. Afraid of taking the risk of abandoning himself in/to the other he succumbed to the tyrannies of pleasure. Afraid of allowing the mysteries of the world to disrupt its rational and practical presence, Sade pursued the pleasures of the flesh without ever losing himself in the flesh. In his fascination with the conflict between consciousness and the flesh, Sade exposed the contradiction of the sadistic enterprise. The contradiction, according to Beauvoir is this: attempting to lose himself in the pleasures of the flesh and in this way to experience both the ambiguity of his being as consciousness made flesh (or flesh made consciousness) and the reality of his being for and with others, Sade substituted the spectacle for the lived experience and accepted counterfeit transactions of domination and assimilation/incorporation for genuine relationships of reciprocity and gratuitous generosity. Centering his life in the erotic, Sade missed the truth of the erotic event. This truth, according to Beauvoir, can be found only by those who abandon themselves to the risks of emotional intoxication. Living this intoxication we discover the subjectivity and passivity of our fleshed existence and experience the ways in which the body turned flesh dissolves the barriers between us. This experience of intoxication guides us to the true resolution of the problem of our age; for here we discover that we are intimately and inextricably related to each other. We learn that we do not need a priori laws to understand that we cannot harm each other without inflicting damage on ourselves. We come to understand that the appeal is the ground of our being for each other, and that as equally vulnerable to the abuse of the appeal, we are also equally available to each other for the task of pursuing justice.

Explaining the origins of the *Sade* essay, Beauvoir tells us that "circumstances and my own pleasure led me to write about Sade."[3] The circumstances were that she was asked to write a preface for *Justine*. The pleasure was discovering that

> Justine's epic extravagance was a revelation. Sade posed the problem of the *Other* in its extremist terms; in his excesses, man-as-transcendence and man-as-object achieve a dramatic confrontation.[4]

Beauvoir's decision to title the essay "Must We Burn Sade?" also tells us something about her interest in the Marquis. Unique as the title seems to us today, Beauvoir's readers would have been struck by its allusions to other authors who, like Sade, were judged to be threats to liberal democratic values. "Must We Burn Sade?" repeats the title of a 1946 symposium in *Action* dedicated to literature *noir* titled "Must We Burn Kafka?" It mimics the title of an article in *Combat* that defended Sartre against his critics titled "Should We Burn Sartre?"[5] Beauvoir does not tell us how she conceives of the relationship, conjured up by her title, between Sartre and the ghosts of Kafka and Sade. Her analyses, however, alert us to the fact that for all of her disputations of his logic and for all of her criticisms of his failures, Beauvoir identifies Sade as an author whose insights into the meanings of evil, freedom, and the erotic must be confronted to adequately address the problem of the relationship between the self and its other(s).

NOTES

1. For an extensive discussion of the relationship between the essay "Must We Burn Sade?" and *The Ethics of Ambiguity* and *The Second Sex*, and for the affinities between Beauvoir and Merleau-Ponty, see Debra Bergoffen, *The Philosophy of Simone de Beauvoir: Gendered Phenomenologies, Erotic Generosities* (Albany: State University of New York, 1997), 113–40.

2. W. E. B. DuBois, *The Souls of Black Folk* (New York: Norton, 1999), 5; Luce Irigaray, *An Ethics of Sexual Difference*, trans. Carolyn Burke and Gillian C. Gill (Ithaca: Cornell University Press, 1993), 5.

3. Simone de Beauvoir, *After the War: The Force of Circumstance I*, trans. Richard Howard (New York: Paragon House, 1992), 243.

4. Ibid.

5. Ibid., 44, 230.

MUST WE BURN SADE?

by Simone de Beauvoir

TRANSLATION BY KIM ALLEN GLEED,

MARILYN GADDIS ROSE, AND VIRGINIA PRESTON

NOTES BY LAUREN GUILMETTE

"Imperious, wrathful, headstrong, extreme in all things, with an unbridled imagination on behavior unparalleled in this lifetime, an atheist to the point of fanaticism. In a few words this is what I am, so kill me with another blow or take me as I am because I will not change."[1]

They chose to kill him, at first in the slow fire of tedium in the dungeon, and later with calumny and omission; indeed, this was the death he had hoped for: "Once covered over, the grave will be sown with acorns so that eventually . . . the traces of my tomb will disappear from the face of the earth, and I flatter myself that my memory will be erased from the minds of men. . . ."[2] Of his last wishes, the latter was the only one respected, and very carefully so. Sade's history was disfigured by imbecilic legends;* his name itself was diluted by the heavy words: "sadism," "sadistic"; his intimate journals were lost, his manuscripts burned—the ten volumes of *Journées*

"Faut-il brûler Sade?" *Les temps modernes* 7:75 (Jan. 1952): 1197–1230; in *Privilèges* (Paris: Gallimard, 1972), 9–89, © Éditions Gallimard, 1972.

* The elderly Sade had baskets of roses brought to him; he smelled them voluptuously and then soiled them in the muddy gutters with a sardonic laugh. Today's journalists show us how this genre of anecdotes is concocted.

44

de Florabelle at the instigation of his own son[3]—his books banned. While, towards the end of the nineteenth century Swinburne and others became curious about him, we had to wait for Apollinaire before a place was given to him in French letters.[4] Still, Sade is far from having won it officially: we can leaf through extensive and detailed works on "The Ideas of the Eighteenth Century," or indeed "Sensibilities of the Eighteenth Century," without once finding his name. We understand that in reaction to this scandalous silence Sade zealots have been led to greet him as a prophet of genius: his works would simultaneously herald Nietzsche, Stirner, Freud and surrealism;[5] yet this cult, founded like all cults upon misconception, in deifying the "divine marquis," betrays him also; where one would like to understand, we are entreated to adore. The critics who make neither a blackguard nor an idol of Sade, but rather a man, a writer, can be counted on the fingers of one hand. Thanks to them, Sade has returned once again to the earth, among us. But where may we properly situate him? What about him merits our interest? Even his admirers readily admit that the greater part of his work is unreadable; philosophically, it escapes banality only to sink into darkness and incoherence. As for his vices, they do not astound us in their originality; in this domain, Sade invented nothing, and we find a profusion of cases at least as strange as his in the annals of psychiatry. In truth, it is neither as an author nor as a sexual pervert that Sade imposes upon our attention: it is by the relation he created between these two aspects of himself. Sade's anomalies take their value from the moment when instead of submitting to them as to a fact of nature, he elaborates an immense system in which to justify them; conversely, his texts engage us from the moment we grasp that beyond their repetitiveness, their clichés, and their clumsiness, he attempts to communicate an experience whose particularity, however, is to want to be incommunicable. Sade tried to convert his psycho-physiological destiny into an ethical choice; and with this act through which he assumes his separation, he claims to set an example and make an appeal: here his adventure takes on a substantial human significance.

Would it be possible to satisfy our aspirations to universality without renouncing individuality? Or is it only through the sacrifice of our differences that we can integrate ourselves into the collectivity? This problem touches us all. For Sade, the differences are pushed to the point of scandal, and the immensity of his literary work shows us the passion with which he hoped to be accepted by the human community: in Sade, we encounter in its most extreme form the conflict that no individual can evade without self-deception. This is the paradox, and in a sense, the triumph of Sade,

45

that for having been so stubborn in his singularities, he helps us to define the human drama in its generality.

In order to understand Sade's development, to grasp in this history the role of his freedom, to measure his successes and failures, it would be useful to know exactly the givens of his situation. Unfortunately, despite the zeal of his biographers, the person and the history of Sade remain obscure in many ways. We possess no authentic portraits of him; and the descriptions of him that his contemporaries left us are extremely poor. The depositions from the Marseilles trial depict him at the age of thirty-two years as "of handsome figure and full face," medium height, dressed in a gray frock and marigold silk breeches, wearing a feather in his hat, a sword at his side, and a cane in his hand. Here he is at fifty-three years, according to a certificate of residence dated May 7, 1793: "Height of five feet and two inches, nearly white hair, round face, receding hairline, blue eyes, ordinary nose, round chin." The description of May 23, 1794, varies slightly: "Height of just over five feet, two inches, medium nose, small mouth, round chin, blonde-gray hair, oval face, high receding hairline, pale blue eyes." He had lost his "handsome figure" since he wrote, a few years earlier, from the Bastille that "I have acquired, due to the lack of exercise, a corpulence so enormous that I can hardly move." It is this corpulence that first struck Charles Nodier when he met Sade in 1807 at Sainte-Pélagie:[6] "An enormous obesity which restricted his movements enough to prevent him from deploying the remainder of grace and elegance that one still finds in his manners overall. His weary eyes, however, kept enough of their brilliant and feverish character which lit up from one moment to the next like a spark on dying coal." These testimonies, the only ones we possess, hardly allow us to evoke an individual face; it has been said* that Nodier's description is reminiscent of the aging Oscar Wilde; it also suggests Montesquieu or Maurice Sachs; it invites us to imagine something of Charlus in Sade, but this is a tenuous reckoning.[7] What is even more unfortunate is the fact we are so poorly informed of his childhood. If we take Valcour's narrative for an autobiographical sketch, Sade would have known resentment and violence from an early age: raised with Louis Joseph de Bourbon, who was the same age, it seems that Sade defended himself against the egotistical arrogance of the little prince with such violent blows and rages that he had to be removed from the court.[8] That his sojourns at the somber castle of Saumane and the decaying Abbey d'Ebreuil may have marked his imagination, there is no doubt; but of

---

* [Jean] Desbordes: *Le vrai visage du Marquis de Sade* [The True Face of the Marquis de Sade (Paris: Éditions de la Nouvelle Revue Critique, 1939)].

his brief years of study, of his time in the army, or of his life as a *charming* and debauched man of the world we know nothing significant. We could attempt to infer such details from his life and works: this is what Pierre Klossowski did, who sees in the hatred Sade devoted to his mother the key to both his life and works;[9] but Klossowski infers this hypothesis from the role played by the mother in Sade's writing; that is, he limits himself to describing Sade's imaginary world from a certain angle; he does not uncover the roots in the real world. In fact, we glimpse, a priori, the importance of Sade's relationship with his father and mother based on general schemas; in their singular detail, they escape us. When we begin to discover Sade, he is already formed and we do not know how he became who he is. Such an ignorance prevents us from accounting for his tendencies and his spontaneous behavior; the nature of his affectivity and the singular traits of his sexuality appear to us as facts we can only record. The result of this unfortunate lacuna is that Sade's private life will always escape us; all explanation will leave behind a residue that only the history of Sade's childhood could clarify. Nevertheless, these limits imposed upon our comprehension must not discourage us; because Sade, as we have noted, did not restrict himself to submitting passively to the consequences of these early choices; what interests us most about him, more than his anomalies, is the way in which he assumed them. He made an ethic of his sexuality, this ethic he made manifest in a body of literature; Sade conquered his true originality through this reflective movement of his adult life. The reason for his tastes remains obscure to us; but we can grasp how he made principles from these tastes, and why he carried them *to the point of fanaticism*.

Superficially, Sade at twenty-three resembles other young men of means of his time; he is cultivated, enjoys theater, the arts, reading; he is dissolute; he keeps a mistress named la Beauvoisin, and frequents brothels; he marries without enthusiasm, according to his father's wishes, a young but wealthy woman of the minor nobility, Renée-Pélagie de Montreuil. At this point, the drama that would have repercussions—and repetitions—throughout his life explodes: married in May, Sade was arrested in October for excesses committed in a brothel he had frequented since June; the reasons for his arrest were serious enough that Sade wrote to the governor of the prison in letters gone astray, begging him to keep the arrest secret; for if he did not, he would be ruined. This episode hints to us that Sade's eroticism already had a disturbing characteristic; what confirms this hypothesis is that a year later Inspector Marais warned madams not to lend girls to the Marquis. But his interest resides less in the information that he gives us than in the revelation that it constituted for Sade himself: on the eve of his adult life he brutally

47

discovered that a reconciliation was impossible between his social existence and his individual pleasures.

The young Sade had nothing of the revolutionary nor even of the rebel in him; he was ready to accept society as it was. Submissive to his father* to the degree that, at twenty-three, he received from him a wife whom he did not like, he envisioned no other destiny than that which was his by heredity: he would be husband, father, marquis, captain, lord of the manor, lieutenant-general. He in no way wished to renounce the privileges that his own rank and his wife's fortunes assured him.[10] However, he was not satisfied by them; he was offered occupations, responsibilities, honors, but no enterprises, nothing that interested, amused, excited him. He did not want to be simply that public figure for whom conventions and routine determined every gesture, but also a vibrant individual. There was only one place where the latter could affirm himself, and that was not the bed where Sade was too coolly greeted by his prudish wife, but the brothel where he purchased the right to unleash his fantasies. It is a place which is common to the majority of young aristocrats of the time. Offspring of a declining class which once held a concrete power but which no longer possessed any real hold on the world, they tried to symbolically resuscitate in the secrets of the bed chamber the conditions of their lingering nostalgia: that of the feudal despot, solitary and sovereign. The orgies of the Duc de Charolais, among others, were celebrated and bloody;[11] it is this illusion of sovereignty for which Sade thirsted. "What do we desire when we reach orgasm? That everything that surrounds you is concerned only with you, thinks only of you, cares only for you . . . there is no man who does not wish to be a despot when he f——."[12] The intoxication of tyranny leads immediately to cruelty because the libertine, by molesting the object that serves him, "experiences all the charms a nervous individual enjoys when he makes full use of his strength: he dominates, he is a tyrant."[13]

In all truth, it is a petty exploit to whip a few girls by means of an agreed-upon payment; that Sade attaches so much importance to it is a fact which opens him fully to question. It is striking that, outside the walls of his "little home," he does not dream of "making full use of his strength"; we glimpse no ambition in him, no spirit of enterprise, no will to power, and I would believe readily that he was even cowardly. This is probably why Sade systematically ascribes to his heroes all the traits society considers degenerate; but

---

* Klossowski was astonished that Sade manifested no ill will towards his father, but Sade does not spontaneously detest authority; he concedes that an individual may both use and abuse his rights. As an inheritor of his father's rights and possessions, he at first opposed society only at an individual and affective level, through women: his wife and his mother-in-law.

he painted Blangis so indulgently that we may justifiably suppose that he projects himself onto this character;[14] and these words have the resonance of a confession: "A determined child would have frightened this colossus . . . he became timid and cowardly, and the idea of the least dangerous combat with a comparable force would have made him flee to the ends of the earth." That Sade, sometimes due to recklessness and sometimes to largesse, was capable of audacious extravagance does not contradict the hypothesis of his fearful timidity with regard to his equals, and, more generally, before the reality of the world. He speaks so much about the firmness of the soul not because he possessed it but because he coveted it: in adversity, he whimpered, he squirmed, he lost his bearings. The fear of having no money, which haunted Sade without respite, translates a more diffuse anxiety; he was mistrustful of everything and everyone because he felt maladjusted. He was: he conducted himself in a disorderly manner, accumulated debts, went into rages at anything, fled or surrendered at inappropriate moments; he fell into all the traps. This world, both boring and threatening, which offered him nothing of value and of which he wasn't sure what to ask, ceased to interest him; he would go seek his truth elsewhere. When he writes that the passion of *jouissance*[15] "subordinates and reunites at the same time" all the others,[16] he gives us an exact description of his own experience; he subordinated his existence to his eroticism because eroticism seemed to him to be the only possible accomplishment of his existence. He devoted himself to it with so much ardor, imprudence and stubbornness, because he attached more importance to the stories he told himself during the voluptuous act than to contingent events: he chose the imaginary.

Sade undoubtedly thought himself safe in his chimerical paradise; an impenetrable barrier seemed to protect him from the universe of the serious world. And perhaps if no scandal had occurred, he might have remained only an ordinary debauchee known in certain circles for somewhat peculiar tastes. There were at the time plenty of libertines who indulged in worse orgies with impunity; but I suppose that in Sade's case scandal was fatal. There are certain "sexual perverts" to whom the Dr. Jekyll and Mr. Hyde myth applies perfectly;[17] they hope to satisfy their "vices" without compromising their official positions; but if they are nevertheless imaginative enough to think of themselves, little by little, with a vertiginous mixture of shame and pride, they unmask themselves: like Charlus, despite and even because of his ruses. To what extent was there provocation in Sade's imprudence? It is impossible to decide. Seemingly he wanted to affirm the radical separation between his family life and his private pleasures; and he apparently also could not find satisfaction in his clandestine triumph without pushing it to the point where it overflowed secrecy. His surprise resembles that of a child who strikes a vase until it breaks. Playing with danger, he still believed himself sovereign, but society was watching; it refused any sharing and claimed each individual entirely; it quickly took hold of Sade's secret and considered it a crime.

It was with prayers, humiliation and shame that Sade first reacted; he begged to be permitted to see his wife again, whom he admitted having grievously offended; he asked for a confessor and opened his heart to him. This was not pure hypocrisy; from one day to the next a dreadful metamorphosis had taken place; natural and innocent behaviors, which until then had only been sources of pleasure, had suddenly become punishable acts, and the agreeable young man found himself transformed into a mangy sheep. It is probable that he knew from childhood onwards—perhaps as a result of his relations with his mother—the odious wrenching of remorse, but the scandal of 1763 rekindled them in a dramatic way: Sade foresaw that he would be a culprit for the rest of his life. He attached too much value to his re-creations to imagine for an instant renouncing them; rather, he would rid himself of shame through defiance. It is remarkable that the first of his deliberately scandalous acts took place immediately after his detention: la Beauvoisin accompanied him to Château de la Coste, and under the name of Mme de Sade, she danced and put on an act before the entire Provençal nobility, while the Abbé de Sade saw himself constrained to mute complicity. Society denied Sade any clandestine freedom; it tried to socialize his eroticism, and in return, the social life of the Marquis from then on played itself out on an erotic plane. As we cannot tranquilly separate good from evil in order to give oneself over to each in turn, it is in confrontation with the good and even as a function of it, that we must claim responsibility for the evil. His subsequent behavior may have its roots in resentment, as Sade confided on several occasions: "There are some souls which appear hard as a result of their sensitivity to emotions and these sometimes go to great lengths: what we take in them for insouciance and cruelty is simply a manner known only to them of feeling more vividly than others."[18] Dolmancé imputes his vices to the wickedness of man: "It was their ingratitude that dried my heart, their perfidy that destroyed in me those disastrous virtues for which I might, like you, have been born."[19] The demonic morality Sade later erected in theory was first of all for him a lived experience.

It was through Renée-Pélagie that Sade learned the blandness and ennui of virtue, merged together in a revulsion that only a being of flesh and bone can provoke. But what he also learns from Renée with great delight is that under its concrete, carnal and individual form, the good can be vanquished in single combat. His wife is not for him an enemy, but like all the wifely figures she inspires for him, a victim of choice: the one who desires to be an accomplice. Blamont's relations with his wife no doubt reflect quite precisely those of Sade and the Marquise: Blamont revels in caressing his wife at the moment when he plots the darkest machinations against her.[20] To inflict *jouissance*—Sade understands this a hundred and fifty years before the psychoanalysts, and many of his victims in his work are subjected to pleasure before they are tortured—can be a tyrannical violence; and the executioner disguised as a lover is enchanted to see his credulous lover swoon with pleasure and gratitude, confusing wickedness and tenderness. To unite such subtle joys with the fulfillment of a social duty was assuredly what encouraged Sade to have three children with his wife. Yet he obtained even greater advantage: virtue allied itself with vice and became its slave. For years Mme de Sade covered her husband's faults: she courageously helped him escape from Miolans, she furthered her sister's intrigue with the Marquis and later the orgies at the Château de la Coste. She went so far as to make herself a criminal, when, to disarm Nanon's accusations, she hid silver place settings in her bags.[21] Sade never showed any acknowledgment of her, and the idea of gratitude was one he attacked with the utmost ferocity; but he clearly felt for her that ambiguous friendship that all despots feel for whatever is unconditionally his. Thanks to her, he could not only reconcile his role of spouse, father and gentleman with his pleasures; but he also established the striking superiority of vice over goodness, devotion, fidelity, decency, and he marvelously ridiculed society by submitting the institution of marriage and all the conjugal virtues to the caprice of his imagination and his senses.

While Renée-Pélagie was Sade's most triumphant success, Mme de Montreuil epitomized his defeat. She embodied the abstract and universal justice against which the individual is broken, and it was against her that he most fiercely demanded his wife's alliance. If he won his trial in the eyes of virtue, the law would lose much of its power, because its most powerful weapons are not the prison or the gallows, but the venom with which it infects vulnerable hearts. Under her mother's influence, Renée became flustered; the young canoness took fright. Hostile society insinuated itself into Sade's home, ruining his pleasures, and he himself came under its sway. Disgraced and dishonored, he doubted himself, which was the supreme infamy that Mme de Montreuil committed against him. A culprit is first of all an accused; it was she who made Sade a criminal. This is why throughout

51

his books he never ceases to ridicule, soil and torture her; in her are all the faults he kills. It is possible that Klossowski's hypothesis has some basis and that Sade may have hated his own mother—the singular nature of his sexuality suggests it—but his enmity certainly would not have remained as undying if Renée's mother had not rendered maternity so hateful to him. And to tell the truth, she played a role important and frightening enough in the life of her son-in-law for one to imagine he attacked only her. In any case, she is certainly held up to savage ridicule by her own daughter in the final pages of *La philosophie dans le boudoir.*

If Sade was finally vanquished by both his mother-in-law and the law, he was complicit in this defeat. No matter what role chance and imprudence had in the scandal of 1763, it is certain that afterwards he sought in danger the exaltation of his pleasures. In this sense, one can say that he desired his persecutions, however suffered in indignation. He was playing with fire when he chose Easter Sunday to lure the beggar Rose Keller into his home in the Parisian suburb of Arcueil; beaten, terrorized, and insecurely locked in, she escaped, naked, unleashing a scandal for which Sade had to pay with two brief periods of detention.

During three years of exile—interspersed with a few brief periods of service—that he spent in Provence, he seemed assuaged. He carried out conscientiously his roles of lord of the manor and spouse: he had two children with his wife, received homage from the community of Saumanne, cared for his grounds, read, and had several dramatic works performed at his theater, including one of his own composition. But he was poorly compensated for this edifying life: in 1771 he was imprisoned for debts. Released, his virtuous zeal had cooled off. He seduced his young sister-in-law, for whom he seemed briefly to have had sincere feelings: canoness, virgin, his wife's sister, these appellations in any case added spice to the adventure. Meanwhile, he sought in Marseilles yet other distractions, and in 1772 "the affair of the aphrodisiac bonbons" took on unexpected and terrifying proportions.[22] While he was in flight to Italy with his sister-in-law, he and his valet Latour were condemned to death in absentia, and both were burned in effigy on the square in Aix. The canoness took refuge in a convent in France, where she would end her days, while he hid in Savoy. Captured and imprisoned in the Château de Miolans, his wife helped him escape, but he was henceforth a hunted man. Whether on the roads of Italy, or shut away in his castle, he knew that a normal existence would no longer be permitted him. From time to time he took his seigniorial role seriously, such as when a troop of actors settled on his lands to present *Le mari cocu, battu et content.*[23] Sade—

perhaps irritated by this title—ordered the posters torn down by the town clerk as "scandalous and detrimental to the freedoms of the Church"; he also chased from his grounds an individual named Saint-Denis—against whom he held grievances—declaring: "I have the right to expel from my land all homeless and disreputable persons." These displays of authority were not enough to amuse him, so he attempted to realize the dream that haunted his texts: in the solitude of the Château de la Coste, he assembled a seraglio obedient to his whims. With the complicity of the Marquise he assembled several handsome valets, an illiterate but attractive secretary, an appetizing cook and chambermaid, plus two young girls furnished by madams. But, the Château de la Coste was not the inaccessible fortress of *Les cent vingt journées de Sodome*; society surrounded him. The girls fled, the chambermaid gave birth to a child whose paternity she attributed to Sade, the cook's father came to the castle to shoot Sade with a revolver, and the handsome secretary was retrieved by his parents. Only Renée-Pélagie conformed exactly to the character assigned to her by her husband; all the others reclaimed their existence, and Sade once again understood that he could not make of this too-real world his theater.

This world was not content to thwart his dreams: it renounced him. Sade fled to Italy; but Mme de Montreuil, who did not forgive him for having seduced her younger daughter, was watching for him; returned to France, he ventured to Paris, and she took advantage of the occasion to have him imprisoned in the Château de Vincennes on February 13, 1777. Brought back to Aix, and put on trial, Sade took refuge at La Coste where he began, under his wife's resigned eye, an affair with his housekeeper, Mademoiselle Rousset. But on November 7, 1778, Sade found himself again at Vincennes "locked up like a wild beast behind nineteen iron doors."

So another history began; during eleven years of captivity—first at Vincennes and then at the Bastille—a man died and a writer was born. The man was quickly broken; reduced to powerlessness, and unaware how long his imprisonment would last, his spirit fled into a delirium of interpretation: through meticulous calculations, none of which were based in fact, he sought to guess the length of his captivity. Intellectually he got his bearings back relatively quickly, as his correspondence with Mme de Sade and Mademoiselle Rousset proves.[24] But his flesh abdicated; he sought in the pleasures of the table compensation for his sexual fast. His valet Carteron, relates that in prison "he smoked like a chimney" and "ate for four." "Extreme in all things," by his own admission, Sade became a bulimic; he ordered his wife to send him enormous baskets of food, and he quickly became fat. In the midst of his complaints, accusations, pleas, supplications, he still amused himself a little by torturing the Marquise: he feigned jealousy, accused her of dark plots, and when she visited him, he criticized her appearance and demanded that she dress in the most austere fashion. Yet these amusements were rare and poor. From 1782 onwards, he would demand of literature alone what life no longer allowed him: excitement, defiance, sincerity and all the joys of the imagination. And here again, he is "extreme," writing as he ate: in a frenzy. From *Dialogue entre un prêtre et un moribond* followed *Les cent vingt journées de Sodome*, *Les infortunes de la vertu*, and *Aline et Valcour*.[25] According to the 1788 catalog he presumably wrote thirty-five plays, a half dozen tales, and the vast majority of *Portefeuille d'un homme de lettres*.[26] Still, this list is undoubtedly incomplete.

When Sade found himself free again on Good Friday, 1790, he could hope, he did hope that a new life was awaiting him. His wife demanded a separation, his sons, one of whom was preparing to emigrate, the other of whom was a Knight of Malta, were strangers to him, as was his "good, fat, farm girl" of a daughter. Freed from his family, he whom the old society treated as a pariah would try to integrate into the new society that had just given him back his dignity as a citizen. His plays were publicly performed, *Oxtiern* even became a great success.[27] Granted membership in the Section des Piques, he was named president of it, and he ardently wrote addresses and petitions.[28] But his idyll with the Revolution was short-lived. Sade was fifty, had a past that rendered him suspect, and an aristocratic temperament that his hatred of the aristocracy had not subdued: he is once again divided. He was republican, and theoretically he even claimed complete socialism and the abolition of property, but he intended to keep his castle and his grounds. This world to which he attempted to adapt was still too real a world whose brutal resistance hurt him; and it was, moreover, a world ruled by the universal laws that he considered abstract, false and unjust; when in their name society authorized itself to murder, Sade withdrew in horror. One must truly misunderstand Sade to be surprised that instead of requesting a post as a commissary of the people in the provinces, which would have enabled him to torture and kill, he was discredited by his humanity. Do we imagine that Sade "loved blood" as one loves the mountains or the sea? "To make blood flow" was an act whose significance for him could be exalting in certain circumstances; but what he essentially required of cruelty was that both singular individuals and his own existence be revealed to him at once as consciousness and freedom and as flesh. He refused to judge, condemn and see anonymous people die at a distance. He hated nothing in the old society more than its claim to judge and punish, of which he had been the victim: he could not excuse the Reign of Terror. When murder became constitutional it was nothing more than the odious expression of abstract principles: it became inhuman. And this is why, named juror for indictment, Sade almost always rendered dismissals in favor of the accused, and refused to harm, in the name of the law, Mme de Montreuil and her family, even when he held their fate in his hands. He was even eventually led to resign from his position as president of the Section des Piques, as he wrote to Gaufridy,[29] "I believed myself forced to leave the seat to my vice-president; they wanted me to put a horror, an inhumanity into practice: I never wanted to." In December 1793 he was incarcerated under charges of "moderantism." Released three hundred and seventy five days later, he wrote with disgust, "My national detention, the guillotine beneath my eyes, caused me a hundred times more pain than all the Bastilles imaginable." It was through these crude slaughters that politics demonstrated with too much evidence that it considered men to be a simple collection of objects, whereas Sade demanded around him a universe peopled with singular existences. The "evil" in which he took refuge vanished when crime was claimed by virtue. The Reign of Terror, which was exercised in good conscience, constituted the most radical negation of Sade's demonic world.

"The excesses of the Reign of Terror made crime ordinary," wrote Saint-Just.[30] Sade's sexuality had cooled not only because he was old and worn, but because the guillotine had assassinated the black poetry of eroticism. To find pleasure in humiliating flesh, or exalting it, one must valorize it. The flesh has neither meaning nor price if one can, in full tranquility, treat men as things. Sade would once again resuscitate in his books his past experiences and revive his old universe; but in his blood and nerves, he no longer believed in it. There was nothing physical in the relationship that attached him to the one he called "Sensible."[31] His only erotic pleasures now came from the contemplation of obscene paintings inspired by *Justine* with which he had decorated a private chamber.[32] He remembered; but was no longer capable of any élan, and the sole enterprise of living overwhelmed him. Delivered from the social and familial surroundings in which he suffocated, but whose solid protection was nevertheless necessary, he now dragged himself from misery to malady. He sold his possessions at La Coste at a loss, and he quickly squandered the revenue. He took refuge with a farmer and later in a garret with the son of "Sensible," earning forty *sous* a day as an employee of the performances at Versailles. The decree of June 28, 1799, which prohibited striking his name from the lists of émigrés, where he had been inscribed as a noble, tore these desperate words from him: "Death and wretchedness, this is the compensation I receive for my constant attachment to the Republic." He received nevertheless a certificate of residence and citizenship, and in December 1799 he played the role of Fabrice in *Oxtiern*. But at the beginning of 1800 he was in the hospital at Versailles "dying of hunger and cold," and threatened with imprisonment for debts. He was so unhappy in the hostile world of so-called free men that one may wonder if he had chosen to return to the solitude and security of prison. At least we can say that to have the imprudence of circulating *Justine* and the folly of publishing *Zoloé*, in which he takes on Josephine, Mme Tallien, Tallien, Barras and Bonaparte,[33] the idea of a new seclusion must not have been entirely repugnant to him. Secret or stated, his desire was fulfilled: there he was, locked up at Saint-Pélagie on April 5, 1801, and it was there, and then at Charenton—where Mme Quesnet would follow him, obtaining a room next to his by passing as his daughter—that he would end his days.

Obviously, once locked up, Sade protested and struggled for years; but at least he could give himself over once again heedlessly to the passion that for him replaced that of *jouissance*: writing. He never stopped. When he left the Bastille, the majority of his papers were lost, and the manuscript of *Les journées de Sodome*—a scroll of 12 meters that he had carefully hidden and which was saved without his knowing it—he believed destroyed. After *La philosophie dans le boudoir*, written in 1795, he began a new project: a completely developed and revised version of *Justine*, followed by *Juliette*, which appeared, and he disclaimed, in 1797,[34] while he had *Les crimes de l'amour* printed publicly.[35] At Sainte-Pélagie, he became absorbed in the immense ten-volume work: *Les journées de Florabelle ou la nature dévoilée*. We must also attribute to him, although the book did not appear under his name, the two-volume *La Marquise de Ganges*.[36]

Apparently, Sade no longer wished for anything but peace in his daily life because henceforth the meaning of his existence resided definitively in his work as a writer. He took walks with "Sensible" in the asylum gardens, wrote and performed plays for the ill, agreed to compose an impromptu on the occasion of a visit by the Archbishop of Paris, and, on Easter Sunday, served holy bread and took up the collection at the parish church. His will shows that he had in no way reneged on his convictions, but he was tired of fighting. "He was polite to the point of obsequiousness," said Nodier, "affable to the degree of unction . . . he spoke respectfully of everything that one respects." According to Ange Pitou, the idea of aging and that of death horrified him. "This man paled at the idea of death and fainted at seeing his white hair."[37] He nevertheless died peacefully on December 2, 1814, of "a pulmonary congestion in the form of asthma."

The most salient feature of this painful experience that was his life is that there was never any solidarity between other men and himself. No common enterprise linked the last scions of decadent nobility. Sade peopled the solitude to which his birth condemned him with erotic games so extreme that his peers turned against him. When a new world was proposed to him, he dragged too heavy a past behind him: divided against himself, suspect to others, this aristocrat haunted by dreams of despotism could not sincerely ally himself with the rising bourgeoisie. And although he was indignant at the bourgeoisie for oppressing the people, the latter were nonetheless foreign to him; he did not belong to any of the classes whose antagonism he denounced; he had no fellow man but himself. Perhaps if his affective formation had been different, he would have been able to counteract this destiny, but all his life he appeared as a fanatical egocentric. His indifference to external events, his obsessive worries about money, the maniacal care with which he surrounded his debauches, the delirium of his interpretation outlined at Vincennes, and the schizophrenic aspect of his dreams reveal a radically introverted temperament. This passionate coincidence with himself, while it had shown him his limits, had also given his life the exemplary character which makes us examine it today.

* * *

Sade made his eroticism the meaning and the expression of his whole existence; therefore it is not idle curiosity to seek to specify the nature of it. To say, as Maurice Heine does, that he tried everything and loved everything, is to evade the problem; and the term "algolagnia" does little to advance our appreciation of Sade's intelligence.[38] He evidently possessed a well defined sexual idiosyncrasy; but it is not so easy to understand it for his accomplices and his victims kept silent, and there were only two flagrant scandals that briefly raised the curtain behind which debauchery is usually hidden. His journals and memoirs have been lost; his letters are prudent, and in his books he invents himself more than he bares himself. "I conceived all that one may conceive in this genre, but I assuredly have not done everything that I have conceived. And I assuredly never will," he wrote. It is understandable that his work has been compared to Krafft-Ebbing's *Psychopathia sexualis*, and nobody would dream of imputing to the latter all the perversions he catalogs.[39] Similarly, Sade systematically established, according to formulas of a kind of combinatory art, a repertory of man's sexual possibilities. Sade certainly did not live or even dream all of these in his own flesh. Not only does he report too much, but he frequently reports incorrectly. His stories resemble the engravings that illustrate *Justine* and *Juliette* in the 1797 editions: the anatomy and the posture of the characters are drawn with minute realism, but the clumsy serenity and the monotony of their facial expressions render their horrible bacchanals perfectly unreal. Through the cold-blooded orgies that Sade devises, it is difficult to discern a convincing live testimony. Nevertheless, there are, in his novels, situations which he treats with particular indulgence, showing some of his heroes a special sympathy. Sade lends many of his tastes and ideas to Noirceuil, Blangis, Gernande, and Dolmancé in particular.[40] Sometimes also in a letter, in an incident, or at the turn of a dialogue, springs forth an unforeseen and living phrase that is not the echo of any foreign voice. These are the scenes, the heroes and the privileged texts that we must examine.

In the vernacular, sadism signifies cruelty: flayings, bloodlettings, tortures, murders. The first striking feature in Sade's work is indeed that which tradition has associated with his name. The Rose Keller episode reveals him whipping his victim with a cat-o'-nine-tails and a knotted whipcord, and, apparently,* hacking her with a pen knife and pouring hot wax on her wounds. In Marseilles, he pulled from his pockets a parchment cat-o'-nine-tails studded with bent nails and ordered heather switches brought to him, and in all his conduct regarding his wife, he manifested evident mental cruelty. He also expresses himself abundantly on the pleasure one can feel by causing suffering, but when he contents himself with repeating the classical doctrine of animal spirits, he hardly enlightens us: "It is simply a question of disturbing the totality of our nerves with the most violent shock possible; now, there is no doubt that since pain affects us more sharply than pleasure, the resulting shocks on us from this sensation produced in the other will be therefore essentially a more vigorous vibration."[41] Sade does not clear up the mystery of how the violence of a vibration may become voluptuous consciousness. Happily, he sketches out more sincere explanations elsewhere. The fact is that the original intuition behind all of Sade's sexuality and ethics is the fundamental identity of coitus and of cruelty. "Would the climax of pleasure be a kind of rage if the mother of the human species† had not intended that the treatment of coitus to be the same as that of anger? In that case, what well-constituted man . . . would not desire . . . to disturb

---

* Sade's statements about the incident do not correspond on this point with Rose Keller's.
† Nature.

his *jouissance*?" In the description that Sade gives us of the Duc de Blangis at the moment of orgasm, one must certainly see a transposition into the epic mode of the author's morals: "Dreadful cries, atrocious blasphemies escaped from his swollen chest, flames seemed to come from his eyes. He foamed, he whinnied . . ."[42] and he carried this to the point of choking. Sade himself, according to the deposition of Rose Keller, "started screaming very loudly and very frighteningly" before he cut the ropes that immobilized his victim. The letter "*La vanille et la manille*," confirms that he experienced orgasm as an attack analogous to an epileptic fit, aggressive and murderous like rage.[43]

How do we explain this singular violence? Some have wondered if in fact Sade was not sexually deficient; many of his heroes—Gernande, who is dear to him, for example—have little means, and great difficulty becoming erect or ejaculating. Surely Sade experienced these torments; but it was the excess of debauchery that seems to have led him to this half-impotence, which is also the case with a great number of his libertines. Among them, however, many are very well-endowed, and Sade often alludes to the vigor of his own temperament. It is, on the other hand, the combination of his ardent sexual appetites with his radical, affective "isolatism" that seems to me to be the key to his eroticism.

From adolescence to his imprisonment, Sade certainly knew in a pressing, indeed obsessive, manner the solicitations of desire; on the other hand, there was an experience of which he seemed absolutely ignorant: that of emotional intoxication. Never does sensual pleasure [*volupté*] appear in his texts as self-forgetting, swooning, or abandon. Compare, for example, the effusions of Rousseau with Noirceuil or Dolmancé's frenetic blasphemies, or the Mother Superior's excitement in Diderot's *La religieuse* with the brutal pleasures of Sade's tribades.[44] For Sade's heroes, male aggression is not attenuated by the ordinary metamorphosis of the body into flesh; not for an instant does he lose himself in his animality. He remains so lucid, so cerebral that, instead of hampering his ardor, philosophical discourse becomes for him an aphrodisiac. In this cold, tense body resistant to all enchantment, we see that desire and pleasure are unleashed in a furious attack: they strike him like some sort of organic accident, instead of constituting an attitude lived in the subject's psycho-physiological unity. Thanks to this disproportion, the sexual act creates this illusion of sovereign *jouissance* which gives it its incomparable value in Sade's eyes; but it lacks for him an essential dimension, the absence for which all sadism strives to compensate. Through emotional intoxication, existence is grasped in oneself and in the other as

59

at once subjectivity and passivity. Through this ambiguous unity, the two partners merge: each is delivered from its self-presence and attains an immediate communication with the other. The curse that weighed on Sade—and which his childhood alone could explain to us—is this *autism* which prevents him from ever forgetting himself and from ever realizing the presence of the other. If he had possessed a cold nature, no problem would have arisen; but he had instincts that pushed him towards these foreign objects with which he was unable to unite, so he had to invent special ways to grasp them. Later, when his desires were depleted, he continued to live in this erotic universe in which, through sensuality, boredom, defiance and resentment, he constructed the only worthwhile universe in his eyes: and the goal of his maneuverings was to provoke erection and orgasm. But even when these were easy for him, Sade needed deviations to give his sexuality the signification that took shape in it without reaching completion: an evasion of his consciousness in his flesh, an apprehension of the other as consciousness through the flesh.

Normally, it is through the vertigo of the other made flesh that each is enchanted in his own flesh. If the subject remains enclosed in the solitude of his consciousness, then he escapes emotional intoxication and can rejoin the other only through representations; a cerebral and cold lover watches very closely for the *jouissance* of his mistress, and he needs to affirm himself as the author of it because he has no other means of attaining his own fleshly condition. One could qualify as sadistic that conduct which compensates for separation with reflective tyranny. Sade knew, as we have seen, that to inflict pleasure could be an aggressive act, and his despotism sometimes takes this form; but it did not satisfy him. First, he was repelled by the kind of equality that shared sensual pleasure creates: "If the objects that serve us have *jouissance*, they often become more occupied with themselves than with us, and our own *jouissance* is consequently disturbed. The idea of seeing another achieve the same pleasure reduces one to a kind of equality which spoils the unspeakable attractions that come from despotism."[45] And in a more trenchant manner, he declares, "All shared *jouissance* is weakened."[46] And then agreeable sensations are too benign; flesh reveals itself as flesh most dramatically when it is torn and bloody. "There is no kind of sensation that is more active, more incisive than that of pain: its impressions are unmistakable." But in order for me to also become flesh and blood through the suffering I have inflicted, I must recognize my own condition in the passivity of the other, thus recognizing that the other is inhabited by freedom and consciousness. The libertine "would have much to complain of if he acted upon an inert object that felt nothing." This is why the contortions and cries of the victim are necessary for the happiness of the torturer, to the extent that Verneuil fitted his wife with a sort of *bonnet* which amplified her cries.[47] In its revolt, the tortured object affirms itself as my fellow creature, and I attain through its mediation that synthesis of spirit and flesh that I was previously denied.

If the sought-after goal is to at once escape oneself and to discover the reality of foreign existences, there is still another way which opens itself: to be abused by the other. Sade is far from ignorant of this; in Marseilles he used switches and cat-o'-nine-tails, both to be whipped and to whip. This was assuredly one of his most usual practices, and all his heroes are happily whipped. "Nobody today doubts that flagellation possesses a virtue of the greatest effect to restore a vigor extinguished by excesses of pleasure."[48] There is still another way to realize his passivity: in Marseilles, Sade was sodomized by his valet Latour, who seems rather accustomed to providing this service for him; his heroes repeatedly imitated him; and he declared loudly, in the most vivid terms, that maximum pleasure is attained by combining active and passive sodomy. There is no other perversion of which he speaks so often and with so much indulgence, or indeed even impassioned vehemence.

For those who like to catalog individuals under well-defined labels, two questions now emerge: Was Sade a sodomite? And, was he deep down a masochist? In terms of sodomy, everything confirms that it was one of the essential aspects of his sexuality: his physical appearance, the role played by his valets, the presence of the handsome, illiterate secretary at La Coste, the enormous importance that, in his writings, Sade attributes to this *fantasy*, and the ardor of his speeches in its defense. Certainly women played an important role in his life as in his work; he knew many girls, kept la Beauvoisin and other less significant mistresses, seduced his sister-in-law, assembled young women and girls in the Château de la Coste, flirted with Mlle Rousset and ended his life at the side of Mme Quesnet. In addition, of course, there were the bonds imposed by society, but which he re-created in his own way, that united him to Mme de Sade. But what relationships did he have with them? It is remarkable that, in the only two testimonies collected on his sexual activity, we do not see that Sade "knew" these partners in the normal way. In the case of Rose Keller, he was satiated by whipping her, but did not touch her. As regards the girl in Marseilles, he proposed to her that she be "known from behind" by his domestic servant or, by default, by himself; since she refused, he contented himself with touching her while he himself was "known" by Latour. His protagonists cheerfully amuse themselves by

61

deflowering young virgins: this bloody and sacrilegious violence appeals to Sade's imagination, but even when they sexually initiate a virgin, they often prefer to treat her as a boy than make her blood run. More than one of Sade's characters professes a profound distaste for women's "fronts"; others are still more eclectic, but their preferences are clear. Sade never praised the part of a woman's body that the *Thousand and One Nights* so joyously celebrated, and had nothing but disdain for the poor *effeminates* who possessed their wives normally. We have seen under what conditions he fathered children with Mme de Sade, and given the strange orgies that went on at La Coste, what proves that he was the one who impregnated Nanon? Of course we must not attribute to Sade the opinions that specialized pederasts in his books profess; but the argument that he places in the mouth of the bishop in *Les journées de Sodome* is close enough to his heart that we may consider it a confession. In terms of pleasure, he says, "The boy is worth more than the girl; consider it from the point of view of evil, which is almost always the true attraction of pleasure; the crime will seem greater to you with a being totally from your species than with one who is not, and from this moment, the sensual pleasure is doubled."[49] Sade may well have written to Mme de Sade that his only fault had been to *love women too much*, but that is from an official and hypocritical letter. And it is through storybook dialectic that he gives women the most triumphant roles in his books: wickedness in them makes a striking contrast with the traditional softness of their sex. When they surmount, through crime, their natural abjection, they demonstrate more strikingly than man that no situation could shackle the flight of a bold heart. But they become the most magnificent torturers in imagination, only because in reality they are born victims: servile, tearful, foolish and passive. Throughout Sade's work, the contempt and disgust that Sade truly felt for them shows through. Was it his mother he despised in them? We might also wonder whether Sade did not hate this sex because he saw in it not his complement, but his double, and that he could receive nothing from it. His great female villains have more warmth and liveliness than his male heroes, and not only for aesthetic reasons, but because they are closer to him. I do not at all believe that he finds himself, as has been claimed, in the bleating Justine, but he certainly recognizes himself in Juliette, who submits to the same treatment as her sister with pride and pleasure. Sade felt himself to be a woman, and he reproaches women for not being the male he desires: he endowed the greatest and most extravagant of all, la Durand, with a gigantic clitoris that allowed her to behave sexually as a man.[50]

It is impossible to say to what degree women were for Sade anything but substitutes and toys, but we can correctly affirm that his sexuality was essentially anal, which is confirmed by his attachment to money. The stories of embezzling inheritances played an enormous role in his life, and theft appears in his work as a sexual practice, the thought of which is enough to provoke orgasm. And if we refuse this Freudian interpretation of his cupidity, it is an unequivocal fact that Sade openly recognized his coprophilia. In Marseilles, he gave sugared almonds to a girl telling her "that they would excite her to break wind," and he was disappointed they did not produce the expected benefit. It is also striking that the two *fantasies* he attempted to explain in the greatest depth were cruelty and coprophagy. To what extent did he engage in these? There is a significant gap between Sade's practices in Marseilles and the excremental orgies in *Les journées de Sodome*, but the importance he attributes to these practices, the care with which he describes the rites and especially the preparations for them, proves that we are not dealing with cold and systematic inventions, but with affective phantasms. On the other hand, Sade's extraordinary bulimia as a prisoner cannot be explained simply by his idleness: eating cannot be a substitute for erotic activity unless an infantile equivalence remains between the gastrointestinal functions and the sexual functions. This is certainly perpetuated with Sade, who closely links the alimentary orgy with the erotic orgy. "No passion is better allied with lust than intoxication and gluttony,"[51] he notes; and this confusion ends up with phantasms of anthropophagy. Drinking blood, swallowing sperm and excrement, and eating children is all to assuage desire by the destruction of its object. *Jouissance* accepts no exchange, no gift, no reciprocity, no gratuitous munificence: its despotism is that of avarice that chooses to annihilate that which it cannot assimilate.

Sade's coprophilia has still another meaning: "If it is the filthy thing that pleases us in the act of lust, the filthier it is, the more it should please us." Among the most evident sexual attractions, Sade ranks at the top old age, ugliness and stench. This connection of the erotic with the *vile* is as primary for Sade as its connection with cruelty, and is explained in an analogous manner. Beauty is too simple; we grasp it with an intellectual judgment that does not tear consciousness from its solitude or the body from its indifference. Instead of being degraded by vileness, the man who has commerce with filth, like the one who wounds or is wounded, realizes himself as flesh; and in his wretchedness and his humiliation he becomes an abyss where the spirit is engulfed and where separate individuals are joined. Sade was able to succeed in abolishing his obsessive presence only when he was beaten, penetrated, or soiled.

Nevertheless, Sade is not a masochist in the popular sense of the word; he fiercely mocks men who make themselves slaves to a woman: "I abandon them to the vile pleasure of wearing the irons with which nature gives them the right to overwhelm others; these animals should vegetate in the baseness that degrades them." The universe of the masochist is magical, and this is why he is almost always a fetishist. Objects—shoes, furs and riding crops— are charged with exhalations that have the power to change him into a thing, and this is what the masochist explicitly seeks: to be abolished by becoming an inert object. The world of Sade is essentially rational and practical; objects—material or human—which serve his pleasures are tools without mystery, and he explicitly sees in humiliation a haughty ruse. For example, Saint-Fond declares: "The humiliation of certain libertine acts serves as a pretext for pride."[52] And elsewhere Sade says of the libertine that "the state of degradation which characterizes the one in which you plunge him to punish him, pleases, amuses, delights him, and he enjoys within himself having gone so far as to deserve such treatment."[53] There is nevertheless between these two attitudes an intimate kinship: the masochist wants to lose himself in order to become fascinated by this object with which he claims to blend, and this effort redirects him to his own subjectivity. By demanding that his partner mistreat him, he tyrannizes him. His humiliating exhibitions and the tortures undergone, humiliate and torture the other as well. Inversely, by soiling and wounding, the torturer also soils and wounds himself. He participates in this passivity which he unveils, and seeking to grasp himself as the cause of the torment he inflicts, he reaches himself both as instrument and as object, which is why these practices are rightly unified under the name *sadomasochism*. We must be careful, however, that despite the generality of this term, such behaviors may concretely offer a great diversity. Sade is not Sacher Masoch.[54] What particularly characterizes him is the tension of a will that is applied to the realization of flesh without being lost in it. In Marseilles, he had himself whipped, but from time to time he threw himself towards the chimney and inscribed with a knife on a pipe the number of lashes he had just received; humiliation immediately turns into bragging. Sodomized, he flays a girl at the same time; and one of his favorite fantasies is to be beaten and penetrated, while beating and penetrating a submissive victim at the same time.

I said that we would misunderstand the meaning and bearing of Sade's singularities if we limited ourselves to thinking of them as simple facts; they are always charged with an ethical significance. After the scandal of 1763, Sade's eroticism is no longer only an individual attitude: it is also a challenge to society. In a letter to his wife, Sade explains how he made principles of his tastes. "These principles and these tastes are taken by me to the point of fanaticism," he writes, "and fanaticism is the work of my tyrants' persecution." The supreme intention that animates all sexual activity is the wish to be criminal: cruelty or befouling are to realize evil. Sade directly experienced coitus as cruelty, laceration, and transgression, and through resentment he stubbornly laid claim to blackness. Since society allied itself with nature in order to deem him criminal in his pleasures, he would make crime itself a pleasure. "Crime is the soul of lust. What would *jouissance* be if crime did not accompany it? It is not the object of debauchery that excites us, it is the idea of evil."[55] Of the pleasure of torturing and ridiculing a beautiful woman, he writes, "there is a kind of pleasure that results from the sacrilege and desecration of the objects offered to our cult."[56] It was not by chance that he chose Easter Sunday to whip Rose Keller; and it was at the moment he sardonically proposed to hear her confession that his sexual excitement reached its paroxysm: no aphrodisiac is more powerful than the challenge to the Good. "The desires we feel for great crimes are always more violent than those we feel for small ones."[57] Did Sade do evil in order to feel guilty? Or did he escape his culpability by assuming it? Reducing him to one or the other of these positions would be to mutilate him. He settles in neither complacent abjection nor stupid impudence, but constantly oscillates dramatically between arrogance and bad conscience.

We therefore perceive the impact of Sade's cruelty and masochism. This man who allied a violent temperament—which was quickly consumed, it seems—with an affective and quasi-pathological "isolatism," sought a substitute for emotional intoxication through pain, inflicted and suffered. His cruelty has an extremely complex meaning. First, it appears as an extreme and immediate accomplishment of the coital instinct and its total assumption. Cruelty affirms the radical separation of the object other and the sovereign subject, aiming at the jealous destruction of what cannot be voraciously assimilated; but especially, rather than crowning orgasm impulsively, it seeks to provoke it in a premeditated way. Cruelty permits grasping the consciousness-flesh unity through the other, and projecting it onto the self; and finally, cruelty freely claims the criminal character which nature and society have assigned to eroticism. On the other hand, by having himself sodomized, flagellated and soiled, Sade also comes to the revelation of himself as passive flesh; he satiates his desire for self-punishment and accepts the

65

guilt to which he had been assigned, and immediately returns from humility to pride through defiance. In the complete sadistic scene, the individual unleashes his nature, knowing it is evil and aggressively assuming it as such; he thereby merges vengeance and transgression, and transforms the latter into glory.

Murder is one act which is proposed as the most extreme end of both cruelty and masochism, because the subject affirms himself in a privileged manner as both tyrant and criminal. It is often maintained that it constitutes the supreme achievement of sadistic sexuality, but in my opinion this interpretation rests upon a misunderstanding. Assuredly it is with an apologetic aim that Sade in his letters denies so forcefully ever having been an assassin; however I think the idea truly repulses him. To be sure, he overloads his accounts with monstrous slaughters because there is no abuse whose abstract signification is as glaringly obvious as murder; it represents the exasperated demand of a freedom without law and without fear. And by indefinitely prolonging the agony of his victim on paper, the author can eternalize the privileged instant in which a lucid spirit inhabits a body that self-degrades into matter; he breathes once more a living past into unconscious remains. But in truth, what would a tyrant do with this *inert object*: a cadaver? There is undoubtedly in the passage from life to death something vertiginous, and the sadist, whom the conflicts of consciousness and flesh fascinate, will gladly dream himself the author of such a radical metamorphosis. But while it is normal for him to occasionally realize this privileged experience, it is not possible that it will bring him supreme satisfaction. This freedom that one claims to tyrannize to the point of annihilation, in being annihilated, slips out of the world in which tyranny had taken hold of it. Sade's protagonists indefinitely multiply their massacres because none of it satiates them. Concretely, massacres bring no solution to the problems that torment the libertine because the goal he pursues is not simply that of pleasure—no one would commit themselves so passionately, so dangerously, to the pursuit of a sensation even had it the violence of an epileptic fit—rather, the final trauma must guarantee, by its own evidence, the success of an enterprise where the stakes infinitely surpass it. But on the contrary, he frequently stops the act without completing it, and if it is prolonged by murder, the death only confirms the failure. Blangis strangles with the fury of orgasm, and there is a hopelessness in this rage where desire is extinguished without being assuaged; the pleasures that he premeditates are less savage and more complex. The following episode from *Juliette* is, among others, significant: inflamed by a conversation with a young woman, Noirceuil, who "had little taste for solitary pleasures," meaning those practiced in isolation with a single partner, immediately calls to his friends. "We are not numerous enough. . . . No, leave me be . . . My passions concentrated on this single point resemble the rays of the sun reunited by an incendiary lens; they immediately burn the object found in their focus."[58] He forbids himself such an excess not because of an abstract scruple, but because he knows that after the murderous spasm he will once again find himself frustrated. Our instincts indicate to us ends we cannot reach if we are content to follow our immediate impulses; we must surmount them, reflect upon them, and invent ingenious means to satisfy them. The presence of foreign consciousnesses will best help us take the necessary distance from them.

Sexuality in Sade does not derive from biology: it is a social event. The orgies in which he indulged were almost always collective: in Marseilles, Sade demanded two girls and was accompanied by his valet; at La Coste he assembled a seraglio; in his novels, the libertines create true communities. The advantage is primarily the number of combinations offered to their debauches, but this socialization of eroticism has deeper motives. In Marseilles, Sade called his valet "Monsieur le Marquis" and wished to watch him "know" a girl using his name rather than "know" her himself: the representation of the erotic scene was more interesting to him than the lived experience. In *Les journées de Sodome, fantasies* are recounted before they are practiced. Through this doubling, the act becomes a spectacle that one looks upon at a distance when it is executed, thereby keeping a signification that a bestial and solitary outburst obscures. For if the debauchee were to coincide exactly with his gestures and the victim with his emotions, freedom and consciousness would be lost in the distractions of the flesh; the latter would be only brute suffering, the former, convulsive voluptuousness; but thanks to the witnesses assembled around them, a presence is maintained that helps the subject himself remain present. He hopes to reach himself through representations, and in order to see himself, he must be seen. While tyrannizing a victim, Sade is an object for those who watch him; inversely, by contemplating the violence that he is undergoing in the flesh he violates, he regains a grasp of himself as subject in the midst of his passivity, and the confusion of the for-itself and the for-others is accomplished. The accomplices are singularly necessary for endowing sexuality with its demoniacal dimension; it is through them that the act committed or undergone takes on a sure form instead of being diluted in contingent moments. In becoming real every infamy turns out to be possible; ordinarily, we familiarize ourselves with it so intimately that we hardly judge it condemnable; to be aston-

67

ished, to be frightened, we must contemplate ourselves from afar, through the eyes of strangers.

But this recourse to the other, as precious as it may be, is not enough to remove the contradictions that any sadistic attempt implies: if we have failed to grasp the ambiguous unity of existence in a lived experience, we will never succeed in reconstructing it intellectually. By definition, a representation can coincide with neither the intimacy of consciousness nor the opacity of the flesh; even less can it reconcile them. Once dissociated, these two moments of human reality are opposed, and once we pursue the one, the other shies away. If he is inflicted with too violent suffering, the subject gets lost, abdicates, and loses his sovereignty. An excess of villainy brings a disgust that goes contrary to pleasure. Cruelty is, in a practical sense, difficult to exercise except within very modest limits, and theoretically it implies a contradiction which is expressed by the following two quotes: "The most divine attractions are nothing when submission and obedience do not offer themselves," and: "One must do violence to the object of one's desire; no more pleasure arises when it gives in." But where can one meet free slaves? One must be satisfied with compromises. Sade crossed the conventional boundaries a bit with paid and abjectly consenting girls, and he permitted himself some violence against a spouse who maintained human dignity in her docility, but the ideal erotic act would never be realized. This is the deeper meaning of the words that Sade places in Jérome's mouth: "What we are doing here is nothing but the image of what we would like to do." Not only are the really considerable infamies practically forbidden; but even those that can be evoked in the most extreme frenzies would still disappoint their author: "To attack the sun, to deprive the universe of it, or to make use of it to set the world on fire, now that would be a crime!" Yet this dream appears satisfying because the criminal projects his own annihilation along with that of the universe; if he survived, he would find himself frustrated once again. The sadistic crime can never be adequate to the intention that animates it: the victim is never more than an analogon, the subject can only grasp himself as an imago, and their relationship is nothing but the parody of a drama that would really set them both in the grips of their incommunicable intimacy. This is why the bishop in *Les cent vingt journées de Sodome* "never committed one crime without immediately conceiving a second."[59] The moment of the plan is a privileged moment for the libertine, because he can ignore the contradiction with which reality will fatally oppose him. And narration plays a primordial role in sadistic orgies—easily awakening the senses upon which objects of flesh and bone no longer act—because the

68

latter can only be fully attained in their absence. In truth, the only way to be satisfied by the phantasms that debauchery creates is to count on their very unreality. In choosing eroticism, Sade chose the imaginary. Only in the imaginary could he succeed in installing himself with certainty and without the risk of disappointment. He repeated this throughout his work: "*Jouissance* of the senses is always ruled by imagination. Man cannot lay claim to bliss except in serving every caprice of his imagination." It is through imagination that he escapes from space, time, prison, the police, the void of absence, opaque presences, the conflicts of existence, death, life, and all its contradictions. Sade's eroticism is not accomplished through murder, but through literature.

* * *

It may seem at first glance that, by writing, Sade simply reacted, as others have, against his situation as a prisoner. The idea was not entirely foreign to him: one of the plays presented at La Coste in 1772 was undoubtedly his composition, and his coffers, forced open thanks to Mme de Montreuil, contained, written in his hand, "little sheets" which were probably notes on sexuality. He nonetheless waited four years, once imprisoned at Vincennes, before beginning a substantial work. In another dungeon in that same fortress, Mirabeau who groaned "I am buried alive in a tomb," was also seeking a diversion in writing.[60] Through translations, scandalous correspondences and an essay on *lettres de cachet*, he attempted simultaneously to kill time, distract his flesh, and undermine hostile society. Sade followed similar motives; he kept himself occupied; and more than once while composing his novels he had to *punch* himself. He too wanted to take revenge on his torturers, and wrote to his wife with a joyous rage, "You have imagined that you have worked wonders, I would wager, in reducing me to an atrocious abstinence from the sins of the flesh. Well then! you are mistaken . . . you have caused me to create fantasies that I must realize." Yet although his detention brought about his decision to write, it nevertheless had far deeper roots. Sade always told himself stories throughout his debauches, but the reality that served as an analogon to his fantasies, while it lent them density, also bothered them by its resistance. The opacity of things submerged their meanings; words, on the contrary, retain these meanings. A child already knows that graffiti is more obscene than the organs or gestures it evokes because the dirtying intention is affirmed in all its purity. Of all sacrilege, blasphemy is the easiest and surest. Sade's protagonists speak incessantly, and in the Rose Keller affair he indulged himself with long speeches. Writing, even better than speech, is capable of giving images the solidity of a monument, and it resists all contestation. Thanks to writing, virtue keeps its lethal prestige in the instant when it is denounced as hypocrisy and foolishness; crime remains criminal in its grandeur; and freedom can still pulse through a dying body. Literature permitted Sade to unleash and fix his dreams, and also to surmount the contradictions implied by all demonic systems. Even better still, writing itself is a demonic act because it aggressively flaunts criminal ghosts, which is what makes it so invaluable. If we find it paradoxical that an "isolationist" engaged himself so passionately in an effort of communication, then we understand him badly. He has nothing of the misanthrope who prefers animals and virgin forests to his own species. Cut off from the other, this inaccessible presence haunted him. Even in the most intimate moments of his life, Sade reclaimed foreign consciousnesses as witnesses, so it is natural that he wished to expose himself before the vast public to which a book could lay claim.

Did he desire nothing other than scandalizing? In 1795 he wrote, "I will offer you great truths; people will listen to them and reflect upon them. If not all of them are pleasing, at least some of them will remain, I will have contributed in some way to the progress of light, and I will be content."[61]*
And in *La nouvelle Justine*, "It is to love men poorly to disguise such essential truths from them, whatever the results may be." After Sade presided over the Section des Piques and wrote speeches and petitions in the name of the collectivity, he must have flattered himself that he was one of the spokespeople for humanity. In his most optimistic moments, he retained from his experience, not the accursed aspect, but its authentic richness. These dreams were quickly dissipated, but it is far too simple to cast Sade as a Satanist. For him, sincerity is inextricably mixed with bad faith. He was pleased that truth could scandalize, but he also made scandal a duty because scandal manifested truth: at the moment when he arrogantly claimed his faults, he proved himself right. His intent was also to send a message to the public whom he deliberately outraged. His writings reflect the ambivalence of his relationship with the given world and with others.

What should be still more surprising is the mode of expression he chose. One would expect someone who so jealously cultivated his singularity to translate his experience in a more singular form, as did Lautréamont for example.[62] But first of all, the eighteenth century offered few lyric possibilities. Sade loathed the bland sensibility which was mistaken for poetry at the time;

* *La philosophie dans le boudoir.*

the times were not ripe for a *"poète maudit."* And nothing disposed Sade to great literary audacity. A true creator must—at least on a certain plane and at a certain moment—be radically freed from the given and emerge in a total solitude beyond other men. But in Sade there is an intimate weakness which his arrogance poorly masks; society had settled into his very heart in the form of guilt. He has neither the means nor the time to reinvent the world, man, and himself: he is in too much of a hurry, too pressured to defend himself. I have already said that in writing, he seeks above all else to win a good conscience; and for that he has to force the other to absolve him, indeed approve of him. He pleads instead of affirming himself; and to make himself understood, he borrows literary forms and proven doctrines from society. Educated in a rationalist era, no weapon seems more certain to him than reasoning. He who wrote, "Every principle of universal ethics is a real chimera," submits docilely to the general conventions of contemporary aesthetics and to the claims of universal logic. His art and his thinking can be explained thus: when he justifies himself, he is always trying at the same time to excuse himself. His work is an ambiguous enterprise to push crime to its very limits while abolishing his guilt.

It is natural and striking that as a consequence Sade's preferred genre was parody. He did not attempt to establish a new universe, but limited himself to deriding that which was imposed upon him by the manner in which he imitated it. And first, he pretended to believe in the chimeras that popu-late it: innocence, goodness, devotion, generosity, chastity. When he paints virtue unctuously in *Aline et Valcour*, *Justine*, and *Les crimes de l'amour*, it is not simply a prudent maneuver; and the "gauzes" with which he covers Justine are more than a literary artifice. One must lend a reality to virtue if one wants to amuse oneself by *vexing* it. In defending his tales against the reproach of immorality, Sade hypocritically writes: "Who would flatter himself to make virtue stand out when the features of vice that surround it are not strongly pronounced?" But he intended the exact opposite: how can one give vice its savor if the reader is not taken in by the mirage of the good? It is still more voluptuous to dupe honest folks than to shock them, and in writing out these sugared circumlocutions, Sade enjoyed the keen pleasures of mystification. Unfortunately, he usually amused himself more than he amuses us; very often his language has the same coldness, the same blandness, as the edifying tales that he undermines, and the scenes develop according to equally dreary conventions. However, it is through parody that Sade obtained his most brilliant artistic successes. Precursor to the *roman noir*, as Maurice Heine has emphasized, Sade is too profoundly rationalist to sink into the fantastic. When he abandons himself to the extravagances of his imagination, we do not know whether we should admire the epic vehemence or the irony; the miracle is that the latter is subtle enough not to ruin his deliria. On the contrary, this irony lends the deliria a dry poetry that keeps our incredulity at bay. This dark humor, which, on occasion he knows how to turn against itself, is more than a simple process. Blending shame and pride, truth and crime, Sade is inhabited with the spirit of contestation. He is at his most serious when he clowns around, and he is most sincere when his bad faith jumps out at us. His extravagance often disguises naive truths, while through the most ponderous reasoning he produces great blunders. His thought busies itself eluding whoever tries to get a hold on it, which is how his thought attains its goal of disturbing us. His style itself tends to disconcert us; he speaks with a monotone and awkward voice and begins to bore us, when suddenly, bitterly, sardonically, obscenely, a truth illuminates his dullness and brings out its brutal force. That is when, in its gaiety, violence and arrogant crudeness, Sade's style becomes that of a great writer.

Nevertheless, nobody would dream of classifying *Justine* alongside *Manon Lescaut* or *Liaisons dangereuses*.[63] Paradoxically, it was the very necessity of Sade's work which imposed upon it its aesthetic limits. He did not take up the indispensable distance of an artist vis-à-vis his work. He lacked the necessary detachment to confront reality in proposing to re-create it. Nor did he confront himself: he was content to project his phantasms beyond himself. His narratives have the unreality, the false precision and the monotony of schizophrenic reverie: it is for his own pleasure that he tells stories, and he is not concerned with imposing them upon a reader. The resistances of the world are not evoked there, nor are the more pathetic resistances that Sade encountered in the secrecy of his own heart. Caves, subterranean passages, mysterious castles, the whole arsenal of the Gothic novel, take on a singular meaning with Sade, symbolizing the isolation of the image. Perception reflects [*renvoie*] the totality of the given, and hence the obstacles enveloped by it. The image is perfectly docile and plastic; we find in it only what we have placed there. It is the enchanted domain where no force can dislodge the solitary despot. Sade was imitating this image even while claiming to give it a literary opacity. Thus he does not bother with the spatial and temporal coordinates in relation to which every real event is situated. The places he evokes are not of this world; and *tableaux vivants*, rather than adventures, take place here. Duration does not bite into Sade's universe; there is no future either for or in his work. Not only do the orgies to which he invites us take place nowhere, in no time, but what is even more serious, no persons are brought into play. The victims are frozen in their tearful abjection, the torturers in their frenzy. Sade complacently dreams himself in them rather than lending them his living depth. They do not know remorse; they scarcely know satiety; they are unaware of disgust; they kill with indifference; they are abstract incarnations of evil. But removed from any social, familial or human base, eroticism loses its *extraordinary* character. No longer conflict, revelation, privileged experience; no longer revealing dramatic relations between individuals, eroticism reverts to its biological coarseness. How can we feel the antagonism of foreign freedoms, or the fall of spirit into flesh if, everywhere, voluptuous or tortured, the flesh alone is flaunted? Horror itself is extinguished in these excesses at which no consciousness is concretely present. An Edgar Allan Poe tale such as *The Pit and the Pendulum* exudes so much anguish because we apprehend the situation from inside the subject, but we grasp the heroes of Sade only from the outside. They are as artificial and move about in the world as arbitrarily as Florian's shepherds; this is why these dark pastorals have the austerity of a nudist colony.[64]

The debauches that Sade presents in minute detail systematically exhaust the anatomical possibilities of the human body rather than uncovering its singular affective complexes. Nevertheless, if he has failed to give these acts an aesthetic truth, Sade foreshadowed sexual forms which were until then undreamt-of, in particular those uniting hatred of the mother, frigidity, cerebrality, passive sodomy, and cruelty. No one more vigorously emphasized the link between the imagination and what is called vice; and in these moments he opened for us, with surprising depth, insights into the relationship between sexuality and existence. Should we therefore admire him as a true innovator in the realm of psychology? It is not easy to decide. We always lend too much or too little significance to precursors; how can we measure the value of a truth that has not yet, to borrow a word from Hegel, *become*?[65] An idea receives its value from the experience that it sums up and from the method that it inaugurates; but we hardly know what credit to give to a formula whose novelty charms us, if no development confirms it. We are tempted either to enlarge it to the full significance with which it is subsequently enriched or, on the contrary, to minimize its impact. Thus, confronting Sade, the impartial reader hesitates. Often at the turn of a page he encounters an unanticipated phrase which seems to open up virgin paths, but the thought immediately stops short; instead of a living and singular voice, we hear nothing but the banal drivel of d'Holbach or La Mettrie.[66]

73

It is remarkable, for example, that in 1795,* Sade would write, "The act of *jouissance* is a passion which, I admit, subordinates all others; but at the same time it brings them all together."[67] Not only does Sade, in the first part of this quote, anticipate what has been called Freud's "pansexualism," he makes eroticism the primordial source of human conduct; moreover, in the second part he posits that sexuality is charged with significations that exceed it. Sade has unquestionably anticipated the great truth that the libido is everywhere and is always more than itself. He knows that the "perversions" commonly considered moral monstrosities or physiological defects envelop what we would now call an intentionality. He wrote to his wife that all "fantasy . . . always traces back to a principle of sensitivity"; and in *Aline et Valcour*, he affirms, "The refinements come only from sensitivity; it is therefore possible to have much of it and still be moved by those things that seem to exclude it." He also understood that our tastes are not motivated by the intrinsic qualities of the object, but by the relationship that the latter sustains with the subject. In a passage from *La nouvelle Justine*, he seeks to explain coprophilia to himself: his answer is mumbled; but what he indicates—by clumsily using the notion of imagination—is that the truth of a thing resides not in its brute presence, but in the meaning it carries for us in the course of our singular experience. Such intuitions authorize us to hail Sade as a precursor to psychoanalysis; unfortunately, he devalues his intuitions when he persists in repeating Holbach's principles of psycho-physiological parallelism. "When anatomy has been perfected, we will easily use it to demonstrate the relationship of the organization of man to the tastes that will have affected him." The contradiction is flagrant in the striking passage from *Les cent vingt journées de Sodome* in which he considers the sexual attractiveness of ugliness: "It is therefore proven that horror, villainy, the ghastly thing pleases us when we f . . . Beauty is the simple thing; ugliness is the extraordinary; and all ardent imaginations undoubtedly prefer an extraordinary thing to a simple one."[68] We wish Sade would define this link that he confusedly indicates between horror and desire, but he brusquely stops at a conclusion that negates the question he had posed: "All these things depend upon our conformation, on our organs, on the manner in which they affect each other; and we are no more the masters of changing our tastes on this than we are of varying the shapes of our bodies." It seems at first paradoxical that this man who had such an ardent predilection for himself forwarded theories that deny individual singularity all signification. He asked

---

* *La philosophie dans le boudoir.*

that we endeavor to better understand the human heart; he searched for and explored its most bizarre aspects; he cries out, "What an enigma is man!" He boasts, "You know no one analyzes things as I do";[69] and yet, he made himself a disciple of La Mettrie who, confusing man with machines and plants, reduced psychology to nothingness. As disconcerting as it may be, this antinomy can easily be explained. It is without a doubt less simple to be a monster than some would seem to believe. Fascinated by his own mystery, Sade is frightened by it; instead of expressing himself, he wants to defend himself. The words he lends Blamont* are a confession: "I have supported my deviations by reasonings; I was not eager to doubt: I conquered, I uprooted, I destroyed in my heart all that could disturb my pleasures." The first of his liberating tasks, which he repeated a thousand times, was to triumph over remorse; and if this meant repudiating all feelings of guilt, what doctrine is more certain than one which saps the very idea of responsibility? But it would be a gross error to want to imprison him in determinism, because he, like so many others, relies on it in order to lay claim to his freedom.

From the point of view of literature, these discourses woven out of commonplaces with which Sade interrupts his bacchanals finally rob them of all verisimilitude and life. Here again, Sade is not so much addressing the reader, but himself. His tiresome whitewashing has the value of a purification rite whose repetition is as natural to him as confession is to a believer. Sade does not hand over to us the work of a liberated man: he makes us participate in his effort of liberation. But it is precisely in this way that he grabs us: his attempt is more true than all the instruments it uses. If Sade were satisfied with the determinism he professed, he would be forced to repudiate all his ethical anxieties; but they imposed themselves on him with an evidence that no logic could obscure. Beyond the facile excuses he fastidiously invokes, he persists in attacking and interrogating himself. It is thanks to this stubborn sincerity, that despite his failure as a consummate artist or coherent philosopher, he merits acknowledgement as a great moralist.

* * *

Extreme in everything, Sade could not adapt to the deist compromises of his century. In 1782, his first work—*Dialogue entre un prêtre et un moribond*—was an atheist text. The existence of God had already been denied earlier, starting with the *Testament de Jean Meslier*, which appeared in 1729, and Rousseau had dared to present a sympathetic atheist, M. de Wolmar,

---

* *Aline et Valcour.*

in *La nouvelle Héloïse*.[70] That did not prevent Abbé Mélégan from having been thrown into prison for having written *Zoroastre* or stop La Mettrie from having to take shelter with Frederic II. Popularized in 1770 by Holbach in *Le système de la nature*, and also, in the same year, by satires assembled under the title *Recueil philosophique*, and professed with vehemence by Sylvain Maréchal, atheism was no less dangerous a doctrine in a century which had to place the guillotine itself under the aegis of the Supreme Being.[71] In flaunting his atheism, Sade was deliberately committing a provocative act, but it was also a sincere act. Despite the importance of Klossowski's study, I believe he betrays Sade when he takes his passionate refusal of God as the confession of a need. We readily accept today the sophism that to attack God is to affirm him; but in truth, this is a notion invented by the men whom the atheist challenges. Sade explains himself clearly when he writes, "The idea of God is the only fault that I cannot pardon among men"; and he attacks this mystification first because as a good heir to Descartes, he proceeds from the simple to the complex, from the crude lie to more fallacious errors.[72] He knows that in order to deliver the individual from the idols in which society alienates him, he must begin by assuring his autonomy in regards to heaven. If man had not been terrorized by the great bogeyman whom he stupidly worships, he would not have sacrificed his freedom and his truth so readily; in choosing God, he renounces himself and therein lies his unpardonable sin. In truth, he is not accountable to any transcendent judge; there is no authority but the earth. Sade is not unaware of how much the belief in hell and in eternity can exalt cruelty. Saint-Fond caresses this hope in order to find delight in the limitless sufferings of the damned; he also amuses himself in imagining a diabolical demiurge in whom is incarnated the diffuse malevolence of nature; but not for an instant does Sade consider these hypotheses anything but intellectual pastimes. He does not recognize himself in the characters to whom he lends these hypotheses, and through the mouth of his spokesmen, he refutes them. When he evokes the absolute crime, he dreams of bruising nature and not of wounding God. We may reproach his declamations against religion for reproducing proven commonplaces with fastidious monotony. Still, Sade gives these a personal turn when, anticipating Nietzsche, he denounces Christianity as a religion of victims that should be replaced, according to him, with an ideology of force. In any case, his good faith cannot be in doubt. Sade's temperament is deeply irreligious; there is no trace in him of metaphysical anxiety: he is far too occupied with claiming his existence to wonder about its meaning and its end. On these matters, Sade's convictions never faltered; although he served mass and flattered a bishop, it was only because, old and broken, he chose hypocrisy; but his testament is unequivocal. Death frightened him to the same degree as decrepitude, as the dissolution of his individuality—the fear of the beyond never appears in his work. Sade wanted to have commerce only with men, and everything that is not human is foreign to him.

Nevertheless, in the midst of men, he is alone. The eighteenth century, to the extent that it attempted to abolish the reign of God on earth, substituted another idol in its place. Atheists and deists came together in the cult they created for this new incarnation of the Supreme Good: Nature. They wouldn't hear of giving up the conveniences of a categorical and universal morality. Transcendent values collapsed, so pleasure was recognized as the measure of the good, and through this hedonism, self-love was rehabilitated: "We must begin by telling ourselves that we have nothing else to do in this world except procure pleasant sensations and feelings," wrote Mme du Châtelet.[73] But these timid egoists proposed a natural order which assured the harmonious reconciliation of individual interests with the general interest; reasonable organization obtained through a pact or a contract was enough for society to prosper for the good of one and all. Sade made himself the tragic rebuttal of this optimistic religion.

The eighteenth century frequently painted love in grave and somber colors; Richardson, Prévost, Duclos and Crébillon, whom Sade cites with great esteem—he pretended not to know Laclos—created more or less satanic heroes; but their wickedness always had its source in a perversion of their spirit or their will, not in their spontaneity.[74] Due to its instinctive character, actual eroticism was, on the other hand, rehabilitated; it was innocent, healthy and useful to the species. Sexual desire according to Diderot is joined with the very movement of life; and the passions it arouses are as good and as fecund as life itself. The nuns in *La religieuse* delight in "sadistic" meanness only because they suppress their desires rather than satisfying them. Rousseau, for whom sexual experience was complex and not very pleasant, also describes it in edifying terms: "Soft pleasures [*voluptés*], pure pleasures, sharp, without any mixture of pain. . . ." And also: "The love that I imagine, that which I have felt, flames up at the illusory image of the perfection of the beloved object; and this same illusion leads it to the enthusiasm of virtue; because this idea always enters into that of a perfect woman."* Even if in the work of Restif de la Bretonne, pleasure has a stormy character,

---

* Cf. Sade: "It is horror, villainy, the dreadful object that pleases us when we f . . . Aren't these better found in a corrupted object? All kinds of people prefer an old, ugly, and even stinking woman for their *jouissance* than a fresh and pretty girl."

77

it is nevertheless rapture, languor and tenderness.[75] Sade was alone in discovering sexuality as egoism, tyranny and cruelty; he grasped an invitation to crime in a natural instinct. This would be enough to give him a unique place in the history of the sensibility of his century, but from this intuition he drew even more singular ethical consequences.

To declare nature evil was not in itself a new idea. Hobbes, whom Sade knew well and whom he readily cites, posited that "man is wolf to man" and that the state of nature is a state of war.[76] An important lineage of English moralists and satirists followed him along this path: Swift among others, whom Sade studied so closely that he came to copy him.[77] In France, Vauvenargues took up the Puritan and Jansenist tradition of Christianity that conflates flesh with original sin.[78] Bayle, and more brilliantly Buffon, established that Nature was not inherently good. While the legend of the noble savage had been current since the sixteenth century, particularly in the works of Diderot and the Encyclopedists, Émeric de Crucé had already attacked it at the beginning of the eighteenth century.[79] History, travel and science had little by little discredited this idea. It was easy for Sade, through a large number of arguments, to support the thesis implied in his erotic experience and which society ironically confirmed by throwing him in prison for following his instincts. But where Sade distinguishes himself from his predecessors is that, after having denounced the blackness of nature, they set it against an artificial moral code that derived from God or society; while from the generally accepted credo "Nature is good; let us follow her," Sade, in rejecting the first point, paradoxically retains the second. The example of Nature retains an imperative value even though its law is a law of hatred and destruction. By what ruse did he turn the new cult against its devotees? This is what we must study more closely.

Sade conceived in different ways the relation of man to Nature; his variations seem to me less like moments of a dialectic than translating the hesitation of a thought that sometimes limits its audacity, and other times unleashes itself without restraint. When he limits himself to seeking hasty justifications, Sade adopts a mechanistic vision of the world. La Mettrie guaranteed the moral indifference of human acts when he declared, "We are no more criminal in following the impulses of the primitive movements that govern us than is the Nile with its floods and the sea with its waves." Thus Sade, to excuse himself, compares himself to plants, beasts and the elements. "I am nothing more in her hands than a machine that she* moves

---

* Nature.

as she pleases." Though he takes refuge a thousand times in analogous affirmations, they do not express his sincere thought. First, nature is not, in Sade's eyes, an indifferent mechanism; there is a meaning in her avatars to the degree that we can amuse ourselves in imagining that a malicious spirit rules her. In truth she is cruel and devouring; the spirit of destruction inhabits her; she "would desire the total annihilation of all living creatures so that she could enjoy the ability that she has to produce new ones." On the other hand, man is not nature's slave; in *Aline et Valcour* Sade already indicates that he could tear himself away from Nature and turn himself against her, "Let us finally dare to outrage this unintelligible Nature to better know the art of enjoying her." And in a more decisive manner, he declares in *Juliette*, "Once created, man is no longer tied to Nature: once nature has created him, she can no longer have any [control] over man." And again he emphasizes this point; in his relationship with nature, man is comparable to "the foam, the vapor that rises from rarefied liquid in a bottle heated by fire: this vapor is not created, it is a result, it is heterogeneous; it draws its existence from a foreign element, it can be or can not be without causing the element from which it emanates to suffer; it owes nothing to that element, and that element owes it nothing." If he matters no more in the eyes of the universe than a bit of foam, this very insignificance guarantees man his autonomy. The order of nature cannot enslave him because he is radically heterogeneous to her; thus an ethical decision is permitted him, and no one possesses the right to dictate it to him. Why, of the paths open to him, did Sade choose one that, through an imitation of nature, leads him to crime? We must grasp the whole of his system to answer this question: the goal of the system being precisely to justify the "crimes" that Sade never envisioned renouncing.

We are always more influenced than we think by the ideas with which we struggle. To be sure, Sade often uses naturalism as an *ad hominem* argument; he found malicious pleasure in claiming for the profit of evil the examples that his contemporaries claimed to exploit in favor of the good; but without a doubt he also took for granted that right is founded in fact. When he wants to demonstrate that the libertine is authorized to oppress women, he exclaims, "Has not Nature proven that we possess this right by giving us the necessary force to subject them to our desires?" We could endlessly multiply his analogous citations: "Nature has created us all equal from birth, Sophie," said la Dubois to Justine.[80] "If fate is pleased to disrupt this first order of general laws, it is up to us to correct the caprice."[81] And the essential reproach Sade addresses to the codes imposed by society is that they are artificial; in a particularly significant text* he compares them to the codes that a community of the blind might establish: "All these duties, being nothing but convention, are by the same token, chimerical. Man has made laws relative to his little knowledge, his little ruses, and his little needs—but there is nothing real in all of this . . . Coming to nature herself, we will easily understand that everything we arrange and decide is as far from the perfection of her designs and as inferior to her as are the laws of this society of the blind to our own." Montesquieu suggested that laws depend on climate, circumstance, indeed the disposition of the "fibers" of our bodies; we can then conclude that in them are expressed the diverse aspects that nature presents across space and time. But when Sade sends us endlessly through Patagonia, Tahiti, and the Antipodes, it is to show us that the diversity of decreed rules definitively contests their value. Because they are relative, they seem arbitrary to him; and it is important to note that *conventional* and *chimerical* are, for him, synonyms. Nature retains in his eyes a sacred characteristic: indivisible and unique; she is an absolute outside of which there is no reality.

That Sade's thought on this point may not be completely coherent, that it has evolved, that all these moments are not equally sincere, is obvious; but these inconsistencies are not so flagrant as we might believe. It would be too simple a syllogism to argue that Nature is evil, so a society that distances itself from her merits our submission. First, society's hypocrisy renders it suspect: society claims to draw inspiration from nature while being hostile towards her; and then despite the antagonism it manifests towards nature, its roots are in nature. In the very way it contradicts nature, society demonstrates its original perversion. The idea of general interest has no foundation in nature: "The interests of individuals are almost always opposed to that of society"; but it was invented to appease a natural instinct, to wit: the tyrannical will of the powerful. Rather than rectifying the primitive order of the world, laws only aggravate its injustice. "We are all alike except in strength," which is to say there is no essential difference among individuals, and the unequal division of forces could have been balanced. Instead, the strong have arrogated all superiorities to themselves and have even invented some. Holbach and many others have denounced the hypocrisy of codes whose only end is the oppression of the weak. Morelly and Brissot among others have shown that ownership rests upon no natural foundation; society has completely fabricated this iniquitous institution.[82] "There is no exclusive property in nature," Brissot writes. "The word is struck from her code;

---

* Cited by Maurice Heine, *Le Marquis de Sade*, p. 83.

the miserable starveling can carry away and devour this bread which is his because he is hungry—hunger is his entitlement." In almost the same terms Sade, in *La philosophie dans le boudoir*, claims that we substitute the idea of *jouissance* with that of property. How can the latter boast about constituting a universally recognized right when the poor rise up against it and the rich dream only of increasing it through new hoardings? "It is through a total equality of fortunes and conditions that we must stimulate the strongest powers, not by vain laws." But in fact, it is the strong who have made the laws for their profit; their excessive arrogance manifests itself in the most odious way in the punishments they assume the right to inflict. Beccaria maintained that the goal of punishment is to make reparation, but that no one should claim the right to punish.[83] Sade, after him, rises up virulently against all punishments of an expiatory character: "O you imbeciles who massacre and imprison, from all reigns and from all governments, when will you prefer the science of knowing man to that of imprisoning him and killing him?" Above all Sade revolts against capital punishment; society attempts to justify it with the notion of *lex talionis*, but that is yet another chimera with no root in reality.[84] First, reciprocity does not exist between the subjects themselves—their existences are not commensurable—next, there is no analogy between a murder committed impulsively from passion or need and assassination coldly premeditated by judges. And how can the latter compensate in any way for the former? Far from attenuating the cruelty of nature, society knows only how to exacerbate it by raising gallows. In truth, society never does more than oppose one wrong with a greater wrong; nothing authorizes it to require our loyalty. The famous contract invoked by Hobbes and Rousseau is nothing but a myth: how would individual freedom be recognized in the order oppressing it? The pact suits neither the strong, who have no interest in abdicating any of their privileges, nor the weak, whose inferiority it entrenches. Between these two groups there could exist nothing but a state of war, and each group's values are irreconcilable with those of the other. "The moment he took a hundred *louis* from a man's pocket, he did a very just thing for him, although the robbed man must have regarded it otherwise."[85] In a speech he attributes to Coeur de Fer, Sade passionately denounces the bourgeois mystification which consists of establishing class interests as universal principles: no universal morality is possible since the concrete conditions in which people live are not homogeneous.[86]

But if society has betrayed its own aspirations, should we not try to reform it? Cannot an individual's freedom be used precisely for this task? That Sade may have occasionally imagined this solution does not seem doubtful to me. It is remarkable that in *Aline et Valcour* he describes with equal indulgence the anarchic society of cannibals, which granted man's instinctive cruelty, and the communist society of Zamé, where evil is disarmed by justice.[87] I do not believe there is any irony in this last image, no more than in the appeal inserted in *La philosophie dans le boudoir* which begins, "Frenchmen . . ."* Sade's attitude during the Revolution proves that he sincerely hoped to become integrated in the community. He suffered profoundly from the ostracism of which he was an object and dreamt of an ideal society from which his individual tastes would not exclude him. In truth, he thought these would not constitute a serious danger for an enlightened society. Zamé assures us he would not be embarrassed by Sade's imitators: "The people you tell me about are rare, they would not bother me at all." And in a letter, Sade affirms, "The opinions or the vices of individuals are not what harms the State, but rather the morals of public figures."[88] The fact is that libertine acts do not bite into the world, they are hardly more than games. Sade took refuge behind their insignificance, and he goes as far as to suggest he would be ready to sacrifice them. Dictated by defiance and resentment, they would lose their meaning in a world without hatred; by abolishing the interdictions that provide crime with its attractiveness, lewdness itself would be eliminated. Perhaps Sade really dreamt nostalgically of the intimate conversion that the conversion of other men would provoke in him; no doubt he expected that his vices would be accepted as exceptions by a community which, respecting individual singularity, would recognize him as an exception. What he was sure of in any case, was that men who are content to whip a girl from time to time are less harmful than a farmer-general.[89] Institutional injustices, official prevarications and constitutional crimes are the real scourge; and this is what necessarily accompanies the abstract laws that claim to impose themselves uniformly upon the plurality of radically separate subjects. A just economic organization would render codes and tribunals useless because crime is born of need and inequality, and would disappear at the same time as its motives. This is a sort of reasonable anarchy which constitutes in Sade's eyes an ideal regime: "The rule of law is inferior to that of anarchy, the greatest proof of this which I propose is that every government must plunge itself into anarchy when it wants to redo its constitution. To abrogate old laws, it is necessary to establish a revolutionary regime in which there are no laws: from this regime new laws

---

* Some have maintained that Sade does not endorse this declaration because he places it in the Chevalier's mouth; however, the Chevalier reads a text by Sade's mouthpiece, Dolmancé, and Dolmancé recognizes the authorship as his own.

82

are born at the end, but this second state is nevertheless less pure than the first because it is derived from it." Doubtless, this reasoning does not seem particularly convincing. But what Sade remarkably understood was that the ideology of his day did no more than translate an economic system, and that by concretely transforming the latter, the mystifications of the bourgeois moral code would be annihilated. There are very few of Sade's contemporaries who developed such penetrating views in so *extreme* a manner.

Yet Sade was not decisively committed to the path of social reforms. The whole of his life and his work was not determined by these utopian reveries; how could he have believed in them for so long from the depth of his dungeons or after the Reign of Terror? Those events confirmed his personal experience: the failure of society is not a simple accident. And besides, it is evident that the interest he shows in its possible success is of an entirely speculative order. His own case is what obsesses him; he had little wish to be converted: much better to be confirmed in his choices. His vices condemned him to solitude, so he would demonstrate the necessity of solitude and the supremacy of evil. Good faith is easy for him here because this maladjusted aristocrat never met men anywhere who were like him. Although he was suspicious of generalizations, he lent his situation the value of a metaphysical fatality. "Man is isolated in the world. All creatures are born isolated without any need for one another."[90] If the diversity of individuals could be assimilated—as Sade himself frequently suggests—to that which differentiates plants and animals, a rational society could succeed in overcoming it. It would be enough to respect each one's singularity. But man is not only subjected to solitude; he claims it against everyone. So it follows that there is an heterogeneity of values not only from one class to another, but also from one individual to another. "All passions have two meanings, Juliette: one very unjust relative to the victim; the other singularly just in relation to the individual who exerts it . . ." And this fundamental antagonism cannot be surpassed because it is truth itself. If human projects claim to be reconciled in a common search for the general interest, they are necessarily inauthentic because there is no other reality than that of the subject enclosed in itself and hostile to any other subject that disputes its sovereignty. What prevents individual freedom from opting for the good is that the latter exists neither in the empty heavens nor on the unjust earth, nor even in a distant ideal: it is nowhere. Evil is an absolute whose only opponents are *fantastical* notions, and there is only one way to affirm oneself when confronting it: and that is to assume it.

For there is one idea that Sade ferociously repudiates throughout all his pessimism: that of submission. This is why he hates the resigned hypocrisy that we decorate with the name of virtue. Hypocrisy is in fact an imbecilic submission to the reign of evil, such as society has re-created it; in hypocrisy, man renounces both his authenticity and his freedom at the same time. Sade has a fine time showing that chastity and temperance are not even justified by their usefulness; and the prejudices that condemn incest, sodomy and all sexual *fantasies* have as their single goal to annihilate the individual by imposing upon him an inept conformity. But the major virtues that the century preached also had deeper meaning: they attempted to offset the all too obvious insufficiencies of the law. Against tolerance, Sade raised no objection, undoubtedly because he saw no one practice it; but he fanatically attacked what is called humanity or good deeds. These are mystifications that claim to reconcile that which is irreconcilable: the unsatisfied appetites of the poor and the egotistical cupidity of the rich. Taking up the tradition of La Rochefoucauld, he shows that humanity and good deeds are nothing but a mask which disguises self-interest.[91] To contain the arrogance of the powerful, the weak invented the idea of fraternity which rests upon no solid base: "Now I beg you to tell me whether I must love a being solely because he exists or because he resembles me and that, due to this unique relationship, I should suddenly prefer him to myself?" What hypocrisy among the privileged who proclaim an edifying philanthropy while they consent to the abject condition of the oppressed! This deceitful sentimentality was so widespread at the time that even Valmont in Laclos is moved to the point of tears when he engages in charity work; and it is obviously this fashion that incited Sade to unleash against *good deeds* all his bad faith and sincerity.[92] To be sure, Sade is clowning when he claims that in mistreating girls, he serves morality: if libertines were allowed to molest their victims with impunity, he claims, prostitution would become such a dangerous occupation that nobody would take it up. But through these sophisms he rightly denounces the inconsistency of a society that protects what it condemns, and which puts the debauchee in the pillory while authorizing debauchery. He proclaims the dangers of giving alms with the same dark irony; if we do not reduce the poverty-stricken to despair, they may revolt, and the safest thing would be to exterminate them all. By attributing this project to Saint-Fond, Sade is expanding upon Swift's famous pamphlet.[93] And although he certainly does not identify with the protagonist, the cynicism of this aristocrat who excessively espouses the interests of his class has more value in Sade's eyes than the compromises of shameful playboys. His thought is clear: either eliminate the poor or eliminate poverty, but do not perpetuate injustice and oppression through half measures; and above all, do not claim to make amends for your extortions by tossing an insignificant dole to those you exploit. Sade's protagonists leave a poor wretch to die of hunger rather than soil themselves with alms that would cost them nothing, because they passionately refuse any complicity with decent folk who appease their conscience at such a vile price.

It is logical that Sade comes to the conclusion that virtue merits no admiration and no gratitude since, far from reflecting the exigencies of a transcendent good, it serves the interests of those who flaunt it. But, after all, if self-interest is the individual's only law, why despise it? What superiority does vice have over it? Sade responded often and with vehemence to this question. In the case where we choose virtue, he tells us, "What lack of movement! What coldness! Nothing rouses me, nothing excites me . . . I ask, is this pleasure? What a difference on the opposite side! How my senses are titillated! How my organs are aroused." And again, "Happiness is only in that which excites, and crime alone excites." This argument has weight in the name of the hedonism professed by his century. Our only objection may be that Sade generalizes his individual case: can certain souls not be *excited* also by the good? Sade refuses this eclecticism. "Virtue can never bring anything but a fantastical happiness . . . there is no true felicity except in the senses, and virtue gratifies none of them." This declaration may surprise us because for Sade, imagination was the wellspring of vice. But through the phantasms on which it feeds, vice apprehends a truth, and the proof is that vice ends in orgasm, that is, in a sure sensation; whereas the illusions which nourish virtue can never be recovered by the individual in any concrete way. Sensation, according to the philosophy Sade borrowed from his era, is the only measure of reality, and if virtue awakens none, then it has no real foundation. Sade explains himself even more clearly in this comparison between virtue and vice: "The first is chimerical, the other is real, the first is attached to prejudices, the other is founded on reason. I f . . . with one and I feel very little with the other." Chimerical and fantastical, virtue encloses us in a world of appearances; whereas the authenticity of what we call vice is guaranteed by its intimate link with the flesh. In using the vocabulary of Stirner, justifiably compared with Sade, we would say that virtue alienates the individual in this empty entity that is Man; and only in crime can he claim himself and accomplish himself as a concrete self.[94] If the poor man resigns himself or if he attempts vainly to struggle for his brothers, he is manipulated, duped, an inert object with which nature plays: he is nothing. What he must to do, like Dubois or Coeur de Fer, is try to move onto the side of the strong. The rich man who passively accepts his privileges also exists only in the manner of a thing, but if he abuses his powers and becomes a tyrant or torturer, then he is somebody; he profits cynically from the injustice that favors him instead of losing himself in philanthropic dreams. "Where would the victims of our wickedness be if all men were criminals? Never cease to hold such people under the yoke of errors and lies," declares Esterval.[95]

Do we then return to the idea that man can only obey malicious nature? Does man not kill his freedom under the pretext of safeguarding his authenticity? No, because although freedom cannot contradict the given, it is capable of tearing itself away from the given in order to assume it. This approach is analogous to the Stoic conversion which also turns reality to its own account through voluntary decisions. It is not contradictory that Sade, while extolling crime, is often indignant about injustice, egoism, or the cruelty of man.* He had nothing but disdain for the timid vices and the thoughtless infamies that limit themselves to passively reflecting the darkness of nature. One must *make himself* a criminal to avoid *being* wicked in the manner of a volcano or a policeman; this is not a question of submitting to the universe, but rather of imitating it in free defiance. This is the attitude taken by the chemist Almani on the rim of Mount Etna: "Yes, my friend, yes, I abhor nature; and it is because I know her well that I detest her. Versed in her awful secrets, I have experienced a sort of inexpressible pleasure in copying her black deeds. I imitate her but detest her all the while . . . Her murderous nets are set for us alone, let us try to envelop her in them . . . In offering me only her effects, she conceals from me all her causes. I am therefore restricted to an imitation of the former; unable to divine the motive which places the dagger in her hands, I was able to wrest the weapon from her and use it as she does."[96] We find the same ambiguous tone in the following words of Dolmancé: "It was their ingratitude that dried my heart."[97] It reminds us that Sade dedicated himself to evil out of despair and resentment. And this is where his hero distinguishes himself from the ancient sage: he does not follow nature with love and joy, but copies her while abhorring her and without understanding her. And he wills himself without approving of himself. Evil is not harmonious; its essence is wrenching.

This wrenching must be lived in a constant tension; otherwise it would be frozen in remorse, and in this form it constitutes a mortal danger. Blanchot has noted that the sadistic hero gives himself over to the worst catastrophes

---

* The analogy with Stirner is striking here. He also condemns "common" crime and only advocates crime when the revolt of the ego is accomplished.

as soon as, by some scruple, he restores to society its power over him.[98] To repent or hesitate, is to acknowledge judgment, and therefore accept being guilty instead of claiming responsibility as the free author of his acts. He who consents to his passivity deserves all the defeats the hostile world inflicts upon him. On the contrary, "The true libertine loves even the reproach that his execrable crimes deserve. Have we not seen those who even love the tortures that human vengeance proposed to them, who submitted to them with joy, and who looked upon the gallows as a glorious throne? This is man at the highest degree of a deliberate corruption." At this supreme degree, man is not only delivered from prejudice and shame, but from all fear. His serenity meets that of the ancient sage who considered futile "things that do not depend upon us," but who limited himself in an entirely negative manner to defending himself against possible suffering; the black stoicism of Sade promises a positive happiness. Thus, Coeur de Fer proposes this alternative: "Either the crime that makes us happy or the gallows that stops us being unhappy."[99] Nothing can threaten the man who knows how to transform even his defeats into triumphs; he fears nothing because all things are good to him. The brutal facticity of things does not crush the free man because it does not interest him: he is only concerned with their signification, and that comes only from him. An individual who is whipped or penetrated by another can be either the master or the slave; the ambivalence of pain and pleasure, of humiliation and pride permits the libertine to dominate any given situation. This is how Juliette knows how to transform into *jouissance* the torment that overwhelmed Justine. Basically, the content of experience is unimportant: what counts is the intention with which the subject animates it. Thus, hedonism is achieved in ataraxia, which confirms the paradoxical kinship of sadism and stoicism: the happiness promised to the individual is reduced to indifference. "I, myself, am happy, my dear, since I have given myself over to all cold-blooded crimes," says Bressac.[100] Cruelty appears under a new form, as an asceticism: "He who knows how to harden himself to the evils of the other becomes inaccessible to his own evils." We must no longer seek excitement, but *apathy*. A novice libertine undoubtedly needs violent emotions to experience the truth of his singular existence; but once he conquers it, crime's pure form is enough to guarantee it to him. Pure crime has "a character of grandeur and sublimity which prevails and will always prevail over the monotonous attractions of virtue" and which makes vain the contingent satisfactions upon which he might otherwise be tempted to count. With a severity analogous to that of Kant and which has its source in the same puritanical tradition, Sade conceives of a free act only as one released of all sensitivity: if he obeyed affective motives, he would once again make us slaves of nature and not autonomous subjects.

Such a choice is permitted to any individual, regardless of his situation. One of the victims trapped in the monks' harem where Justine languishes manages to escape by proving her valor: she stabbed one of her company with such savagery that she won the admiration of her masters, who made her queen of the seraglio. Those who remain on the side of the oppressed do so because of the baseness of their hearts, and they must be refused all pity. "What do you expect there could be in common between somebody who can do anything and someone who dares nothing?" The opposition between these two verbs is significant, because for Sade, to dare also means to be able. Blanchot emphasized the austerity of this moral code: the criminals in Sade almost always have violent deaths, and it is their merit that transforms their ordeals into glory. But in fact death is not the worst of failures, and whatever end he reserves for them, Sade guarantees his heroes a destiny which allows them to accomplish themselves. This optimism rests upon an aristocratic vision of humanity, which, enveloped in its implacable harshness, involves the doctrine of predestination, because this quality of soul which permits the elect few to rule over the herd of the condemned appears as an arbitrarily dispensed grace. Since the beginning of time Juliette was saved, and Justine was lost. What is more interesting still is that merit can not be followed by success unless it is *recognized*; the force of spirit of a Valérie or a Juliette does them no good if it does not merit the admiration of their tyrants. Divided and separated, we must admit that these figures collectively kneel before certain values. Indeed, under the diverse guises of orgasm, nature, or reason— which are all equivalent for Sade—they choose reality, or more precisely, reality is imposed upon them. Through their mediation the hero's triumph is assured; but what saves him in the last resort is that he bet on truth. Beyond all contingencies, Sade believed in an absolute that would never disappoint a person who invoked it as the supreme authority.

All men do not embrace such a sure moral code only because of their pusillanimity, for no valid objection can oppose it. It could not offend a God who is only a chimera; and since Nature is division and hostility, even in attacking her we would still conform to her. Ceding to his naturalist prejudices Sade writes, "The only real crime would be to outrage nature." And he adds immediately, "Is it even possible to imagine that nature would give us the capacity for a crime that would outrage her?"[101] Everything that is, is integrated by her, even murder, which she welcomes with indifference, since "the life principle of all beings is nothing other than that of death which is only imaginary." Man alone attaches importance to his own existence, but he "could totally annihilate his species without the universe feeling the least alteration." He claims to possess a sacred character that renders him untouchable, but he is only one animal among others. "It is only man's pride that would establish murder as a crime."[102] In truth, Sade's defense is so energetic he winds up denying any criminal character in crime. He realizes this himself, and he tries, in a convulsive effort, to reanimate the flame of Evil in the last part of *Juliette*. But if there is no God, if man is but a vapor, if nature consents to everything, then the worst devastations—volcanoes, fires, poison, plague—fall into indifference. "The impossibility of outraging nature is in my opinion man's worst torture!"[103] groans Sade. And if he had staked everything on crime's demoniacal horror, his ethic would lead him to a radical failure; but he himself subscribes to this failure because he is also waging another battle: his profound conviction is that crime is good.

In the first place, crime is not simply inoffensive in regards to nature: it serves her. Sade explains in *Juliette* that "the spirit of the three kingdoms" would become so violent if no obstacle prevented it, that it would paralyze the working of the universe: "There would no longer be gravity or movement." Bearing this contradiction in her breast, nature is rescued by human crimes from this stagnation which would also threaten a too virtuous society. Sade undoubtedly read *La ruche murmurante* by Mandeville, which had enjoyed great success at the beginning of the century.[104] The author showed there that the passions and faults of individuals serve the public prosperity; it is even the greatest villains who work most actively for the common good, and when an untimely conversion makes virtue triumph, the hive finds itself destroyed. Sade himself declared many times that a collectivity that "fell" into virtue would by the same stroke be precipitated into inertia. Here, we see a foreshadowing of the Hegelian theory according to which the "restlessness of the spirit" cannot be abolished without bringing about the end of history. But for Sade immobility does not appear as a frozen plenitude, but as pure absence. Humanity, with all its conventions, tries fiercely to break all attachment with nature, and would turn into a pale phantom were it not for a few resolute souls who maintain within it, yet in spite of it, the rights of truth; and truth is division, war and agitation. It is already enough that our limited senses forbid us from attaining reality in the very heart of humanity, says Sade in the singular text where he compares us to blind men; let us not willingly mutilate ourselves again; let us instead try to exceed our limits. "The most perfect being of whom we can conceive is the one who distances

himself farthest from our conventions and finds them the most distasteful."
If we return it to its context, Sade's declaration makes us think of Rimbaud's
demand in favor of a "systematic deregulation" of all the senses;[105] and also
of the surrealists' attempts to penetrate beyond human artifice into the mysterious heart of the real. But more than as a poet, it is as a moralist that
Sade seeks to break the prison of appearances. The mystified and mystifying
society against which he struggles evokes the Heideggerian "one" that swal-
lows up the authenticity of existence, and it also means for him recuperat-
ing the latter through an individual decision.[106] These comparisons are not
games. We must situate Sade within the great family of those who, beyond
the "banality of daily life," wished to conquer an immanent truth in this
world. From this perspective, crime appears to him as a duty: "In a criminal
society, one must be criminal." This formula encapsulates his ethic. Through
crime, the libertine refuses all complicity with the darkness of the given of
which the masses are nothing but a passive, and therefore abject, reflection.
He prevents society from going to sleep in injustice, and creates an apoca-
lyptic state that compels all individuals to assume in an incessant tension
their separation, and hence their truth.

It seems, however, that one could raise the most convincing objections
against Sade in the name of the individual because the individual is real and
because crime is really an outrage against him. Here Sade's thought reveals
itself as *extreme*: nothing has truth for me other than what my experience
envelops, and the intimate presence of the other radically escapes this experience; therefore it does not concern me, and cannot dictate any duty to
me. "We mock the torment of others: and what would this torment have in
common with us?" And again, "There is no comparison between what others experience and what we feel; the strongest pain for others must surely
be nothing to us, and the least tremor of pleasure we experience touches
us." The fact is that the only sure links between men are those they create
by transcending themselves in a common world through common projects.
The hedonistic sensualism professed by the eighteenth century proposed no
other project to the individual than to "procure agreeable sensations and
sentiments"; it froze him in his solitary immanence. In a passage from *Justine*, Sade shows us a surgeon who plans to dissect his daughter to help the
progress of science and thus humanity: grasped in its transcendent becoming, humanity thus has value in his eyes; but reduced to his vain presence to
himself, what is a man? A pure fact stripped of all value that touches me no
more than an inert stone. "The neighbor is nothing to me; there is not the
least relationship between him and me."[107]

These declarations seem contradictory to Sade's living attitude; it is immediately apparent that if there is nothing in *common* between the torment of the victim and the torturer, the latter cannot draw any pleasure from it. But in truth, what Sade contests is the a priori existence of a given relation between me and the other upon which my conduct should be regulated in the abstract. He does not deny the possibility of establishing one; and if he refuses the other an ethical recognition founded on the false notions of reciprocity and universality, it is in order to give himself the authority to decisively break the carnal barriers that isolate consciousnesses. Each consciousness can only bear witness of itself, and has no right to impose upon the other whatever value it attributes to itself, but it can claim this value in a singular and living manner through acts. This is the role the criminal chooses; and through the violence of his affirmation, he becomes real for the other, while also unveiling the other as truly existent. But we should note that—unlike the conflict described by Hegel—this process does not constitute any risk for the subject: his primacy is not at stake, and no matter what happens to him, he will not accept a master. Defeated, he would return to a solitude that would end in death, but he would remain sovereign.

Thus, the other does not represent for the despot a danger which could reach the heart of his being; nonetheless, this foreign world from which he is excluded bothers him, and he wishes to penetrate it. Paradoxically, in this forbidden domain he is able to provoke events, and the temptation is all the more vertiginous because the events will be incommensurable with his experience. Sade a hundred times insisted upon this point: it is not the other's misfortune that excites the libertine, it is knowing that he authored it. For him this is much more than an abstract and demoniacal pleasure, for when he plots his dark machinations, he sees his freedom metamorphose into the other's destiny. And because death is more certain than life, and suffering than well-being, he assumes this mystery through persecutions and murder. But to impose himself in the name of fate upon the stupefied victim is not enough. He possesses the duped and mystified victim, but only from the outside. In disclosing himself to her, the torturer incites the victim to manifest her freedom in her cries or her prayers, but if the freedom is not revealed, the victim is unworthy of the torture, and is either killed or forgotten. It can also happen that through the violence of her revolt, flight, suicide, or victory, she escapes the tormentor, but what the latter demands is that in oscillating between refusal and submission, rebellion or consent, she recognizes in any case her destiny in the freedom of the tyrant. Then she is united with him by the tightest of bonds; they form a veritable couple.

91

There are rarer cases where the freedom of the victim, without shying away from the destiny that the tyrant creates for her, succeeds in surmounting it. She turns her suffering into pleasure, her shame into pride, and becomes an accomplice. Then the debauchee finds himself fulfilled, "No pleasure is keener to a libertine spirit than making proselytes." To deprave an innocent creature is evidently a satanic act; but given the ambivalence of evil, in winning an adept for evil, one performs an authentic conversion. The taking of virginity, for example, appears in this light as a ceremony of initiation. Just as we must outrage nature in order to imitate her, although the outrage is abolished since she herself demands it, so, in violating an individual, we force him to assume his separation and thereby he finds a truth which reconciles him with his antagonist. Torturer and victim recognize themselves as fellow men in astonishment, esteem and indeed admiration. It has rightly been shown that no definitive alliance exists among Sade's libertines—their rapport implies a constant tension—but the fact that Sade makes egoism triumph systematically over friendship does not stop him from endowing the latter with reality. Noirceuil takes great care to let Juliette know that he keeps her simply because he finds pleasure in her company, but such a pleasure implies a concrete rapport between them; both feel confirmed in themselves through the presence of an *alter ego*, which is an absolution and an exaltation. Collective debauchery realizes genuine communion between Sade's libertines: each grasps the meaning of his acts and his own face through the consciousness of others. Fellow man truly exists for me when I experience my own flesh in a foreign flesh. The scandal of coexistence does not let itself be thought, but we can vanquish the mystery of it in the way that Alexander severed the Gordian knot: we must settle into it through our acts.[108] "What an enigma is man!—Yes my friend, and this is why we must say to a man with much spirit that it is better to f . . . him than to understand him."[109] Eroticism seems for Sade to be a mode of communication, and the only valid one. We could say, in parodying Claudel that, for Sade, "the dick is the shortest path from one heart to another."[110]

* * *

We betray Sade if we dedicate to him a too easy sympathy; because it is my unhappiness he wants, my subjection and my death; and each time we take the side of the child whose throat has been cut by a lecher, we rise against him. But he does not prohibit me from defending myself; he allows that the father of a family will avenge or prevent, even by murder, the rape of his child. What he demands is that in the struggle which opposes irreconcilable existences, each engage himself concretely in the name of his own existence. He approves of vendettas but not of tribunals: we can kill, but not judge. The judge's pretensions are more arrogant than those of the tyrant since the latter is limited to coinciding with himself whereas the former tries to erect his opinions as universal law. His endeavor rests upon a lie, because each is enclosed in his own skin, and he cannot become the mediator between separate individuals from whom he himself is separated. And although a large number of these individuals may form a league, and together may alienate themselves in institutions which none of them rule any longer, this does not give them any new rights: the number has nothing to do with it. There is no way of measuring what is incommensurable. To escape the conflicts of existence, we take refuge in a world of appearances and existence itself hides. Believing we are defending ourselves, we annihilate ourselves. Sade's immense merit is that he proclaimed the truth of man against the abstractions and alienations that are only flights. Nobody was more passionately attached to the concrete than he. He never gave credit to what "they say," which is easy nourishment for mediocre spirits, but adhered only to the truths that were given to him in the evidence of his lived experience; he also surpassed the sensualism of his epoch in order to transform it into an ethics of authenticity.

This does not mean that the solution he proposes can satisfy us. Although the greatness of Sade comes from his efforts to grasp the very essence of the human condition in his singular situation, this is also the source of his limitations. He considered the outcome he chose for himself to be valid for all, and at the exclusion of any other outcome, but in this he was doubly mistaken. Despite all his pessimism, he was socially on the side of the privileged, and he did not understand that social inequality affects the individual even in his ethical possibilities. Revolt itself is a luxury that requires culture, leisure, and a certain distance from the necessities of existence, and although Sade's protagonists pay for their revolt with their lives, at least it had first endowed their lives with a sense of value; whereas for the vast majority of men revolt coincides with imbecilic suicide. Contrary to his wishes, it is luck and not merit that selects the criminal elite. If we object that he never aimed at universality, that it was enough for him to obtain his own salvation, we do not do him justice because he made himself an example by writing—and with such passion—about his experience. And no doubt he did not expect this appeal to be heard by all, but he did not think he addressed it solely to the privileged classes, whose arrogance he detested. He believed in a sort of predestination that he conceived as democratic, and he would not have wanted to discover that it depended upon economic circumstances from which, in his thinking, it must be allowed to escape.

On the other hand, Sade did not suppose any path other than individual rebellion could exist. He knew of only two alternatives: abstract morality or crime. He was unaware of action. If he suspected that a concrete communication between subjects could be permitted through an enterprise that integrated all men in the general project of being men, he did not pursue it. Instead, he refused the individual his transcendence, and doomed him to an insignificance which authorized doing violence to him. But this violence exercised in a void becomes derisory, and the tyrant who seeks to affirm himself through violence discovers only his own nothingness.

To this contradiction, however, Sade can oppose yet another, because the eighteenth-century's fond dream of reconciling individuals within their immanence is in every sense impracticable. In his own way, Sade was the pathetic embodiment of the necessary denial of this dream by the Reign of Terror as the individual who does not agree to renounce his singularity, and whom society repudiates. But if we choose to recognize in each subject only the transcendence that unites him concretely with his fellow men, we are led to alienate all of them in the new idols and their singular insignificance will seem all the more evident; we would sacrifice today for tomorrow, the minority for the majority and the freedom of the individual for collective accomplishments. Prison and the guillotine would be the logical consequences of this renunciation. False fraternity ends in the crimes in which virtue recognizes its abstract face. "Nothing more closely resembles virtue than a great crime," says Saint-Just. Is it not better to assume evil than to subscribe to this good that leads to abstract slaughters? It is doubtless impossible to elude this dilemma. If the totality of men who people the earth were present to everyone, in all their reality, no collective action would be permitted and for each the air would become unbreathable. At any given instant thousands of people suffer and die, in vain, unjustly, and we are not affected: our existence is possible only at this price. Sade's merit is not only that he cried aloud that which each person shamefully admits to himself, but that he did not reconcile himself to it. He chose cruelty over indifference. That is undoubtedly why he finds so many echoes today, when the individual knows he is the victim less of men's wickedness than of their good conscience; we come to his aid by undermining this terrifying optimism. In the solitude of the dungeons, Sade realized an ethical night analogous to the intellectual night that enveloped Descartes; he did not make a self-evident truth burst forth; but at least he contested all the too-easy answers. If we can ever hope to surmount the separation of individuals, it is on the condition of not underestimating it; otherwise, the promises of happiness and justice will entail the most serious threats. Sade lived the moments of egoism, injustice and unhappiness to the utmost, and he claimed the truth of them. What constitutes the supreme value of his testimony is that it disturbs us. He obliges us to call into question once again the essential problem which, under many faces, haunts these times: the true relationship of man to man.

NOTES

The three essays appearing in the *Privilèges* volume ("Must We Burn Sade?" "Right-Wing Thought Today," and "Merleau-Ponty and Pseudo-Sartreanism") were preceded by the following foreword, written by Simone de Beauvoir and translated by Kim Allen Gleed, Marilyn Gaddis Rose, and Virginia Preston: "Written in different periods and from different perspectives, these essays nonetheless respond to the same question: how can those who are privileged think their own situation? The old nobility was ignorant of this problem: they defended their rights and used them without bothering to legitimate them. The emerging bourgeoisie, on the other hand, crafted an ideology that favored its liberation; having become the dominant class, it cannot contemplate repudiating its heritage. But all thought aims at universality: to justify the possession of particular advantages on universal grounds is not an easy enterprise.

There is a man who dared to systematically assume particularity, separation and egoism: Sade. It is to him that our first study is devoted. Descended from that nobility which affirmed its privileges with blows of the sword, seduced by the rationalism of the bourgeois philosophers, he attempted a curious synthesis of the attitudes of the two classes. He demanded in its most extreme form the reign of his own pleasure and believed he could ideologically found this demand. He failed. Neither in his life nor in his works did he surmount the contradictions of solipsism. At least, however, he had the merit of strikingly demonstrating that privilege can only be willed egotistically, that it is impossible to legitimate in the eyes of all. In positing as irreconcilable the interests of the tyrant and those of the slave, he foresaw the class struggle. This is why the average privileged individual is frightened by this extremist. To assume injustice as such is to recognize that there is another justice; it is to bring one's life and one's self into question. This solution cannot satisfy the Western bourgeois. He wishes to rest in the possession of his rights without effort and without risk: he wants *his* justice to be *the* justice. In our second essay we have examined the procedures used by present day conservatives to valorize iniquity. Our last article is the analysis of a particular case. Because culture is itself a privilege, many intellectuals side with the most favored class: we will see through what falsifications and sophisms one of them endeavors to conflate the general interest and the bourgeois interest. In each of these cases, the failure is fatal: it is impossible for the privileged to assume their practical attitude on the theoretical plane. They have no other recourse than heedlessness and bad faith."

1. This quote is from a letter Sade wrote to his wife from prison in 1783. His correspondences from 1759 to 1814 can be found in vol. 12 of the 1966–67 edition of *Oeuvres complètes*, or see *Lettres à sa femme* (Arles: Actes Sud, 1997). For an English translation, see *Letters from Prison*, trans. Richard Seaver (New York: Arcade Publishers, 1999).

2. There are two French editions of *Oeuvres complètes du marquis de Sade* (Complete Works of the Marquis de Sade). The first one, in 16 volumes, was edited by Gilbert Lely (Paris: Cercle du livre précieux, 1966–67) and the second one, in 15 volumes, was edited by Annie Le Brun and Jean-Jacques Pauvert (Paris: Pauvert, 1986–91); This quote is from *Oeuvres complètes*, vol. 1 (1966–67), 632.

3. Notes for *Les journées de Florabelle, ou la nature dévoilée* (The Days of Florabelle, or Nature Revealed) can be found in vol. 15 of *Oeuvres complètes* (1966–67) and vol. 11 of *Oeuvres complètes* (1986–91).

4. Algernon Charles Swinburne (1837–1909) was an English poet; Guillaume Apollinaire (1880–1918) was a French poet.

5. Friedrich Wilhelm Nietzsche (1844–1900) was a German philosopher; Max Stirner (Johann Kasper Schmidt) (1804–86) was a German philosopher and translator; Sigmund Freud (1856–1939) was an Austrian neurologist.

6. Charles Nodier (1780–1844) was an author of romantic tales.

7. Oscar Wilde (1854–1900) was an Irish playwright, poet, and novelist; Baron de Montesquieu (1689–1755) was a French political philosopher; Maurice Sachs (1906–45) was an Austrian-born French art writer; Charlus is a character in Marcel Proust's *A la recherche du temps perdu* (*Remembrance of Things Past* or *In Search of Lost Time*).

8. Valcour is a character in Sade's *Aline et Valcour, ou le roman philosophique* (Aline and Valcour, or the Philosophical Novel) in vols. 4–5 of both editions of *Oeuvres complètes*; Louis Joseph de Bourbon, older brother of Louis XVII, died June 4, 1789.

9. Pierre Klossowski (1905–2001) was a French artist and writer who published a great deal of criticism on Sade.

10. Simone de Beauvoir is referring here to Pierre Klossowski's "Nature As Destructive Principle" in Klossowski's *Sade, mon prochain* (Sade, My Kinsman) (Paris: Éditions du Seuil, 1947).

11. The Duc de Charolais was a famous rapist and murderer in Paris. However, his acts went unpunished.

12. *La philosophie dans le boudoir* in *Oeuvres complètes*, vol. 3 (1966–67), 530; for a published English translation, see *"Justine," "Philosophy in the Bedroom" and Other Writings*, trans. Richard Seaver and Austryn Wainhouse (New York: Grove Press, 1965), 345.

13. Ibid.

14. Blangis is a character in Sade's *Les cent vingt journées de Sodome* in vol. 13 of *Oeuvres complètes* (1966–67) and vol. 1 of *Oeuvres complètes* (1986–91). For a published English translation, see *"The 120 Days of Sodom" and Other Writings*, trans. Austryn Wainhouse and Richard Seaver (New York: Grove Press, 1966), 201–202.

15. The term *jouissance* has several meanings in French; it can mean "pleasure," "sexual pleasure," or "orgasm" (which is usually how Sade uses the term), and it can also mean "the possession, use or enjoyment of something."

16. *La philosophie dans le boudoir* in *Oeuvres complètes*, vol. 3 (1966–67), 529; for a published English translation, see *"Justine," "Philosophy in the Bedroom" and Other Writings*, 345.

17. These characters represent two sides of an individual personality in the novel *The Strange Case of Dr. Jekyll and Mr. Hyde* (1886) by Scottish writer Robert Louis Stevenson.

18. From Sade, *Aline et Valcour*.

19. Dolmancé is a character in Sade's *La philosophie dans le boudoir* in vol. 3 of both editions of *Oeuvres complètes*; for a published English translation, see *"Justine," "Philosophy in the Bedroom" and Other Writings*, 341.

20. Blamont is a character in Sade's *Aline et Valcour*.

21. Nanon is the chambermaid at Château de la Coste who accused Sade of fathering her baby.

22. Sade gave candies laced with the aphrodisiac Spanish Fly to young women. When they fell ill, he was prosecuted for attempting to poison them.

23. See Jean de la Fontaine (1621–95), author of Aesop's fables; "The Cudgeled and Contented Cuckold" in *The Tales and Novels of J. de la Fontaine, Volume 2*. Available online through the Gutenberg Project's Web site. Also available in translation in *The Complete Works of Jean de la Fontaine* (Evanston Ill.: Northwestern University Press, 1988).

24. See Sade, *Lettres à sa femme*.

25. *Dialogue entre un prêtre et un moribond* in vol. 1 of *Oeuvres complètes* (1986–91). For an English translation, see *Dialogue between a Priest and a Dying Man*, trans. Richard Seaver and Austryn Wainhouse in *The Complete Justine*, 1965; *Les infortunes de la vertu* in vol. 14 of *Oeuvres complètes* (1966–67) and vol. 2 of *Oeuvres complètes* (1986–91). For an English translation, see *The Misfortunes of Virtue and Other Early Tales*, trans. and ed. David Coward (New York: Oxford University Press, 2000).

26. *Fragments de portefeuille d'un homme de lettres* (Fragments from the Portfolio of a Man of Letters) in *Oeuvres complètes*, vol. 1 (1986–91).

27. *Le comte Oxtiern, ou les dangers du libertinage* in vol. 11 of *Oeuvres complètes* (1966–67). For an English translation, see *The Plays of the Marquis de Sade: "Count Oxtiern," "The Bedroom," "The Madness of Misfortune," "The Haunted Tower," "The Shyster," Vol. 1*, trans. and ed. John C. Franceschina and Ben Ohmart (Durango: Hollowbrook Publishing, 1993).

28. Section des Piques was located in the most radical district in post-Revolution Paris; it had a citizen's organization that championed Robespierre.

29. Gaufridy was Sade's business agent and lawyer in Provence.

30. Louis de Saint-Just (1767–94) was a French politician.

31. "Sensible" is the name Sade gives to a female correspondent.

32. *Justine, ou les malheurs de la vertu* (Justine, or the Misfortunes of Virtue) in vol. 3 of both editions of *Oeuvres complètes*. For a published English translation, see *"Justine," "Philosophy in the Bedroom" and Other Writings*, trans. Richard Seaver and Austryn Wainhouse.

33. *Zoloé, et ses deux acolytes, ou quelques décades de la vie de trois jolies femmes* (Zoloé and His Two Acolytes, or Several Weeks in the Life of Three Pretty Women) (Paris: Bibliothèque des curieux, 1926); Josephine de Beauharnais (1763–1814) was the wife of Napoleon; Thérésa de Cabarrus Tallien (1773–1835) was a French revolutionary who saved many émigrés by her entreaties; Jean Lambert Tallien (1767–1820) was an anti-Jacobin revolutionary; Paul François Barras (1775–1829) was a leader in the post-Revolutionary Directorate; Napoleon Bonaparte (1769–1821) was the French emperor from 1804 to 1815.

34. *Juliette ou prospérités du vice* (Juliette, or Vice Amply Rewarded) in vols. 6–9 of *Oeuvres complètes* (1966–67) and vol. 8–9 of *Oeuvres complètes* (1986–91). For a published English translation see *Juliette*, trans. Austryn Wainhouse. (New York: Grove Press, 1968).

35. *Les crimes de l'amour* in vol. 10 of both editions of *Oeuvres complètes*. For a published English translation, see *Crimes of Love*, trans. Margaret Crosland (London: Peter Owen Ltd, 1998).

36. *La Marquise du Ganges*, ed. Beatrice Didier (Paris: Livre de poche, 1974). Also published in vol. 11 of both editions of *Oeuvres complètes*.

37. Louis-Ange Pitou (1767–1842) was a songwriter and singer who was sympathetic to the Royalist cause during the French Revolution. He shared a prison cell with Sade.

38. Maurice Heine (1884–1940), a scholar and biographer, was the father of modern Sade studies and author of *Le Marquis de Sade* (Paris: Gallimard, 1950); *Algolagnia* is sexual pleasure derived from inflicting pain.

39. Richard von Krafft-Ebing (1840–1902) was a German neurologist whose *Psychopathia sexualis* (1886) was originally written in Latin. English translations are available through Velvet Publications (1997) and Arcane Publications (1998).

40. Noirceuil is a character in Sade's *Juliette*; Gernande is a character is Sade's *Justine*.

41. *Les cent vingt journées de Sodome* in *Oeuvres complètes*, vol. 1 (1986–91), 292; for a published English translation, see *"The 120 Days in Sodom" and Other Writings*, trans. Richard Seaver and Austryn Wainhouse (New York: Grove Press, 1966), 489.

42. For a published English translation, see *"The 120 Days in Sodom" and Other Writings*, 201.

43. *La vanille et la manille* (Paris: Collection Drosera, 1950) was a letter written from prison to the Marquise detailing Sade's physical difficulties in ejaculating. He used vanilla as an aphrodisiac to promote orgasm, and "manille" (which means the second best trump or honor in a card game) was Sade's code word for masturbation. For more information, see *The Marquis de Sade: A Life* by Neil Schaeffer.

44. Jean-Jacques Rousseau (1712–78) was a French (Swiss-born) philosopher and writer; Denis Diderot (1713–84) was a French philosopher and critic. *La religieuse* was written by Diderot in 1780 and published posthumously in 1796 (repr., Paris: Gallimard, 1994). For an English translation, see *Memoirs of a Nun* (New York: Knopf, 1992); tribade is an archaic term for lesbian.

45. *Oeuvres complètes*, vol. 3 (1966–67), 529; for a published English translation, see *Philosophy in the Bedroom*, 344.

46. Ibid.

47. The Marquis de Verneuil is a character in Honoré de Balzac's *Les chouans* (*The Chouans*).

48. *Oeuvres complètes*, vol. 8 (1986–91), 313; for a published English translation, see Wainhouse, *Juliette*, 286.

49. *Oeuvres complètes*, vol. 1 (1986–91), 264; for a published English translation, see *The 120 Days in Sodom*, 458.

50. La Durand is a character in Sade's *Histoire de Juliette*.

51. *Oeuvres complètes*, vol. 8 (1986–91), 404; for a published English translation, see *Juliette*, 421.

52. Saint-Fond is a character in Sade's *Juliette*.

53. *Oeuvres complètes*, vol. 1 (1986–91), 298; for a published English translation, see *The 120 Days in Sodom*, 496.

54. Leopold von Sacher-Masoch (1836–95) was an Austrian writer whose erotic works led to the creation of the word "masochism."

55. *Oeuvres complètes*, vol. 1 (1986–91), 182; for a published English translation, see *The 120 Days in Sodom*, 364.

56. Ibid.

57. Ibid.

58. *Oeuvres complètes*, vol. 8 (1986–91), 181; for a published English translation, see *Juliette*, 186.

59. *Oeuvres complètes*, vol. 1 (1986–91), 182–83; for a published English translation, see *The 120 Days in Sodom*, 364.

60. Honoré-Gabriel Riqueti, Count de Mirabeau (1749–91) was a French orator and statesman.

61. *Oeuvres complètes*, vol. 3 (1966–67), 478; for a published English translation, see *Philosophy in the Bedroom*, 296.

62. Comte de Lautréamont, Isidore Ducasse (1846–70) was a Uruguayan-born French poet.

63. *Manon Lescaut* (1731) is a novel by Antoine François Prévost; *Liaisons dangereuses* (*Dangerous Liaisons*) (1782) is a novel by Pierre Ambroise François Choderlos de Laclos.

64. Edgar Allan Poe (1809–49) was an American poet and short-story writer; Jean-Pierre Claris de Florian (1755–94) was a French fabulist and satirist.

65. Georg Wilhelm Friedrich Hegel (1770–1831) was a German philosopher.

66. Paul Henri Thiry, Baron d'Holbach (1723–89) was a German-born French philosopher who supported naturalistic views; Julien Offray de La Mettrie (1709–51) was a physician and philosopher.

67. *Oeuvres complètes*, vol. 3 (1966–67), 529; for a published English translation, see *Philosophy in the Bedroom*, 345.

68. *Oeuvres complètes*, vol. 1 (1986–91), 59–60; for a published English translation, see *The 120 Days in Sodom*, 233.

69. *Oeuvres complètes*, vol. 1 (1986–91), 299; for a published English translation, see *The 120 Days in Sodom*, 497.

70. *Testament de Jean Meslier* (Testament of Jean Meslier) (Hildesheim: G. Olms Verlag, 1974); *La nouvelle Héloïse*, translated as *Julie, or the New Heloise*, by P. Stewart and J. Vaché (Hanover: Dartmouth College Press, 1997).

71. Abbé Mélégan and *Zoroastre*—there are two possibilities here: Abraham-Hyacinthe Anquetil-Duperron (1731–1805) gave up priesthood in order to devote himself to Eastern languages. When the British reduced the French presence in India, he returned to France and published a three-volume Zend-Avesta in 1771, crediting him with the introduction of Zoroastrianism in France. However, Zoroastra already was a presence in French intellectual life. Jean-Philippe Rameau (1683–1764) produced a lavish lyric opera *Zoroastre* at the royal court in 1749; *Le système de la nature* is d'Holbach's most famous work. For an English translation, see *The System of Nature*, trans. Alistair Jackson and H. D. Robinson (Manchester: Clinamen, 1999); Pierre Sylvain Maréchal (1750–1803) established the French Revolutionary calendar.

72. René Descartes (1596–1650) was a French mathematician and philosopher.

73. Emilie du Châtelet (1706–49) was a mistress of Voltaire.

74. Samuel Richardson (1689–1761) was an English novelist whose works include *Pamela* (1740) and *Clarissa* (1747–48); Antoine François Prévost d'Exiles, a.k.a. Abbé Prévost (1679–1763) was a French novelist, journalist, and cleric; Charles-Pinot Duclos (1704–72) was a

French novelist and grammarian; Crébillon (Prosper Jolyot) (1674–1762) was a French tragic poet; Pierre Ambroise François Choderlos de Laclos (1741–1803) was a French novelist and general.

75. Restif de la Bretonne, Nicolas Edme (1734–86) was a French novelist.

76. Thomas Hobbes (1588–1679) was an English philosopher.

77. Jonathan Swift (1667–1745) was an Irish satirist.

78. Luc de Clapiers de Vauvenargues (1715–47) was the French author of *Maximus*.

79. Pierre Bayle (1647–1706) was the founder of eighteenth-century nationalism; Georges-Louis de Buffon (1707–88) was a French nationalist; Émeric de Crucé (1590–1648) was a political philosopher.

80. La Dubois is a character in Sade's *Justine*.

81. *Oeuvres complètes*, vol. 3 (1966–67), 80; for a published English translation, see *"Justine," "Philosophy in the Bedroom" and Other Writings*, 481.

82. Morelly (ca. 1715–ca. 1780) was an early French communist whose views were embraced by the Revolution; Jacques Pierre Brissot de Warville (1754–93) was a French revolutionary and journalist.

83. Cesare Bonesana Beccaria, Marchese di Beccaria (1738–94) was an Italian criminologist, economist, and jurist.

84. *Lex talionis* is the notion of retaliation or exacting compensation.

85. *Oeuvres complètes*, vol. 3 (1966–67), 97; for a published English translation, see *"Justine," "Philosophy in the Bedroom" and Other Writings*, 498.

86. Coeur de Fer is a character in Sade's *Justine*.

87. Zamé is a character in Sade's *Aline et Valcour*.

88. *Letters from Prison*, Letter 83 (to Madame de Sade, Nov. 1783), 328.

89. A farmer-general was an official in the French Ancien Régime.

90. *Oeuvres complètes*, vol. 3 (1966–67), 93; for a published English translation, see *"Justine," "Philosophy in the Bedroom" and Other Writings*, 494.

91. François La Rochefoucauld, Duc de la Rochefoucauld (1613–80) was a French writer.

92. Valmont is a character in *Liaisons dangereuses* by Pierre Choderlos de Laclos.

93. The pamphlet Beauvoir is most likely referring to is Jonathan Swift's *A Modest Proposal* (1729), a satirical work proposing that poor Irish families sell their children as food to the rich.

94. Recall that Max Stirner (Johann Kasper Schmidt) (1804–86) was a German philosopher and translator.

95. Esterval is a character in Sade's *La nouvelle Justine* (The New Justine), which can be found in vol. 6–9 of *Oeuvres complètes* (1966–67) and vol. 6–7 of *Oeuvres complètes* (1986–91).

96. Almani the Chemist is a character in Sade's *La nouvelle Justine*.

97. *Oeuvres complètes*, vol. 3 (1966–67), 526; for a published English translation, see *Philosophy in the Bedroom*, 341.

98. Maurice Blanchot (1907–2003) was a French novelist and literary critic.

99. *Oeuvres complètes*, vol. 3 (1966–67), 94–95; for a published English translation, see *"Justine," "Philosophy in the Bedroom" and Other Writings*, 495.

100. The Marquis de Bressac is a character in Sade's *Justine*.

101. *Oeuvres complètes*, vol. 3 (1966–67), 421; for a published English translation, see *Philosophy in the Bedroom*, 237.

102. *Oeuvres complètes*, vol. 3 (1966–67), 422; for a published English translation, see *Philosophy in the Bedroom*, 238.

103. *Oeuvres complètes*, vol. 1 (1986–91), 182; for a published English translation, see *The 120 Days in Sodom*, 364.

104. Bernard Mandeville (1670–1733) was a British scientist; *La ruche murmurante* is translated as *The Fable of the Bees* (1705).

105. (Jean-Nicolas) Arthur Rimbaud (1854–91) was a French poet.

106. Martin Heidegger (1889–1976) was a German philosopher.

107. "Eugenie de Franval" in *Oeuvres complètes*, vol. 2 (1986–91), 447–48; for a published English translation, see *"Justine," "Philosophy in the Bedroom" and Other Writings*, 432.

108. The Gordian knot was a knot tied by Gordius, the king of Phrygia, which could only be untied by the future king of Asia. Alexander the Great cut it with his sword.

109. *Oeuvres complètes*, vol. 1 (1986–91), 299; for a published English translation, see *The 120 Days in Sodom*, 497.

110. Paul Claudel (1868–1955) was a French poet, playwright, and diplomat.

3

Right-Wing Thought Today

INTRODUCTION

by Sonia Kruks

In the late 1940s, Simone de Beauvoir, Jean-Paul Sartre, Maurice Merleau-Ponty, and other members of the team that edited the journal, *Les temps modernes*, advocated what they called a "third way" in politics: they sought to develop a democratic socialist path, to delineate a middle way between capitalism and Soviet-style communism. Given this project, the journal was anti-American but also kept a certain distance from the Communists, offering them only what it described as "critical support." However, with the hardening of the lines of the Cold War, notably after the outbreak of hostilities in Korea in 1950 (which brought growing fears of a nuclear war), Sartre became convinced that no effective political space remained for a "third way." From 1952, when he wrote the first part of *The Communists and Peace*,[1] until the Soviet invasion of Hungary in 1956, Sartre was a close fellow traveler with the Parti Communiste Français (PCF; French Communist Party)—and Beauvoir accompanied him. However, Beauvoir notes in her autobiography that she agreed to accompany Sartre in this about-turn only after she had been repeatedly challenged to reconsider her "old prejudices." Her resistance became worn away and so, she writes, "I liquidated my ethical idealism and ended up by adopting Sartre's point of view as my own."[2]

But once convinced, Beauvoir became a staunch fellow traveler in her own right, as is evidenced in "Right-Wing Thought Today."

Beauvoir's essay was written in late 1954, and was originally published in *Les temps modernes* in 1955.[3] She wrote it for a special issue of the journal about the problems and possibilities of "the Left" in France. The editorial board (of which she remained a member) felt it was urgent to clarify what did and did not constitute properly Left politics. The difficulties were brought about by the French defeat in Indo-China in 1954, the heightening of conflict in Algeria, the fall of the Mendès-France government, and various domestic issues, all of which were dividing leftist parties and groups. In addition, the Cold War was increasingly being fought out on the cultural plane. The CIA-funded "Congress for Cultural Freedom" was supporting a range of organizations and periodicals in Europe that combined intense anticommunism with liberal or social-democratic positions. Among these was the Parisian intellectual journal *Preuves*, which began publication in 1951. Its aim was to compete for the minds of people such as *Les temps modernes* readers, softly persuading them toward more pro-American political positions.[4] All in all, it was becomingly increasingly difficult to see who belonged to the Left. As Beauvoir later wrote, "It became evident to us that we would have to make distinctions between our real allies and our adversaries in this new 'Left.' The *Temps modernes* team took upon itself the task of elucidating the meaning of this now devalued label."[5] The journal wanted to clarify both the term's historical and its present usages, and to offer its own vision of Left politics. The short editorial with which the special issue began asserted that " the crisis of the Left is one with the crisis of French politics itself," and it went on to ask, "do the notions of 'Left' and 'Right' still have a meaning?"[6] In order to answer this question (to which the answer was, of course, to be a resounding "yes"), it was necessary also to analyze the "Right." For, the editorial argued, the Left "defines itself essentially as negativity; it is the negation of a certain social regime and of the ideas that accompany this regime and help to conserve it; understanding this allows one to better understand certain reactions of the left today." Thus, it continued, "We have thought it useful to present in [the] first place the ideologies and attitudes of the contemporary right"[7]—and this presentation was Beauvoir's task.

The special issue was published in May 1955. However, even though it ran to nearly five hundred pages, more material was assembled for it than could be published. Thus it was decided to divide Beauvoir's essay into two parts. The first part (which consists of the sections up to and including "The

Mission of the Elite") was the lead essay in the special issue.[8] It was placed directly after the editorial and was followed by a range of essays on the definitions, history, and tasks of the Left. The issue concluded with a second editorial, which urged the need for a new "Popular Front," in which socialists would once again cooperate with the PCF, as they had done in the 1930s.[9] The second part of Beauvoir's essay was published in the subsequent issue of the journal (June-July 1955).[10]

Meanwhile, in April 1955, Merleau-Ponty published *Adventures of the Dialectic*, in which he made public his disagreements with Sartre's new procommunist politics and also attacked aspects of Sartre's philosophical work. Beauvoir took it upon herself to reply to Merleau-Ponty. Her speedily written and angry response to him, "Merleau-Ponty et le pseudo-sartrisme," was also published in the June-July issue of *Les temps modernes* along with the remainder of "Right-Wing Thought Today." Then, in September of the same year, she republished both essays (as well as her earlier essay on Sade) as a book that she entitled *Privilèges* (Privileges).

In the short foreword Beauvoir wrote for *Privilèges*, she suggests that what links all her essays together is their focus on the inevitable incoherence of the thought of the privileged. The thinkers of the privileged classes (among whom she now included Merleau-Ponty) have to engage in the dubious task of trying to justify their particular class interests in the language of the universal. Alluding to Marx's notion (in *The German Ideology*) that the ruling class must represent its own interest as the common interest of all members of society, Beauvoir also observes that the thought of the privileged must of necessity mask the actual practices of their class. However, in an existential twist, she adds that the privileged thinker is therefore necessarily in "bad faith," for he is engaged in a process of active self-delusion.

Thus, in "Right-Wing Thought Today," Beauvoir's focus is not on what Marx had called the "active members" of the ruling, or "bourgeois," class, but rather on the producers of the ideologies that legitimize their domination— that is, on "right-wing" intellectuals and their thought.[11] Throughout the text, Beauvoir variously refers to this group also as the producers of "bourgeois thought," as the "Elite," the "Elect," or the "privileged." In *Force of Circumstance*, she says that she read extensively in right-wing thought in order to write her article. She also remarks that, just as in *The Second Sex* (1949) she had set out and exposed the myths "spun around woman through the ages," so similarly here it was "a matter of laying bare the practical truths—the defense of the privileged by the privileged—whose crudity is concealed behind systems and nebulous concepts."[12] She describes the reading she undertook for this essay as irritating but adds, "I did it joyfully, since all of this nonsense was a sign of the ideological collapse of the privileged classes."

Beauvoir's essay is sometimes rambling and repetitive. One has the feeling that she read and wrote with such haste that, at times, she lacked sufficient distance from her material to be selective. The amount of detail and the number of examples she provides often tend to obscure the thrust of her argument. Moreover, her peremptory and dismissive tone can be off-putting to present-day readers who, with hindsight, know that her pro-Communist stance and triumphalist rhetoric were not to be justified by historical events. However, Beauvoir made no apologies for her tone, instead observing in *Force of Circumstance*, "I take too peremptory a tone in my essays, some people have told me . . . I don't think so. The best way to explode a bag of hot air is not to pat it but to dig one's nails into it."[13]

In spite of its prolixity, the key ideas in the essay may be easily summarized. What above all characterizes right-wing thought in the twentieth century, Beauvoir claims, is that it has become no more than a "counter-thought." The optimism of nineteenth-century bourgeois thought, that of a class that was still rising, had begun to wane already by the First World War. Since the advent of the Soviet Union, the main task of right-wing thought has been to oppose itself to communism. To do so effectively, it must justify the status quo and preach passivity and inaction to those who might otherwise challenge the class order. Right-wing thought thus lacks a positive content: it is no more than a range of disparate and often inconsistent reactions; a mishmash of counter-assertions. All that these share is their common opposition to the coherent and forward-looking theory and practice of communism. Because its main task is to legitimize the privilege of the few, both in their own eyes and in those of the many, right-wing thought is *essentially* inconsistent. For, Beauvoir argues, the proper endpoint of thought is to seek truths that are universal, and which thus apply to all. But since right-wing "thought" instead aims only at the legitimation of particular interests, it denies this endpoint and is, as such, intrinsically irrational. This explains why it may take on so many and such contradictory forms.

The greater part of Beauvoir's essay consists of a survey of diverse writings, involving extensive quotation as well as her own critical commentary. She draws on the work of a wide range of recent Western thinkers: novelists, sociologists, essayists and men (there are no women mentioned) of letters, historians, and philosophers. But although a vast array of thinkers are mentioned in passing, the bulk of her account addresses the work of only relatively few. These include, among novelists, Drieu La Rochelle, an active fascist and Nazi collaborator, and Henry Montherlant, whose work glorified masculinity and militarism; the liberal sociologist Raymond Aron and the nationalistic and (at that time) pro-Gaullist sociologist Jules Monnerot; and the fascist-inspired journalist and man of letters Thierry Maulnier. Other thinkers to whom Beauvoir repeatedly refers include the historians Oswald Spengler and Arnold Toynbee; the American ex-Trotskyist James Burnham; and, among philosophers, Karl Jaspers and Max Scheler, while Nietzsche is frequently invoked as an important precursor.

Through her extensive presentations and analyses, Beauvoir documents at length how right-wing thought takes on apparently antithetical forms: the defense of brutal *real politik* on the one hand, and a spiritualist withdrawal and quietism on the other; celebrations of the organic and harmonious nature of human society and, in direct contradiction, an atomistic view of society that affirms the inevitability of competition and conflict; an insistence on the naturalness of hierarchy, and yet also an emphasis on the need for the Elite to impose order, and so on. But what these diverse doctrines have in common is that each, in its own way, justifies the status quo and opposes itself to the bearers of equality and freedom—that is, to the communist movement. At the end of the essay Beauvoir argues that, since all right-wing thought is merely epiphenomenal, there is no point seriously engaging in argument with the thinkers of the Right. For they are not concerned with arriving at the truth, but only with obscuring it.

In many ways, "Right-Wing Thought Today" cuts uncomfortably across the grain of Beauvoir's less polemical essays on politics. For example, in *The Ethics of Ambiguity* (1947), Beauvoir had warned against the dangers of that triumphalist form of communism that believed it had Truth and History unambiguously on its side. To accept any ready-made values is to fall into the form of bad faith, which she called "seriousness": "The serious man puts nothing into question," she had written, and for "the serious revolutionary" the revolution becomes an inhuman "idol" and one "to which one will not hesitate to sacrifice man himself."[14] In the late 1940s, although strongly committed to socialism as a politics of freedom, Beauvoir had also insisted that we pay attention to the ambiguities of political judgment and complexities of political action. By contrast, "Right-Wing Thought Today" is marked by a striking Manichaeism: either one is with the Communists, or one is against them. If with them, then one is on the side of the masses; if against, on the side of the Elite. "Today, it is no longer possible to be against the bourgeoisie without positively allying oneself with its adversaries," she writes. Beauvoir's position realistically reflects the increasingly polarized world of the Cold War but, even so, the essay is methodologically troubling.

Beauvoir's critique involves a degree of abstraction that is, in her own terms, problematic. In claiming that such a diverse array of ideas are no more than epiphenomenal manifestations of class interests, she precludes making discriminations among various nonsocialist doctrines: whatever is not deemed to be Left thought comes to be defined as equally dangerous. Thus alongside the Nazi collaborator, Drieu le Rochelle, Beauvoir casts humanistic existential thinkers such as Max Scheler or Karl Jaspers, as well as the liberal sociologist Raymond Aron, as on the side of the enemy, as if there were no significant political or intellectual divergences among them. This erasure of important differences sits in paradoxical tension with Beauvoir's philosophical commitment (developed in many other works) to valuing the specificities and concrete contexts of thought and action.[15] There is also sometimes a naive rationalism in Beauvoir's text that again runs counter to her emphasis, in other writings, on the ambiguity of political life. For at points in the essay, she appears to hold a rather uncritical faith in scientific reason and empiricism, and to suggest that it is merely a ruse of right-wing thought to see history as contingent or discontinuous.

Yet, in spite of these difficulties, Beauvoir's essay still offers flashes of remarkable insight. For example, she is highly attuned, well ahead of most other Left social critics of her day, to the Eurocentric and masculinist tones of Western elite thought, describing it as a thought that "monopolizes the supreme category—the human" for itself. Similarly, both her critique of meritocracy as a ruse that justifies privilege and her observations on the elitism of the cult of "elegance" also address issues that still are current today. About meritocracy she perceptively observes that "the idea of a competition opened to thousands of individuals and in which only the worthiest succeeds implies the necessity of thousands of failures." The myth of "merit," she points out, always justifies the status quo, for it implies that "by making others responsible for their own lot, I am in the right to wash my hands of the matter." With regard to the cult of elegance, Beauvoir insightfully describes how previous notions of nobility as a quality acquired by blood are recast in the modern age: now new forms of superiority, based instead on the "innate" possession of good taste, are affirmed. But, like noble blood, "elegance is defined by a principle of exclusion" and so it becomes yet another justification for elite privilege.

"Right-Wing Thought Today" is now perhaps mainly of historical interest. Its primary significance is as a document that reveals Beauvoir's thinking in the context of the Cold War, a political conjuncture that has long passed. Yet, as the examples above suggest, elements of the essay also remain of enduring relevance. It continues to offer prescient insights that still bear on debates about inequality, elitism, and privilege today.

NOTES

1. *The Communists and Peace* was originally published as a series of essays in *Les temps modernes* between July 1952 and April 1954.

2. Simone de Beauvoir, *Force of Circumstance* (1963), trans. Richard Howard, Introduction by Toril Moi (New York: Paragon, 1992), 2 vols., vol. 2, 12.

3. In an interview published in the Communist paper, *L'Humanité-Dimanche* on December 19, 1954, Beauvoir tells her interviewer that she has just completed an article for *Les temps modernes*, "which is a critique of contemporary right-wing thought." The interview is reprinted in Claude Francis and Fernande Gontier, ed. *Les écrits de Simone de Beauvoir* (Paris: Gallimard, 1979), 358–62, see esp. 361. However, in *Force of Circumstance*, Beauvoir gives the impression that her essay was written somewhat later. For here she refers to the fall of the Mendès-France government, which occurred in February 1955 (mainly over his support for decolonization in North Africa), as one of the key events that precipitated the decision at *Les temps modernes* to engage in the political inquiry of which her essay was a part. See *Force of Circumstance*, vol. 2, 39. It is possible that Beauvoir revised the essay between its initial completion at the end of 1954 and its publication in May 1955.

4. The first meeting of the Congress was held in 1950 in the American sector of occupied Berlin. Raymond Aron and François Mauriac were among the French participants, although both later said they did not know about the CIA funding. *Preuves*, for which Aron wrote extensively, began publication in 1951. For information on the Congress and the network of CIA-supported organizations and periodicals that were formed under its aegis, see Frances Stonor Saunders, *The Cultural Cold War: The CIA and the World of Arts and Letters* (New York: The New Press, 2000). On *Preuves*, see in particular Saunders, 101–2; 217–19, and Pierre Grémion, "Présentation," in Pierre Grémion, ed. *Preuves, une revue Européenne à Paris* (Preuves: A European Review in Paris) (Paris: Julliard, 1989), 9–22. See also David Drake, *Intellectuals and Politics in Post-War France* (Basingstoke: Palgrave, 2002), 87–89.

5. Beauvoir, *Force of Circumstance*, vol. 2, 39.

6. Editorial, *Les temps modernes* 10:112–13 (May 1955): 1537.

7. Ibid., 1538.

8. *Les temps modernes* 10:112–13 (May 1955): 1539–75.

9. "Vers un Front Populaire?" ("Towards a Popular Front?") *Les temps modernes* 10:112–13 (May 1955): 2005–15.

10. *Les temps modernes* 10:114–15 (June-July, 1955): 2219–61.

11. Marx writes: "The division of labor . . . manifests itself also in the ruling class as the division of mental and material labor, so that inside this class one part appears as the thinkers of the class (its active, conceptive ideologists, who make the perfecting of the illusions of the class about itself their chief source of livelihood), while the others' attitude to these ideas and illusions is more passive and receptive, because they are in reality the active

members of this class," *The German Ideology*, in Robert C. Tucker, ed. *The Marx-Engels Reader* (New York: Norton, 1978), 173.

12. Beauvoir, *Force of Circumstance*, vol. 2, 39.

13. Ibid., 41.

14. *The Ethics of Ambiguity* (1947), trans. Bernard Frechtman (New York: Citadel Press, 1967), 49.

15. I explore this paradox more fully in "Ambiguity and Certitude in Simone de Beauvoir's Politics," *PMLA (Journal of the Modern Language Association)* 124:1 (January 2009): 214–20.

RIGHT-WING THOUGHT TODAY

by Simone de Beauvoir

TRANSLATION BY VÉRONIQUE ZAYTZEFF

AND FREDERICK M. MORRISON

NOTES BY VÉRONIQUE ZAYTZEFF, FREDERICK M. MORRISON,

SONIA KRUKS, AND ANDREA VELTMAN

Truth is one, but error is multiple. It is not just by chance that the right wing professes pluralism. Right-wing doctrines that give expression to pluralism are far too numerous for this article to seriously examine them all. Yet, bourgeois thinkers—who forbid their adversaries the use of Marxist methods if they do not accept the entire system as a whole—still have no qualms themselves about eclectically pulling together ideas borrowed from Spengler, Burnham, Jaspers, and many others.[1] Such an amalgam constitutes the common fund of the modern ideologies of the right and is the topic of this present study.

The Present Situation of Bourgeois Thought

We know that today's bourgeois is frightened. This panic is immediately obvious in all the books, articles, and speeches that reflect his thinking. Ac-

"*La pensée de droite, aujourd'hui*," *Les temps modernes* 112–13, (May 1955): 1539–75; 114–15 (June-July 1955): 2219–61; in *Privilèges* (Paris: Gallimard, 1955), 93–200, © Éditions Gallimard, 1972. This translation is of the *Privilèges* text.

cording to a formula dear to Malraux, "Europe has ceased to think of itself in terms of freedom in order to think of itself in terms of destiny."[2] However, the destiny of the West, like that of all civilizations, according to Spengler, whose terminology is borrowed here, is its death: the death of Europe, the waning of the West, the end of a world, the end of the world. The bourgeoisie lives with the imminence of the cataclysm that will abolish it.

Around 1945 Fabre-Luce wrote: "Weeping about future ruins is already heard amidst the ruins."[3]

"Today too many disasters are forcing man* to worry about what he does and to doubt the value of civilization itself. No sooner does he begin to wonder than he despairs and laughs nervously" (Caillois, *Liberté de l'esprit* [Freedom of the Spirit], 1949).[4]

"Society is in need of supermen, for no longer is it capable of self-direction and Western civilization is shaken to its foundations" (Alexis Carrel, *Réflexions sur la conduite de la vie* [Reflections on the Conduct of Life], 1950).[5]

"Today, we find ourselves between an end and a beginning. We too have our terrors. The process to which we are committed [*engagés*] will be lengthy and terrible" (Soustelle, *Liberté de l'esprit*, 1951).[6]

"All of us know the threat weighing on the freedom of spirit, our most precious jewel in Western civilization" (Rémy Roure, *Preuves* [Evidence], 1951).[7]

And so forth.

The phenomenon is not entirely new. Conservatives have always fearfully anticipated that former barbarisms will return in the future.† "To be on the right, is to fear losing what exists," Jules Romain aptly wrote at a time when he did not yet share this fear.[8] In the shape that it has assumed today, this "small fear of the twentieth century," as denounced by Mounier, had begun to spread as early as the end of the First World War.[9] That was when the optimism of the bourgeoisie began to be seriously undermined. For in the preceding century, the bourgeoisie had believed in the harmonious development of capitalism, continual progress, and in its own eternity. When it felt the need for justification, it could invoke the general interest to its own

---

* In order to grasp the scope of the texts I quote in this article, it will be necessary to remember that in the eyes of the thinkers on the right, the man of privilege is the only one endowed with a genuine existence. In the language of the bourgeois, the word *man* means *bourgeois*. Europe and the West mean the bourgeoisie of Europe and the West, or more exactly, this is the Idea of man forged by European and Western bourgeois thinkers. As for the non-privileged man, he is usually referred to by the term "the masses" and is granted only a negative reality.

† For example, in 1880, Pobedonostsev, Supreme Procurator of the Most Holy Synod, wrote: "In comparing the present with the distant past, we feel that we are living in some strange world *in which everything is retreating to primeval chaos*, and, in the midst of all this fermentation, we feel we are helpless." Quoted by Trotsky in *My Life* [New York: Charles Scribner's Sons, 1930].

advantage—the growth of science, technology, and industries based on capital ensured abundance and happiness to future humanity. The bourgeoisie was particularly confident in its future and it felt strong. While it did not ignore "the threat posed by the workers," it had numerous weapons against that threat. "To the strength of garrisons, we can add the omnipotence of religious hopes," wrote Chateaubriand in full seriousness.[10]

By the beginning of the twentieth century, the situation had already quite changed. Monopolies had succeeded the system of free trade, and capitalism, thus transformed, had begun to see its own contradictions. Furthermore, "the threat posed by the workers" had become considerably worse, religious hopes had lost their omnipotence, and the proletariat had become a force capable of defeating the force of the garrisons. The bourgeoisie itself began to distrust the illusions it had built up. The progress in technology and industry turned out to be more menacing than promising: they had learned not how to fertilize the earth but how to destroy it. It goes without saying that bourgeois economists still maintained that only capitalism was capable of achieving universal prosperity; they admitted however that it would be necessary to adapt it considerably. In the light of wars and crises it had been discovered that the development of the capitalistic regime hardly resembled an upward march toward a new golden age. One even began to suspect that in the history of humanity it might be nothing more than a temporary form. By mistaking its own lot for that of the entire earth, the bourgeoisie proceeded to prophesy somber apocalypses. Its ideologists took up the catastrophic vision of history as it had been outlined by Nietzsche.[11]

"After the First World War," writes Jaspers, "twilight fell over all civilizations. Humanity's demise [fin] was foreseen in this crucible in which all peoples, all men are melted down once again either to disappear or to be reborn. This was not yet the end, but almost everywhere the end was envisaged as an eventuality. Everyone was spending their time waiting, either in anguished dread or in resigned fatalism. The end was either reduced to natural, historical, and sociological laws or it was given a metaphysical interpretation ascribing it to a loss of substance. These differences of atmosphere were very marked in Klages, Spengler, and Alfred Weber.[12] However, none of them doubted that the crisis was here, and that it was graver than it had ever been."* [13]

At the same time, anguished voices were being raised in France as well. Valéry tolled the knell in an essay that caused a great stir at the time: our civilization had just discovered that it was mortal.[14] In 1927, Drieu la Rochelle

---

* *Origine et sens de l'histoire* [*The Origin and Goal of History*], 290.

wrote in *Le jeune Européen* [The Young European], "All the values by which we have lived up to now are disappearing." And further on, he wrote, "I try to come as close as possible to the characteristics of my time, so that I can touch them with my fingertip. I find them so abominable and so powerful that man in his weakened state will no longer be able to escape the fatality they express and will soon perish at their hands."[15] Following which, he predicts at length the death of humanity.

However, the bourgeoisie still contemplated humanity's end, that is to say its own demise as a class, as only an "eventuality." Because it still had one hope: fascism. Nazi ideology converted pessimism into the will-to-power. When Spengler announced the decline of the West, he believed that his book could "serve as a basis for the political organization for our future." He proposed the following alternative to Western man: "Do what is necessary or do nothing,"[16] that is to say that he exhorted him to accept a new Caesarism. Drieu, in the somber prophecies of his youth, was leaning toward the PPF.[17] He saluted fascism as a modern Renaissance. "Totalitarianism offers Twentieth Century man chances of a dual corporeal and spiritual restoration," he wrote in his *Notes pour comprendre ce siècle* [Notes for Understanding this Century]. In 1940, he congratulated Europe on having finally discovered "the sense of the tragic." He declared that "it was essential to reintroduce the tragic into French thought." However, what he meant was that France quite simply had to become integrated into a Nazi Europe.

So now the necessary has been done: in vain. Fascism has been vanquished. The defeat weighs heavily on today's bourgeoisie. In the "twilight" that is now shrouding civilization, the bourgeoisie can not catch sight of a heroic light, of a Caesar. Nothing can defend it from the doubts now besetting it. "Two world wars, concentration camps, and the atomic bomb were necessary to shake our good conscience," wrote Soustelle in *Liberté de l'esprit*. "We began to ask ourselves the terrible question: is it possible that our civilization might not be *the* Civilization?"

The question having been asked, an immense chorus answers, it is not. All the peoples that are not a part of the West, that is to say, all those who do not recognize the suzerainty of the USA, and in the West all men who are not bourgeois, refuse to accept Western bourgeois civilization. What is even more critical is that they are in the process of creating a different civilization. Prior to the last war, the bourgeois sensed that something was about to end and he did not know what would be born thereafter. Now barbarity has a name: communism. Communism has the "Medusa face" whose sight makes the blood of civilized people run cold. It already rules one-fifth of the globe. It is a cancer that will soon have eaten away at the entire world. The sole remedies considered by the right are the bomb and culture. One is quite radical while the other is decidedly not. In anger or in terror, the right appropriates the Marxist prophecies in its own name: it knows that it is doomed.

The ideas of the defeated are defeated ideas. To decipher the present-day ideologies of the right, we must always remember that they have been formed under the sign of defeat. It goes without saying that they are linked to the past by numerous threads. Idealism is one such thread that has lost none of its importance since the time Marx denounced it. Cut off by his work and his lifestyle from any contact with matter, shielded from any need, the bourgeois is oblivious to the resistances of the real world. Idealism is as natural to him as breathing. Everything encourages him to systematically develop this tendency in which his own situation is immediately reflected: he has a fundamental interest in denying the class struggle, and can only blind himself to its existence by refusing reality as a whole. For reality, he substitutes Ideas whose meaning he defines to his own liking and whose extension he limits arbitrarily. The method considered in its generality* is too well known. Marx and Lenin have attacked it so spectacularly that there is no need for another word about it. It is enough to underscore that the various developments of bourgeois thought all involve and tend to confirm an idealist attitude.

In earlier times, beautiful, arrogant systems were built on this base, but the times when a Joseph de Maistre or a Bonald prospered are long gone.[18] Maurras's doctrine itself, despite its weakness, is still too positive a doctrine so it has been buried too.[19] The bourgeois theoretician, knowing that he has no hold on the future, no longer tries to build; he defines himself with respect to communism and against it, in a purely negative way. For example, Aron, in the conclusion of *Le grand schisme* [The Great Schism],[20] does not ask himself "What do we believe in?" but "What can we oppose to communism?" He answers, "The affirmation of Christian and humanist values." For one who has read his books, it is evident that the above-mentioned values are the least of his concerns. The defeat of communism is the sole thing that interests him. The same is true of the type of manifesto that opens the second issue of *Preuves* in which Rougemont starts by declaring, "We are rather weak against totalitarian propaganda," and as an agenda, proposes counter-propaganda themes.[21] Things have gotten to such a point that in a 1950 edition of *Liberté de l'esprit*, Léon Werth answered to a survey on free-

---

* We will return to its most modern aspects.

117

dom by declaring that "In 1950, a regime of freedom defines itself by its op-posite—the Stalinist regime."[22] His friends praised this answer highly. This is a confession that the contemporary right no longer knows what it is de-fending. It just defends itself against communism and does so without any hope. Those that Nizan called "the watch-dogs" of the bourgeoisie, today are trying to justify the survival of a society whose impending death they themselves announce.[23]

This justification itself is not an easy task: its historical failure reveals to the bourgeoisie the theoretical contradictions in which its thought is en-tangled. In an article published in March 1952 in the review *Preuves*, Jules Romains pathetically expounded his ideological drama: bourgeois society has become a victim of the principles it had created for its own use and which are now indiscreetly spreading all over the world. "Until now, every civilization capable of organizing itself and, above all, of surviving, had done so only to the extent to which it was able to preserve the differences, acqui-sitions, and inequalities it had slowly accumulated to its advantage, all of which could appear iniquitous and monstrous in the eyes of the barbar-ity, savagery, famine, and verminous poverty that surrounded it." Yet, "The concept of justice or, more exactly, the concept of equal rights is like a bush fire. One would like to stop it at the firebreaks, but it jumps right over them. The eradication of privileges, of advantageous differences, and of localized acquisitions is a chain reaction which will only cease when it has nothing left to devour."

This naive text straightforwardly poses the problem our modern watch-dogs have to resolve. The Atlantic Pact forced the bourgeois to go beyond [*dépasser*] the old nationalism toward what they call Europe, the West, and Civilization. We are not bothered by it: as long as we are counted among the privileged ones, we can well erase a few frontiers. That is the point: we would like to live with our own kind. But all of a sudden, the "barbarity, savagery, famine, and verminous poverty" get stirred up; they act out, raise their voices, and threaten. How then can one still deny that they exist? Even if Mr. de Rougemont declares that "Europe is the world's consciousness [*conscience*]," the Western bourgeois is forced to admit that he is no longer the only consciousness, the absolute subject; there are other men. To these other men the privileges of the civilized ones *appear* iniquitous: how can one dispel this appearance? Until now, thanks to the firebreaks that it had been able to carve out, the bourgeoisie easily reconciled the idea of justice and the reality of its interests. Can it still do so now? Renouncing the prof-itable inequalities is, of course, out of the question. Will it be necessary to throw the idea of justice overboard? This is a painful dilemma, given the traditions of bourgeois ideology.

This entire problem stems from the fact that the bourgeoisie thinks. The nobility fought for its privileges and did not worry very much about justifying them. Therefore, as Drieu la Rochelle nostalgically reminds us, "To think, after all, was to strike or be stricken with a sword."[24] For the bourgeoisie, to the contrary, thought was an instrument of liberation and today, the bourgeoisie finds itself encumbered by the ideology it forged for itself at the time when it was a rising class. "Each new class," Marx wrote, "has to give its ideas the form of universality, and represent them as the only rational, universally valid ones."[25] Its claim, he adds, is justified insofar as this class rises up in revolution. However, the bourgeoisie has now become, in its turn, a ruling class. Rather than fighting against outside privileges, today it defends its own privileges against the rest of humanity. The bourgeoisie can not entirely repudiate the philosophy of the Enlightenment whose truth it experienced in the French Revolution; however, this is a double-edged sword that, today, is turned against the bourgeoisie. How is it indeed possible to provide a universal justification for specific advantageous claims? It is quite natural for everyone to prefer himself, but it is impossible to establish this preference as a system that is valid for all.

The bourgeoisie is aware of this paradox and so for this reason has an ambivalent attitude towards thought. Marx rightly indicates that there is a definite antagonism between "the active members" of the ruling class and "the active and conceptive ideologists whose specialty it is to create the illusions that this class has of itself."[26] These specialists are viewed with suspicion. On the right, the word "intellectual" easily takes on a derogatory meaning. It is true that the proletariat also views intellectuals with suspicion, but only to the extent that they are also bourgeois. Among the bourgeoisie, Marx recognized the intellectuals in particular as capable of attaining "the theoretical intelligence of the historical movement as a whole," whereas the typical bourgeois distrusts thought itself.[27] "Any good reasoning offends," Stendhal used to say.[28] Any progressive system of government fights illiteracy while, on the contrary, reactionary regimes, such as Franco's and Salazar's, deliberately favor it.[29] As soon as the right feels strong enough, it substitutes violence for thought—as was seen in Nazi Germany. In France, too, the "Royalist supporters" and other fascists claimed that, if one was part of the majority, it was better to strike than to argue.

Drieu had already sighed, "Today, men have no more swords."[30] The bourgeoisie feels even more disarmed today than twenty years ago. Americans, it is true, have the atomic bomb which is, precisely, their substitute for thought. However, in France and Germany, spiritual sublimations are more necessary than ever. The bourgeoisie wants to convince others as well as itself that it is aiming at universal ends in defending its specific interests. The task assigned to its "active and conceptive ideologists" is to invent a superior justice in whose name injustice will find itself justified.

Practically vanquished, theoretically cornered by insurmountable contradictions, why, one should ask, does the Western intellectual persist in defending a condemned civilization that doubts its own value? Since our civilization is not *the* Civilization, but merely a moment in human history, why not surpass it toward the totality of history and humanity? Mounier rightly indicates in *Petite peur du XXe siècle* that the idea of Apocalypse through which "the European guilty conscience" is expressed, is falsified by fear; for, in truth, the Apocalypse is not a song of catastrophe but "a poem of triumph, the affirmation of the final victory of the just and the ecstatic song of the final reign of plenitude." As regards the "active members" of the bourgeoisie, the reason for this falsification is obvious. The final reign of justice and plenitude would appear as a disaster to the privileged who dug in their heels in defense of their unjust privileges. It would seem natural that the intellectuals, being in love with universals, would take a stand for humanity in general rather than for the particular interests of a condemned society. Why is it that so many of them persist in identifying Man with the bourgeois, even if it means prophesying in fear the end of man?*

This attitude offers such a paradox that Thierry Maulnier himself was amazed at it.[31] In May 1953, in *La table ronde* [The Round Table], he asked the Western bourgeois, all things considered, what do you have to offer against communism? Up until now, we have been fighting against it in the name of the terror it evokes in us. What if this terror were to come to a

---

* Drieu's case is interesting to consider from this point of view. In 1927, he wrote in *Le jeune Européen*, "If the human dies, from the moment he dies, this universe, which is going to feed on the dissolution of our dear and beautiful categories, does not matter much. I am suffering too much, I am standing down." However, in September 1940, preaching the integration of France into a Nazified Europe, he wrote: "Metamorphosis, the lives of nations are a series of metamorphoses. A nation crosses the centuries only by changing its image, and each time it takes on a new image, it discards the old one as if it were dead skin, rags of flesh—a horrifying sight for the one who amorously reveled in this former shape. . . . So, once again it is time for the metamorphosis: necessary, inevitable, in the sweat and anguish and blood of disaster. France must renounce all the old forms of nationalism. France must turn away from the national in order to immerse itself into the social." Drieu thus acknowledges that in order to save Man, it is necessary to know how to renounce certain particular forms of the human. However, the surpassing he preached served, in fact, the interests of his class, as today the surpassing toward Civilization serves the West. The *metamorphosis* becomes unacceptable as soon as it contradicts these interests.

stop? "If communism abandons terror, if it can, if it *dares* to abandon terror, then you will have to give up trying to find within communism itself the weapons to fight against it. You will be left to find those weapons within yourselves. . . . Until now the defense of the Western world has been negative. The Western world does not want communism. Fine. However, this can not indefinitely substitute for a future proposed to man, nor for a meaning given to this future." It would seem logical to conclude that if the reasons for being anti-communist are found only within communism and if, precisely, these reasons are no longer there, then let us renounce anti-communism. However, the meaning of Maulnier's article is different. What he wants is assistance in finding a positive justification for this struggle. Once again, why this obstinacy?

To answer that the anti-communist intellectuals are themselves bourgeois is not enough. Many of them hardly enjoy the material advantages reserved for the bourgeoisie and, moreover, the "active members" of their class keep them at some distance. However, by their very reaction to this situation, they created their own ideological interests which they are passionately eager to safeguard. The superior justice which they were charged with inventing and which contradicts worldly justice, can only be situated in the heavens, and that is where they situate themselves. There, they coin eternal Truths and absolute Values. They are more attached to these illusions of universality than are other bourgeois, since it is they who have crafted them. Moreover, the intelligible world is for them an arrogant refuge from the mediocrity of their condition. They escape from their own class and ideally reign above all classes over all of humanity. This is the reason their loathing of Marxism is much fiercer than that of the active bourgeois—Marxism knows only the earth and brutally hurls them [the anti-communist intellectuals] back among men. It goes without saying that they do not own up to the true reason for their hate. They prefer to confess shamelessly to puerile nightmares. "If the Red Army were to enter France, if the Communist Party were to seize power, I would be deported and executed." They write science-fiction novels "not to be read at night," and together with Thierry Maulnier they whine "Marxism wants my death." In fact, they dread ideological liquidation, or more exactly, they know that this liquidation has already occurred. Marxism sees them not as sacred mediators between Ideas and men, but as bourgeois parasites, a mere emanation of capitalistic powers, an epiphenomenon, and a nothingness; this is just not acceptable to someone who, for want of finding his place in this world, alienated himself in eternity.

Thus, while upholding the pretense that his thought is universal, the

121

bourgeois ideologist does not abdicate the particularistic will of his class. He is left with a single way out, which is to deny particularity the very instant he claims the right to it. Every bourgeois has a practical interest in disguising the class struggle.* The bourgeois thinker is forced to do it, if he wishes to adhere to his own thought. He refuses therefore to grant any importance to the empirical singularities of his situation, and correlatively, to the ensemble of empirical singularities that define concrete situations. In societies, material factors have only a secondary role. Thought transcends those contingencies. Humanity is ideally homogeneous. Man, as he soars in the intelligible, unique, indivisible, unanimous, and perfect heavens is expressed through the mouth of the thinker.

The entire philosophy of man elaborated by bourgeois intellectuals, and in particular their theory of knowledge, aims precisely, as will be seen, at supporting this claim. However, given the negative attitude I mentioned earlier, their positive doctrine matters much less than their self-defense. Their very first concern is to get rid of Marxism. They will be able to take their ideas seriously only when they have, first, invalidated the system that calls them into question. Their thought is, first and foremost, a counter-thought. Most of their writings are, in fact, attacks on communism.

There is a strange paradox here: because the bourgeois thinker lives in terror of prophecies, he takes great pains to deny Marxism any prophetic or even methodological value. He evades this contradiction by a catastrophic pessimism that changes necessity into accident. Socialism will triumph; however its advent will not be the outcome of a rational dialectic, but just the result of a meaningless cataclysm. This is why the Western intellectual takes pleasure in his fear and changes the Apocalypse into a song of horror. He would rather have humanity doomed to absurdity and nothingness than question himself.

Anti-Communism

"All problems are a matter of opinion," asserts Brice Parain.[32] All anti-communist systems postulate this opinion. Although there are minor differences, their convergence here is remarkable. A man's material reality and situation count for nothing; only his subjective reactions matter. Socialism is explained not by the force of a system of production, but by the play of

---

* "When I am asked," noticed Alain, "if the break between the right and left parties, or between men of the right and men of the left, still has a meaning, the first idea that comes into my mind is that the man who asks this question is certainly not a man of the left."

wills whose motives are either ethical or affective. Economic necessity is nothing more than an abstraction—the economy, when all is said and done, is the concern of psychology. Classes in general and the proletariat in particular are defined by their state of mind.*

Nietzsche was the first one to propose a psychologistic interpretation of history and of society. "The weak are filled with a desire for vengeance and resentment while the strong have an aggressive pathos." The idea of resentment has had extraordinary good fortune among thinkers on the right. Scheler used it not to attack Christianity, which, according to him was a positive doctrine of love, but to destroy any socialist ethic—socialism necessarily expresses a resentment of God and of anything that is divine in man.[33] Scheler, with some nuance, made Rathenau's statement his own: "The concept of justice rests on envy."[34] Aware of its baseness, the "ethical proletariat" wishes to debase those who are superior to it. Challenging the right of ownership, in particular, "rests on the working class's envy of classes that have not earned their wealth by their own work." The revolutionary idea is reduced to the "uprising of slaves driven by resentment."†

This psychology might have appeared too superficial. To give it more depth, they resorted to psychoanalysis. Eastman in *La science de la révolution* [The Science of Revolution] interpreted working-class mentality in accordance with Freud.[35] De Man, whose book *Au-delà du marxisme* [Beyond Marxism] had considerable success in France around 1928, preferred Adler—in psychoanalyzing the proletariat, he diagnosed a very pronounced inferiority complex.[36] The spirit of the class struggle was engendered by a profound instinct of self-worth. The unskilled worker protects himself against feelings of deficiency with "compensating reactions." The revolutionary attitude is one of these reactions. The inferiority complex appears, in many subsequent studies, as the consequence of a more general affective phenomenon—frustration. The feeling of frustration makes the worker despondent and causes neuroses that are sublimated into the revolutionary attitude. When all is said and done, the proletarian's affliction comes from the fact that he thinks of himself as a proletarian. This conclusion concurs with Spengler's affirmation "From the economic point of view, there is no working-class."‡ The same thesis is developed by Toynbee.§[37] "The proletariat is,

---

* See on this topic the book by Pierre Naville: *Psychologie, marxisme, matérialisme* [Psychology, Marxism, and Materialism] where this question is studied in detail.

† *L'homme du ressentiment* [The Man of Resentment], 145.

‡ *Déclin de l'Occident* [The Decline of the West], Volume 2, 440.

§ *L'histoire* [History], 416.

in effect, a state of mind rather than the consequence of external conditions.
. . . [It is] an element or a social group that exists inside a given society but
is, nevertheless, not truly* part of it. . . . The true mark of the proletariat is
neither poverty nor humble birth, but the awareness and the resentment of
being disinherited." In *La guerre en question* [The War in Question], Monnerot repeats this definition almost word for word. According to him, the
word proletariat refers to "[t]hose who, in terms of power and action within
a civilization, feel deprived."[38]

A naive reader is tempted to ask: why *do they feel* deprived? Monnerot, in
Sociologie du communisme,† sketches out an answer. He develops endlessly
the idea that the class struggle is nothing more than a set of mental reactions
whose origin is resentment. Marxism is made up of a "*detonating mixture:
dialectics and resentment* . . . The resentment, wherein the dialectics is mobilized, coincides with the resentment of a social category whose birth is
appalling and whose resentment is a historical necessity.

" . . . It was necessary that an individual resentment, aided by a great
power of intellectual keenness and synthesis, *interpret* a collective resentment, a historical resentment, so that this doctrine of revolution could then
be born."‡

Therefore, Monnerot admits that the proletariat's resentment is "historically a *necessity.*" Such a concession, were it taken seriously, would suffice to
ruin all his theories—necessity exists only on the side of reality. If one were
to admit that reality imposes a revolutionary awareness [*prise de conscience*]
on the proletariat, then the entire psychologism collapses and a Marxist
model appears again. In a note that increases the confusion, Monnerot adds,
"Here, we concur with Hegel in seeing the role of *evil* as a historical driving
force." This rapprochement glaringly reveals his bad faith: evil is an objective reality. To see in it a historical driving force is to define History as an
objectively founded process; while by assimilating the idea of evil to that of
resentment, Monnerot psychologizes it. As a matter of fact, in the remainder of the work, historical *necessity* is carefully passed over in silence. The
"detonating power" of resentment is explained by the intervention of factors
radically external to the lived situation.

---

* In another passage, Toynbee wrote "morally" instead of "truly."

† I will often quote this book, which appears to be one of the essential works on contemporary
anti-communism. By the care he takes to conceal his sources, Monnerot aims at originality: he
never quotes even when he plagiarizes. As a matter of fact, he is of interest to us only because of
the number of platitudes he exploits: among others, the theme of resentment.

‡ Monnerot's emphasis.

What are those factors? Well, first and foremost, the action of ringleaders, i.e., communists. The Communist Party, which Monnerot baptizes as the Enterprise, seeks to exploit and organize vague unrests: "The Enterprise uses, maintains, and attempts to bring resentments of classes, masses, and individuals to a decisive degree of active virulence, which specifically consists in outsiders organizing the various discontents and discontented peoples."

Of course, these maneuvers are not explained by an objective finality either. The Party, radically foreign to the proletariat, pursues no aim that might be of concern to the proletariat—it only acts upon it from the outside, in a mechanical, absurd fashion. For instance, when the Party "works on the colonial masses," it is not because it takes to heart their desire for emancipation—but in order "to aggravate and poison all the contradictions of the capitalistic world."*

Fine. But, why this type of politics? Here, Monnerot borrows his response from Burnham. Burnham had learned from the "Machiavellians" and taught the dazzled right-wing thinkers the following profound truth: when seeking power, chiefs, States, and parties always aim for power alone. When a man of action offers an objective purpose, such as the common good or freedom, it is only in order to mystify the world and it would be very naive to believe him. In truth, the sole topic of political science is "the struggle for power under various forms whether avowed or concealed." This postulate allows Burnham to define communism as "a world-wide conspiracy to bring about the conquest of a monopoly of power at the time of the decline of capitalism."[39] Monnerot, too, equates the Enterprise with a secret society seeking to rule for the sake of ruling—the very name with which he baptizes it is chosen to underscore its private and egoist character.

Machiavellianism harmoniously completes the psychology of resentment. Subjective in its motives, revolutionary action is equally subjective in its ends. Men driven by a "will-to-power" amplify feelings of inferiority, envy, and hate in those who know themselves to be powerless.

The advantages of such an interpretation are obvious. All things considered, all the hardships of men are imaginary and ideal remedies are sufficient. Changing the world is useless; it is enough to modify the opinion that certain people have of it. Nietzsche proposed giving the underprivileged an illusion of *dignity*. De Man suggests reducing the inferiority complex suffered by unskilled workers by granting them certain social advantages.

---

* *Sociologie du communisme*, 19.

The enlightened right wing readily recognizes that it is necessary to *morally* integrate the proletariat into society. In a word, it proposes to transform the mentality of the oppressed, but not the situation oppressing them. In America this is the way that Big Business* operates cynically. It uses Public Relations to spread among the exploited masses the slogans profitable to the exploiters. It has perfected the technique of Human Engineering that is devoted to concealing the material reality of the worker's condition through moral and affective mystifications.[40] By means of appropriate education and carefully thought out methods of command, they endeavor to convince the proletarian that he is not a proletarian, but an American citizen. If he refuses to be manipulated, then he is considered abnormal and a therapy of "psychological release" has been invented for his cure.

One of the duties of humanity is clearly to fight the ringleaders interested in exacerbating the revolutionary neurosis. It goes without saying that the doctrine they invoke to serve their devious goals could not aspire to any truth—our anti-communists are not so naive as to ascribe to it a content that would reflect some reality. They have learned from Sorel that myths are a dynamic force to be evaluated not intellectually but in terms of their efficacy.[41] From the Machiavellians they learned that ideas are weapons of war aimed at creating affective and active attitudes. Some specialists profess to know and critique Marxism scientifically, but the great majority of its opponents disdain any knowledge of it. Thierry Maulnier confesses that the doctrine of Marx, Engels, and Lenin "is surely almost unknown to those who fight it or believe they are fighting it." Burnham approvingly quotes this sentence by Pareto: "Determining the social value of Marxism and knowing whether the Marxist theory of surplus value is true or false, is about as important as knowing whether baptism wipes away sin when one seeks to determine the social value of Christianity—and this is of no importance whatsoever."[42]

Marxism, like the situation it claims to interpret, is explained by subjective chance. It is one of the forms of this modern humanitarianism that, according to Scheler, "is nothing more than the outcome of a repressed hatred of family and social milieu." Love for "anything with a human face" reveals a hatred of God. It is also "a protest against love for the fatherland." More fundamentally it is a way of running away from oneself and of assuaging one's self-hatred. De Man considers socialism more kindly—its true motive is an individual sense of morality. The socialist, for tactical reasons, is led to

---

* For more details, refer to the article by Michel Crozier: *Human Engineering*, in *Les temps modernes*, July 1951.

attribute to his doctrine an objective scope; however, it is nothing more than a disguise. Marx, for one, "presented socialism as necessary only because he considered it as desirable, following a tacitly presupposed moral judgment." A similar idea is found in Spengler: "Political parties, today as during Hellenistic times, have in some way ennobled certain economic groups, whose standard of living they wished to improve, by elevating them to the rank of a political order, as Marx did for industrial workers." Monnerot thinks that Marx obeyed an irrational impulse rather than an ethical concern. Marx and Marxists after him had been too greatly stricken by the birth and the apogee of capitalism. "The aftershock of an affective trauma determined their particular perspective." And, of course, Marx is a man of resentment, as are those whom he addresses and who rally to him.

Resentment, ethical will, or trauma: in every case, an individual metamorphosis is at the origin of Marxism. And its success is explained by extrinsic reasons. According to Pareto, it is a social fact that can be accounted for by sociological laws: in particular the law of "derivations," and the law of "the residue," both invented by Pareto. Toynbee sees in Marxism "the disguise of the Jewish Apocalypse." Caillois sees orthodoxy in it. Aron attributes its explosive might to the conjunction of a Christian theme with a Promethean theme and a rationalist theme. Yet mainly, the authors all keep repeating tirelessly that Marxism panders to the religious instinct of the masses: it is a religion.

De Man writes: "There is no socialism without some sort of religion. The psychological impulse toward socialism has its cause beyond any worldly reality."

"The USSR is a superstition," writes Aron. In *Les guerres en chaîne* [*The Century of Total War*]* he develops at length this idea borrowed from Toynbee: "Marxism is a Christian heresy."

In June 1949 in *Liberté de l'esprit*, Stanislas Fumet thanks Berdyaev for long ago having revealed to him that Marxism was a religion,[43] and concludes, in Pareto's style, "Its dogmas are of no importance. What does count is the hold it has upon souls, and as long as there are souls, what counts is that magical or tactical operation of the priest, whose action subjugates minds and thereby allows him to bend wills in the name of some divinity or other."

Monnerot's book is entirely based on this equation: communism is the "Islam of the twentieth century." The Enterprise is "the religious image of a

---

* [Raymond Aron, *Les guerres en chaîne* (Paris: Gallimard, 1951), trans. E. W. Dickes and O. S. Griffiths (Derek Verschoyle: London; printed in U.S., 1954)] Page 136 and following.

division of humanity." "The communist enterprise is a religious enterprise." "Communism offers itself both as secular religion and universal State. As a secular religion, it channels resentments, organizes and makes effective the impetus that sets men against the societies in which they were born; communism accelerates the societies' state of separation from themselves and the scission of a part of their native resources, thus hastening the rhythms of dissolution and destruction." Socialism is a "messianism of the human race."

One must also mention Thierry Maulnier's article "Fanatisme des marxistes" [The Fanaticism of the Marxists] in which he tries to transpose Marxism into religious terminology. Paradise, he says, has been moved from heaven into the Future. Since Marx elevated historical creation to an absolute value, one finds in his doctrine a supra-historical transcendence of values and the promise of salvation in another world. Hence, there is a Marxist religion: "the religion of humanity to be conquered or of humanity to be built."

The method of severing communism from all its real bases and defining it as a pure form is even more evident in another work by Thierry Maulnier: *La face de Méduse du communisme*. The author asks, why does every revolution imply a terror? He arrogantly dismisses all the objective reasons. The idea that an expropriating enterprise could not be successful without violence is, among other things, utterly foreign to him. For he says that one has to search for the explanation of Terror in "the dark forces of the collective man." Terror is "the very foundation of the collective unconscious upon which the apparatus of revolutionary justice is erected." There was a Terror in 1793 because at the end of the eighteenth century "people began to get bored." Terror is born from the "tragic fascination with death" and from "the intellectual guilty conscience inherent in any fanaticism." It has its sources in fear and will-to-power. Maulnier says further that "Revolution is the victorious surge of resentment." It is an enterprise in "social sorcery" and, as such, it demands expiatory victims. Terror represents "the ritual of conjuration and purification, the liturgical pomp, the office and the Mystery." "Once the feast is over, the ritual is established. The orgy of Terror becomes the Church of Terror." It is understood that this Church is Machiavellian. Its aim is to carry out "a total confiscation of the individual for the benefit of society."

Thus, they got even with Marxism: it was reduced to a psycho-sociological phenomenon without any internal signification. A mere instrument in the hands of the Enterprise that exploits human credulity for its own benefit, neither Divinity nor dogmas count in this religion, only the Machiavellianism of its priests.

128

Nevertheless, a problem remains that particularly bothers right-wing in-tellectuals—the existence of left-wing intellectuals. They are neither under-privileged proletarians nor do they exhibit the will-to-power that drives the ringleaders. How does one explain their aberration? There is no point in looking too far; a few accommodations will suffice and the notion of resent-ment will again be useful in this case. It is decreed that members of the *Intel-ligentsia*—even if they were born in some bourgeois French family—feel ex-iled within society. In any case, they do not occupy the highest ranks, which is enough to provoke their hatred of society and themselves. The intellectual, Aron says, detests the bourgeois. It does not cross his mind for one second that this hostility could be the reverse side of his positive feeling toward other men.* In his opinion, it is obviously the result of an inferiority complex. In-tellectuals "can only arrive at the top by eliminating the social category that, in the West, owes its power to wealth and this wealth to the chance of busi-ness transactions, heredity, or exceptional talents." Thus "One flees towards the red metropolis because he detests the society in which he lives."†

Monnerot attempted to provide slightly more subtle explanations. How-ever, he only succeeded in feigning complexity under the cover of a total obscurity. One must quote, among others, the passage where he evokes the manner in which communists succeeded in countering the atomic bomb: "By using psychological methods and playing on religious, ethical, and metaphysical motives, communists attacked the scientists who permitted the manufacture of such weapons. Their efforts were aimed at those whose calculations and discoveries were at the heart of this new weaponry and

---

* One remembers the dialogue between Jeannette Vermersch and a right-wing deputy. The latter cried, "So much hatred in a woman's heart!" She answered, "One cannot love the people without hating their oppressors." However, bourgeois psychology recognizes only negative feelings as original and authentic.

† *Les guerres en chaîne*, 461–465. It may be a surprise that Aron adopts Françoise Giroud's concept of the intellectual that represents him as a bitter man fascinated by wealth and social prestige. This is evidently the logic of a subjectivism pushed to the point of absurdity. Cut off from his activity, which in turn is cut off from its goals [*fins*], the intellectual, from the Machiavellian perspective, is no longer anything but a barely satisfied will-to-power. But is this really how Aron himself grasps his projects? And does he sincerely believe that Irène Joliot-Curie trembles in vexa-tion at the thought of the Duchess of Windsor, or that Einstein gnashes his teeth because he is not the Aga-Khan? If such feelings exist, it could in any case only be for bourgeois intellectuals who, in fact, recognize bourgeois values. Moreover, it is true that "the active members" of their class show disdain for those conceptive ideologues and barely allow them into their drawing rooms. As for the left-wing intellectual, he has no desire to be seated there in the first place; he absolutely does not admit that power and wealth put men *at the top*. It is only through a phenomenon of projec-tion that Aron or Monnerot can attribute to the left-wing intellectual a kind of valorization that is perfectly foreign to him.

they tried to force them to develop an ethical imperative *to deliver their recipes not directly to Russia and Russian soldiers, but to the servants, the messengers, and protagonists who have a concept of a 'more just' world.*"*

How is this work carried out? What are the methods used? Monnerot develops this point a bit further.

"Communist policies know that every man can be caught by playing on the need, passion, vice, or weakness that magnetize him. The *weak point* of each individual whose help it would be useful to secure represents the *strong point* of such groups."

We thus assume that a team of communist psycho-technicians roams America offering atomic scientists money, honors, women, drugs, whiskey, and little boys, according to each scientist's weak point. In what way does the exploitation of this weak point bring about the awakening of an "ethical imperative" in the hearts of scientists? The process remains mysterious. To elucidate this mystery, it behooves us to turn to in-depth psychology. In the chapter devoted to the "psychology of secular religions," Monnerot explains that individuals suffering from private neurosis discover that participation in a collective neurosis brings about a relief of their own pains. He describes at length the various frenzies which plague communist intellectuals as a group, but, once again, how does one catch this disease? Why didn't Monnerot catch it, for example? As a last resort, Monnerot recalls Aron's explanation—the left-wing intellectual is driven by resentment.

Communism "presents itself as a promotion for those who think they have nothing to lose and everything to gain from a radical change, namely, all those who, without being truly under-privileged, nevertheless feel they are on the fringes of society (this is the particular case of those who constitute the *Intelligentsia*)."

Thus, despite the socio-psychoanalytic jargon he uses, Monnerot does not provide any clear solution to the problem of why certain intellectuals are on the left. Koestler looked for answers in physiology.[44] According to him, it was necessary to bring in to play "the fatigue of synapses."† This fatigue originates from "a general weakening of the connections between cerebral cells through which the nerve impulse must pass. . . . This fatigue might be produced by the indefinite rape of the subject's consciousness." In a recent issue of *Preuves*, Koestler has taken the trouble to write a "Petit

---

* *Sociologie du communisme*, 130. Monnerot's emphasis.
† *Les hommes ont soif* [*The Age of Longing* (Paris: Calmann-Lévy, 1951)].

guide des névroses politiques" [Short Guide to Political Neuroses].* Nevertheless, these explanations on the whole seem insufficient for the people on the right themselves. They merely mention that the USSR and the communists have "psychological methods" that are all the more formidable as they are more secret. The newspaper *Dimanche-matin* [Sunday Morning], when explaining Geneviève de Galard's letter to Ho Chi-Minh as well as certain statements made by the wife of General de Castries, alluded to techniques of "brainwashing." As the holder of drugs, philters, evil spells, and glamour, the Communist Party is a sorcerer to whose obscure spells the masses and some individuals passively submit.

The Theory of the Elite

The most striking feature of all the anti-communist texts we have just examined is the idea of man that they unanimously offer us. Whether he is a proletarian or an intellectual, man is radically cut off from reality—his consciousness is passively subjected to ideas, images, and affective states that leave their mark by chance. At times these states are produced by the purely mechanical play of external factors. At other times, they are fabricated by the subject himself, beset by deliriums of imagination. In spite of these refinements borrowed from psychoanalysis and sociology, this philosophy simply perpetuates the old psycho-physiological idealism already refuted by Bergson: "Perception is a hallucination that is true."[45] One merely fits Taine's old saying into the current fashion.[46] The hallucinating person has no means of ascertaining whether by chance the proletarian's revolt or the intellectual's indignation is justified by the situation. He is hopelessly locked in his immanence. He reacts to his hallucinations with kinds of perfectly irrational psychological discharges that are explained either by the mystery of organic forces or by the quirks of subjectivity. Nevertheless insofar as these reactions have a certain finality, this finality is purely egoist. Separated from the world, the individual is *a fortiori* separated from his fellow men. He does not communicate with them and he does not have any positive feeling toward them. His sole motive is self-interest which is expressed either by empty ambition or, if this ambition remains unfulfilled, by resentment.

---

* Monnerot and Koestler are only plagiarizing the ideas that inspire the American techniques of *Human Engineering*, whose essential originality, says Michel Crozier (quoted article) is "to consider all the opponents as patients and to treat the subversive opinions and the spirit of revolt as a form of neurosis."

Nor is this ethics new—it repeats the platitudes of the old Christian pessimism and those of naturalistic skepticism. Monnerot, for example, explaining how left-wing intellectuals are "taken in," resembles those mothers and spouses, fortified by spiteful wisdom, who accuse their sons or husbands of having "let themselves be hoodwinked" by a harlot. This world is a world of scoundrels and dupes who are plagued by agitations devoid of ends and meanings—man is an evil and stupid animal. This is what right-wing thinkers postulate.

There is nothing gratuitous in this disillusioned cynicism. We have seen it before—nothing bothers the privileged more than the existence of other filthy, half-starved and barbaric men. However, if man deserves only contempt, then scruples are no longer necessary—one is authorized to consider him a total zero. This is the reason why all the literature discrediting him without any chance of appeal plays the game of the right-wing. Vautel, Céline and Léautaud find in the right-wing the heartiest of welcomes.[47]

There is, nevertheless, a major problem: aren't those who denounce man's destitution men themselves? If every consciousness is hallucinated, if every action is motivated by self-interest, how can they convince us that they are bearers of truth and that their ends are objectively valid? If one were to stretch cynicism to its very limit, one would be forced to concur with Sade's conclusion: "There are two sides to every passion, Juliette. The passion is very unjust for the victim, whereas for the one who exercises this passion, it appears singularly just."[48] However, if this is the case, we renounce any pretension to universal justice—everyone fights for himself. Such realism would lead to the recognition of the class struggle and this is precisely what they want to avoid. The bourgeoisie greatly values having Right on its side. For this, its thinkers have to elevate it above coarse humanity.

* * *

Religion has long taken the place of ideology for the privileged. Man, blind, guilty, and corrupted by original sin, appears as an anti-value in the light of Christianity. There is only one salvation for him—to submit himself to God's will that manifests itself through the world as it is. The privileged man, in all humility, accepts the place assigned to him—he is chosen by God which is sufficient for the foundation of his rights. As for the underprivileged, only resignation will allow them to deserve the celestial compensations that re-establish justice through eternity. Around the year 1,000 a monk of Saint-Laud wrote, "All power comes from God. God himself wanted some men to be lords and others to be serfs, so that the lords would have to worship and love God and serfs would have to worship and love their lords." The capitalist bourgeoisie, in its turn, immediately drafted God into its service. In 1761, while giving a speech to those he called "stewards of Providence," the Reverend Father Hyacinthe de Gasquet declared, "Jesus-Christ himself is your guarantor. You still place capital within his divine hands and on his adored head."[49] Eighteenth century philosophers fought for freedom of thought. However, as soon as the bourgeoisie came to power, it understood how necessary it was to keep "religious hopes" alive among the people and, by the same token, secure for itself a good conscience. Even nowadays there is a Christian thought that justifies the exploitation of one man by another in the name of God. Claudel, in his *Mémoires improvisés* [Improvised Memoirs] writes, "Man is the raw material of which one must ask all the necessary questions in order to draw out everything that can be given. Consequently, it is nonsense to find fault in the exploitation of one man by another. On the contrary, man is a thing that begs to be exploited."[50] Yet Christianity has become an ambiguous doctrine. Considering that every man is God's creature, certain Christians underscore the dignity of each man and the fundamental equality of all, denying that God is in the pay of the powerful of this world. At any rate, resorting to religion cannot be sufficient for the bourgeois because of the very fact that he creates God in his own image—not as a grand lord with an arbitrary will, but as an enlightened mind whose decisions are rationally motivated. The bourgeois is not averse to invoking him as a guarantor of the established order, but he still needs to first demonstrate that this order merits divine support. Finally, the fact is that God's rating has gone down quite a bit. His existence is too uncertain, too remote, and his designs are too hidden for man to succeed in making him intervene in a convincing manner as a guarantor of earthly hierarchies. Something else has to be found.

It must be found. One would sink into a nihilistic indifference if, after having debased man, one then failed to save the bourgeois. Having denied the importance of material differences that concretely set the classes against each other, the bourgeois then reestablishes between them a different type of heterogeneity—the privileged class participates in a transcendent reality that purifies its existence. Reactionary cynicism is necessarily coupled with a mystique. Drieu was well aware of this when he deplored his inability to believe in God. "There is only one excuse to run away from man, and that is God."* That was too candidly sincere. Later on, still an unbeliever, he

---

* *La suite dans les idées* [Coherence of Ideas].

managed to subordinate the "human aspect" to something else he called the *divine*. In his *Notes pour comprendre ce siècle*, wanting to demonstrate the necessity of accepting fascism, he wrote, "Man, in losing his sense of glory, loses his sense of immortality, and in losing the sense of immortality, he loses his sense of divinity.

"However, if divinity dies, nature tarnishes, and the physical human, withering imperceptibly, becomes boring."

As an atheist, Drieu evidently does not think of divinity as a positive and concrete reality. For him and many others,* it is the transcendent projection of a quality immanent in certain men that elevates them above humanity. According to the circumstances this singular virtue will take on various forms—we see that the Nazi defeat brought about curious metamorphoses in this area. However, at any rate, its definition is negative—it is said to be superhuman because it is inhuman. It is *other* than man and it is not found among men. The bourgeois thinker transforms this absence into a mysterious substance that would exclusively belong to the bourgeois. Through its mediation, the interests of the bourgeoisie are changed into values. The existence of privilege becomes sacred, its possession a right, and its exercise a duty. The privileged are called the Elite, their privileges are called superiorities, and together they are called Civilization. The masses, on the other hand, are nothingness. Thus one can assert that inequality achieves justice.

The most radically aristocratic attitude consists in splitting humanity in two and then considering this schism a given. Nietzsche borrowed the hierarchy opposing masters to slaves from Machiavelli and Gobineau, and as they did, he founded this opposition on the fact of race.[51] Only the existence of the rich and powerful—nobles and heroes—has significance; all other men constitute the masses: "The sand grains of humanity: all are very equal, very small, and very round."[52] Nietzsche declares, "In my opinion, the masses are worthy of attention only from three points of view . . . as a diffuse copy of great men . . . as a resistance encountered by the rich and powerful . . . as an instrument of the rich and powerful. As for the rest, the devil and statistics damn them."[53]

Prior to the last war, Nietzsche's tradition was still very much alive. Spengler, in particular, again took up the idea that nobility is explained by "the elemental facts of blood" and that only nobility possesses a historical existence, a real existence. "The chance [*le hasard*] called man" is nothing but a

---

* Scheler, among others, constantly spoke of the *divine* without God being positively defined: Jasper's transcendence was also nothing but the reverse side of an absence.

moment in the history of the planet, and it depends on the "unfathomable mystery of cosmic fluctuations." Life and History are one. "In the supreme sense, politics is life and life is politics." However, it would be simpleminded to believe that life, which is the very substance of human reality, inhabits every living individual. Life is embodied in races. In its immediate form, race is realized in the peasantry that is, so to speak, nature. In higher cultures, it rises to the highest power and is accomplished in nobility. "Nobility is properly speaking *the order*, the quintessence of race and blood, and an existential current without any possible completed form." There is a profound affinity between the nobility and the people, founded on realities of race, language, and landscape, which is endowed with a soul and which itself also possesses a substantial reality. However, in the other orders this reality withers. The clergy is, actually, a non-order, and it is opposed to nobility as space is opposed to time; it is "the non-race, the free and alert being, atemporal and ahistorical." As for the bourgeoisie, it stems from the conflict between the city dwellers and the rural people. Its unity is "simply a unity of contradiction," and it has no substance at all. The economy and science develop with the bourgeoisie, which forms parties and brings about the advent of the masses through which History is destroyed. "The masses are the formless absolute that spitefully hounds every type of form, all differences in rank, constituted property, and constituted knowledge." The masses are the "expression of History that leads to non-History: the masses are the end, the radical nothingness." Opposing the Elite man, the Hero, to the man of the masses, the individual considered in his material existence as subjugated by need, Spengler writes, "To feed oneself and to fight: the difference in degree between these two sides of life is given to us in their relationship with death.* . . . There is no greater opposition than the one between *death by starvation and the death of the hero*. From the economic point of view, life is threatened, degraded, and belittled by hunger. . . . Politics sacrifices men for a purpose [*fin*] . . . the economy only destroys them. War creates and hunger annihilates all great things. . . . Hunger arouses this type of loathsome, vulgar, and entirely a-metaphysical anguish under which the formal mold of a culture suddenly breaks and the human beast's pure fight for existence begins."[54]

The bourgeoisie speaks in unison with Spengler each time it accuses those men of "sordid materialism" who allow themselves to go hungry. However,

---

* We will come back to this essential fact: the man of the right subordinates life to death. He conceives life through death.

it is slightly embarrassed by this exalted warrior ethics. Nietzsche had specifically included all the bourgeois among the grains of sand composing the masses. In the intentional confusion of Nazi ideology, many of these bourgeois had linked their cause to that of the "race of the lords." The lords lost the war. Even though the bourgeoisie remains respectful of blood hierarchies, it no longer has any reason to subordinate all others to them—spiritualism takes precedence over racism. From this viewpoint the bourgeoisie is closer to Scheler than to Spengler. For Scheler, after all, value is defined by, "[a] certain vital nobility that brings us closer to the divine." Scheler maintains an essential point—value is not something that can be acquired. Since it is vital it remains linked to race: it is innate, but the raw racial fact is no longer sufficient to found it—it appears as a mediation toward a transcendence. Certain spiritual graces are dispensed to men according to an organic predestination. Among the exemplary figures whose radiance helps men to rise toward God, the Hero occupies an elevated position; however the position of the Genius is even higher, and the Saint towers at the apex of the hierarchy. Except for these nuances, Scheler's ethics is as pitiless as Nietzsche's and Spengler's ethics for the "human beast."

We have already seen that Scheler is unable to ascribe solely to resentment "the love of everything that has a human face." After all, such a love "first attaches itself onto *the lowest and most animal* aspects of human nature, that is to say, exactly onto what all men have in common."* He adds, "Piercing under this humanity, one can feel a true hatred of positive values that are clearly not part of the generic." The generic whole of men is the "moral proletariat" that, out of hatred and resentment against the holders of values, claims to be a creator of values. Ridiculous pretense! "The masses are governed absolutely by the same laws that govern herds of animals. In the masses in their pure state, man would simply become an animal again."†

The transition from racism to spiritualism is achieved in Jaspers. A German, with a lively interest in Nazism, Jaspers holds forth today in a defeated Germany; he transposes the arrogant ideas of Spengler and Scheler into the language of the defeated. He declares that Man, reduced to himself, seems to him, as to them, to be devoid of any signification. "It is not man as a specimen of empirical existence that is worthy of love, but the possibility of nobility in each individual." However, the idea of nobility has been profoundly modified. Today's nobility is no longer the prerogative of a class, a race, or a

---

* *L'homme du ressentiment* [The Man of Resentment]. Scheler's emphasis.
† *Le saint, le génie, le héros* [The Saint, the Genius, and the Hero].

caste. It is a quality of the soul, a certain "opening to the Transcendent," for above the empirical world, there is the Transcendent—only it really exists, only it has value. Men have dignity only to the extent that they participate in its Being. Everyone *can* participate in it: in this sense Jaspers's ethics claims to have a democratic appearance; in fact, it calls for a pluralistic and hierarchical society. Indeed, the Transcendent offers itself only to individualized forms—to "people" who "have a soul" and not to the shapeless masses. It offers itself to individuals rooted in such substantial forms as fatherland, family, race, and civilization, but not to the man from the masses. Therefore, nobility is reserved for a handful of beings. "The problem of human nobility nowadays consists in *safeguarding the activity of the best, who are reduced to a minority.*" The immense majority of men, enclosed in their empirical existence, with only contingent ties between them, are nothing more than a *mass* in which human substance is denied. "When man belongs to the mass, he is no longer himself. The mass is, to begin with, a dissolving element." "The mass does not know hierarchy; it is unconscious, uniform, and quantitative, without type or tradition, amorphous, and empty. It is the chosen field of propaganda, for it is suggestible, irresponsible, and has the lowest level of consciousness."

There is unanimity: the man who embodies only himself—not blood, life, or the transcendent—is a "radical nothingness." They have tried to show us that he has no existence in any domain. His own history escapes him and he is incapable of transcending it.

History

History escapes men in general and the masses in particular. In order to establish this thesis, the authoritative views of Burnham, Spengler, and Toynbee are quoted the most often. It would be beyond the scope of this article to examine their systems in detail here, but we will attempt to bring out their spirit.

Human nature is bad and immutable, asserts Burnham, faithful to Machiavellian principles, and this pessimism suffices to condemn History. If man stays the same, progress is impossible and no external change has any meaning. Burnham borrowed his theory of the "movement of the elites" from Pareto. History is not made by the masses, but by the staff officers. It only changes and renews itself when there are conflicts between elites coveting power: some are liquidated while others triumph. To this diversity corresponds the pluralism of civilizations, between which exist certain ties of causality, but their succession is nevertheless discontinuous; the replacement of one team by another is a change devoid of any finality. On one hand, individuals leading the world have no objective aim—they want power for the sake of power. On the other hand, no social evolution could succeed in improving man's lot. Claiming to ever free him from need is, among other things, a mystification, for he is by definition "an animal that desires."* Such a doctrine is not exactly catastrophic; it talks neither of decadence nor of the Apocalypse. Burnham foresees a rational evolution of capitalism: the regime favoring property owners must be succeeded by "the era of the organizers" that will subordinate capital to technocracy. However, this evolution denies any meaning to History; the latter appears as an imbecilic marching in place. The elites are fighting absurdly over a power they never use: men never gain anything.

When anti-communists want to dispel the charm of politics and ruin the idea of revolution, they readily plunder Burnham. Aron and Monnerot, among others, copy him and plagiarize him for pages on end. In order to fight "revolutionary romanticism," Aron is forever repeating that revolution boils down to a change in the ruling staff. The disillusioned skepticism inspiring his articles has its direct source in Burnham's Machiavellian vision. As for Monnerot, he writes that "[w]orld revolution signifies world trouble in the movement of the elites."† "Revolutions betray the fact that elites leave something to be desired." And so forth.

Yet, we have seen that the pessimism of the right wing must necessarily be accompanied by a mystique. Now, although Burnham supplies polemical weapons against the "illusions" of socialism, his work's positive opposing view is clearly deficient. Having shown that History is absurd, in what name will he save this Elite that specifically makes History? If they blindly aim at an empty power, how will the Elect interest us in their cause? To be quite honest, Burnham is so frenetically alienated in anti-communism that he does not feel the need to justify it. He is American: he wants America to dominate the world; that is all there is to it. Yet, it happens that, with feigned naïveté, he asks the question, "Is a communist world empire desirable?"‡ His answer is remarkably awkward. "A world communist economy would

---

* We see here how much the subjectivist formalism of the right serves its egoism. To assimilate need and desire, it is necessary to empty them of all concrete content: The exigencies of the famished and the reverie of the sybarite are reduced to the same uncertain state of mind. This self-interested merging of a pseudo-realist cynicism with idealist abstraction is characteristic of the right.

† Naturally without quoting Burnham or Pareto in *La guerre en question*.

‡ For the domination of the world.

not increase the material well-being of the majority of humanity" he asserts. However, two pages further, he concedes that "more than half of the earth's inhabitants are already at the lowest possible level; their material condition could not get much worse, and could even improve."[55] More than half, isn't that the majority? Unless an Elect is worth two or ten ordinary inhabitants of the earth? Burnham hastily abandons the uncertain field of mathematics. There are economic values other than material well-being such as security, freedom. And besides economic values, our civilization has "ideals" whose abolition, incidentally, "might be considered preferable" (sic)—but these are ideals that are nevertheless "at least partially operative." They are: the absolute value of the human person, the ideal of liberty and individual dignity, and also the ideal of an objective truth. Finally, Burnham concludes, "Even though in our history and all other histories, force has usually determined in practice what the laws decree as being just, we have always rebelled against the idea that force could really be just." Upholding the idea of a practically nonexistent justice is not a very exalting "ideal," and it seems not very logical to condemn "more than half of the earth's inhabitants" to remain "at the lowest possible level" in the name of "the absolute value of the human person." As for the "objective truth," one wonders in what way it could be of interest to a firm believer in Machiavelli. To be quite honest, Burnham's disciples are as embarrassed as he is when they are asked why they are fighting. Aron only feels at ease when he combats his adversaries' puerile illusions; however, as soon as he has to find ethical reasons to support America and capitalism, he lacks conviction. He does not try to either define or found "the old Christian and humanist values" that one can offer against communism. "For me, truth remains the supreme value" he once said. Why? And what truth are we talking about? In fact, Machiavellian pessimism is as harsh for the Elite as it is for the masses; from such a vantage point the absurd play of human passions can only be contemplated with a hopeless cynicism. One will have to look elsewhere to invent a mystique.

Spengler's and Toynbee's systems offer more possibilities. Their vision of the world is more tragic than the vision of the Machiavellians. In subordinating History to the Cosmos, in dooming to death the multiplicity of civilizations whose birth is controlled by inhuman chance, they sever humanity from any future and proclaim humanity's insignificance. But precisely because something else exists for them besides man, they can propose for certain men a supra-human salvation. Within every historical cycle, they exalt forms that transcend History, forms whose existence is fortuitously linked to the interests of the privileged.

"In History, the matter at issue is life, always and uniquely life, race, the victory of the will-to-power, and not that of truths, inventions, or money," writes Spengler in the conclusion to his book.[56] Not only does the role of technology and economy appear as secondary to him, but man as producer, as the "product of his product," is expelled from History. The object of History and its reality has nothing to do with "the existence of the human beast."

"I see in living History the image of a perpetual formation and transformation, of a future, and of a miraculous death of organic forms," he writes.

These forms are cultures; and they all show among themselves analogies founded on "the impenetrable mystery of cosmic fluctuations." However, they develop separately, in a discontinuous fashion; one after the other. They grow until the moment when, having realized their destiny, that is to say, a civilization, they decline one after the other. "A culture is born the instant a great soul awakens; a culture dies when the soul has realized the entire sum of its possibilities in the shape of peoples, languages, religious doctrines, arts, States, and sciences, and it returns to the primary psychic state." Spengler, in his conclusion, summarizes the drama of all these births and deaths in this way: "The drama of an exalted culture, all this marvelous world of divinities, arts, thoughts, battles, and cities still ends in the elemental facts of eternal blood, which is one and the same as the cosmic flow in eternal circulation. The clear awakened being, endowed with a rich plasticity, again falls silently into the service of being, as the Chinese empires have taught us. Time triumphs over space and with its inexorable march, confines to this planet the fleeting chance called culture in the chance called man, a form in which the chance called life goes on for a moment, while to our eyes the fluid horizons of terrestrial history and planetary history open up in the luminous world in front of us."

In this cosmic evocation, through the unintelligible play of chance, what clearly stands out is the importance given to the "elemental facts of blood." Life, as we have seen, is embodied in nobility which is "History made flesh." The defeat of the nobility, the advent of the masses, lead to the end of History; humanity sinks into silence, unconsciousness, and nothingness.

There are several differences between Spengler and Toynbee. Spengler counts eight civilizations, each lasting one thousand years and each with a fatal end. For Toynbee there are twenty-nine of them; their duration varies and their evolution leaves a place for human free will and for divine will. Toynbee allows for certain influences between civilizations and he vaguely evokes an idea of progress, but the progress in question is a spiritual one appreciable only by God, and not a human conquest. Both systems agree on the essentials. Toynbee also sees the succession of civilizations as discontinuous and economic factors have only a secondary importance. History depends on a cosmic factor: the alternating rhythm of stasis-dynamism (in pre-Chinese language the yin and the yang). The yang is released as a reaction to a challenge thrown down by milieu, race, and so forth. However, after a period of ascent the civilization shatters; it is then that an "internal proletariat" and an "external proletariat" break away. Civilization reacts to this period of unrest by creating a universal State; however, caught between both proletariats, the State dies. If a civilization were ever to survive, it would lead us up to the stage of the superhuman. However, unless God grants us a reprieve, the future of the West seems to be truly jeopardized: we have already entered the period of unrest. And Toynbee concludes, "The Spirit of the Earth, while weaving and arranging its threads on the chain of time, composes man's history as it is manifested in the genesis, growth, decline, and disintegration of human societies. In all this confusion of life and turmoil of actions, we can hear the beat of an elementary rhythm. This rhythm is the alternating movement of yin and yang. The movement provoked by this rhythm is neither the fluctuation of an indecisive beat nor the cycle of a disciplinary mill. The perpetual rotation of a wheel is not a pointless repetition if, with each revolution, it brings the vehicle closer to its destination. The music originated by the rhythm of yin and yang is the chant of creation."*[57]

The symbol of the wheel proposed by Toynbee is in great favor today. It has been taken up by, among others, Abellio whose prophecies have been taken seriously by some right-wing intellectuals.[58] According to him, History presents itself in the form of cycles: Involution-Evolution separated by Floods; the whole lies within a unique cycle that ends with an Apocalypse. The totality of cycles constitutes a spiral. There is, as for Toynbee, a vague future for humanity; however, we have no practical hold over this cosmic process. Today's man is trapped in his singular Flood. Action, which would necessarily be either a pointless gesture or treason, is forbidden to him. The sole recourse is to build an "ark" to cross from one world to the other. This ark should gather, in a kind of spiritual order, "spirits that are more in love with light than with power." "This society of spirits considers with equal indifference the political regimes with which it integrates while having a clear awareness of their relativity."

---

* In the last volumes he has just published, Toynbee makes every effort towards optimism; he believes that a coexistence between the USSR and the USA is possible. However, due to the fact that he puts all his hopes into a "super-religion" which would reconcile Buddhism with Christianity, one can consider his philosophy of History as catastrophic as Spengler's which he claims to oppose.

It is striking that today any type of pluralist-cyclic-catastrophic rant is certain of reaching some part of the public. An attempt was made to make a success of the woolly daydreams of a Guénon who deciphers the coming end of the West through obscure symbolic systems.[59] Hindu philosophy is being rediscovered, insofar as it is cosmological, anti-historical and preaches non-action: the Wheel of Shiva casts its great shadow over the life and death of civilizations. Having defined human nature as immutable, the conservative furthermore likes to think that History runs in circles: nothing ever changes. The Nietzschean idea of eternal return is not exactly accepted; however, it is acknowledged that such profound analogies exist between cultures that any attempt at reforming the world is condemned in advance. Even though, from an ethical point of view, the structure of society is deplored for what it is, any yearnings for a better world remain in the realm of utopia: the lucid realist bows before morphologic necessity which dooms future societies to repeat this society's injustices and abuses. Whether History follows a circle or a spiral, any evolution initiates a decadence and any future is frozen in the bosom of the Cosmos. Humanity fruitlessly marches in place, lost in a submerging immensity. The relationship of man to society appears secondary—what is essential is his relationship to the Universe, over which he has no power.

Yet, amidst these fateful cycles, there are more or less somber moments; the West long ago started its own decline. However, Spengler still believed that Caesarism could delay its death and he preached the fascist commitment in thinly veiled terms. All its hopes dashed, the right-wing presently thinks that catastrophe is imminent and action impotent. Through Jaspers, vanquished Germany tries to come to terms with [assumer] this pessimism. Jaspers attributes to it an even more definitive figure, but less dramatic than that of Spengler. Instead of Burnham's, Spengler's, and Toynbee's cynical, aggressive, or resigned despair, he proposes a transcendental wisdom to man. Yes, History is Failure, but it is good that it is so.

According to Jaspers, historical reality is constituted by a plurality of substantial forms: races, civilizations, and peoples. It is this pluralism that dooms History to failure; despite a certain possibility of communication between these forms, their diversity necessarily leads to conflicts and destructions. But on the other hand, to claim to unify humanity would be to sin against the Transcendent. To abolish the frontiers that divide classes and nations is "an enterprise of leveling that one cannot imagine without fear." Indeed we have seen that man opens up to the Transcendent and accomplishes himself as Existence only through his affiliation with a community that possesses the immanent unity of a soul and is thus limited and differentiated. The masses are closed to the Transcendent and would only be capable of pursuing earthly ends, such as the happiness of humanity. "Finitude, as immanent happiness, is demeaning when it becomes the final aim—man relinquishes his transcendence." Humanity would find happiness solely at the expense of the dignity of Existence. In the name of the superior interests of Being, it is thus necessary that the failure of History and the misfortune of men be perpetuated. On the empirical plane, this failure is obviously unsettling and History does not have a clear meaning: "Humanity with its ancient cultures is carried away by a current toward who knows what destruction or what renovation." However, from a superior point of view, we must congratulate ourselves, for this earthly failure is the ultimate "cipher of transcendence." "History is the progressive revelation of Being" inasmuch as it leads precisely nowhere. "What is historic is what fails, but it is the presence of the eternal in time." To meet the demands of the Transcendent, I must assume my historicity, that is to say, lay claim to my roots and consider History as the horizon of my present and as the manner in which the eternal gives itself to me. But I must not count on action for it is only the appearance of the certitude of being, constantly threatened by ruin.

Thus, the perversity of human nature, cosmic fatality, and the demands of the Transcendent all concur in condemning action. All that is left to be done is to ponder fate with clarity, to pray to God with Toynbee, to take refuge with Abellio in an "ark," or, according to Jaspers's example, to open up to the Transcendent. However, for those who have an interest in maintaining the status quo, when all is said and done, despair is an excellent alibi—catastrophic quietism is at the service of the established order. These somber perspectives offer at least a morose consolation to a class aware of its condemnation—its liquidation will be a spiritual disaster.

The Mission of the Elite

Yet, although an ethics of ataraxia works to the advantage of individual bourgeois egoism, his class egoism remains pugnacious: in condemning History, he, nevertheless, wants to valorize the moment of History that grants him his privileges. Having reduced man to nothingness, the Elite saves itself by deifying itself and, here, its approach is comparable. According to the Elite, Forms, Ideas, and Values exist that transcend History and demand to be defended.

Stephen Spender writes that the struggle taking place all over the world today pits "those who want to maintain eternal values against those who deem good whatever means are necessary so that their political principles may triumph—even if these principles are respectable in themselves."[60] Mircea Eliade declares, "The sole justification of organized collectivities—society, nation, and state—is, in the last analysis, the creation and conservation of spiritual values. Universal history itself only takes into account peoples that are creators of cultures."[61] We have seen that in order to exalt values and eternal truths, the most Machiavellian and the most skeptical of our thinkers, such as Burnham and Aron, discovered, when they felt like it, that they had a Platonic soul.

In all the systems we have examined, there is a common thesis that greatly aids the bourgeois in claiming the defense of bourgeois interests as his duty: pluralism. Pluralism is the foundation of historical pessimism; however, pluralism also allows the buttressing of this pessimism with a combative ideology. All right-wing thinkers have decided to consider pessimism as a truth definitely acquired. "However, for us," Monnerot, among others, writes,* "there are *certain types* of slavery, *certain types* of feudalism, *certain types* of capitalism, each with its own history, that have profoundly changed during the course of this history and each one, in the course of its own history, reaches a point when it differs from itself as much or almost as much as it differs from the others." To Marx's "simplistic" schema opposing exploiters and exploited, one substitutes a design so complex that the oppressors differ among themselves as much as they differ from the oppressed, with the result that this last distinction loses its importance. However, most of all, pluralism authorizes the civilized man to dig these "trenches" dreamed of with such nostalgia by Mr. Jules Romains who well understood how difficult it is to defend capitalistic Europe in the name of the universal. One needs to have the enormous naïveté of a Rougemont to write that we Europeans must "see ourselves as responsible for a very distinctive culture. This culture is the heart† of a civilization that *itself* ‡ has truly become universal for better or for worse." Much more logically Spengler declares, "There are no eternal truths. The sole criterion for a doctrine is its necessity for life." Indeed, a pluralistic thought could not, without contradiction, annex eternity. However, pluralism provides us with the means to get round the difficulty it causes: to the ideal of universality it substitutes

---

* *Sociologie du communisme*, 258.

† *Sic, Preuves*, January 1954. [The original reads "le cour" with a note saying it was a typo in *Preuves*: the typo must have been a missing "e," which would make it "le coeur" in French, "the heart."]

‡ Rougemont's emphasis.

the recognition of a multiplicity of truths, and we have to confine ourselves to the truth imposed on us by a vital necessity. Western bourgeois civilization is the only one to which we are substantially connected. Not only will tomorrow's civilization realize no progress over it, but we find ourselves separated from this distant future by a radical abyss. For want of having any hold over it, this future is for us nothing but an empty concept; our sole business is this Form to which we belong. The decline threatening it does not include the promise of a new Form. It simply announces the triumph of the formless. Beyond, there is nothing but silence and night. Therefore, let us worry about Europe and the West—nothing else is of any concern to us. Here, Jaspers again confirms Spengler's thesis. According to him there is a plurality of truths that communicate through their connection to Being, but which must be lived in their separation. "My truth, what I am as freedom, insofar as I exist, collides with another, also existent, truth. It is through it and with it that I become myself. It is not unique and alone, but it is unique and irreplaceable insofar as it exists in relation to the other." To be oneself, this is the supreme moral law; it is to open oneself to the Transcendent. I only reach this authenticity by assuming my finitude instead of claiming to surpass it. Therefore, my duty as a Western bourgeois is to want Western bourgeois civilization unconditionally.

The salvation of civilization will, of course, operate against the masses, for the masses intervene in the course of the world solely as elements of dissolution. They break up orders, they provoke schisms, they deny the Transcendent and drain human reality of its substance; through them everything is lost and nothing is created. It falls to the Elite to save "the marvelous world" of cultures. Today, *Western man* feels that he has been assigned a mission; however, it will be demonstrated that the unprivileged does not deserve the name of *man*. Denied its claims as a historic agent, the masses are moreover excluded from the world of thought and the world of ethical and aesthetic values: we will see by what ruses this is accomplished.

Thought

"Common sense is the most widely shared thing in the world."[62] The right-wing could never subscribe to so grossly democratic an assertion. What the collection of "human beasts" share among themselves is only their animality. Far from constituting a common basis through which all men can recognize each other, thought, in the eyes of the bourgeois, is a faculty of distinction that distinguishes.

It has been seen that bourgeois theoreticians profess a psycho-physiological subjectivism: ideas reflect not the object thought, but the mentality of the thinking subject. This mentality is a rather mysterious complex depending in part on external factors, but which, first of all, translates a certain essence: there is a black soul, a Jewish character, a yellow wisdom, a feminine sensitivity, a peasant common sense, etc. The nature of his essence defines the area of being that is accessible to each one. For this subjectivist philosophy is anti-intellectualist, too: this is a philosophy not of consciousness but of being. The "co-naissance,"[63] according to Claudel's coined word, is communion; it falls under neither comprehension nor reason. The man of the right scorns as "simplistic" the systemized knowledge that is communicated methodically and can be drawn from books. He only values the *lived experience* that singularly unites a subject and an object participating in the same substance.* Therefore, among conscious individuals a hierarchy exists; those endowed with the highest "vital nobility" and a greater "substantial wealth" realize the most perfect communion with being. The masses, deprived of substance, are condemned to an animal slumber interrupted by hallucinations and delirious states. Individuals rooted in a substantial form, that is to say those accepting the bourgeois order, all have something legitimate to reveal: in their place and within their limits they grasp truths that escape the rationalist theoretician. The woman who bleeds and gives birth will have a deeper "instinct" of the things of life than the biologist. The peasant has a more accurate intuition of the earth than a licensed agronomist. The colonist listens with irony to the ethnographer's theories: it is by beating a Negro that one truly learns to understand him. Spengler explains that this concrete form, race, cannot be grasped by the scientist who analyzes and weighs, but rather it is revealed to the man of breeding:

"Pure human races," he writes, "differ among themselves absolutely in the same spiritual way as those that are impure. An identical element that reveals itself only to the most delicate palate, a sweet aroma present in each form, unites beneath all the high cultures in Caucasia, the Etruscans with the Renaissance; on the Tigris the Sumerians of the year 3000 with the Persians of the year 500 and other Persians of the Islamic era. . . . All this is *inaccessible to the scientist who measures and weighs.* This element exists for

---

* This is the source of the taste for "gossip" by right-wing people. Rather than methodically established facts, or scientifically demonstrated laws, they prefer the anecdote whispered from ear to ear. The privileged experience of one of their kind is inscribed in it, and it is transmitted in a privileged manner. They want no other warranty of its truth but the quality of the elect who are spreading it. We see examples of this methodology almost daily in *Le figaro.*

the *feeling* that perceives it with an unerring certainty at first glance, but not for scientific analysis. I, therefore, come to the conclusion that race, just like time and fate, is something decisive for all vital questions, something that everyone has a *clear* and *distinct* knowledge of as soon as one stops trying to grasp it through analysis and classification that dissociate. . . . This is why the only means of delving into the totemic side of life is not at all through classification, but through the *physiognomic touch.*"[64]

One will recognize in Spengler's phraseology one of the right wing's most cherished clichés. Maurras taught that a Jewish man would never be able to *feel* a verse written by Racine.* Drieu la Rochelle in his novel *Gilles* denounced the "modern" side of the Jewish people whose rational thinking loses what is instinctive and complex in the world. A person without roots, a person lower in status would never be able understand the class or the race upon which he forces himself. In *Les déracinés* [The Uprooted (1897)] by Barrès, Racadot, despite all his intelligence, is doomed to err because he has no roots, while the moronic Saint-Phlin, well-settled on the property of his ancestors, effortlessly moves about in the truth.[65] Bourgeois parents readily convince themselves that their son, even if he is the dunce of the class, has a "je ne sais quoi" that the most brilliant scholarship holder lacks.

"The active and conceptive ideologists" who have elaborated this system put themselves in a most favorable position. The system allows them to restore to their benefit the method of authority. Only he, the superior individual, whether by blood, nobility, or his openness to the Transcendent, is capable of feeling in its quasi-totality the ensemble of forms that constitute reality. Thanks to this postulate, the right-wing thinker easily overcomes the seeming contradictions of his position. When he attacks Marxists, the anti-communist sees in their ideas nothing more than a superficial rationalization of unconscious instincts and dark forces. When it comes to his own ideas, he declares them objectively founded. He is a pluralist when he reflects on foreign truths, but he considers his own truth as an absolute. But this lack of reciprocity is, according to him, perfectly justified: the singularity of certain men—the elect, to whom he belongs—is specifically to reach the universal. By confining his adversaries in an empty immanence, and his inferiors in their limited particularity, he towers above them as a master whose revelations must be accepted by an act of faith. This position is both infinitely weak and unassailable. The true Abraham is never sure of being

---

* The moment "Mediterranean thinking" claims its singularity, it becomes Spenglerian and therefore German; it contradicts the essence to which it aspires at that very same moment: a lucid and universally valid rationalism.

Abraham, however no one can demonstrate to the Napoleons confined in asylums that they are not Napoleon. This ambiguity explains the sharp tone readily taken up by right-wing writers. They do not submit their ideas to the judgment of others: the truths enunciated by them have, as their sole and sufficient guarantee, the writers' personal merit. To offer proof would be to demean oneself: the Master is beyond any possible questioning and he demands an unconditional adherence.* What truth would one offer against him since the supreme truth is precisely the one that is revealed to him?

This theory of knowledge necessarily implies that reality itself is irrational. Here we find again one of the paradoxes of bourgeois thinking: the "active members" of the bourgeoisie believe in science; they practice and apply it, yet, its ideologists devote themselves to discrediting it. We know, for example, what whimsical interpretation they gave of the indeterminacy principle by claiming that matter itself is disorder and contingency. As a matter of fact, the belief in natural necessities is, conversely, the first condition for a human liberation. In a chaotic universe that is impossible to master by thought, man is crushed, passive, and enslaved. His misery is striking; he is decidedly nothing but a contemptible beast. He feels lost and he is ready to docilely listen to the voice of the Elect offering to guide him. This is why the right-wing thinker asserts that nature is caprice and mystery. The science that analyzes and classifies it grasps only superficial appearances. Nature is driven by a secret life filled with invisible fluids. Its profound reality is not the empirical world as it is revealed to us, but a hidden Being, a cosmic substance or a transcendent spirit. According to Spengler, external reality is only "an expression and a symbol. The morphology of universal history necessarily becomes a universal symbology."[66]

Jaspers who, as we have seen, spiritualizes Spengler's theses according to the needs of post-fascist Germany, borrows his idea of physiognomic touch and puts it to use in order to decipher the transcendence in the physiognomy of things. Instead of dissociating the real, as science does, he says we must understand it through "ciphers" that give us totalities. Nature is an indefinitely equivocal cipher, and History is too, insofar as it is failure. Consciousness in general is cipher and the ultimate cipher is existence itself.

---

* Gurdjieff, who played the magus, pushed and parodied this attitude to the extreme when, by peppering his terrorized disciples with enigmatic sentences, he would then furiously refuse to explain them. Still, thousand of examples of such a disdainful tone are to be found among more serious people, from Montherlant to Aron. What is called "impertinence" of the young writers of the right is one form of this useful arrogance.

This esotericism confirms the Master's importance. The revelation of secrets is reserved for those few initiates endowed with a certain innate grace. It is not surprising that from here some thinkers turn toward occultism, alchemy, and astrology. Hitler believed in horoscopes. If, thanks to the "physiognomic touch," one can learn everything about a man by studying the shape of his cranium, why cannot one do the same by studying the lines of his hand or the configuration of the sky? The cosmic stream penetrates and links everything—one is able to know anything through anything. If man is tuned not to other men, but to the spirit of the Earth, then his fate hinges on the stars or on tea leaves rather than on public squares. Mysticism leads to magic. This explains the success among the right-wing of symbology more or less inspired by the Orient, the warm welcome given to books written by Guénon, Daumal, Schmidt, Abellio, and the credibility given to a Gurdjieff.[67]

Mysticism also leads to silence. Right-wing anti-intellectualism is manifested in its relation to language. To trust speech, common to everyone, is a basely democratic attitude. Truth, hidden behind symbols and ciphers comes under the ineffable. Nietzsche considered language as treason: "What sheer folly speech is!" Spengler writes, "In the end, language and truth exclude each other. . . . The more profound is a communication, the better it succeeds, for this reason, in renouncing the sign. . . . The purest symbol of understanding that language has ever given is that of an old peasant couple, sitting in the evening in front of the farm and communicating in silence."*[68] Brice Parain concludes his essay on language by asserting, "The closer we are to silence, the closer we are to freedom." Ciphers, according to Jaspers, lead to the ineffable. The triple language of transcendence finally resounds in the silence; failure is this silence. The ultimate cipher is silence. This mute peace is the supreme revelation. "The non-being revealed by the failure of everything accessible to us is the Being of the transcendence." Indeed, the word, adapted to the life of society and empirical existence cannot express man's truth that is his relationship to the Cosmos, to the Transcendent. Articulate conversation only suits the masses. Authentic men communicate through the substance in which they are rooted all together. An identical mysterious fluid flows through them and an identical Form dazzles them. Right-wing literature excels in describing such wordless harmonies and in singing the praises of such mute insights. The truth of the humble ones—peasants, women, natives, servants, and poor craftsmen—could not be better expressed than by silence.

---

* [*The Decline of the West*] Volume 1, 122.

Still, right-wing intellectuals do a lot of talking. Freedom of expression is indeed one of those freedoms they most passionately demand and, by and large, they do not much believe in séances. The majority remain faithful to a certain rationalism. However, they always leave just enough room for the irrational in order for them to impose their authority. If truth were universally demonstrable, thought would be democratically open to everyone. So they substitute loose and debatable connections for the rigorous and necessary connections established by science. According to them, the task assigned to the thinker is to reach beyond the empirical given and feel the singular relationships between "forms" accessible only to the "physiognomic touch." Thus, Spengler intends to create a morphology; his entire system is based on formal links between forms, on Analogy. For all the right-wing doctrinarians, Analogy plays an immense role. For one, it is the sole type of explanation used by Monnerot in *Sociologie du communisme*. In the first chapter, he assimilates communism to Islam and the rest of the book simply develops the consequences of this rapprochement. Furthermore, he dwells on the oft-repeated analogies between communism and the Church, the Twentieth Century and the high Middle Ages. Does he wish to explain Lenin? He writes, "The problem of the pleb's powerlessness had already been given a solution *analogous** to Lenin's and that is *mutatis mutandis* militarization. . . . The *analogy*† holds. . . . Lenin, without knowing it, was the first theoretician and the first practitioner of *Caesarism* in our times." To account for the fact that certain civilizations stagnate while others progress, Toynbee limits himself to suggesting to us the following image: during their climbs, tired mountaineers often rest on a ledge; some fall asleep and others start climbing again: that is the key to History.

One sees what freedom is thus left to the whim of the theoretician. Facts impose no interpretation on him. From Spengler to Jaspers, including Toynbee and many others, each author strings the facts together according to his fancy. Regarding Aron's ideas on History, Pouillon, in a *Les temps modernes* article,‡[69] clearly demonstrated how the idea of objective contingency furthered subjective arbitrariness: "He thus does not soften historical determinism, but limits himself to disputing its unity and cuts it to pieces. This is what he calls contingency. For him this contingency does not imply a new notion of the causal relation, but is purely and simply a solution of continu-

---

* My [Beauvoir's] emphasis.
† Monnerot's emphasis.
‡ June 1954.

ity that he handles carefully in several selected passages, according to what he wishes to prove." This is another advantage of pluralism—introducing into the universe discontinuities that favor self-interested interventions by the thinking subject.

Moreover, the theory of forms satisfies this fundamental tendency of bourgeois thought that we have already pointed out—idealism. We are assured that forms exist in a substantial way, but their existence is subterranean and inaccessible. If we confront them with the empirical world, they appear as pure myth. In 1914, Boutroux, when defining war as "the struggle of Descartes against Kant," gave an admirable example of how Myth allows one to elegantly evade reality.[70] Nowadays, the Korean War is defined as the struggle of civilization against barbarism; and the Koreans are conjured away. In *L'Islam du XXe siècle* [Twentieth Century Islam],[71] who can find the flesh and blood proletarians who joined the Communist Party? Exploiters, colonists, and the privileged believe they are well hidden behind those great idols represented by English democracy, French works, and culture.

Transcendental idealism happily complements psycho-physiological idealism for the conservative: the latter isolates the things of consciousness and the former substitutes abstractions for them; deprived of both presence and existence, these abstractions become absolutely nothing. From this point on, everyone embroiders as he pleases in the intelligible heavens. One is entitled to inscribe thereon ideal relations that correspond to no terrestrial incarnation: thus Burnham justifies the capitalistic regime by the *ideal* of rights not based on force, while at the same time recognizing that, today, in fact, rights are based on force. Others link capitalism to Truth, Honor, and Freedom: thus Ideas in heaven, like words on paper, coexist without any trouble.

Yet, idealistic sublimation is not, in general, totally arbitrary. Using pluralistic substantialism as an excuse to strip the man of the masses of his dignity of thought, the bourgeois doctrinarian utilizes idealism to exclude him from the world of values. The "beautiful categories" he projects on the heavens, are, in fact, bourgeois categories. It'll be easy for him to assert that his fate is linked to that of the privileged and that the oppressed have no share in it whatsoever.

We know quite well, for example, that the concept of freedom is defined in extension and in comprehension on the basis of bourgeois freedoms. Freedom exists where the bourgeois are free. Mr. Larteguy straightforwardly says it in his *Paris-Presse* report, "Quinze jours à Hanoï" [Two Weeks in Hanoï].[72] He writes: "Haïphong is one of the ugliest cities in the world. ... The smells are atrocious, the poverty and filth turn one's stomach, and prostitution flourishes. Nevertheless, it is still freedom." The prostitutes, the filthy and the paupers can not contest the freedom enjoyed in Hanoi by Mr. Lartéguy and a handful of privileged people—it is *freedom*. Moreover, the meaning of the word is positively defined by the bourgeois condition. In a sentence already quoted, Léon Werth clearly admits it. To define a regime of freedom by its opposite, the Stalinist regime, is to define it positively by the capitalistic regime. In earlier times, for proslavery Americans, the idea of Freedom included the right to possess slaves; for the bourgeois of today it includes the right to exploit the proletariat.

Culture and intelligence are likewise defined on the basis of bourgeois norms; therefore one finds them in the bourgeois. Crozier* points out that in America, intelligence tests—called IQ tests—inevitably prove that the rich are more intelligent than the poor. "Children of rich people always have a much higher average IQ than children of poor parents. Since the knowledge and the attitudes mentioned in the IQ tests are knowledge and attitudes of the rich people, the contrary would be rather amazing. Even the American norm is a norm for rich people."†

Certain Ideas happen to shine with implacable purity, even some whose incarnation the bourgeoisie fails to discover in its breast. For example, it is often proclaimed today that Woman is being lost, that she is lost. How about Man himself? In this mid-century, is there a worthy model still to be found? If the catastrophic Elite sometimes seems to exclude itself from humanity, it is simply because it knows itself to be in danger. It is fascinated by the image of what it used to be, because it nostalgically condemns the present in the

---

* *Human Engineering*, in *Les temps modernes*, June 1951.

† In *La physiologie du mariage* [Physiology of Marriage] (1830), Balzac gave the crudest example of this process. He intended to speak about woman. There are, he said, about fifteen million women in France. However . . . "'We will begin by subtracting from this total sum about nine million creatures who, at first glance, seem rather to bear some resemblance to a woman. . . . The nine million beings we are talking about here do present, at first glance, all the characteristics attributed to the human species . . . but for us to see women in them, that is what our Physiology will never accept. . . . A woman is a rare variety of the human race. One generally recognizes her by the whiteness, the fineness, and the softness of her skin. She does not devote herself to any harsh work. . . . For her, walking is tiring. Does she eat? That is a mystery. . . . Are these traits, taken at random among thousands of others, recognizable in these creatures with weather-beaten skin and with hands black as those of monkeys? . . . Alas! Although there are in the world female storekeepers sitting all day long among candles and light brown sugar, farm wives milking cows, unfortunate females used as beasts of burden in factories or who carry a basket, a hoe, or a street vendor's tray, although there exist unfortunately too many vulgar creatures for whom the life of the soul, the benefits of education, and the delightful storms of the heart are an unreachable paradise, and although nature wanted them to have a coracoid process, a hyoid bone, and thirty-two vertebrae, let them remain, in the eyes of the physiologist, in the genus orangutan! . . . The man with feelings, the drawing room philosopher, will cast them out of womankind as we do ourselves."

name of a happier past. Nevertheless its pretention remains intact. Beyond singular categories, it monopolizes the supreme category—the human. We have seen that bourgeois thinkers need to believe that Man, the indivisible, unanimous, and unique Man speaks through their mouths. The bourgeoisie is eager to posit itself as a universal class. Hence, the concept of Man will be formed on the basis of bourgeois particularities. "Man is what men are," said Marx, and this realism forbids any kind of cheating. However, the idealist ascends to the Idea by eliminating in its incarnations anything that he deems accidental. It is his responsibility to decide what he considers essential, and once it is posited that only he incarnates Man, who has the right to contradict him?

Among Western thinkers, Man is readily referred to by the expression "human Person." This Idea brings us into the domain of ethics. We are going to take a closer look at the magic tricks used to forbid this domain to the masses.

Ethics

Prior to the last war, right-wing ethics was ardently heroic.* Following Nietzsche's example, Spengler had an arrogant idea of the hero: "Only the hero, the man of destiny, is definitively in the real world." It is he who makes History; he takes action and wages war. Spengler takes up Nietzsche's praise of the warrior's life and of death in battle. True communication between men, the one that language fails to realize, is obtained through violence. "The sword is the shortest path from one heart to another," Claudel wrote. The pluralism of races and cultures, and the radical separation of individuals imply that the truth of man is not friendship, but conflict. "It is not true that the universe wants to be happy and united. It is divided, and its parts oppose each other," wrote Drieu. And also: "The struggle to exist is not meant to be won." In this age, one lauds violence even if it is devoid of heroism: Man asserts his power through massacres and pogroms. Separation which is the same thing as existence is fully realized in the blood of the other: one proves *his* truth by killing or, at least, by dreaming of murder. "Nothing is done unless it is done in blood," wrote Drieu again in *Le jeune Européen*. "I hope for a blood bath like an old man on the verge of death."

---

* "To serve by commanding, and from that to imagine a life without fear or reproach, in the manner of Bayard to whom fidelity and courage were sufficient; and when one's chest measurement is not enough, to feel tears swell in one's eyes at the mere thought of it: that is the lyricism of the right." (Alain)

Gilles, in the novel by the same name, after having searched for his own identity for four hundred pages, found his true self when he took a rifle to shoot Spanish workers. Drieu admired the dynamism of young Nazis, and he took a stand at Doriot's side.[73] At that time, one saluted the incarnation of the Hero in Mussolini and in Hitler.

The bloodshed did not serve the interests of the bourgeoisie. The rifle, as well as the sword, became an outdated weapon. The generic and anonymous murder committed by the atomic bomb cannot in any way be seen as an affirmation of existence. Today, some Westerners positively wish for war simply because they feel drawn to terror. The vanquished right wing has an idea of greatness that is much more modest than formerly. Its moralists no longer preach heroism, but wisdom. Jaspers, as we have seen, took up the task of thinking through this transmutation of Fascist turbulence into bourgeois spiritualism. The practical moral code he proposes to the postwar Elite follows from his philosophy of the Transcendent.

Jaspers still calls the elite man a hero and, according to him, nobility still remains the supreme virtue of the hero. However, these words have undergone a great change in meaning: "The sole heroism that remains accessible to man today is that of a lusterless achievement, of an action without glory. . . . The true hero is characterized by the faithfulness he brings to his vocation. Today, the hero resists the ordeal of the elusive masses. The modern hero as *martyr* is unable to catch sight of his adversary, and what he himself truly is remains invisible."[74]

Thus, the hero has become a martyr. He is defined above all negatively: by his resistance, a blind resistance, to the masses. He is not particularly sure what he's fighting against nor does he know the meaning of his fight; this is the situation of many anti-communists. Jaspers nevertheless intends to give a positive content to the idea of *vocation*. "The best men in the sense of a nobility of humanity . . . are . . . men who are themselves." He says more specifically, "The marvelous, the sole authentic being I encounter is the man who is himself. . . . By questioning everything in reflecting upon himself, he comes to the encounter with himself in the concrete instant by leaning on himself. . . . He comes to himself as to a gift. Reflecting on oneself is surpassed, as a matter of fact, by Existence itself." Such is the aim of this obscure fight: one has to maintain the possibility of being oneself. However, here, it is not a matter of an anarchic individualism, analogous to that of Gide when he exhorted Nathanaël to make himself "the most irreplaceable of beings." Authenticity, according to Jaspers, is a surpassing toward the Transcendent: "There where I am myself, I am not only myself." Authenticity is not acquired by executing more or less gratuitous acts, but by *faithfulness*. Here, Jaspers draws closer to Barrès in preaching the individual's deep-rootedness in "the earth and the dead." In order to accomplish himself, each must claim his ties to his race, family, country, traditions, and friendships. From his past onward he must assume the particularity of his present situation; by the acceptance of his finitude, he achieves depth and opens himself to the Transcendent. This achievement is not a solitary one: "True nobility is not the feat of an isolated being. It is in the link between independent men. The nobility of minds that are themselves is found dispersed throughout the world. The unity of this dispersal is like the universal Church of a *corpus mysticum* formed by an anonymous chain of friends."

Jaspers's precept, "to be oneself," constitutes one of the platitudes that the right wing keeps on repeating most complacently. I quote at random: "It is necessary to give back his personality to the human being standardized by modern life. The sexes must once again be clearly defined. ... Then it is necessary for him to develop himself in the specific and manifold wealth of his activities" (Alexis Carrel, *L'homme cet inconnu* [*Man, The Unknown*], 1935). "The revenge on an era claiming to count only by the masses ... is that some individualities remain there impregnable as fortresses. Nothing can be done against them. Here an Englishman, there a German, and a few scattered others, will, alone, have 'dominated the debate.' The rest is nothing but a joke." (Braspart, regarding Jünger, 1948, in *La table ronde*).[75]

Claude Elsen, in *Liberté de l'esprit*, boasted in 1949, "The sole commitment that is worthwhile is the one that one makes to oneself, only to oneself, the lucid accomplishment of oneself and of one's solitary destiny—irreplaceable."[76]

Jacques Laurent wrote in 1954 in *La Parisienne* [The Parisian], "For the writer, the problem is not rejecting or ignoring politics but ... going beyond politics. There, he is himself, and a writer that is not himself is redundant."[77]

And so forth.

Among a number of these irreplaceable individuals one also runs into the dream of a *corpus mysticum*. Abellio wishes to gather them in a sort of ark. Monnerot suggests the creation of an order destined, naturally, to fight communism. One recognizes the formula that has proliferated everywhere during these past ten years: "There are still some of us who . . ." He who enunciates it asserts his membership in an elite that is heroic in its minority.

But after all what concrete content is to be given to the motto, "to be oneself"? The answer is unanimous: one must differ. The *faithfulness* Jaspers preaches is the affirmation of our singular finitude, hence the claim of our difference. Mr. de Rougemont, among others, underlined the importance of this notion. He took from Scheler the opposition between the individual, a simple element of the masses, and the *person* who he defines as "The individual charged with a vocation which distinguishes him from the masses, but which links him practically to the community."[78] To be free, to be oneself is one and the same thing: again and always it is to distinguish oneself. "The only freedom of any value to me," says any true* European, "is the one in which I am able to realize myself, search, find, and believe in my truth. . . . Therefore there will never be any real freedom except in the need, the right, and the passion to differ from my neighbor." It is in the name of the Person, thus of Difference, that Rougemont zealously preaches the defense of Europe against barbarism. The entire right wing speaks with one voice. Aron, himself, abandoning his Machiavellian skepticism, is romantically carried away to boast of "the irreplaceable vocation of each human being, this spark that is everything."† It is evidently in the sense of "Person" that one must take the word "individual" in Claudel's statements:‡ "The individual [is] above anything else, and society only exists to draw from the individual everything he can give." "The individual is irreplaceable. . . . It is not a matter of realizing humanity in general, but realizing the individual." The nostalgia for a civilization where every individual "is charged with a vocation" inspired Mr. Paul Sérant§ to a remarkable medley of clichés used by the right wing. He wrote about the soldiers of Dien-Bien-Phuh [*sic*]: "They bear witness to a *civilization* where things were not done by just anybody, but where there were *vocations*, and their particular vocation as soldiers was rightly honored among the highest. The modern world vowed death to this civilization . . . The notion of vocation has been dishonored at the same time as *honor* itself, for honor is made flesh solely in the accomplishment of a vocation. However, this *hideous disorder* is not accepted by the *best* of men: despite the *enterprise* of *leveling* and *standardization*, despite everything, *personalities* assert themselves and destroyed *castes* reconstitute themselves."

There is nevertheless something a bit awkward in this affair. Rougement curiously speaks of individuals *charged with a vocation*. Charged by whom?

---

* "If he does not say it, he is not genuine; he is not European; I suspect that he is not a man." Here is again an example of the manner in which the right fabricates Ideas. Published in *Preuves*.

† *Les guerres en chaîne*, 479.

‡ *Mémoires improvisés* [Improvised Memoirs].

§ *La Parisienne*, June 1954. My [Beauvoir's] emphasis.

This word that escapes him is significant. A vocation, in order to earn its name, must be an appeal made by oneself to oneself. However, while one understands quite well that *advantageous differences* are claimed by the privileged as conditions of their authenticity and freedom, who then, will claim disadvantageous differences? These differences could not exist without each other: no wealthy people without poor people, no masters without slaves. Was there ever a time when men passionately claimed the freedom to distinguish themselves through poverty or slavery? To tell the truth, it is a grim joke to depict the past as an era when serfs, craftsmen, workers—in short, the oppressed—lived *honored* lives, in accordance with the appeal of a *vocation*. It requires a shameful bad faith to suggest that in a capitalistic Europe, a proletarian can search for and find *his* irreplaceable truth.* Alexis Carrel, who nevertheless had no qualms about it, admitted that, "It seems that the modern organization of business and mass production is incompatible with the development of the human person."†

Moreover, Rougemont and the other true Europeans admit in fact that only the Elect realizes himself as a Person. According to Jaspers, the hero defines himself by his resistance to the masses. No masses, no heroes. The existence of an undifferentiated humanity is necessary so that certain ones distinguish themselves by differing. Hence, this distinction is a priori reserved to the few. To attribute to all men the dignity of a person would be to posit their equality; it would be leveling, standardization, and socialism. However, there is no need to hold this exclusivism against civilization. Since "each human being" is distinguished by an "irreplaceable vocation," the laborer, the unskilled worker is not a human being. In this case, it does not matter that this regime will not allow him to make a Person of himself. The only ones who deserve the name of man are those for whom this achievement is possible; hence, it is possible for all men worthy of this name.

If one were to allow oneself to be duped by the self-interested idealism of people devoted to thought, one would be surprised by their strange conception of ethics. For all true moralists, for the sages of antiquity or for Spinoza,

---

* One of Chardonne's texts in *Lettres à Roger Nimier* [Letters to Roger Nimier (1952)], provides an excellent example of the calculated confusion created by the right between *vocation* and *oppression*. "I have seen the movie *Le salaire de la peur* [*The Wages of Fear*]. The escapade of these two men offends scrupulous men, because a salary is involved. As soon as the capitalistic claw appears, they balk. He who climbs the Himalayas runs the risk of similar dangers, but he does it for nothing. Curiosity drives him; he wants to be the first one to enter into the unknown. That's commendable. The editor should say to the author, 'This is beautiful work, but, well, I am not going to pay you for it. It would be a real pity, for it would spoil everything.'"

† *L'homme cet inconnu*. Moreover, Carrel completely ignores this remark that is sufficient to pull down his entire system.

ethics is a certain way of living the reality of the world.[79] Here, to the contrary, they suggest rigging this world in order to maintain outdated values. The masses do exist; our ideologists admit it. Therefore, they should offer to define an ethics for the masses. To the contrary, they violently come out against "the modern world," against the present and the future, in the name of an imaginary past. However, their goals are so transparent that it is not worth the time to judge them in this area. The issue is, once again and as always, to deny the masses for the benefit of the Elite. In the field of aesthetics, the same process is used in pursuit of the same goal.

Art

One of Drieu's heroes, admiring the hands of a very beautiful woman, declares,* "When I would see her feet and hands, I would bless the cruelty of her family who, for three centuries had been trampling on the Indians in order to secure the perfection of leisure time shown in such delicate and firm fingers." This provoking sally expresses one of the aristocratic dogmas of the right wing: one must prefer Beauty to men. Beauty is one of the highest figures of this inhuman reality which constitutes the truth of the Human and that must be maintained *against* men. "To maintain the Human, to act in such a way that, for a long time to come, there will be a human expression of the world through songs, dances, and monuments": such is the supreme goal, according to Drieu, and the masses hinder it since "humanity is ugly, whether it originates in Chicago or Pontoise."

The fate of Beauty is immediately linked to that of Art: it is a given reality that lets itself be grasped in aesthetic contemplation. However, it is fully accomplished only in the Art that re-creates it. Man definitively surpasses himself in Art and this surpassing is more important than the living creatures that are its instrument. Such is the meaning of the following text by Malraux in *La psychologie de l'art* [*The Psychology of Art* (1947–49)]: "Let the gods, on the day of the Last Judgment, raise up the people of statues in front of the forms that used to be alive! The world they have created will not bear witness to their presence, but rather the world of statues will!" The shapes expressing human existence prevail over the contingency of its incarnations; the latter are playthings of fate. Art, to the contrary, is an antifate; it anchors us in eternity. What is the ephemeral individual in the eyes of the eternal? Aesthetes of the West reproach this empirical world not only

---

* *L'homme à cheval* [The Man on Horseback (1943)].

for its perishable character, but also its disorder and absurdity. To this chaos, Art substitutes a well-ordered, significative universe. Caillois congratulates Saint-John Perse for having shown that "the universe exists only when distributed in types and kinds, in grades, ranks, categories, and promotions."[80] Through the grace of his poetry, "for one moment and in one place, ritual and ceremony bring the universal rioting to a halt."

What the supporters of the West most readily put forward are the interests of Art. Other eternal values are equivocal and elusive. Art is endowed with an irrefutable reality. The man of the left recognizes it as much as does the conservative, and he attaches to it the highest importance. However, precisely for that very reason, he wonders in amazement what gives the bourgeoisie the right, in reviews, congresses, and festivals which are more numerous every year now, to mistake the cause of Art for its own cause?

This confusion is a rather new phenomenon. In the last century, and even in the beginning of the present century, literature often constituted an authentic revolt against the bourgeoisie: it's sufficient to cite Rimbaud, Mallarmé, and the surrealists.[81] The negative moment of the revolution—which is precisely the revolt—had not yet been surpassed; an individual insurrection, whether it was of an intellectual, moral, or aesthetic order, had a meaning and an impact. Today, it is no longer possible to be against the bourgeoisie without positively allying oneself with its adversaries: whether he likes it or not, the artist finds himself committed [engagé]. If he wants to safeguard an anarchic independence, the bourgeoisie immediately annexes it, accepting his insolence and escapades with maternal indulgence, thus showing that culture enjoys freedom in its midst. In retrospect, the bourgeoisie has reclaimed Rimbaud and Mallarmé. The modern rebel cannot ignore this state of affairs: either he lines up on the side of the revolution or he consents to serve the cause of Western civilization. While, in earlier times, poetry was built on the ruins of bourgeois values, presently the bourgeoisie uses it as a weapon against the masses.

Once again, what gives the bourgeoisie such a right? They explain that the last pagans had desperately defended a civilization they believed was unique, against Christian barbarity. Nevertheless the Western bourgeois admires cathedrals as much as he admires temples. He has learned, according to Soustelle's remark: "One is always someone else's barbarian." How can he use his own singular culture as an excuse to refuse the one that will dawn tomorrow? The civilized man answers by saying that he deals exclusively with this present civilization and that his destiny is carrying him toward an era that will be the triumph of the formless. Our duty is to delay this death;

future births that will take place in the ages to come are of no concern to us. The argument, which we have already encountered in its generality, appears to be singularly formal in this domain. One observes here the same perversion as the one found in the field of ethics: like morality, authentic art confronts the world through its living becoming; to try to freeze the human and endlessly copy dead forms, is to work against it. The works that are most greatly prized by today's intellectual bourgeois are pastiches; however, Stendhal or Madame de Lafayette whom they parody were great precisely due to their novelty.[82] If Art is an anti-fate, it will defeat time tomorrow as well as today. The first concern of a new Rimbaud* would be to jump over these barriers that feign to protect him.

They retort that man is only able to counter destiny at a certain moment of his destiny and that the near future will resurrect the barbarity of the High Middle Ages. This future, according to the prophecies of the catastrophic Elite, is communism, and there is an incompatibility between communism and culture. A number of intellectuals and artists disagree with this claim. Aron and Monnerot even accuse them of joining communism because they expect a "promotion." Would the communist regime thus favor them? The fact that they believe it proves nothing: it has been established that they are spiritually false; their opinion, corrupted by resentment, is worthless. Infallible facts go against their aberrations. Art itself spoke through the mouth of Mr. Stanislas Fumet.† "Therefore, it is not we, writers and artists, who refuse the servitude promised us, it is *the essence of art* and the purity of its intention that shies away from it. If your philosophy does not recognize it . . ., Art, with its infallibility, tells your philosophy that it is an error and that its moral application is an imposture. Aesthetics shows that ethics is ridiculous."

The freedom that Art requires is bourgeois freedom, the one that gets on well with filth, poverty, and corruption; the survival of these defects is even necessary to it. For freedom is difference: thus evil and good, poor and rich must be side by side. There is a new way of justifying injustice: the Western artist asserts that it is necessary for his work. Let us rather listen to Montherlant:‡ "I am a poet, and nothing but a poet; and I need to love and live

---

* In his book *Le communisme* [Communism], regarding young people "who acclaim Malraux while he talks about the eternal rights of the great individual, the creative genius, Goya, Rembrandt, and Cézanne," [Dionys] Mascolo pointed out: "What young genius could be found among them? What future Rimbaud would ever applaud these defenses of genius periodically delivered by Malraux? . . . [They] are only anxious to have their irreparable lack of needs protected under the alleged shelters demanded by genius. But that's just it: genius never had any shelter."

† *Liberté de l'esprit.*

‡ *Aux fontaines du désir* [At the Fountains of Desire (1927)].

the whole diversity of the world and its so-called opposites, because it represents the substance of my poetry which would rot away from starvation in a universe where only the true and the just reign, as we would die of thirst were we to drink only chemically pure water."[83]

Thus it is good that millions of men die of starvation so that Montherlant's poetry be spared this fate; many Western geniuses agree: let famines, squalor and barbarities continue if such is the price of my work! Distinguished minds acquiesce: to eliminate evil would be to make the earth dull and would eliminate this "poignant salt"* which gives life its taste. One of the virtues of our civilization is precisely that it is guilty, Thierry Maulnier has explained. Men's misfortune is necessary to the Transcendent, Jaspers asserts, and we are assured that it is furthermore indispensable to Beauty and Art. Doctrines and politics aiming at humanity's happiness are basely a-metaphysical and grossly anti-aesthetic. Let us thus preserve this world as it is.

Once again, it is difficult to conceive why a renovated humanity would be unable to manifest itself through "songs, dances, and monuments." The conservatives repeat that "there will always be misfortune on earth" so often that one can turn the argument against them: once oppression is swept away, the true history of humanity will begin and no one has said that it would be easy; to tell the truth, it is impossible for us to foresee it. Whoever a priori distrusts novelty is perhaps an academician, and is surely not an artist. Mascolo† justly remarks, "To whatever degree it might be reduced, it is not being too optimistic to think that enough 'destiny' will always remain to provoke the artistic act which represents its negation." He adds, "This art, an accomplice of misfortune, can not be a great art. It ends up betraying misfortune and thus betraying itself."

But it would be naive to take seriously the self-interested chatting of Western geniuses: their intention is too manifest. Drieu, who often spoke unguardedly in his youth, frankly confessed: "I don't know how to love. Love of beauty is a pretext to despise men." These words confirm what Sartre demonstrated so well in *Saint Genet* [1952]: "Aestheticism does not in the least come from an unconditional love of beauty; it is born out of resentment." It is a weapon used, on one hand, to justify the established order and on the other hand to allow one to despise those whom this order oppresses and sacrifices.

Some members of the American Elite once used the following argument with me: "Hemingway's books are best-sellers; the general public likes only

---

* Claudel.
† *Le communisme.*

bad literature; therefore, Hemingway writes bad literature." The syllogism is rigorous as soon as we accept the premise that the masses and value are mutually exclusive. This principle of exclusion is the foundation of right-wing aesthetics. Only the uncommon is precious, and by making itself too available to a large audience, it destroys itself. This is, for example, the case of elegance, which is a purely negative notion. The elegant woman asserts herself by differing from other women; if all of them became elegant, none of them would any longer be elegant and the notion itself would vanish. This is why elegance—among aesthetic values—is the one that the Elite most readily exalts. The Elite also appreciates refinement which is, by definition, the prerogative of a few. Beauty itself is conceived as being difficult, secretive, and elusive to the common people: what they like is immediately brought into disrepute.

There is, however, an aesthetic concept whose core seems more positive and that is quality. As a matter of fact, its fate is closely linked to that of hierarchical societies. Each human, if he quietly remains in his own place, possesses a certain substantial value. This value manifests itself in the gracefulness of a feminine gesture, in the nobility of a peasant's gesture, and especially in the quality of the object manufactured by an artisan. However, artisans produce little: an object of quality is rare, thus enjoyed solely by a handful of connoisseurs of artisanship, the only ones trained to appreciate it. It is not so much its noticeable charm as its aristocratic character that imparts value to it. An old wine reveals a *substantial form*—the real France—to the gourmet savoring it. Yet were it to have the exact same savor and same bouquet, such a wine, when mass-produced, would no longer provide connoisseurs with a pretext for distinction; even if they were to still drink it with pleasure, they would no longer be interested in it. For example, lacework made by a machine—such a perfect copy of lacework made by hand that it even imitates its defects—by being mass-produced and accessible to the masses has no value whatsoever, neither economic nor aesthetic, and the two go hand in hand. Despite appearances, the idea of quality also contains a principle of exclusion: one can assert that in a humanity reduced to masses, Art and aesthetic values would be absent, for one defines as valuable solely what is denied to the masses.*

---

* It is hardly useful to point out the argument: artists and art lovers come exclusively from the elite. Regarding Blacks, Bernard Shaw said to the Americans: "You force them to be shoeshine boys and from that you conclude that they are good for nothing but shining shoes." Today we can see rather well why an unskilled worker could not write *Du côté de chez Swann* [*Swann's Way*] and would appreciate it with difficulty.

Value and Privilege

This is how the Elite thus justifies the order that favors it. Men are nothing: only the supra-human reality that is exclusively incarnated in hierarchical societies counts; the Elite participates in it to the highest degree. If the individual wishes to attain a truth, realize himself as a person, and manifest beauty, he has no other choice but to accept the hierarchy. Then the Elect recognize him as one of them; they grant him the famous "equality in difference."[84] The fact is that those on whom this difference is imposed feel less equal, as Orwell would say, than those who choose it: the majority of them do not feel in the least equal. Their lack of discipline makes them fall into the masses whose crude, empirical existence is legitimized by nothing. The masses attain neither the True, nor the Good, nor the Beautiful. Were it common to everyone, the divine would become human and thus would perish; however, it does not run this risk since its definition is based on a principle of exclusion. We have seen how under the pretext of defending values, civilization forbids men as a whole the rights and advantages it conceals under this name. The Western thinker nonetheless continues to maintain that values are universal: by his careful doing, the universe has been reduced to the few.

There is nevertheless a difficult crossing to make: what synthetic link unites vital or spiritual values to material values? And do not these two last words clash with each other since materiality is an unworthy thing? Saints considered that virtue was in itself its own end; if they hoped for a reward, they imagined it to be of the spiritual order, as virtue itself. One could, if need be, conceive that the Wise and the Hero intend to guide other men and be honored by them; but one could not think that they demand to be paid better than other men. Yet, through the idea of *merit*, bourgeois ethics mysteriously unites value to enjoyment. Scheler does not hesitate to state: "Values of enjoyment, as the objects or the relations representing them, must therefore be distributed among men not according to 'justice' but in such a way that men could lay claim to them in proportion to their life worth. And any 'just' distribution of the values of enjoyment—realized or in the process of being realized—would constitute a blatant injustice toward those who represent superior life worths."

The demand for material goods in the name of immaterial virtues rarely takes on such a naively cynical character. One will prefer to plead, for example, that fortune, leisure, and bourgeois liberties are necessary for the fulfillment of superior virtues, of elevated qualities: it was necessary to trample on

163

the Indians so that the hands of the beautiful Camilla would be so perfect. However, this detour is dangerous; when one begins to introduce materiality into a system, it soon becomes difficult to take it into account. If the merits the Elite boasts about are subordinated to the empirical conditions of its existence, may one not suppose that if all men were equally favored, they all would be able to elevate themselves to the same lofty heights? We can see where such a hypothesis might lead us.

The most serious argument is the one pointed out by Jaspers. The survival of a "nobility of humanity" and the demands of the Transcendent require the upholding of a hierarchical society, thus entailing material inequalities. If the Elite did not have sufficient economic force to control the collectivity, the latter would turn into the masses. The noble soul thus does not directly demand empirical advantages; it only wishes that the situation advantageous to it be perpetuated for the spiritual good of all.

The system is highly coherent: it has the coherence of a tautology. And the postulate on which it is based is as arbitrary as an act of violence: one declares that the masses are deprived of substance and everything else ensues. Yet, how can one recognize the ontological richness of a group or an individual? Substance does not belong to the empirical world; it is revealed only through signs and the sole sign distinguishing the Elect is privilege: it is through privileges that the Elite recognizes itself, asserts itself, and separates itself.

The entire trick consists in making privilege into the manifestation of a value whose presence would bestow on the privileged the right to privilege. He must have economic power in order to defend the good incarnated in him, and of which his power is the sign. In other words, the Elect deserves the values of enjoyment because he owns them. The conclusion is straightforward since the possessors established the merit scale in order to legitimize their possessions. Camouflaged in the depth of vast systems, bourgeois ideology amounts to this truism: privilege belongs to the privileged.

Guido Piovene, a most hardened anti-communist, confirms exactly those conclusions in demonstrating the necessity of "the cold war."*[85] He confesses that the justifications proposed by the endless amount of anti-communist literature are all nonsense. "The majority of these arguments leave us puzzled, and—if we go beyond a practical adherence—reveal themselves to be not very explicit, as superficial and temporary—as much, or almost as much, as those thrown against us by the adversary. They always aim too high or too low. . . . I will set aside the arguments that come under ideal-

---

* "La guerre froide" [The Cold War], *La table ronde*, August 1953.

ism under all its guises and that boast of the 'priority' and the 'superiority of the mind' and 'the spirit that makes history'; all those arguments that have henceforth fallen into banality. It is equally unhelpful to enlarge on the patriotic arguments. . . . However, idealism is an argument dear to the intellectuals, and in all its varieties, supports thousands of books and pamphlets. It focuses on the lies of the communist world and its contempt for the truth. . . . We all undergo in various degrees the same crisis of the truth and the soul; no one is able to decide definitely." Piovene concludes: "In our countries, the bourgeoisie is not very convinced and has few valid reasons to defend itself, save for the instinct of self-preservation and the intention of its members to keep hard at it, endowed with the values they carry within themselves by the simple fact of living."

The Life of the Elect

Since the privileged one's superiority is the ultimate justification of the system that favors him, it is necessary to study this exalted figure of Man more closely. The elect have excluded the rest of humanity from their spiritual universe. Once alone with themselves, what kind of marvel are they going to make out of themselves?

Considering what has been said, it is not in action that one must search for the "cipher" to their existence. The fact is that, in this empirical world, the active members of the bourgeoisie pursue ends that they deeply take to heart, and its ideologists mystically lend an objective importance to the defense of the civilization of values. The men who undertake this fight presumably surpass themselves authentically toward transcendent realities. Yet, we have seen that today's struggle is more negative than conquering, and that bourgeois ethics consequently leans toward quietism: its vision of the world and its psychology of immanentism are pointed in this direction.

The bourgeois thinker justifies quietism by historical catastrophism, and this pessimism is often accompanied by a cosmological optimism: History is condemned, but the universe is roughly good. Aesthetic hindsight, at any rate, allows him to consider it as being good. Nietzsche preached the *amor fati* [love of fate]: it was necessary, he taught, "to say yes to life." Following his teaching, those occupying the best places in this world courageously resign themselves to accept it. Montherlant, for example, never ceased to proclaim throughout his life that, "All is well." In 1925 he wrote,* "Yes, everyone is

---

* *Aux fontaines du désir.*

right, always. The Moroccan and the government that machine-guns him. The hunter and the game. The law and the outlaw. And I when I cold-bloodedly write this. And I if I were to curse it in the heat of violent emotion." He repeated it in his *Carnets* [Notes] in 1938: "In what frame of mind, can we, being happy, bear the misery of the world? Just as we bear that it is night in New York when the sun is shining in Paris." And, in 1951, he said the following: "What else have I done for the last forty years, but accept? Accept others, accept myself, and accept circumstances: accept while approving . . . Presently, I live in a world where everything is stamped with the triple seal of madness, baseness, and horror. And yet, this universal adherence still makes me quiver when I hear this sentence that already mysteriously moved me in the secret depth of my twentieth year . . . : '*In spite of my misfortunes, my advanced years and the greatness of my soul enable me to see that all is well.*'"*

All is well if our soul is great enough to bear the misery of others and our own privileges; Montherlant's comparison subtly suggests that men's fate imitates great natural cycles: tomorrow, the unemployed will become, in his turn, a millionaire and Montherlant, a miner underground. And if the wheel is not turning fast enough, many a wise man preaches to us the equivalence of everything and nothing: God's absence is equivalent to his presence, the nothingness of consciousness refers to the plenitude of Being, man's misery makes his greatness, and through dispossession one attains true wealth. A mutilated dialectic where thesis and antithesis are immediately identified without their common surpassing toward a higher synthesis taking place, such is the method readily used by the right to confuse the issue and stop History. The slave does not have to become the master; he already is master, at least this is what the master asserts. The right's philosophy can take on many other countenances; but whether it is founded on stoicism, mysticism or naturalism, this attitude of consent, so marveled at by Montherlant, is most widespread among the privileged. Pingaud advocates it in his *Eloge du consentement* [In Praise of Consent],† "Consent is the opposite of conquest."[86] The consenting man "cannot allow himself to be linked with anyone . . . he refuses to belong to anyone, even to himself . . . he does not seek to realize any undertaking, is not an activist for any cause, and does not put forward any rule. He has eternity on his side for he already lives arbitrarily in eternity. He is not afraid

---

* Quote from Sophocles, *Œdipe à Colone* [*Oedipus at Colonus*]. When Oedipus, miserable, blind, overwhelmed with years and misfortunes, uttered this sentence, he, in fact, showed the greatness of his soul. This sentence takes on a totally different meaning in the mouth of a well-to-do young or old bourgeois.

† *La table ronde*, May 1953. My [Beauvoir's] emphasis.

of dying for he is already dead. And because he is already dead, because he already lives in eternity, this man can, without remorse and with no ulterior motive, accept [*assumer*] history. He accepts it not as a task from which he will profit or as a conquest from which he will emerge stronger, but as *an obvious fact he can only observe*. . . . The man of consent thus will be the friend and the servant of all. . . . His love and his faithfulness are universal."

One sees in this text how closely the ideas of consent and ataraxia are linked: one must not take a stand, one must do nothing. This way of accepting history by restricting oneself to observing it is, more or less, what Jaspers teaches. He is interested in *denial* under the triple form of suicide, mysticism, and irony—but not under the form of revolutionary action, and he essentially emphasizes faithfulness. Faithfulness consists in anchoring the finitude of our present situation in the past and submitting to it such as it is given to us. Tinged with irony and melancholy or enlightened by mysticism, bourgeois wisdom very generally puts forward this motto: accept.

Does this motto entirely exclude action? On this matter, the right-wing intellectuals do not all agree. Not long ago Claude Elsen and Claude Mauriac debated it at length in *Liberté de l'esprit*; so did Jacques Laurent and Thierry Maulnier more recently.[87] Elsen and Laurent are uncompromising quietists: the faintest action is a taint, sufficient to cloud the pure miracle of being themselves. Claude Mauriac admitted that to safeguard the values that surpass action, it was sometimes necessary to act. Thierry Maulnier believed that some eternal principles must actually be defended. What is certain is that, in any case, the individual appears to all of them as something other than his actions. These acts do not define him; his truth is elsewhere.

In fact, the value that distinguishes the elite man is not something that is acquired: vital or spiritual, nobility is an innate grace. And how could an enterprise seriously be of interest to a lucid individual, since he knows himself to be bound by his own immanence? His only authentic relationship is with his own self; any exterior end remains foreign to him. If he does pursue one, it is not because he is objectively sought by it; he does it out of a subjective whim. The criticism leveled at Marxism by the anti-communists is entirely based, as we have seen, on this radical dissociation between the subject and his ends; allegedly disinterested enterprises are nothing more than selfish purposes in disguise. This interpretation is evidently projective: action is a superfluous luxury and a gratuitous game for the bourgeois, whose situation is already comfortably guaranteed and who is fundamentally confined to egoism. In *La suite dans les idées*, Drieu emphatically expressed this indifference toward the contents of commitment [*engagement*]: "Why shouldn't we change the flag? Why shouldn't we prefer red to white? It's the way of love. We want something new. If it is offered to us, let's take it. . . . Something new, something new. Let's drop the bombs!"

As a matter of fact, Gilles, Drieu's hero, chooses an ideology for himself as he would choose a shirt at Charvet's. First he opts for communism then, disgusted by it he becomes a fascist. Having performed a similar 180-degree turn, Ramon Fernandez stated at that same time, "I only like departing trains."[88] With whom was he traveling? What was the train's destination? It did not matter to him. If one acts, it is in order to give oneself subjective satisfactions: an impression of novelty, or motion, or courage. Anyone who imagines himself aiming at a goal outside himself would be a dupe. This is what Montherlant asserts in *Service inutile* [Useless Service (1935)]: "You will tell me that there is no cause worth dying for. That is quite probable. However, it is not for this cause that one suffers or dies. It is for the idea that this suffering and death give us of ourselves. . . . One must be absurd, my friend, but one must not be a dupe. No pity for the dupes."

Montherlant preaches again this Machiavellian wisdom in *Le solstice de juin* [The Summer Solstice (1941)]: "The adversary as a person and the ideas he is supposed to represent are thus of no importance whatsoever." "Fighting without faith, is the formula to which we are necessarily led if we want to maintain the only acceptable idea of man: the one where he is, at the same time, the hero and the sage."

When, during an interview, Nimier said in substance: "No, I have not been a militiaman: blue did not suit me," he was keeping up with this tradition.[89] The affected frivolity of his sally meant that he refused to grant any truth to the outside world in order to grant it to himself alone. Chardonne follows the same trend when he writes in *Lettres à Roger Nimier*, "Our opinions signify that we are made this way; that's all there is to it! . . ."[90]

" . . . I consider my own opinions and those of others as trifles; this is the point to which my studies led me. Presently, the political opinions of a Frenchman are the opinions of a nervous woman; and the ideas of a nervous woman, I know where they come from. I don't like that."

The contempt for objective ends appears, among other things, in the mythology of the chief, as he is conceived by the right. It is not his work that is of interest, but his figure. Drieu's poems on *Le dictateur* [The Dictator], and his novel *L'homme à cheval* [The Man on Horseback] are revealing. The hero of *L'homme à cheval* becomes dictator by chance, without any motive. He has no definite agenda, yet he invents a cause for himself because, being a dictator, he needs a pretext to reveal himself. But in reality he is indifferent to all parties, isolated from his own country and the entire world. Dictator-ship, in the end, serves him only to exalt the nobility of his soul. A mediocre prince limits himself to exercising power for the sake of power. The chief, if he is of good quality, makes an asceticism out of power, and becomes the greatest of all because he is the most separate. Having no equal, he differs from others more than anyone else: he is more himself. In him, the elite man realizes the highest level of individuality, and it is precisely thence that his authority comes. His supporters obey him not because they take up for themselves the objective ends he is pursuing, but because they submit to the ascendancy of his personality. Like the Master, for the same reasons, he demands an unconditional adherence in the name of a certain Grace that is within him. Prior to the last war, Max Weber suggested a portrait of the "charismatic chief" that Aron* summarized thus: "Entirely devoted to the task, passionate, but nevertheless lucid, he is the master of his troops; he triumphs by the ascendancy of his personality, and not by flattery or dema-gogy."[91] He is akin to the Jewish prophet "who castigates the people and who stands out as a chief because he is endowed with extraordinary virtues." The myth has lost much of its splendor since the deaths of Mussolini and Hitler. However, it does survive. For example, it is striking that when speaking of General de Gaulle in *Paris-Match*, Malraux did not say a word to indicate that the Gaullist agenda or enterprise had ever interested him: he simply declared he had been seduced by the greatness of the man.

The meaning and impact of the subjectivist attitude are expressed nowhere more obviously than in the essay† in which Thierry Maulnier claims for man "the right to be wrong." He declares, "The right to be wrong is the fundamen-tal right of the human being that envelops all the others." It is true that the recognition of this right necessarily envelops a global conception of man, one that by reducing him to his immanence authorizes all the selfish demands of the bourgeois. For a man who believes in the importance of his ends, failure is an absolute tragedy. It is impossible to redeem, other than by repairing it objectively. Thierry Maulnier would probably hesitate in letting a switchman who has caused a serious accident remain at his job, in the name of the right to error, for even though one can find excuses for him, he is objectively dis-qualified. The *right to be wrong* thus implies that ethics is not situated in this empirical world, but on a transcendent plane, that is to say, in fact, on a sub-jective plane. Good is somewhere in the heavens and the quality of the soul

---

* Raymond Aron, *Sociologie allemande* [*German Sociology*]. Let us point out that Aron does not in the least claim this description as his own.

† *La face de Méduse du communisme.*

seeking it does not depend on its success, but on the purity of its intention. The ethics of intention blends perfectly with bourgeois subjectivism, but it contradicts the very idea of attempt: why would one aim at empirical ends if they have in themselves no ethical signification? Contemplation is then the only conceivable link to the Transcendent. The most troubling element in this business is that the "errors" defended by Maulnier are of a very concrete nature: they are political mistakes that put human lives at stake. Should one accept that murder is not a matter of ethics? Perhaps so, if the empirical existence of human beings counts for naught. But then consenting to the crimes committed against them is not a "wrong" either, so one might as well follow Sade and state that one is authorized to trample on human beings.

Yet, bourgeois subjectivism does not take this extreme form. The bourgeois is integrated into the order he defends, and even if he believes that, in the final analysis, he deals only with himself, he must still interact with others. For want of acts, behaviors are demanded of him. Which law will these behaviors follow?

Social hierarchy provides an answer to this question. In the bourgeois world, the relationships that individuals maintain with each other are never immediate. Each is recognized by others through the function he carries out which valorizes him. This recognition is governed by rituals and ceremonies, and its character is institutional. Morals and laws define the relationships between parents and children, husband and wife, leader and his subordinates, and inversely. Politeness and good manners constantly remind the bourgeois that they must exclusively communicate through the intermediary of society. The respect shown to each other by peers expresses their deference toward the form or the institution incarnated in each one of them. When two generals salute each other, they are saluting the army. Insofar as singular circumstances surpass the predictions of the established code, beings of quality are recognized by the fact that they instinctively invent an appropriate behavior. This instinct is the sense of honor. "Honor is a question of blood, not of comprehension," declared Spengler. "One does not think, or one is already dishonored." Honor dons various shapes: for the inferior it is fidelity and devotion, while between peers, it is loyalty. For the Master, the essential virtue is justice. One well knows the mythologies where this morality is exalted: the simple dignity of those of humble extraction, the abnegation of wives and good servants, disciplines accepted, responsibilities assumed, father and son, commander and soldier, marriage, home, and family. From Henri Bordeaux to Claudel, a vast literature extols bourgeois institutions and the elevated virtues to which they give rise.[92]

The trouble is that, today, these myths look slightly old-fashioned. The old hierarchies are shaky, the order of the world is uncertain, honor is withering: this is the theme of a great many complaints. Faced with masses that nothing inhuman can transfigure, the Elect returns to solipsism: "Everything that is human is foreign to me," as the hero of Le hussard bleu [1950] concluded. This is logical, since the right wing accepts only mediated relationships between men. As soon as the institution perishes, as soon as the mediation vanishes, only isolated atoms remain present. Henri Bordeaux leads directly to Nimier.

Skeptical and no longer right-thinking, the youthful literature of the right thus shuts itself away in subjectivism. No real communication between human beings exists. Love, for example, is not union, but solitude. A psychological idealism, inspired by Proust, and a certain interpretation of psychoanalysis, allows love to be considered as an immanent phenomenon, as the classic example of "false hallucination," where the object is nothing but pretext, and the lover is alone with his pleasure, desire, myths, complexes, and deliriums. Just as easily, his behavior toward his beloved concerns only himself. For example, Costals, in Les jeunes filles [The Girls (1936)], through Solange Dandillot and the small worries and entertainment with which she provides him, only has a relationship with himself.[93] His gestures are determined by the image he wishes to form of himself. The system extends to all human relationships. For example, generosity toward an inferior is a valued virtue, but the generous act, as understood by the right, is not an answer to a call from outside, or motivated by the needs of the others. It is a pretext for the superior man to manifest his "vital nobility," or—as with Claudel's king of Naples—to prove his detachment from worldly goods. However, the Elect can, just as easily, capriciously deny generosity. For amusement's sake, he will demonstrate his indifference toward others, or the sovereignty of his free will, or his refusal of conventional virtues. In any case, by being founded on nothing, his conduct is gratuitous. Montherlant's apologia of the caterpillars has the same meaning: the strong one can play any kind of games with the weak, for he alone is the master.

The sole concern of the Elect will thus be the cult of his ego, that is to say, the cultivation of his differences. The male Elite proudly asserts its virility, according to a well-known sexual mythology.* The majority of the elect lay claim to a racial specificity which they grasp as a superiority. They think and

* The case of women is more complex because the sexual difference for them is inferiority; in any case, they do not assume it in arrogance.

live as a Breton, a Mediterranean, or a sailor's son, as descendants of valiant knights, great bourgeois, or the old peasantry of France. They identify themselves with their social function: incarnated in them are the mother, the grandfather, and the husband. As much as possible, they give their trade the sacred character of a vocation. If they wish to acquire additional individual qualities—or if this is their only resource—they take pains to create for themselves what is called a personality. They take on a character, and become enthusiasts, connoisseurs, or partisans in one or another field. They singularize their image with their way of dressing, the style of their furniture—even the choice of objects they will take with them to the grave. Therefore, their behaviors must, of course, be singular. A hero of Montherlant's suddenly moves away from the woman he was embracing, because too many couples were repeating this same embrace at the same moment. Here again, the negative carries the day: it's a matter of not being like everyone else. In a decadent society, where vocation and honor no longer have great credibility, the only positive morality is of an aesthetic nature. Gestures are a substitute for action, but gesture is an action devoid of its content and considered from afar as an object of contemplation. This withdrawal is obtained precisely through aestheticism. However, the most highly regarded value in this field is elegance, and elegance is defined by a principle of exclusion. The sole rule, all things considered, is to shock and to surprise: to prove, once again, that one is different. Such a formal law could not generate any plenitude. Cut off from his kind and from any real purpose, the Elect leads a life without any content: he does nothing and he has a hold over nothing. In the eyes of someone who evaluates him with objective criteria, he is nothing.

Yet he has discovered a way to evade this judgment: he ascribes depth to his objectively empty life by interiorizing it. This is how one assesses the conversion carried out by the right wing after the Nazi defeat: inner life was substituted for heroism. Educated by history, the catastrophic Elite knows that it is more prudent to confront oneself secretly rather than to square off openly with an adversary. The nobility of blood was inscribed in spilled blood; the nobility of the soul hides in the recesses of the soul. The philosophies of the Transcendent are deliberately developed to allow the individual to take refuge in his immanence. He who sincerely believes in the Transcendent experiences his faith in anguish. Saints knew that it is difficult to tell God's voice from the devil's voice, to tell grace from pride, and not one of those who were looked upon as saints ever boasted of being a saint; such pretense would have been sufficient to spoil his virtues. Our modern heroes have fewer scruples because the Transcendent is nothing but a ghost who plays the role of a medium between self and self. They drew it out of themselves by projecting onto it their advantageous characteristics. They thus discover in themselves the evidence of its presence and this evidence is good enough to justify these modern heroes. To tell the truth, only empirical action and a man's practical surpassing toward terrestrial ends tear him from his immanence and define him objectively. Yet on earth the Elect disdains to take a chance, define himself, or size himself up. He prefers to assert, fortified by his sole authority, that in the silence and the solitude of his soul, he knows his worth, his merit, and his participation in the inhuman that deifies man.

No challenge could reach this intimate evidence. Even intellectual life escapes it, since the truth reveals itself in a singular experience, often ineffable, and never entirely communicable. The man of the right readily takes refuge in the strength—as irrefutable as unjustifiable—of his subjective intuition: there must be something about the Jews, since I cannot stand them. Without providing any objective proof, each can believe himself to be the most clear-sighted, the most discerning, and the most profound of men: his own acquiescence is sufficient for him.* The ethical and aesthetical qualities of nobility, delicacy, greatness, and authenticity are even easier to claim, for no object is called into question, and the subject deals only with his states of mind. He compares them, combines them, contemplates them, and reflects upon them so that he generates new ones. Soul-searching and psychological analysis are pretexts for him to distinguish himself, with no risk, in his own eyes. This is the great advantage of inner life: it gives each one the license to prefer himself to everyone else.

Yet, this hidden life is readily exteriorized through conversations, letters, intimate diaries, essays, and novels. Eventually, one gets tired of the silence, the solitude, and the emptiness, and a recourse then presents itself: to profess them in the form of literature. Literature is more or less the sole activity that seems to be separated enough from reality so that an intransigent quietist might agree to devote himself to it.

* * *

* On this matter, it is strongly recommended that one read the foreword, written by Pauwels, to his book devoted to Gurdjieff. Pauwels *feels* that there are mysterious affinities between Lazareff and Paulhan: those who feel as he does belong, he says, to the same family of minds, the only one that was worth something; the others are grossly blind. Who, therefore, would justifiably contradict him, since the value of the other is measured by his adherence? Within groups of "initiated ones," inner life is lived together, without losing its characteristics.

Writing, however, must not constitute an action: nothing inspires more horror to today's right wing than "committed" literature [*littérature engagée*]. Since 1944 things have also changed in this field. Drieu, before and during the last war, threw himself headlong into political literature. In a conference given during the occupation, Maxence violently reproached the scholars of the between-the-wars period for having kept themselves out of the melee.[94] That was because, at the time, right-wing intellectuals believed themselves to be on the side of the victorious: it was the era of heroism. Repulsed by action, now they want a literature that will stay outside the world and help them camouflage, deny, or at least, flee from reality. A life without any content naturally demands books without any content. Literature has a value insofar as it distinguishes writers and readers from the common herd. The more esoteric it is, the better it plays this role. Reserved for the Elite, literature serves the pretext of self-justification. Therefore, literature must exist and will be even granted great importance, provided that it says nothing. Jacques Chardonne was congratulated for having managed so well, in his *Lettres à [Roger] Nimier* to speak about trifles, that is to say, to speak about nothing.

This is not that easy. Mascolo* noticed regarding the writer: "He always speaks about man. He might have a taste only for forms. It is always the human form that is depicted in the end. This form carries with it the entire baggage of ideas, values, and principles that are precisely what one did not want to find in it. . . . Yet, it is impossible to talk about man, that is to say, to talk, without talking about what man carries. He is a carrier. Even visual arts do not escape this law."[95] The fact is that the fiercest opponents of committed literature let themselves be swept along as soon as they venture into a positive undertaking. All Thierry Maulnier's essays revolve around political questions, and *La maison de la nuit* [The House of the Night (1951)] is the typical committed play. When Jacques Laurent, in *Le petit canard* [The Little Duck (1954)], tries to move us with the fate of a young militiaman, he writes a tendentious novel, to say the least. His so-called uncommitted [*dégagée*] review, "La Parisienne," is so tendentious that it borders on fanaticism. Claude Elsen does not live in an ivory tower, but in a polemical one in *Dimanche-matin*. One neither succeeds in living solipsism to the end nor in writing a book without any content.

At least, this content can be so devoid of signification that it verges on nothingness. Before the Nazi defeat, the young and dynamic right wanted a

---

* *Le communisme.*

militant literature, but most conservative writers exploited themes that allowed them to string sentences together without putting anything at stake. Emmanuel Berl's* 1927 inventory of them remains more or less valid today.[96] Today's authors describe the gentle pleasures of bourgeois life less complacently than before, leaving this to the female novelists across the Channel. On the other hand, the virtues of the so-called psychological novel have never been praised so highly. "Psychology," Berl observed, "knows how to substitute for judgment the fact that things require a collection, infinite for that matter, of separate facts from which no judgment can arise. Psychology has become a certain way of disqualifying the mind." The bourgeois psychological novelist is not interested in the situation of his heroes; he studies the human heart in general and in its pure immanence. In telling us a love story, the beloved object barely exists and the world in which the lovers live exists even less. Or he dissects the states of mind of a hallucinating, solitary character. Or, by bringing together several hallucinating characters to whom any communication is forbidden—since language is a lie—he describes for us the curious phenomena resulting from their coexistence.

The only reality that the bourgeois writer decides to take into account is the inner life. Taken out of his inner life, he only seeks to escape either to the past, or through space, or into the unreal. Childhood recollections occupy a special place in bourgeois libraries; themes of taking root, such as landscape, house, and ancestors, are readily developed in them. The child—irresponsible, asocial, and separated—is the model that the right-wing intellectual would like to perpetuate throughout life. His naive vision of the world abolishes its hard resistances and reveals it as marvelous: how many a pastiche of Le grand Meaulnes [1913] has been written!† The specialists in exoticism also provide us with a certain degree of the marvelous, devoting themselves to depicting strange countries in their incommunicable mystery. Through the irreducible picturesqueness of the sites, and the impenetrable mentality of the inhabitants, they make man appear as something other than man. Tales of dreams, adventures, and fantastic evocations are meant to make us forget both about this world and ourselves.‡

---

* Mort de la pensée bourgeoise [Death of Bourgeois Thought (1929)].

† See among others, La grange aux trois belles [The Barn of the Three Beauties], circa 1938, by Robert Francis, who was the brother of Maxence, and like him, a determined fascist.

‡ It goes without saying that it is the marvelous that is on the right, not poetry. And that it is not impossible, far from it, to demonstrate the truth of man through childhood recollections, tales of voyages, and fantastic stories.

Obviously there is no question here of attempting to draw a picture, even a rough one, of today's bourgeois literature. Therefore, we shall restrict ourselves to a few remarks. We will only examine a bit more closely the two closely associated themes that play the greatest role in the Elite's thinking and morality: the themes of Nature and death.

* * *

"Nature is on the right," said Ramuz.[97] What is true is that Nature is one of the great idols of the right: it appears as the antithesis of both History and praxis.

Against History, Nature gives us a cyclic image of time. We have seen that the symbol of the wheel ruins the idea of progress and favors the quietist philosophies. The great cosmic round is concretely embodied in the indefinite resumption of seasons, days and nights. The evident repetition of winters and summers makes the idea of revolution laughable and demonstrates the eternal. Drieu, among the "modern" and absurd characters of his novel *Gilles*, portrayed a "handsome figure" of an old French peasant, who participates in the great silence of the earth, but from time to time, utters some ponderous sentences for Gilles's benefit. Showing an oak, he murmurs, "There is something of the eternal in man. What this oak says will be told again, under one form or another, always."

Among these immutable truths and essences revealed by Nature, human nature comes first. Humanity is then grasped as a given species, and not as a product of its product: the idea of nature contradicts that of praxis.

Regarding the development of natural species, action has, as a matter of fact, only a secondary influence. At most, it helps the full bloom of possibilities hidden in the seed or egg, but it would not know either how to create them or modify them. Nature is used as an authority for those wishing to assert the pluralism of races and castes, as well as their inequality. For them, the human species is divided like other animal species into originally differentiated varieties whose qualities are hereditarily transmissible. Even though the Elite gave a spiritual dimension to the idea of nobility, it still wishes to think that its superiority is innate. It is as impossible for the common people to acquire it as it is for a seed of barley to produce a grain of wheat. On the other hand, a seed of wheat needs only to be sown in good ground to ripen marvelously. The privileged man likes to imagine that the comfort and leisure he enjoys promote a slow and secret improvement of himself with no effort on his part. To act matters little; one must be. The bourgeois ideologist demands of Nature the confirmation of this truth.

Not only does the conservative assimilate humanity as a species and each human individual to the fruits of the earth, but he does it as well for societies as a whole. It was often pointed out* that the right wing accords preeminence to organicist images. Spengler and Toynbee see societies as organisms: pluralism and the correlative notion of substantial form require it. Only living organisms possess a positively unified individuality that is radically distinct from any other. By subordinating men to a hierarchical form and subjugating them to a pre-established order, the ideology of the right thus necessarily sees men as having the same relationship as limbs do to the stomach, or bees to the hive. With these images, it denies individuals their autonomy and their ability to achieve immediate solidarities among themselves. Above all, it denies the struggles that divide them. All of them seem equally interested in maintaining the form to which they belong. Violence is concealed behind the gentle harshness of a vital necessity.

Naturalistic optimism claims to be even more universal: Nature is harmony, as was proven by Bernardin de Saint-Pierre's melon;[98] in Claudel it sings the Creator's praises, proclaiming by its splendor that what is must be. Nature assigns each one his place in this concert. Nationalism, for one, exalted itself through nature claiming that the individual accomplishes himself only by modeling himself on his native soil. Spengler told us that the substance of a country revealed itself in its landscapes. Barrès wanted young French people to revel in French landscapes, and he showed us how Sturel and Saint-Phlin, bicycling along the Moselle, discovered the Lorraine's reality.[99] In Austria and Germany, the young Nazis gaily alternated pogroms and walks in the forest. The neo-fascists of the Upper Adige today still love to pick edelweiss.

Nationalism no longer pays. When Heidegger strolls through the woods today, he is no longer searching for a communion with a particular country, but with Being. However, Being is today the great alibi of the civilized Western man, who justifies his indifference toward other men by claiming to be dedicated to the Transcendent. Dreaming alone up and down hill and dale, he convinces himself that he is united with the Whole. In the silence of things, he grasps the felicitous affirmation of this hidden Reality, the only one that is valid.

This calm picture of Nature is not the only one that presents itself. One can also see in it a disorganized jungle where inequality disputes the idea of

---

* In an article on Gustave Thibon, Debidour points out, "It is curious to notice that, in order to celebrate the social link, right-wing thinkers have always used a set of images borrowed from the biological field: the limbs and the stomach, the tree, the beehive which are symbols of order."

justice and where might invalidates any right. Man is a wolf to man; life is a struggle where the strongest win. Although this concept seems to contradict the previous one, it benefits the oppressors in exactly the same way, allowing them to make Nature shoulder their responsibilities for them. Inequalities are not unfair when they are givens; men's misfortune is not a crime if no one caused it. To the utopians who would like to modify the course of the world, Nature opposes its immutable fate. "One will never overcome the injustice in which this world is steeped; society will always be, as nature, a chaos of iniquities," Chardonne wrote in *Lettres à Roger Nimier*.

To tell the truth, Nature is easy because it relays the words one dictates to it. In the voice of the wind, the sea, and of a swaying palm tree, man never hears anything but his own voice. The Lorraine teaches Barrès the greatness of land ownership because, as Berl noticed,* he chose to contemplate only the hills covered with vineyards and mirabelle plum trees. He ignored the smelting furnaces burning throughout the plains. In a recent interview Giono declared that he sensed the value of a book by reading it outdoors.[100] Rare were those books, he said, that resist this confrontation with the sky and the earth. This means, in fact, that from the style of life he has chosen for himself, few books are of interest to Giono. The challenge comes only from himself and not from the landscapes of Provence. In reality, Nature offers a convenient alibi to the elect who claim to answer only to themselves. They search in it for a sensible image of the abstractions they make up for themselves and of their elusive states of mind. Nature is one of the figures of the Transcendent they exploit in order to repudiate men. Certainly, for one who loves men, love of Nature is not forbidden, far from it. However, one must distrust anyone who draws lessons from it.

* * *

Winter begets summer and summer begets winter. Nature ranks life with death. For Barrès, the cult of the ancestral soil and the cult of the dead are inextricably linked: the earth is an immense cemetery. Nature is so greatly revered by the right-wing writers mainly because it helps them to assert the preeminence of death over life.

* * *

"A revolver is solid; it is made of steel; it is an object. To come up finally against the object," Drieu writes at the end of *Le feu follet* [*The Fire Within*

---

* *Mort de la pensée bourgeoise.*

(1931)], hereby giving us the reason for the right wing's profound fascination with death. It is the sole *real* event that can take place within a life withdrawn into its own immanence, a life without any content. Cut off from the world, cut off from his fellow men who are all strangers to him, without love and without aim, the man of the right is trapped in an empty subjectivity, where nothing takes place except in thought. Death alone *happens* to him while, at the same time, remaining interior to him. Absolutely solitary, without any relation with the other, without object, and without future, death realizes radical separation. One dies alone. This is the reason that the man of the right decides to see in death the truth of life. Death confirms his belief that everyone lives alone and separated. In its light I answer solely to myself; this self is foreign to all those who are foreign to my death: to everyone.

If life is an empty form whose sole real content is death, it behooves us to show the preeminence of death in one's behaviors. The living have no other valid occupation than to play with death, defy it, elude it, and accept it. Heroism is exalted because it helps found the right to egoism. He who, by risking his life, demonstrates that he despises life, has no need to care about the other's life. By choosing to "live dangerously," the masters, according to Nietzsche, assert their right to keep slaves in bondage. "There is contempt for life in any victory," says Nietzsche. He who holds life in the highest contempt and risks it most generously will be victorious and, by the same token, will justify his life. Nietzsche also calls this contempt "love." He places suicide on a level even higher than death in combat. "For love of life one should desire a free and conscious death, without chance or surprise."[101] Contempt bears on the content and love on the pure form of life; the supreme affirmation of the form is the radical abolition of the content by suicide. It is true that only suicide realizes egoism in a decisive and coherent way, but it is not coherent to keep on living, comfortably protected by the shadow of death.

At the time when the right wing was bellicose, it spoke highly of war and murder. By spilling blood, one asserted one's own existence and fertilized the furrows, preparing future harvests. On this point again, the negative carries the day. By killing, the soldier no longer seeds the soil, but rather cleanses it, which is less exalting. Death is no longer either accomplishment or promise. What makes it attractive is that death effectively reduces to nothingness this humanity the Elect wishes to consider as nothingness.

Vanity of vanities. You are dust and you shall return to dust.[102] The catastrophic Elite readily sweeps along into the great terminal night this world that condemns it. "This world that, as any other planet, will one day cease to be fit to live on, is it of any real concern to us?" Chardonne wondered in *Lettres à Roger Nimier*. The privileged man prefers to think that he is not concerned; thus he can peacefully keep on cultivating his garden in the face of surrounding "famines, destitution and barbarities." In the light of the great funereal equality, it would be quite frivolous to fight him for the ephemeral advantages he enjoys.

Meditation on death is the supreme wisdom of those who are already dead.

Conclusion

If we were to let ourselves be enticed into the field where bourgeois thought claims to be situated, it would appear to us as a tissue of inconsistencies. Realistic, hard, pessimistic, and cynical, it is also spiritualistic, mystic, and feebly optimistic. It is a philosophy of immanence and a religion of the Transcendent; substantialistic and pluralistic, it nevertheless rallies to a monistic idealism. At times it claims to be synthetic, and at other times it postulates atomism. However, to criticize it from that angle would be to fall into the trap of idealism, considering bourgeois ideology as an original phenomenon, based on the pursuit of Truth. Its ambivalence warns us not to be duped. Every thought unfolds not among Ideas, but on earth, and it discloses a practice; bourgeois thought is so muddled because there is a contradiction between the practice and its disclosure.

The first of their difficulties comes from the very nature of thought; thought wants to bite into things and claims to be universal. However, one knows to what unacceptable conclusions the apprehension of reality in the universal mode leads: to no more distinctions between men, to a horrible leveling. The right-wing ideologist dissociates the two demands he cannot satisfy together. A realist, he will characterize thought by the nature of the object thought and by that of the thinking subject. The Mediterranean man, for example, thinks the Mediterranean reality concretely and singularly. Symmetrically, when he aims at universality, he makes his object unreal and he makes a pure Idea out of it. He talks of Man to everyone, in the name of everyone, but of an abstract Man such as he has concocted. The schema suggested by this dissociation is the following: at the core of the empirical given there is a substance-value, and Ideas-Values reign above the given. Situating itself sometimes on one plane and sometimes on another, bourgeois thought jumps from the real to the universal and from the universal to the real without ever reuniting them. Between the two there is a Dedekind cut, in the mathematical sense of the word, and like the irrational number, the world of men remains outside of either area: it has no legitimate existence.

The superposition over the subterranean world of "substantial forms" and of a heaven where the One reigns, reflects another hesitation on the part of the right: it defends *this* civilization in the name of truths and eternal values. Historical pluralism is not easily compatible with Platonic monism.

It is on the ethical plane that this dualism is the most interesting. The right wing is both naturalist and artificialist. There is, according to it, a human nature, and the privileged are elevated above the species by natural selection. Yet, the distinctive feature of the Elite is to impose an order founded on artifice: the "universal riot" is foiled by ideas, ceremonies, ethical and aesthetic laws. This work is very different from a practice—it is a question of regulating, not creating, and of maintaining a static order, not progressing. Ethics and art aim at perpetuating the past, not surpassing the present toward the future. Some mystery comes into these operations. How does one explain the change from vital values to spiritual values? How can one be *naturally* endowed with a singular aptitude for grasping the Transcendent and making it come down to earth through art and artifice? No system answers this question. What is certain is that artificialism, through which a transcendence is evoked, appears as necessity because of human nature's perversity. We have often pointed out the contrast between the right-wing's aesthetico-mystical fervor and its bitter cynicism. It hunts down the illusions that men build up about themselves in this empirical world, denouncing their egoism and treating their projects frivolously. However, casualness becomes gravity as soon as the Elite talks about itself and the order it supports. The bourgeoisie believes in Clément Vautel and is stirred by Déroulède.[103] It draws the darkest portraits of men in order to demonstrate the necessity of a God that it conceives in its own image.

When bourgeois thought tries to understand society, it is also torn by two opposing tendencies. It readily uses organicist comparisons because it sees society as synthetic wholes. It assumes the existence of forms that are decipherable by a syncretic intuition and whose truth prevails over that of their elements. Yet, it insists upon the discontinuity of History; between its various forms there are no relationships or only vague analogies. Individuals are isolated as if they were atoms, each one closed on itself and cut off from all the others. Simone Weil—whose thought was excessively exploited by the right even though she frequently attacked the bourgeoisie—often stressed this attitude of the bourgeois which consists in denying relations.[104] It is, she says, because he flees responsibility. In turn, atomism allows one to fail to recognize the responsibilities that the capitalist system has with regard to the condition of those it disadvantages. They appear not as victims of the regime, but as the playthings of chance, sometimes even as the very creators of their own ills. The right wants to ignore statistical laws, opposing them to the individual's abstract odds, and considering that the exception refutes the norm even if its singularity is normally predictable. One ticket out of a hundred wins the lottery. From this the right concludes that everyone can win, instead of acknowledging that ninety-nine must necessarily lose. The notion of merit reinforces the notion of chance: if he is intelligent and hard working, the worker's son will rise above his class. But even presupposing that it is well founded, the idea of a competition opened to thousands of individuals and in which only the worthiest succeeds implies the necessity of thousands of failures. One of the greatest mystifications of liberalism is to take the contingency of individual cases, globally subject to statistical necessity, as the measure of authentic freedom. The advantage of this lie is that by making others responsible for their own lot, I am in the right to wash my hands of the matter. Another way of fleeing responsibility would be to consider oneself as predetermined. However the bourgeois is keen on thinking of himself as supremely free, and only individualistic atomism allows him to reconcile freedom with irresponsibility. The man of the left, on the contrary, thinks of himself as both conditioned and responsible.

All the contradictions of bourgeois thought come down to a single one: it is impossible for the bourgeoisie to assume its practical attitude in thought.* Such is the curse that weighs on its ideology. The proletariat recognizes its particularity as a class, but it works towards its destruction, and in doing this, reveals itself as a universal class. The bourgeoisie strives in practice to maintain its particularity. In order to posit itself as universal, it is obliged to deny this in thought thereby turning its back on reality. Bourgeois ideologists find themselves in conflict with the active members of their class, because they have to disguise with illusions and not express the truth lived by the latter. In practice, the bourgeoisie is committed to the class struggle. It defends, even imposes a politics, and it takes action. Its ideologists preach catastrophism, quietism, skepticism, and a philosophy of immanence that condemns any project. The bourgeoisie believes in science, yet its ideologists contest it. The bourgeois are keenly interested in their empirical exis-

---

* This is the reason that the bourgeoisie always endeavors to confuse the issue and refuse this decision of thought, which is judgment. For the bourgeoisie, Berl noted, "Reflection is no longer that which allows us to judge, but that which allows us to postpone judgment. Faced with a problem, the first issue is the question of finding a bias on which to deviate from the living center where this problem consists of a yes or a no."

tence, yet their moralists despise it in favor of the Transcendent, and they exalt death. The bourgeoisie wishes to have mirrors made so that it can gaze upon itself, but it demands that they be distorting mirrors.

The bourgeois illusionist is not unaware that he distorts the truth of his class. He is annoyed with it for refuting in practice the myths he fabricates for it and knows that it is suspicious of him. His claims brutally dismissed by the opposing class that sees in him nothing but an epiphenomenon, he is doomed to a solitude which he raises to the status of a system. It is to him that the idea of resentment applies. His aestheticism, skepticism, and religiosity are directed against men. He forbids himself from hating them only by forcing himself to hold them in contempt. Gloomy or arrogant, he is the man of refusal; his real certitudes are all negative. He says no to the "modern world," no to the future, that is to say, to the living movement of the world, yet he knows that the world will prevail over him. He is afraid: what is he to expect from these men of tomorrow whose opponent he has become? He arms himself against them with abstract principles: all human life must be respected; respect mine! He speaks in the name of the universal because he dares not speak in his own name, or—like Thierry Maulnier in *La maison de la nuit*—he urges them to have pity as a precaution. However, he is doubtful of being heard. Thus, his supreme resource is to sweep all of humanity along with him into death. The bourgeoisie wants to survive, but its ideologists, knowing themselves to be condemned, foretell universal ruin. Today, the expression "bourgeois ideology" no longer refers to anything positive. The bourgeoisie still exists, but its catastrophist and empty thought is nothing but a counter-thought.

NOTES

The three essays appearing in the *Privilèges* volume ("Must We Burn Sade?" "Right-Wing Thought Today," and "Merleau-Ponty and Pseudo-Sartreanism") were preceded by a foreword written by Simone de Beauvoir. This foreword, translated by Kim Allen Gleed, Marilyn Gaddis Rose, and Virginia Preston, can be found in the notes following the "Must We Burn Sade?" essay in this volume.

1. Oswald Spengler (1880–1936) was an ardent German nationalist, known for his contribution to philosophy of history. He argued, in *The Decline of the West* (1919–22) that history has been marked by a series of great cultures, each of which sprang into being, flowered, and then declined, in accord with a predetermined historical destiny. His ideas were used as a justification for German expansionism. He is sometimes accused of having helped prepare the way intellectually for fascism, although he actually opposed Hitler's rise; James

Burnham (1905–87) was an American-born Marxist who was active in the U.S. labor movement in the 1930s. He edited the Trotskyist *The New Intellectual*. After undergoing a dramatic change of heart, he later wrote works critical of Marxism and communism. These include *The Managerial Revolution* (1941) and *The Machiavellians* (1943). In the former, he argued that the nature of capitalism had changed, so that revolution is no longer appropriate; Karl (Theodor) Jaspers (1883–1969) was a German philosopher in the Christian existentialist tradition. Like Kierkegaard, he argued that attempts at total intellectual systemization must fail and that we require a leap of faith that goes beyond reason. He taught psychiatry and philosophy at the University of Heidelberg and philosophy at the University of Basel in Switzerland. His main work is *Philosophie*, 3 vols. (1932).

2. André Malraux (1901–76) was a French novelist, politician, and art critic. Prominent in antifascist activities in the 1930s, he also fought on the Republican side in the Spanish Civil War and was in the French Resistance during World War II. By the late 1940s his political views shifted, and he served as a minister in Gaullist governments. In the prewar period he wrote politically engaged novels, including *La condition humaine* (The Human Condition, or *Man's Fate*) (1933) and *L'espoir* (Hope, or *Man's Hope*) (1937), and he later wrote extensively on art. Simone de Beauvoir often quoted from memory; this passage is slightly paraphrased from Malraux's *Les conquérants* (Paris: Grasset, 1928), translated as *The Conquerors* by S. Becker (Chicago: University of Chicago Press, 1992), 188.

3. Alfred Fabre-Luce (1899–1983) was a French writer and journalist.

4. Roger Caillois (1913–78) was a French sociologist, poet, literary critic, and essayist. In the 1930s, he was linked briefly with the surrealists, and engaged in left antifascist activities. He later attacked communism as a form of imperialism in *Description du marxisme* (Description of Marxism) (1950); *Liberté de l'esprit* was a journal edited by Claude Mauriac and published monthly from February 1949 to June/July 1953.

5. Alexis Carrel (1873–1944) was a French physiologist, surgeon, philosopher, and winner of the 1912 Nobel Prize in Physiology or Medicine. In 1941, he created the *Fondation pour l'étude des problèmes humains* (Foundation for the Study of Human Problems). His aim was to demonstrate the interdependence of physical and psychical phenomena in order to react against the excesses of civilization and medicine that, according to him, distorted human nature.

6. Jacques Soustelle (1912–90) was a French politician and strong supporter of de Gaulle. However, as Governor-General of Algeria he later opposed de Gaulle's policy of Algerian independence. Soustelle was also an avid researcher of the Aztec culture, and he published twelve books on the subject.

7. Rémy Roure (1885–1966) was a French journalist and author of the 1951 editorial in the first issue of *Preuves*, an anti-Soviet monthly published by the Congress for Cultural Freedom. See Pierre Grémion, *"Preuves* dans le Paris de guerre froide" (*Preuves* in Paris during the Cold War), in *Vingtième siècle: revue d'histoire* (Twentieth Century Review of History) 13 (January–March 1987): 63–82.

8. Jules Romains (pen name of Louis Farigoule) (1885–1972) was a French novelist, dramatist, poet, and member of the Académie Française. He was particularly known for his *roman-fleuve*, *Les hommes de bonne volonté* (Men of Good Will) (1932–47).

9. Emmanuel Mounier (1905–50) was a French thinker and leading progressive Catholic philosopher of the 1930s and 1940s. Author of *Traité de caractère* (Treatise on Character)

(1946), his longing for justice and his Christian faith combined in "Personalism," a movement oriented by its focus on the free development of individual human potential. He founded the journal *Esprit* (Spirit) in 1932. In the postwar period *Esprit* advocated dialogue with the communists and anticolonialism, quite often agreeing with positions put forward in *Les temps modernes*. His essay, *La petite peur du XXe siècle* (Small Fear of the Twentieth Century) (Paris: Les Éditions du Seuil), was published in 1959.

10. Vicomte François René de Chateaubriand (1768–1848) was a prominent man of letters, statesman, and apologist for Christianity. Often read as a precursor of romanticism, he was the author of *Le génie du Christianisme* (The Genius of Christianity) (1802) and *Mémoires d'outre-tombe* (Memoirs from beyond the Grave) (1847).

11. Friedrich Nietzsche (1844–1900) was a German existentialist philosopher who challenged the foundations of traditional morality and Christianity.

12. Ludwig Klages (1872–1956) was a German physiologist and philosopher, and the leading figure in the field of characterology; Alfred Weber (1868–1958), a German economist and sociologist, was a leader in intellectual resistance to Hitlerism in Nazi Germany.

13. Jaspers's original *Vom Ursprung und Ziel der Geschichte* (1949) was translated into French as *Origine et sens de l'histoire* by Hélène Naef and Wolfgang Achterberg (Paris: Plon, 1954). We have translated the French as Beauvoir quotes it in her text. For a published English translation of the German original, see *The Origin and Goal of History*, trans. Michael Bullock (New Haven: Yale University Press, 1953).

14. Paul Valéry (1871–1944) was a major French poet, essayist, and thinker who was influential in the development of symbolist and postsymbolist schools of poetry. His poetry generally focused upon "inner" experience, and is sometimes said to have strong affinities with phenomenology. He wrote also on philosophy and language. Beauvoir may be referring to his 1931 essay, *Regards sur le monde actuel* (A Glance at Today's World) (Paris: Gallimard, 1988).

15. Pierre Drieu la Rochelle (1893–1945) was a French novelist and essayist of the interwar period. Initially involved with the surrealists, he moved rapidly to the right, experiencing a "conversion" to fascism in 1934 and embracing a cult of action. He was best known for his semiautobiographical novel, *Gilles* (written in 1939) (Paris: Gallimard, 1942), which celebrates the possibility of purification through war. A Nazi collaborator, he committed suicide to escape the justice of the Liberation.

16. See Spengler, *The Decline of the West* (1922), abridged English edition prepared by Arthur Helps from the translation by Charles Francis Atkinson, ed. Helmut Werner (New York: Oxford University Press, 1991), 415.

17. The *Parti Populaire Français* (PPF) (French Popular Party) was a fascist political party led by Jacques Doriot before and during World War II. It is generally regarded as the farthest to the right, most pro-Nazi, of France's collaborationist parties.

18. Joseph de Maistre (1755–1821) was a French writer and diplomat. He was violently opposed to the French Revolution and its doctrine of individual rights and is considered a foundational thinker in conservative thought. He wrote *Considérations sur la France* (Considerations on France) (1797); Louis vicomte de Bonald (1754–1840) was a French Catholic philosopher and politician who was opposed to democratic spirit and enlightenment rationalism in any form. His most important works are *Théorie du pouvoir politique et religieux* (Theory of Political and Religious Power) (1796) and *La législation primitive* (Primitive Legislation) (1802).

19. Charles Maurras (1868–1952) founded the right-wing organization "Action Française" in 1899. He was a leader of the French intellectual right, from the Dreyfus Affair until the 1940s. His politics were clerical, anti-Semitic, antirepublican, and highly nationalistic. He actively supported the Vichy regime during the war and was sentenced to life imprisonment afterward.

20. *Le grand schisme* (Paris: Gallimard, 1948) was written by Raymond Aron (1905–83), who was an eminent French liberal sociologist and journalist and friend of Sartre and Beauvoir in the late 1920s. He wrote for the Resistance papers *France libre* and *Combat* during the war. After the war he was briefly on the editorial board of *Les temps modernes*, but he left because of political disagreements and became a vigorous critic of Marxism. He was later renowned for his polemics against left-wing intellectuals, notably Sartre, in such works as *L'opium des intellectuels* (*The Opium of Intellectuals*) (1955) and *Marxismes imaginaires* (Imaginary Marxisms) (1970). He also produced major works of sociological theory.

21. Denis de Rougemont (1906–85) was a writer and cultural historian. Born in Switzerland, he moved to Paris where he participated in founding the "Personalist" reviews, *Esprit* and *Ordre nouveau* (New Order) and authored *L'amour et l'Occident* (*Love in the Western World*) (1938). In Geneva, he founded the Center of European Culture and was a staunch proponent of European federalism.

22. Léon Werth (1877–1955) was a French novelist and author of a pacifist novel *Clavel soldat* (Soldier Clavel) (1919).

23. Paul Nizan (1905–40) was a militant French Communist, journalist, and writer. At the *Ecole Normale*, he became Sartre's close friend. Before being killed in the war, Nizan authored *Aden, Arabie* (1931), *Les chiens de garde* (The Watch Dogs) (1932), *Antoine Bloyé* (1933), and *La conspiration* (*The Conspiracy*) (1938).

24. See Drieu la Rochelle, *Gilles*, 338.

25. The quote is from the first volume of *The German Ideology* (written in 1845 and first published in 1932 by the Marx-Engels Institute in Moscow) by Karl Marx and Friedrich Engels.

26. Beauvoir often quoted from memory; this quote has been published in English as follows: "inside this class one part appears as the thinkers of the class (its active, conceptive ideologists, who make the perfecting of the illusion of the class about itself their chief source of livelihood)," from Karl Marx and Friedrich Engels, *The German Ideology*, in Robert C. Tucker, ed. *The Marx-Engels Reader* (New York: Norton, 1978), 173.

27. See the *Communist Manifesto* (first published in 1848 by the German Workers' Educational Society in London), ch. 1, where Marx writes of "bourgeois ideologists, who have raised themselves to the level of comprehending theoretically the historical movement as a whole."

28. *Stendhal* (1783–1842) was the pseudonym of Marie-Henri Beyle, a French writer who played a major role in the development of the modern novel. See Beauvoir's chapter on Stendahl in *The Second Sex*. This quote is paraphrased from *Le rouge et le noir* (*The Red and the Black*) (Paris: Levasseur, 1830).

29. Francisco Franco (1892–1975) was a Spanish military general who led the Nationalists against the Popular Front government in Spain during the Spanish Civil War; as head of state from 1936 until his death he established a right-wing authoritarian regime and used severe measures to suppress opposition; António de Oliveira Salazar (1889–1970) served as the prime minister of Portugal from 1932 to 1968. He founded and led the Estado Novo (New

State), the authoritarian, right-wing government that presided over and controlled Portugal from 1932 to 1974.

30. See *Gilles* (Paris: Gallimard, 1942), 338.

31. Thierry Maulnier (pen name of Jacques Talagrand) (1909–88) was a French writer and journalist, and prominent right-wing intellectual. Influenced by Maurras, he was active in the movement "Action Française," and claimed to elaborate a noncapitalist alternative to communism on the basis of nationalism as a unifying force. He was involved with the journals of the intellectual right: *Preuves* and *La table ronde*. His political essays include: *La crise est dans l'homme* (The Crisis Is in Man) (1932), *Mythes socialistes* (Socialist Myths) (1936), and *Au-delà du nationalisme* (Beyond Nationalism) (1938), and (in the postwar period) *Violence et conscience* (Violence and Conscience) (1945) and *La face de Méduse du communisme* (The Medusa Face of Communism) (1952). Merleau-Ponty published a critique of his work in *Sense and Non-Sense* (1948).

32. Brice Parain (1897–1971) was a French philosopher of language. He wrote *Recherches sur la nature et les fonctions du language* (Research on the Nature and Functions of Language) (1942), *Embarras du choix* (So Many Choices) (1947), and *Sur la dialectique* (On Dialectics) (1953). He argued that, since language is the source of error and of creativity, it engages man's responsibility.

33. Max Scheler (1874–1928) was a German philosopher, influenced by Husserl's phenomenology. Much of his work focuses on the phenomenology of emotions. *The Nature of Sympathy* (1913) is one of his best known works.

34. This quote appears as a footnote in Scheler's *Ressentiment* (1912), trans. William H. Holdheim (New York: Noonday, 1973), where he attributes the idea to Walther Rathenau (1867–1922), who was a German industrialist, banker, intellectual, and politician, of Jewish origin. During the Weimar period, Rathenau preached that German greatness should be attained through economic, not military, means. He wrote that the idea of justice is based on envy in his *Reflexionen* (Leipzig: Hirzel, 1908).

35. Max Eastman (1883–1969) was an American political thinker and activist who became acquainted with Leon Trotsky, served as his literary agent in the U.S., and translated some of his works into English, including *The Revolution Betrayed*. The original English title of the book Beauvoir refers to here is *Marx and Lenin: The Science of Revolution*. Eastman wrote extensively on Russia and socialism, especially on what he saw as the failure of the Russian Revolution. His books include *The End of Socialism in Russia* (1937) and *Reflections on the Failure of Socialism* (1955); Sigmund Freud (1856–1939) was an Austrian neurologist and founder of psychoanalysis.

36. Henri (Hendryk) de Man (1885–1953) was a Belgian socialist writer and politician. In *Au-delà du marxisme* (1927), he criticized Marxism as deterministic and argued for a non-Marxian socialism based instead on a psychological interpretation of the worker's movement; Alfred Adler (1870–1937) was an Austrian medical doctor, psychologist, and cofounder, with Freud, of the psychoanalytic movement. He later formed an independent school of psychotherapy and personality theory. His most famous concept is the inferiority complex.

37. Arnold (Joseph) Toynbee (1889–1975) was a British historian whose twelve-volume *A Study of History* (1934–54) argued for recurring patterns in history: each of twenty-one civilizations have passed through similar stages of growth, breakdown, and dissolution.

38. Jules Monnerot (1909–95) was a prominent French sociologist in the postwar period, and an ardent critic of Marxism and communism. He was the author of numerous books, including *Sociologie de communisme* (Sociology of Communism) (1949) and *La guerre en question* (1951). He was a politically active Gaullist in the early 1950s.

39. From Burnham, *The Struggle for the World* (New York: John Day, 1947).

40. "Big Business," "Public Relations," and "Human Engineering" are in English in the original.

41. Georges Eugène Sorel (1847–1922) was a French philosopher and theorist of revolutionary syndicalism who originated an influential notion of the power of myth in people's lives.

42. This quote is from Burnham, *The Machiavellians: Defenders of Freedom* (New York: John Day, 1943); Vilfredo Pareto (1848–1923) was a prominent Italian economist and sociologist known for his application of mathematics to economic analysis and for his theory of the "circulation of elites." He argued in *The Mind and Society* (1935) that, because society will always be composed of an elite and a mass, the establishment of socialism will merely produce a new elite.

43. Stanislas Fumet (1896–1983) was a French Catholic writer and prolific critic of art and literature. Founder of the liberal Catholic review, *Temps présent* (Present Time) and (after World War II) of the Catholic publishing house, Desclée de Brouwer; Nikolai Alexandrovich Berdyaev (1874–1948) was a Russian religious and political philosopher. A Christian existentialist, Berdyaev was expelled from Bolshevik Russia in 1922 and lived in exile in France until his death.

44. Arthur Koestler (1905–83) was a Hungarian exile, living in Britain. After supporting communism in the 1930s, he became its resolute critic, notably in his book *Darkness at Noon* (1940). Merleau-Ponty criticized Koestler at length in *Humanism and Terror* (Paris: Gallimard, 1947).

45. Henri Bergson (1859–1941) was the leading French philosopher in the early twentieth century, winning the Nobel Prize for literature in 1927. He was an important early philosophical influence on Beauvoir, whose 1926 diary quotes at length from his *Essai sur les données immédiates de la conscience* (*Time and Free Will*) (Paris: Alcan, 1889). This quote is from his *Matière et Mémoire* (*Matter and Memory*) (Paris: Les Presses Universitaires, 1896), trans. N. M. Paul and W. S. Palmer (New York: Zone Books, 1990).

46. Hippolyte Adolphe Taine (1828–93) was a French critic and historian and a major figure in mid-nineteenth-century positivism, and deeply anticlerical and antiromantic. His reputation as a leading critic of spiritualism was made with *Les philosophes français du XIXième siècle* (French Philosophers of the Nineteenth Century) (1857).

47. Clément Vautel (1875–1974) was a popular French novelist; Louis-Ferdinand Céline was the pen name of the influential and controversial French writer, Louis-Ferdinand Destouches (1894–1961); Paul Léautaud (1872–1956) was a French writer who used the pen name, Maurice Boissard, in many of his works.

48. Donatien Alphonse François, Marquis de Sade (1740–1814) was a French aristocrat, revolutionary, and writer best known for his erotic novels, which combined philosophical discourse with pornographic depictions of sexual fantasies with an emphasis on violence, criminality, and blasphemy against the Catholic Church. He was a proponent of extreme freedom, unrestrained by morality, religion, or law. His novel, *Juliette*, published 1797–1801 as *Histoire de Juliette ou les prospérités du vice* (*Juliette, or Vice Amply Rewarded*), is the sequel to his novel, *Justine ou les malheurs de la vertu* (*Justine, or Good Conduct Well-Chastised*).

49. Hyacinthe Antoine de Gasquet (1707–92), also known as Father Hyacinthe of the Lorgues Commune, was strongly opposed to the practice of usury and wrote *L'usure démasquée* (Usury Unmasked) in 1766.

50. Paul (Louis-Charles-Marie) Claudel (1868–1955) was a prominent and prolific French poet and playwright, known for his role in the revival of poetic drama in France, and for poetry in the "Christian symbolist" tradition.

51. Joseph Arthur, comte de Gobineau (1816–82) was a French diplomat and man of letters best known for his theory of inequality between the races and attribution of the decline of civilization to racial miscegenation, in his *Essai sur l'inégalité des races humaines* (Essay on the Inequality of Human Races) (1853–55).

52. Beauvoir may be paraphrasing a passage from Nietzsche's *Thus Spoke Zarathustra* (1883–85), published in *Basic Writings of Nietzsche*, trans. Walter Kaufmann (New York: Random House Modern Library, 2000), in which Nietzsche compares people with sand grains as being "frank, honest and kind to one another."

53. From Nietzsche's essay *On the Use and Abuse of History for Life*, which was published with three other essays in *Untimely Meditations* (Leipzig: Fritzsch, 1874), trans. R. J. Hollingdale (Cambridge University Press, 1997), and more recently translated as *Unfashionable Observations* by Richard T. Gray (Palo Alto: Stanford University Press, 1998).

54. From *The Decline of the West* (1922), the unabridged edition, which has been published in the United States in two volumes, *Form and Actuality* (New York: Knopf, 1926) and *Perspectives of World History* (New York: Knopf, 1928), both translated by Charles Francis Atkinson. Also available online at http://www.archive.org/details/Decline-Of-The-West-Oswald-Spengler (accessed October 21, 2011).

55. From Burnham, *The Struggle for the World* (New York: John Day, 1947).

56. Spengler, *The Decline of the West*.

57. The quote is from Toynbee's *A Study of History, Volume 1: Introduction; The Geneses of Civilizations* (New York: Oxford University Press, 1934).

58. Raymond Abellio (pen name of Georges Soulès) (1907–86) was a French writer, active in socialist politics before the war, but suspected of Nazi sympathies during it. He wrote semiautobiographical novels portraying his journey from the Left to the Right: *Heureux les pacifiques* (Happy Are the Pacifists) (1946) and *Les yeux d'Ezéchiel sont ouvertes* (Ezekiel's Eyes Are Open) (1949). He also wrote on esoteric religions.

59. René Guénon (1886–1951) was a French philosopher and orientalist. His influential *Crise du monde moderne* (*The Crisis of the Modern World*) (1827) argued that the West, unlike the East, had lost its spiritual tradition. His ideas were influential in the development of theories of "spiritual" fascism.

60. Stephen Spender (1909–95) was a British leftist intellectual, poet, and critic. He was coeditor of the magazines *Horizon* (1939–41) and *Encounter* (1953–57). He fought in the International Brigades in the Spanish Civil War.

61. Mircea Eliade (1907–86) was a Rumanian-born philosopher of comparative religion and man of letters who taught at the Sorbonne in the late 1940s. Distinguished for his research in the symbolic languages used by various religious traditions, he wrote *Technique du yoga* (Yoga Technique) (1948), *Traité d'histoire des religions* (Treatise on the History of Religions) (1949), and *Mythes, rêves et mystères* (*Myths, Dreams, and Mysteries*) (1957).

62. From René Descartes, *Discourse on the Method* (1637), available online in English at http://www.gutenberg.org/ebooks/59 (accessed October 21, 2011).

63. This is a play on words between *connaissance* (knowledge or consciousness) and *co-naissance* (co-birth or be born with).

64. Spengler, *The Decline of the West.*

65. Maurice Barrès (1862–1923) was a French novelist and politician of the Right, known especially for his anti-Dreyfusard and anti-Semitic sentiments. A staunch French nationalist, he advocated the return of Alsace-Lorraine to France and wrote novels on nationalist themes.

66. Spengler, *The Decline of the West.*

67. René Daumal (1908–44) was a French poet and spiritualist writer who collaborated in the *Cahiers de pataphysique* (Pataphysics Notebooks). Influenced by the mystic, Gurdjieff, he became a devotee of Eastern spiritualism. He was best know for *La grande beuverie (A Night of Serious Drinking)* (1938), and for his volumes of poetry; George Ivanovitch Gurdjieff's original name was George S. Georgiades (1877(?)–1949). He was a Greco-Armenian mystic and philosopher who founded an influential quasireligious movement based on Eastern principles. His Institute for the Harmonious Development of Man, founded in 1922, was based near Paris.

68. Spengler, *The Decline of the West.*

69. Jean Pouillon, "Staline: catoblépas ou phénix?" (Stalin: Catoblepas or Phoenix?) *Les temps modernes* 103 (June 1954): 2232–47.

70. Emile Boutroux (1845–1921) was a French philosopher who worked primarily in the area of philosophy of science, notably on issues of necessity and contingency. He was best known for *De la contingence des lois de la nature (The Contingency of the Laws of Nature)* (1874). Although the source of this particular quote has not been identified, and could be Beauvoir's summary or paraphrase of Boutroux's ideas, Boutroux wrote on this topic in several of his works, including *Philosophy and War*, trans. Fred Rothwell (London: Constable and Company, 1916) and *L'idée de liberté en France et en Allemagne* (The Idea of Freedom in France and in Germany) (Paris: Foi et Vie, 1916).

71. *L'Islam du XXe siècle* is the first part of *La sociologie du communisme* by Jules Monnerot.

72. Jean Lartéguy, born Jean Pierre Lucien Osty (1920–2011) was a former secretary to Jean-Paul Sartre. As a journalist he reported on many late-twentieth-century wars (including in Palestine, Korea, Algeria, and Vietnam), and also wrote novels set in war situations.

73. Jacques Doriot (1898–1945) was a French politician, initially as General Secretary of the Communist Youth and a member of the Central Committee of the French Communist Party. However, he was excluded from the Party in 1936 when he protested against Soviet influence in it. He then founded the fascist-oriented PPF (*Parti Populaire Français*). During the Occupation, he collaborated with the Germans.

74. From Jaspers, *Man in the Modern Age* (1931), trans. E. Paul and C. Paul (London: Routledge, 1933).

75. Michel Braspart, pseudonym of Roland Laudenbach, (1921–91), was a French writer, journalist, literary critic, and filmmaker. He founded the French publishing house, La Table Ronde, in 1944, and the journal, *La revue de la table ronde* (The Round Table Review), in 1948; Ernst Jünger (1895–1998) was a conservative, militarist German writer, regarded by many as one of Germany's greatest modern writers.

76. Claude Elsen, pseudonym of Gaston Derycke, was a right-wing Belgian writer, translator, and literary critic, condemned in Belgium as a Nazi collaborator during World War II. See

"Reconciling France: Jean Paulhan and the 'Nouvelle Revue Française,' 1953," by Martyn Cornick and Christopher Flood, *South Central Review* 17:4 (Winter 2000): 26–44.

77. Jacques Laurent-Cély (1919–2000) was a French journalist, novelist, and essayist. A militant royalist in his youth, he was later associated with the right-wing literary movement called the Hussards. He founded the literary journal, *La Parisienne*, in 1952.

78. From Denis de Rougemont, *Love in the Western World* (1939), trans. Montgomery Belgion (New York: Harcourt, 1939) and reprinted in 1983 by Princeton University Press.

79. Benedict de Spinoza (1632–77), a Dutch-Jewish philosopher, was the foremost exponent of seventeenth-century rationalism.

80. Saint-John Perse, (pen name of Alexis Léger) (1887–1975) was a French poet and diplomat who went into exile and was stripped of French nationality by the Vichy regime. He won the Nobel prize for literature in 1960. His *Anabase* (1924) was translated into English as *Anabasis* by T. S. Eliot.

81. Jean Nicolas Arthur Rimbaud (1854–91) was a French poet who influenced modern literature, music and art; Stéphane Mallarmé (1842–98), pseudonym for Étienne Mallarmé, was a French symbolist poet and critic whose work inspired artistic movements including Dadaism, Surrealism, and Futurism.

82. Marie-Madeleine Pioche de La Vergne, comtesse de La Fayette (1634–93), better known as Madame de Lafayette, was a French writer, the author of *La princesse de Clèves* (*The Princess of Cleves*), one of the earliest novels.

83. Henry (Marie-Joseph-Millon) Montherlant (1896–1972) was a French novelist and dramatist. Some of his prewar novels celebrate war as the source of virility, heroism, and fraternity, notably *Le songe* (*The Dream*) (1922) and *Les olympiques* (The Olympics) (1924). A noted misogynist, he turned to drama after the war, focusing in his plays on the irrationality of human action.

84. This phrase, which is analogous to the racist Jim Crow policy of "separate but equal" treatment of Blacks condemned by Beauvoir, was made famous by Ernest Legouvé (1807–1903), an influential French dramatist and essayist, in a series of lectures on the history of women beginning in 1848, in which he argued for women's emancipation based on their distinctive physiological, mental, and emotional differences from men, and on the dignity of their social role as mothers. See Karen Offen's "Ernest Legouvé and the Doctrine of 'Equality in Difference' for Women: A Case Study of Male Feminism in Nineteenth-Century French Thought," in *Journal of Modern History* 58:2 (June 1986): 452–84.

85. Guido Piovene (1907–74) was a prominent Italian journalist and novelist.

86. Bernard Pingaud (1923–) is a French novelist and literary critic who wrote on Sartre and Camus, among others, and collaborated with *Les temps modernes* for a time.

87. Claude Mauriac (1914–96) was the son of François Mauriac. He was a film critic for *Le figaro littéraire* (The Literary Figaro); author of critical essays on Marcel Proust, André Breton, his own father, André Gide, and others; and a great believer in the *nouveau roman* and the importance of form, as demonstrated in his own numerous novels.

88. Ramon Fernandez (1894–1944) was an esteemed literary critic who became, from 1936 to 1943, the self-appointed "minister of culture" for a fascist populist movement led by Jacques Doriot.

89. Roger Nimier (1925–62) was a French writer. Although he dedicated his first novel to Sartre, he was central to a group of young right-wing intellectuals who opposed existentialism. The group, who called themselves "les hussards" (the hussars), taking their name from

his novel, *Le hussard bleu* (*The Blue Hussar*) (1950), criticized the earnestness associated with the continuing Resistance ethos in postwar France, and insisted that the Right be playful and do as one pleases.

90. Jacques Chardonne (pen name of Jacques Boutelleau) (1884–1968) was a French writer. He was one of the heirs of the Cognac house, and co-owner of the Stock publishing house. He authored novels about intimate relationships, and many essays. He was briefly imprisoned after World War II for his compromises with the Vichy regime. Here Beauvoir refers to his *Lettres à Roger Nimier* (1952), an essay in fictional letter form, in which Chardonne expressed nostalgia for a return to a world in harmony with nature.

91. Max Weber (1864–1920) was a German sociologist and philosopher of history, who is regarded as one of the founders of the discipline of sociology. His work included the study of power, religion, and economy, among other topics. His major work was translated into French in 1922 as *Economie et société* (Economy and Society).

92. Henri Bordeaux (1870–1963) was a prolific and popular French novelist and essayist.

93. Pierre Costals and Solange Dandillot are characters in the novel, *Les jeunes filles* by Henri de Montherlant.

94. Jean-Pierre Maxence, pseudonym of Pierre Godmé (1906–56), was a conservative French writer and journalist.

95. Dionys Mascolo (1916–97) was a French writer and political activist. Disillusioned with Communism following Stalin's purges in Hungary, he responded by writing *Le communisme* (1953), for which he was condemned as a "revisionist" by the party.

96. Emmanuel Berl (1892–1976) was a French writer and journalist who analyzed the spiritual decadence of the bourgeoisie, notably in *Mort de la pensée bourgeoise* (1929). After World War II, he wrote and gave radio broadcasts advocating the end of colonialism.

97. Charles Ferdinand Ramuz (1878–1947) was a Swiss writer and poet. This quote is from his *What Is Man*, trans. Gouverneur Paulding (New York: Pantheon Books, 1948).

98. Jacques-Henri Bernardin de Saint-Pierre (1737–1814) was a French writer and disciple of Rousseau; he refers to the melon in his novel, *Paul et Virginie* (Paul and Virginia): "God made the melon with ribs to show that it was to be sectioned and eaten by the family." (Paris: Garnier, 1895), 44–45, cited in "*Un coeur simple* [A Simple Heart] as an Ironic Reply to Bernardin de Saint-Pierre," by English Showalter Jr., *The French Review* 40:1 (October 1966): 47–55.

99. Sturel and Saint-Phlin are two characters in Maurice Barrès's 1900 novel, *L'appel au soldat* (The Soldier's Call), the second volume of the *Roman de l'énergie nationale* (A Novel about National Energy) trilogy recounting the adventures of seven young men from Lorraine who set out to seek their fortune in Paris.

100. Jean Giono (1895–1970) was a French author renowned for his works of fiction set in the Provence region of France.

101. This quote is from Nietzsche, *Twilight of the Idols* (1889), trans. Duncan Large (New York: Oxford University Press, 1998). This and the other Nietzsche quotes in this paragraph are given in Jaspers, *Nietzsche: An Introduction to the Understanding of His Philosophical Activity* (1935), trans. Charles F. Wallraff and Frederick J. Schmitz (Tuscon: The University of Arizona Press, 1965), which perhaps Beauvoir had read since it had been published in French in 1950 as *Nietzsche: introduction à sa philosophie* (Paris: Gallimard).

102. "Vanity of vanities. All is vanity!" *Ecclesiastes* 1:2; "You are dust, and to dust you shall return." *Genesis* 3:19 (*The Holy Bible*, Revised Standard Edition).

103. Paul Déroulède (1846–1914) was a French poet, dramatic actor, novelist, and militant nationalist.

104. Simone Weil (1909–43) was a French philosopher. As an active socialist and Catholic mystic, she chose to live among the poor and work in a factory. Her posthumous book based on these experiences, *La condition ouvrière* (The Condition of the Workers), was published in 1951. Other works include *La pesanteur et la grâce* (*Gravity and Grace*) (1947) and *L'enracinement* (*The Need for Roots*) (1949).

4

Merleau-Ponty and Pseudo-Sartreanism

INTRODUCTION

by William Wilkerson

Simone de Beauvoir, Jean-Paul Sartre, and Maurice Merleau-Ponty had a long and complex history together. All three met as students in the late 1920s. Beauvoir's initial descriptions in her diary of "Ponti"—as she refers to him—were laudatory, happy, and show an affection bordering on love: "Ponti, for whom my sympathy has become profound affection."[1] The friendship between Merleau-Ponty and Sartre was initially cooler, as he (along with Beauvoir) rejected the Catholicism to which the young Merleau-Ponty clung. Merleau-Ponty would eventually court Beauvoir's friend Elizabeth Mabille, her beloved Zaza, but the courtship fell apart when the girl's parents intervened, producing a crisis that Beauvoir believed led to the girl's death. This episode was not only a great early tragedy in Beauvoir's life, but led both Sartre and Beauvoir to view Merleau-Ponty as too hesitant and too trusting in "Catholic pieties."[2]

After school, the three stayed in contact. Beauvoir, of course, continued her lifetime companionship with Sartre; but while he was detained in a prison camp, Merleau-Ponty helped Beauvoir escape the hardships of the Nazi occupation of Paris. By this point Merleau-Ponty had left Catholicism and converted to Marxism, and when Sartre returned to Paris, the

197

three attempted to form a resistance group that soon fell apart. Nonetheless, all three wrote and published major works during the war and then, at the end of the war, together founded a periodical that could express both their political and philosophical views, *Les temps modernes*. All three had deep sympathies for communism, although they remained separate from the Communist Party of France. Beauvoir, although not on the masthead of the journal, was heavily involved with it and writes in her biography that she often saw Merleau-Ponty during this period.[3]

The Korean War produced a crisis among the intellectual left in France and particularly among these three friends. Seeing all the more clearly that they were caught between Soviet imperialism and U.S. imperialism, those on the Left were forced to choose their allegiance and their ideals.[4] Beauvoir partly dramatized this situation in *The Mandarins*, perhaps her best and most successful novel, and one composed during the same period as the breakup of Sartre and Merleau-Ponty. This break occurred in stages, but it was largely political: Merleau-Ponty retreated from both communism and Marxism and resigned as political editor of *Les temps modernes*. Sartre, conversely, embraced both Marxism and the importance of the Communist Party. In 1952 he published the essays that would become *The Communists and Peace*,[5] a strident defense of both communism and the party's role in creating the society of the future. Merleau-Ponty's response to Sartre's radical position came in *Adventures of the Dialectic* (1955), containing the lengthy chapter, "Sartre and Ultrabolshevism."[6]

There, Merleau-Ponty unveils an unrelenting criticism of both Sartre's philosophy and his communist politics. However much Sartre acknowledges the social character of human existence, Merleau-Ponty argues, he nonetheless builds this social existence out of individual freedoms that must come together, rather than starting in an already social "interworld." Sartre's social ontology arises from his views on consciousness, freedom, and temporality, which begin with a consciousness that must bestow meaning in an unbroken activity of nihilation. This ontology jeopardizes Sartre's attempt to provide a philosophical understanding of the relationship between the Communist Party, the proletariat, and the making of revolution. In Merleau-Ponty's view, Sartre's ontology makes impossible both an interworld and a genuine historical meaning independent of a sense-bestowing consciousness, so it will be impossible for the Communist Party to act in anything but the same fashion: the party will impose its meaning on a brute and meaningless mass. Sartre must either abandon the ontology of *Being and Nothingness* or change his political view. He cannot consistently hold to both.

Beauvoir came to Sartre's defense, publishing "Merleau-Ponty and Pseudo-Sartreanism" in *Les temps modernes* in 1955. In her autobiography, she claims that Merleau-Ponty never really understood Sartre,[7] but in this polemical essay, Beauvoir famously goes further and claims that Merleau-Ponty *deliberately* misunderstands Sartre's thinking, creating a straw man "Pseudo-Sartre" whose position can easily be refuted.[8] The main "mistakes" of this pseudo-Sartreanism can be summarized in two points: 1) Merleau-Ponty ignores the centrality of facticity in Sartre's thinking, and thus fails to see how Sartre includes both the interworld and embodiment; and 2) Merleau-Ponty does not see how Sartrean meaning arises as the product of a meeting of world and consciousness, but rather attributes to Sartre an entirely "centrifugal" subjectivity that bestows meaning outward, so that he cannot grasp genuine historical meaning. Underneath both of these criticisms lurks the problem of immediacy: Merleau-Ponty charges that Sartre strives to get mediation out of the pure immediacy of the for-itself.[9] While Beauvoir acknowledges this criticism, she nonetheless claims that Sartre never adopted the view of immediacy Merleau-Ponty falsely attributes to him.

Whether Beauvoir or Merleau-Ponty interprets Sartre correctly,[10] the seldom discussed political dispute that closes both "Merleau-Ponty and Pseudo-Sartreanism" and Merleau-Ponty's *Adventures* is more interesting and more important for a volume on Beauvoir's political writings. As for the argument over Sartre, I will limit myself to two comments.

My first comment concerns the difficulty of fairly judging philosophical disputes. Beauvoir charges Merleau-Ponty with misreading Sartre, often on the basis of Sartre's stated allegiance to such notions as facticity, the interworld, and mediation. For Merleau-Ponty, according to Beauvoir, "Sartre's paradox is that he does not think what he thinks." But here Beauvoir simplistically asserts that a philosopher who claims a view also has a justified position for that view. She ignores the possibility that whatever philosophers may want to say, they may nonetheless lack convincing arguments for their view and may even hold other positions that undermine their view or render their view impossible to establish. Such is the case with Sartre in Merleau-Ponty's view. Merleau-Ponty knows that Sartre has commitments to facticity, a social world, history, and so on, but he believes the ontology of *Being and Nothingness* renders these commitments impossible to cash out.

My second comment concerns a critic's responsibility to be fair to the whole of an author's work. Beauvoir claims that Merleau-Ponty ignores Sartre's development as a thinker by disregarding *Saint Genet* and other texts Sartre wrote after *Being and Nothingness*. In the same vein, Merleau-

Ponty seeks a "comprehensive and definite philosophy of history" in what was essentially a timely political polemic. Here she has a fair criticism. Merleau-Ponty disregards both the essentially political and occasional character of *The Communists and Peace* and also the evidence in that text that Sartre was already moving in the direction of *The Critique of Dialectical Reason* and developing a more ambiguous concept of freedom. Merleau-Ponty thus interprets Sartre's attempts in the early 1950s to understand a complex social formation like the revolutionary proletariat through the ontological lens of *Being and Nothingness*. As a consequence, Merleau-Ponty charges that such an ontology will not do the work Sartre requires in *The Communists and Peace*, but unfairly assumes that Sartre is working with the same ontology or is even interested in ontology in that text.[11]

These preliminary comments aside, the style of most of "Merleau-Ponty and Pseudo-Sartreanism" consists of Beauvoir quoting Merleau-Ponty, and then quoting Sartre, and then arguing that the quote from Merleau-Ponty misreads the quote from Sartre. She derides Merleau-Ponty as "delirious" and occasionally resorts to psychological explanations of his thinking that border on *ad hominem* attacks, such as her claim that Merleau-Ponty's "mood regarding communism seems . . . to be the reflection of a religious soul's bitterness towards a world that is all too human."[12] These parts of the essay make for neither her most engaging nor her most inspiring read. However, the final pages of the essay drop the defense of Sartre and engage Merleau-Ponty's political thinking directly, and here we find a truly provocative dialogue, one that reveals Beauvoir's own political thinking at this critical moment in history.

To grasp the point of this dispute, one must return to the epilogue of *Adventures of the Dialectic*, where Merleau-Ponty leaves the attack on Sartre and critiques revolutionary thought and action itself. Merleau-Ponty argues that, "revolutions are true as movements and false as regimes."[13] As essentially negative responses to an intolerable political or economic situation, revolutions function only negatively. They draw their power and strength from a denial of current conditions, but this leaves them unable to establish themselves as a positive form of life and government without betraying the very negation of conditions from which they drew power. The Soviet and the French revolutions both turned totalitarian for this reason: without something to negate, the revolution becomes a cause unto itself and thus turns absolute. This insight might lead one to the Trotskyite ideal of a permanent revolution, but Merleau-Ponty denies this possibility as well. If a revolution is to be permanent in the sense of continually transforming itself, it must also be "relative"—that is, it must emerge as a play of inherently conflicting multiplicity and plurality such that it can never really be a singular revolution. A relative revolution must be democratic in a radical sense, but such a relative revolution cannot act with the force necessary to overthrow society, since it is by nature uncertain and ambiguous. Revolution will either be an absolute revolution, which will crush all plurality within it, or it will be relative and fail as *revolution* because it is pluralistic democracy and cannot move in a single direction. "The very nature of revolution [*Le propre d'une révolution*] is to believe itself absolute and not to be absolute precisely because it believes itself to be so."[14]

As a result of this thinking, Merleau-Ponty embraces a noncommunist Left and turns back to liberalism and reformism. Yet—quite aside from Beauvoir's criticism of this text—Merleau-Ponty's return to liberalism seems impossible in the form he offers it. On the one hand, he argues that democracy must be so open as to let "even what contests it enter its universe, and it is justified in its own eyes only when it understands its opposition."[15] On the other hand, after advocating this radically plural democracy, he offers as the actual instrument of this democratic reform little more than the status quo: "Parliament is the only known institution that guarantees a minimum of opposition and truth."[16] The hope for a kind of democracy so open as to be untheorizable or unthinkable in advance (a view that Hannah Arendt was to articulate just a few years later in *The Human Condition*) is dashed. Such a "true democracy" would be little more than utopian dreaming and we must work with the institutions we have.[17]

Beauvoir responds with two main points, each indicative of her own political thinking. First, she claims that Merleau-Ponty fails to see revolution as something arising out of a genuine human need, and he fails to see it as a real motion of people involved in a process of democratic self-deliberation. Instead, he characterizes it as monolithic, terrified of dissent, and absolutist. His peculiar characterization of revolution arises because he analyzes a fairly abstract *concept of revolution* rather than the actual fact of people *making* revolution. In contrast, Beauvoir points out, "One kills from hunger, anger, and despair. One kills to live. The stakes are infinite for they are life itself with its infinity of possibilities, but they never assume the positive and utopian image of a paradisiacal society." This claim resonates with many dimensions of Beauvoir's thinking: her commitment to leave behind overly abstract philosophy and turn to the lived experience of real people, and also her belief that free human beings should strive to create an *open future* rather than a closed utopia. The commitment to concrete, lived experience leads her toward phenomenology and existentialism, toward literature rather than the abstract essay, and toward a politics that works from the real situation of oppressed peoples. In her most famous work, *The Second Sex*, she develops from the lived situation of women a wholly new political prac- tice oriented around gender. In all of her work, Beauvoir shows that utopia is not a viable human option: real, lived human beings cannot transcend their failings and become gods who live in a utopia. The most we can hope for is to open the future for each other's freedom to express itself—an inher- ently unknowable and risky enterprise.

Second, Merleau-Ponty's return to liberalism is already a return to the dominance of capitalism. Even if he wants a participatory democracy so open that it includes elements capable of subverting it, the fact remains that Parliament is more a tool of those in power than a tool of those out of power. He cannot genuinely claim that it will provide the sort of radical democ- racy and progress he hopes for. Radical, pluralistic democracy is one thing; liberal parliamentary democratic process is altogether another. Beauvoir thinks that one cannot be neutral with respect to a situation of oppression, since neutrality simply gives the dominant side the freedom to continue their oppression.[18] In "Merleau-Ponty and Pseudo-Sartreanism," Beauvoir accepts the Marxian view that democratic institutions under the conditions of capitalism are a tool of the bourgeoisie, so that Merleau-Ponty has "sided with the bourgeoisie" in opting for Parliament. His neutrality fails to be any- thing more than an endorsement of the dominance of capital and its domi- nance of the working class.

Beauvoir's commitment to fight oppression is also a clear endorsement of a more revolutionary political action that "cannot be integrated into the harmonious development of the world" but would rather "explode at the heart of the world and . . . break its continuity."[19] Beauvoir believed that po- litical movements build themselves organically from the genuine situation of people living under domination, and that this could rarely be resolved through reform; those in power do not cede power willingly. This revolu- tionary commitment poses a difficult problem for Beauvoir, one that con- sumes much of the final pages of *The Ethics of Ambiguity*. Since she remains committed to the undeniable value of all human freedoms, and believes even that each person's freedom is in all of our interests, she must retain a commitment to a value of each human life. Yet humans inevitably fail to realize perfect freedom, and fall into situations of inequality and oppres- sion (class oppression, sexism, racism, even ageism) that must be contested by means that require a denial of freedom and, at the limit, actual violence.

Beauvoir offers no easy solution to this problem in *Ethics*, arguing that this antinomy cannot be fully overcome. In "Merleau-Ponty and Pseudo-Sartreanism" she offers no solution either, and limits herself to exposing the false consciousness of a commitment to liberalism. In short, one might say, whatever problems revolutionary action brings, these problems must be posed against the problems of staying with the status quo of liberal capitalism, a fact Merleau-Ponty fails to see.

In assessing the merits of each position of the debate, it should perhaps be said that both thinkers are quite correct, and yet also terribly wrong. Merleau-Ponty's analysis of the failure of revolution to establish something positive, however abstract, provides a clear assessment of why revolutions struggle with tyranny once they have achieved their goal. Although Beauvoir may be (partly) right that he analyzes the *concept* of revolution, rather than actual revolution,[20] she fails to provide any genuine engagement with the question of why revolutions turn to terror. Moreover, in the context of supporting Sartre's party politics, her support for revolutionary action comes perilously close to a support of all that was tyrannical in the USSR. However, she is certainly right that Merleau-Ponty cannot pretend that he defends radical democracy by defending an institution that undoubtedly serves the interests of the ruling class more fully than it serves those of the underclass.

In short, they were both delirious: Beauvoir, the champion of the oppressed, nearly defends an oppressive regime in the name of freedom; Merleau-Ponty, defender of radical democracy, defends nothing more than the status quo. Yet they were both sober in recognizing and pointing out the other's delirium. And here we have one of the central problems that plagued the Left throughout the twentieth century (and is a central issue of Beauvoir's novel, *The Mandarins*): what must be done?

NOTES

1. Simone de Beauvoir, *Diary of a Philosophy Student, Volume 1, 1926–27*, ed. Barbara Klaw, Sylvie Le Bon de Beauvoir, and Margaret Simons, with Marybeth Timmermann (Urbana: University of Illinois Press, 2006), 283.

2. The whole story of this affair, which was quite complex, can be found in Deirdre Bair, *Simone de Beauvoir: A Biography* (New York: Summit Books, 1990).

3. Simone de Beauvoir, *Force of Circumstance*, trans. Richard Howard (New York: G. P. Putnam's Sons, 1965), 61.

4. See the excellent and detailed history of this moment in Jon Stewart, ed., *The Debate between Sartre and Merleau-Ponty* (Evanston: Northwestern University Press, 1998), xxi–xxx.

5. Jean-Paul Sartre, *Les communistes et la paix*, in *Situations VI* (Paris: Gallimard, 1964), *"The Communists and Peace"* with *"A Reply to Claude Lefort,"* trans. Martha Fletcher, John R. Kleinschmidt, and Philip R. Berk (New York: George Braziller, 1968).

6. Maurice Merleau-Ponty, *Les aventures de la dialectique* (Paris: Éditions Gallimard, 1955), *The Adventures of the Dialectic*, trans. Joseph Bien (Evanston: Northwestern University Press, 1973).

7. Beauvoir, *Force of Circumstance*, 61–62.

8. Yet, ironically, Beauvoir writes in *Force of Circumstance* that Merleau-Ponty "did not hold a grudge against me for it, or at least not for long; he was able to accept the existence of purely intellectual anger. And in any case, though we both felt great friendship for each other, our differences of opinion were often violent; I would often get carried away, and he would smile," 318–19. Much could be said about this and the other claims she makes about Merleau-Ponty in the autobiography: in both this passage and in her claim that Merleau-Ponty never understood Sartre, Beauvoir positions herself close to Sartrean thought and even as a Sartrean, although all the evidence points to a much greater philosophical independence and a view that had much in common with Merleau-Ponty's.

9. This, in my contention, is Merleau-Ponty's "master argument" against Sartre, from the time of the *Phenomenology of Perception* through *Adventures of the Dialectic* and into the final words of *Visible and the Invisible*. See my "Time and Ambiguity: Reassessing Merleau-Ponty's Critique of Sartrean Freedom" in *Journal of the History of Philosophy* 48 (April 2010): 207–34.

10. And the general view is that Beauvoir defends a Sartrean philosophy that is actually closer to Beauvoir's own philosophy: see Christine Daigle "Where Influence Fails: Embodiment in Beauvoir and Sartre" in *Beauvoir and Sartre: The Riddle of Influence*, ed. Christine Daigle and Jacob Golomb (Bloomington: Indiana University Press, 2009), 30–48 at 31-4.

11. Some examples of Sartre's possible development in *Communists and Peace*: "the historical whole determines our powers at any given moment, it prescribes their limits in our field of action and our *real* future; it conditions our attitude toward the possible and the impossible, the real and the imaginary, what is and what should be, time and space" (*Communists and Peace*, 80). Sartre thus argues that the moment's meaning goes beyond individuals' capacities for bestowing meaning, so the bourgeoisie will not be able to use hunger as a weapon unless "the future is carefully blocked off, [because] the future is born of action and turns back on it in order to give it a meaning; reduced to the immediate present the worker no longer understands his history" (*Communists and Peace*, 81). In both passages, Sartre wants a freedom and motivation to mix and go beyond mere immediacy. His subsequent argument that the proletariat can form neither as passive thing nor as a spontaneous movement is built around this same view. However, Sartre remains fairly silent on exactly what explains these features of human existence and meaning; it could be his old concepts of in-itself and for-itself, or a somewhat different picture of being and existence that is just coming into view. It should also be said that Sartre does not help matters by writing to Merleau-Ponty that all the claims of *Being and Nothingness* are just as true at the time of the dispute as they were at the time of *Being and Nothingness*. See Sartre to Merleau-Ponty, July 30, 1953, in *The Debate between Sartre and Merleau-Ponty*, 351.

12. And as we have seen, there is a deeply personal and very old reference behind this charge: within only a few months of knowing him, she already noted in her student diaries that he remained attached to his Catholicism in a way that she could not and that "He likes

religious things (prayers, mass, gospel) in an earthly way." Simone de Beauvoir, *Diary of a Philosophy Student*, 304. See also pages 282–86. As reported in *Force of Circumstance*, Beauvoir claims that even after he lost his attachment to religious things, he retained a nostalgia for a religious "paradise lost," 61.

13. Merleau-Ponty, *Aventures*, 279; *Adventures*, 207.

14. Merleau-Ponty, *Aventures*, 298; *Adventures*, 222.

15. Merleau-Ponty, *Aventures*, 304; *Adventures*, 226.

16. Ibid.

17. Merleau-Ponty, *Aventures*, 290; *Adventures*, 216.

18. Simone de Beauvoir, *"Pour une morale de l'ambiguïté," suivi de "Pyrrhus et Cinéas"* (Paris: Éditions Gallimard, 2008), 104; Simone de Beauvoir, *The Ethics of Ambiguity*, trans. Bernard Frechtman (New York: Citadel Press, 1976), 83.

19. Simone de Beauvoir, *Pour une morale de l'ambiguïté*, 106; *The Ethics of Ambiguity*, 84.

20. And it should be pointed out that Merleau-Ponty does spend some time analyzing the actual history of the French Revolution, so his analysis is not totally abstract.

MERLEAU-PONTY AND PSEUDO-SARTREANISM

by Simone de Beauvoir

TRANSLATION BY VÉRONIQUE ZAYTZEFF

AND FREDERICK M. MORRISON

NOTES BY VÉRONIQUE ZAYTZEFF

When Merleau-Ponty discovered in the light of the Korean War that up until then he had confused Marx and Kant, he realized that he had to give up the Hegelian idea of the end of history and decided on the need to liquidate the Marxist dialectic. I do not intend to examine here the value of the logical process which slowly developed "in conjunction with events" and led him to write *Adventures of the Dialectic*. But Merleau-Ponty involves Sartre in his own enterprise. He claims to find in *The Communists and Peace* an acknowledgment of the failure of dialectic; he criticizes Sartre for not having drawn the necessary conclusions and ascribes this failure to the "madness of the Cogito" which allegedly defines Sartrean ontology. Sartre has so often been criticized without being read or, at least, without being understood, that the very excess of errors committed in his regard usually deprives such errors of any importance. Merleau-Ponty, however, enjoys a certain philosophical prestige; he has known Sartre long enough that the public imagines that he knows

"Merleau-Ponty et le pseudo-sartrisme," *Les temps modernes*, 114–15 (June-July 1955): 2072–22; in *Privilèges* (Paris: Gallimard, 1955): 201–72, © Éditions Gallimard, 1972.

his thought as well. Recently he has so forcefully exhorted his adversaries "to learn how to read" that one can presume that he knows how to interpret a text without prejudice and how to quote it without omission. Under these conditions, his travesty becomes a breach of confidence and it must be denounced.

Sartre wrote *The Communists and Peace* in specific circumstances with a specific purpose;*[1] Merleau-Ponty decides to look through it for a comprehensive and definite philosophy of history. He fails to find one there. Instead of admitting that Sartre did not include one, he calls Sartre's deliberate silences *concealments*, and in light of the Sartrean ontology proceeds to reconstruct what Sartre *must* think. He admits that when Sartre moved from one period in his philosophy to the next "each time his previous views were at the same time preserved and destroyed by a new intuition."† How do we *deduce* this *intuition* from Sartre's system? Merleau-Ponty's method, to say the least, is bold. But what is even more serious is that the philosophy to which our exegete refers contradicts on almost all points what Sartre has always professed. Since all Merleau-Ponty's interpretations presuppose the existence of this pseudo-Sartreanism—which he explicitly exposes only at the end of his study—I shall begin by showing the distance which separates his pseudo-Sartreanism from the authentic Sartrean ontology. Even a layperson will easily realize the enormity of the falsification.

I

Pseudo-Sartreanism is a philosophy of the subject; the subject merges with consciousness which is pure transluscence and is coextensive with the world; its transparency is opposed to the opacity of being-in-itself which possesses no signification [*signification*]; meaning [*sens*] is imposed on things by a decree of consciousness which is motivated *ex nihilo*. The existence of the Other does not break this tête-à-tête since the Other never appears except under the figure of another subject. The relationship between the I [*Je*] and the Other is reduced to the look; each lives alone at the heart of his own universe over which he reigns as sovereign: there is no interworld.

Sartre's philosophy has never been a philosophy of the *subject*, and he seldom uses this word by which Merleau-Ponty indiscriminately designates consciousness, the Me, and man. For Sartre, consciousness, pure presence

---

* "The purpose of this article is to declare my agreement with the communists on precise and limited subjects. I seek to understand what is happening in France, today, before our very eyes."

† *Aventures de la dialectique* [Paris: Gallimard, 1955], 253; hereafter referred to as Ad. [Translated by Joseph Bien as *Adventures of the Dialectic* (Evanston: Northwestern University Press, 1973), 188; hereafter referred to as AD.]

to itself, is not a subject: "It is as the Ego that we are subjects,"*[2] and "the Ego appears to consciousness as a transcendent in-itself."† On this basis Sartre has built his entire theory of the psychical field: "We, on the contrary, have shown that the self on principle cannot inhabit consciousness."‡ The psyche and the Me which is its pole, are construed [*intentionnés*] by consciousness as objects. Merleau-Ponty has so forgotten this fundamental thesis that he asserts, "Sartre used to say that there is no difference between imaginary love and true love because the subject is by definition what he thinks he is."§

His reconstructionist delirium leads him to contradict word for word the author he claims to interpret, for Sartre has developed at length in *The Psychology of Imagination* the concept that one must "distinguish between two irreducible classes of feelings: real feelings and imaginary feelings." "The real and the imaginary by their very essence cannot coexist. It is a matter of two types of objects, of *feelings* and of actions that are completely *irreducible*."**

By applying to love—the psychic object—what Sartre used to say about pleasure—the immanent *erlebnis* [experience]—Merleau-Ponty shows that he confuses consciousness, immediate presence to self, with the subject whose unveiling requires mediation. Thus, when he objects to the pseudo-Sartre, "It is always through the thickness of a field of existence that my presentation to myself takes place,"†† he only repeats one of the leading ideas of *Being and Nothingness*. Faithful on this point to the Heideggerian thesis that human reality announces what it is *based on the world*, Sartre has always insisted on the reciprocal conditioning of the world and the me: "Without the world, there is no selfness [*ipséité*], no person; without selfness, without the person, there is no world."[3] "The pure self is itself over there, beyond its grasp, in the far reaches of its possibilities."‡‡ This is what Sartre calls the "circuit of selfness," and this idea is radically opposed to the one that Merleau-Ponty attributes to him when he remonstrates, with pointless common sense: "The subject is not the sun from which the world radiates, the demiurge of our pure objects."§§

If the subject creates the world by shedding light on it, the latter could not, of course, surpass the consciousness I have of it. "It is a misunderstand-

---

* EN, 203.
† EN, 141 [BN, 79].
‡ EN, 148 [BN, 79].
§ Ad, 178 [AD, 132].
** *L'imaginaire* [*Psychologie phenomenologique de l'imagination* (Paris: Gallimard, 1940)], 187–88. [Translated as *The Psychology of Imagination* (New York: Philosophical Library, 1948), 209–10].
†† Ad, 268 [AD, 199].
‡‡ EN, 148 [BN, 79-80].
§§ Ad, 268 [AD, 199].

ing," writes Merleau-Ponty, "to believe that for Sartre transcendence opens up consciousness. . . . It does not open *onto* a world, which goes beyond its capacity of meaning [*signification*]; it is exactly *coextensive with the world*."*

What Merleau-Ponty simply fails to grasp here is the theory of *facticity*, one of the foundations of Sartrean ontology. My consciousness can only surpass the world by engaging itself in it, that is, by condemning itself to grasp the world in a univocal and finite perspective, and therefore to be perpetually overwhelmed by it: this is why there can be only an embodied consciousness. "We must be careful to remember that the world exists confronting consciousness as an indefinite multiplicity of reciprocal relations which consciousness surveys without perspective,"† writes Sartre. "Thus by the mere fact that there is a world, this world cannot exist without a univocal orientation in relation to me. I must *lose myself* in the world for the world to exist and for me to be able to transcend it. To surpass the world is precisely not to survey it but to be engaged in it in order to emerge from it, to necessarily effect *this* perspective of surpassing. In this sense *finitude* is the necessary condition of the original project of the For-itself."[4] The body expresses "the necessity that there be a choice, that I not be everything at once."[5] Throughout his entire work, from *Nausea* to *Saint Genet*, Sartre devotes himself to describing the passion of the embodied consciousness; he has always portrayed man as surpassed by "the threatening and sumptuous opacity"‡ of the world. How can one, then, without bad faith, define Sartrean consciousness as being *coextensive with the world*, when consciousness only discloses the world through the condition of *losing itself* in the world?

This is not an inconsequential mistake. Merleau-Ponty's entire argument rests on the following thesis: for Sartre, signification is reduced to the consciousness that a subject has of it. But "for Sartre, realization [*la prise de conscience*] is an absolute: it *gives* meaning."§ Sartre's philosophy "is a philosophy in which meaning, seen as wholly *spiritual*, as impalpable as lightning, is absolutely opposed to being, which is absolute weight and absolute opacity."**

It would suffice to skim through just one of Sartre's books to be dumbstruck with astonishment in the face of such assertions. Sartre never denied the principles which rule existential psychoanalysis. Quite the contrary, he deepened and developed them by applying them to various fields. For the

---

* Ad, 266 [AD, 197].
† EN, 368 and following [BN, 282].
‡ *Situations II* [Paris: Gallimard, 1948], 254.
§ Ad, 156 [AD, 115].
** Ad, 168 [AD, 124].

task that Sartre assigns to existential psychoanalysis is "to explain the meaning which *really belongs to things*. The *material* significations, the human meaning, of needles of snow and grained wood, of crowded and greasy, etc. are as real as the world, neither more nor less, and to come into the world is to emerge from the middle ground [*milieu*] of these significations."* The secret meaning of snow is "an ontological meaning" and in order to decipher it one has "to compare strictly objective structures."[6]

"Sartre," says Merleau-Ponty, "always moves from open and uncompleted significations to the pure model of a *closed* signification, such as is offered to lucid consciousness."†

But Sartre has written, "By meaning I denote the participation of the being of a present reality in the being of other realities, whether present or absent, visible or invisible, and gradually, in the *universe*."‡

Therefore, far from being given by consciousness and closed, significations are real, objective, and infinitely open onto the universe.

The falsification here is so glaring that Merleau-Ponty himself takes note of it. He could not be unaware that Sartre's work presents a world in which every consciousness is engaged in things, a world in which all things bear a human meaning. Awakening for an instant from his delirium, the author recognizes that Sartre's work made him "famous by describing a middle ground between consciousness and things, weighty as things and fascinating for consciousness,—the root in *Nausea*, the viscous and the situation in *Being and Nothingness*, here the social world."§ It would seem natural in explaining an author to take into account the author's work. Our exegete, however, disregards it due to a process which we see him use again and again and which I shall call "the ruse of paradox" [*le coup du paradoxe*]. Sartre's paradox is that he does not think what he thinks. "Sartre's thought is in revolt against this middle ground."[7] Merleau-Ponty equivocates with regard to the word "revolt," for he defines it as a will to surpass and implicitly makes it a radical negation. Against *Nausea*, *Being and Nothingness*, against everything Sartre has written, he maintains that Sartreanism acknowledges nothing between the subject and being-in-itself.

To support this thesis, Merleau-Ponty makes use of another process, which is also typical of him, and which I shall call "the ruse of oversig-

---

* EN, 691 [*Existential Psychoanalysis*, trans. Hazel E. Barnes (Chicago: Henry Regnery Company, 1962), 177].

† Ad, 193 [AD, 144].

‡ *Saint Genet [comédien et martyr]* [Paris: Gallimard, 1952], 283 [*Saint Genet. Actor and Martyr*, trans. Bernard Frechtman (New York: George Braziller, 1963), 304].

§ Ad, 185 [AD, 137].

nification" [*le coup de la sursignification*]. He takes a sentence out of context, which by itself is nothing but a trite commonplace, assigns it a singular meaning and makes that a key to Sartre's thought. In a passage where Sartre challenges the myth of a fetishized proletariat, of an entity, he writes, "There are men, animals, and things."[8] This simply means that Sartre situated the debate on earth, in this world. Since he has explained himself frequently enough on the relationship of men and things, there is no need to treat that here. Merleau-Ponty chooses to understand that "Men and things are radically separated: between the two of them there is nothing." Thanks to this short sentence, arbitrarily interpreted, Merleau-Ponty allows himself to throw overboard all Sartre's writings and to invent, as he pleases, a pseudo-Sartreanism.

The consequences of this travesty are of utmost importance; what will result are a philosophy of history and political conceptions radically opposed depending on whether the subject is enclosed in his subjectivity or deciphers objective meanings in the world. Summarizing the debate he initiated, Merleau-Ponty writes, "The question is to know whether, *as Sartre says*, there are only men and things or whether there is also the interworld, which we call history, symbolism, truth-to-be-made."* When he writes that for Sartre, "Consciousness which is constitution, does not *rediscover* a system of *already-present meanings* in what it constitutes: it constructs or creates,"† he means to ban the idea of an interworld from the Sartrean philosophy. Therefore, it must be emphasized that Sartre explicitly repudiates this theory of a creative consciousness: "In *my* world there exist objective significations which are immediately given to me as *not having been brought to light [mises au jour] by me*. I, by whom significations come to things, I find myself engaged in an already signifying [*signifiant*] world which reflects to me significations which I have not put into it."‡

To recall the existence of an objective meaning of things for Sartre is really belaboring the obvious; for example, one can reread *Saint Genet*. There one will see how Genet the child emerges in a world filled with meanings which impose themselves on him. Nevertheless, Merleau-Ponty unflaggingly repeats that for Sartre, "Things are *mute* and the meaning lies only within men."§ "*Wills* do not continue living a decadent or fertile life in the things they mark."[9]

---

* Ad, 269 [AD, 200].
† Ad, 186, note [AD, 138].
‡ EN, 592 [BN, 486].
§ Ad, 247 [AD, 184].

Now here are two passages of Sartre's among many others: "The industrial products that make up the urban landscape are the *social will bottled and canned*; they *speak* to us of our integration in society; men address us through the silence of these products, etc."*

"We dominate matter through work, but our surroundings [*milieu*] dominate us in turn by the rigified swarm of thoughts we have inscribed there."†

We feel like smiling here when we see Merleau-Ponty oppose to Sartre the thought of Marx who wrote: "It is man who makes the unity of the world, but man is spread out everywhere. Men can see nothing around them that is not in their image; everything speaks to them of themselves. Their very landscape is animated."[10] For Sartre had not waited for Merleau-Ponty's lessons to think, like Marx, that: "The world is human," and to show us that urban or agricultural landscapes, streets, public gardens, utensils, and natural elements are mirrors where at every step man rediscovers his own image; that they are voices which relentlessly speak to him of himself.

Merleau-Ponty stubbornly maintains that Sartre ignores any interworld because an interworld would be a mediation between subjects, and all intersubjectivity must first be challenged in order to lead to the negation of history and the dialectic. Merleau-Ponty states, "For Sartre there is a plurality of subjects but no intersubjectivity."‡

"Contrary to appearances, being-for-itself is all Sartre has ever accepted, with its inevitable correlate: pure being-in-itself. There is no hinge, no joint or *mediation*, between me and the other; I immediately feel myself seen, I *assume* this passivity but at the same time I *reintegrate* it into my universe."§ This passage calls for several comments. First of all one finds in it a surprising confusion between *assuming* and *integrating*. To assume my alienation is an ethical attitude that does not eliminate the reality of alienation; the existence of the other means that I am thrown into a universe which, on principle escapes me.

"The fact of the other is incontestable and touches me to the heart. I realize it through uneasiness; through him I am perpetually in danger in a world which is this world and which nevertheless I can only glimpse."**

---

* *Saint Genet*, 241 [*Saint Genet*, 257].

† RL, 1605 ["Réponse à Claude Lefort," *Les temps modernes* VIII:89 (April 1953): 1571–1629; reprinted in *Situations VII* (Paris: Gallimard, 1965), 58; hereafter referred to as RCL; trans. Philip R. Berk as "A Reply to Claude Lefort" in *"The Communists and Peace" with "A Reply to Claude Lefort" (New York: George Braziller, 1968)*, 271; hereafter referred to as ARCL].

‡ Ad, 275 [AD, 205].

§ Ad, 190-191 [AD, 142].

** EN, 334 [BN, 251].

We ought to quote all the pages where Sartre describes this sort of "internal hemorrhage" through which *my* world flows toward the other. "*The flight is without limit*; it is lost externally; the world flows out of the world and I flow outside of me. The other's look makes me be beyond my being in this world and puts me in the midst of the world which is at once this world and beyond this world."*

"The appearance of the other causes the appearance in the situation of an aspect which I did not wish, of which I am not master, and which on principle escapes me since it is for the other. That ignorance which, however, is lived as ignorance, that total opacity which can only be felt as a presentiment across a total translucency—this is nothing but the description of our being-in-the-midst-of-the-world-for-others."†

Here we are quite far from the idea of a consciousness coextensive with the world which reintegrates the other into its universe through an instantaneous decree. On the contrary, we see signs of the beginnings of a fluid relation between the I and the Other, a relation which develops with time, which is never still, in short, the possibility of a dialectic. Sartre has given a precise example of this phenomenon in *Saint Genet*: when Genet assumes his being for the other, when he assumes the role of the burglar, he is far from finding himself as the "demiurge of his pure objects." The acts through which he attempts to recapture his being shape a new face for him that the other sees and which again escapes him. It is a process which does not result in any definitive synthesis: "A fathomless abyss separates the subjective certainty which we have of ourselves from the objective truth which we are for others."‡

The other mistake Merleau-Ponty makes is no less monumental: he imagines—and this is the central theme of his study—that for Sartre the I and the Other have no other relation than the look which brings their pure subjectivity into presence. However, Sartre writes, "Inasmuch as the Other is for him (the For-itself) the Other-as-look, there can be no question of techniques or of foreign significations; the For-itself experiences itself as an object in the Universe beneath the Other's look. But as soon as the For-itself by surpassing the Other toward its ends makes of him a transcendence-transcended . . . the Other-as-object becomes an *indicator of ends*. . . . Thus the Other's presence as transcendence-transcended reveals given complexes of means to ends."§

---

* EN, 319 [BN, 237].
† EN, 324 [BN, 241-42].
‡ *Saint Genet*, 548 [*Saint Genet*, 597].
§ EN, 603 [BN, 496].

Thus, the Other is present to me in things under the guise of meanings and techniques: "The For-itself arises in a world which is a world for other For-itselves. Such is the *given*. And thereby, as we have seen, the meaning of the world is *alienated* to the For-itself. This means simply that each man finds himself in the presence of meanings which do not come into the world through him."*

Therefore, it is amusing to see Merleau-Ponty argue that "A consciousness that is truly engaged in a world and a history which surpass it is not insular. . . . Unlike the Sartrean consciousness, it is not only visible for the other . . . It *can see him*, at least out of the corner of its eye. Between its perspective and that of the other there is a link, these relationships are no longer the encounter of two For-Itselves but are the meshing of two experiences which, without ever coinciding, belong to a single world."†

Throughout *Being and Nothingness* Sartre makes this point. And in *A Reply to Lefort*, he writes: "The other is there, immediately accessible—if not decipherable—and his experience is there, *completing itself in my own or mine completing itself in his*. All these imperfect significations, badly defined and interrupted, which constitute our real knowledge, are taken into account there, in the other who perhaps knows the answer."[11] And in a note, Sartre adds, "But in any case while these values and these points of view, which are not ours although *combined* with ours, while they are given to us as systems of comprehensible relationships, they will always keep their irreducibility: always other, always foreign; immediately present, yet inassimilable."‡

We can see that if Merleau-Ponty's thought is original in comparison with that of the pseudo-Sartre, it is less original when confronted with Sartre himself; this meshing without coincidence that he describes is exactly the mixture of the irreducible experiences so often evoked by Sartre.

Yet, Merleau-Ponty is aware of the text I have just mentioned, and admits that for Sartre "there is, then, a social field."§ But he maintains that the social, according to Sartre, does not exist: "'Sociality' as a given fact is a scandal for the 'I think.'"** "From the fact that the social is a totality, it does not follow that it is a pure relationship of consciousnesses; and yet, that is the very thing which, according to Sartre, goes without saying."††

---

* EN, 602 [BN, 496].

† Ad, 269 [AD, 200].

‡ RL, 1581 [RCL, 22; ARCL, 245].

§ Ad, 186 [AD, 138].

** Ad, 208 [AD, 155].

†† Ad, 214 [AD, 159].

Indeed, Merleau-Ponty says, Sartrean consciousnesses open onto a social field, but "it is facing them, not prior to them, that its unity is made."[12] Intersubjective realities in Sartre "do not have their own energy, they are something constituted."*

We have already said that the For-itself is necessary for a world to exist—Merleau-Ponty also accepts this idea—but the For-itself is far from *constituting* meanings, techniques, a reality that it would project out of itself in the manner of the Hegelian Spirit and where consciousness would find again exactly what it initially put there. The unveiling of the world, performed in the dimension of intersubjectivity, reveals realities which resist consciousness and possess their own laws. It is difficult to know what Merleau-Ponty means by *own energy*, but he certainly insinuates that for Sartre intersubjective realities exist and relate to one another only through a subjectivity which supports them; whereas Sartre, when he defined existential psychoanalysis, wrote, "The signifying, because of the very structure of transcendence, is a reference to other transcendents which can be interpreted without recourse to the subjectivity which has established it."†

Merleau-Ponty is clearly in error when he writes that according to Sartre, "Language only exists as carried by a consciousness which constitutes it."‡

For in *Saint Genet* Sartre sums up his conception of language as follows: "Language is *nature* when I discover it within myself and outside myself with its resistances and its laws which *escape me*. Words have affinities and customs which I must observe, must learn: language is a *tool* as soon as I speak or listen to an interlocuteur; and words sometimes display surprising independence, creating unions in defiance of all laws and thus producing puns and oracles within language; thus, the word is miraculous."[13]

Merleau-Ponty must be victim of a strange delirium to think that Sartre denies the existence of mediating regions between the different topics called culture and literature. According to Sartre, the ideology of a class, for example, is an intersubjective reality, endowed with its *own energy* since it *produces* ideas. He writes in *Henri Martin*, "In other environments [*milieux*], children are immediately thrust into the ideology of their class; it enters them as the air they breathe; they read it *on things*; they learn it with the language: they never think about it, but always through it, since it is this ideology which *produces* and governs ideas."§ He recognizes the same energy in

---

* Ad, 191 [AD, 142].
† EN, 691 [692; BN, 121].
‡ Ad, 191 [254; AD, 189].
§ [*L'affaire*] *Henri Martin* [Paris: Gallimard, 1953], 24.

literature whose moments are born without recourse to a subjectivity; one only needs to read *What Is Literature?* to be convinced. For example, one reads the following regarding Surrealism: "It is the last phase of a lengthy dialectic process: in the 18th century, literature was negativity; under the reign of the bourgeoisie, it went to the absolute and hypostatized state of negation, and became a many-colored process shimmering with annihilation," etc. The idea of dialectic implies objective relations, and it also supposes that the unity of the social field is made both facing and behind consciousness, for each stage is born of the preceding one. Merleau-Ponty claims that, according to Sartre, "the social is never cause or even *motive*, it is never behind the work, it is facing the writer."* In fact, Sartre refuses the deterministic explanation of Taine, who saw a work as the product of its environment;[14] however, Sartre declares that he is far from "ruling out the explanation of the work by man's *situation*." Now, the situation is founded on the given, which "is always discovered as a motive;"† the situation envelops a past which is also always given as a motive for our choices; the situation is defined by its relation to the society to which I belong. All of Sartre's analyses show us the literary work as created based on a society for a public which is itself defined by the historical moment; the social field appears both facing and behind the literary work and it can not be otherwise, since for Sartre, past and future are inextricably linked.

Merleau-Ponty is so convinced of the insularity of Sartrean consciousnesses that he has reduced reading, according to Sartre, to being merely a subjective act. In a book, there would be, "Nothing between scribbling, a book in its physical existence, and the meaning put there by the reader's consciousness."‡ On the contrary Sartre thinks that "all literary works contain in themselves the image of the reader for whom they are intended." The reader is engaged in the story, so are the authors. "Between these men who are immersed in a same story and who equally contribute to it, a contact is established through the medium of the book." And Sartre explains that all reading happens within a *context* which is precisely intersubjectivity.§ Besides, one knows just how many studies Sartre has devoted to "this concrete and imaginary object which is a literary work."** Not one of his critical essays would have been possible had he seen nothing in a book but

---

* Ad, 209 [AD, 156].
† EN, 568 [BN, 463].
‡ Ad, 189 [AD, 141].
§ *Situations II*, 177 and following.
** *Situations II*, 93.

scribbling and a subjective signification. He is so far from holding such an opinion that he used to reproach Mauriac for reducing the novel to an ensemble of signs and intentions, when it should have the thickness of a thing: "If it is true that a novel is a thing, like a painting or an architectural edifice, if it is true that one makes a novel with free consciousnesses and duration . . . *La fin de la nuit* is not a novel; at most it is a collection of signs and intentions."*[15]

Sartre had also written regarding *Sartoris*: "With the passing of time, novels become completely similar to natural phenomena: one forgets that they have an author; one accepts them as stones or trees . . ."†[16]

Nevertheless, Merleau-Ponty passes over all these texts which represent literature and reading as a mode of intersubjectivity. And he maintains his thesis: "Whether as permanent spectacle or as a continued creation, the social is in any case facing consciousnesses and constituted by them."‡

This is blatantly untrue. Sartre opposed the spontaneity of the masses, as envisioned by the Trotskyites,[17] with the idea of a passivity in which the weight of the social is *endured*: "Suppose the spontaneous action of the masses, instead of having the future in view, were reduced to being only a rebound of the past,"[18] he objected to the Trotskyites. And throughout *The Communists and Peace* his analyses defined the workers' condition by a social field whose unity is behind them.

To counter Merleau-Ponty's interpretation, I shall also quote the following passage—one of many possible texts—which is particularly conclusive: "We cannot all be objects unless it be for a transcendent subject, nor *can we all be subjects unless we first undertake the impossible liquidation of objectivity*; as for absolute reciprocity, it is masked by the historical conditions of race and class. . . . Thus, we usually live in a state of familiar and unthinking vagueness. . . . we are not quite objects and not quite subjects. The Other is that instrument which follows the dictates of the voice, which regulates, divides, distributes, and it is, at the same time, that warm, diffused atmosphere which envelops us."§

We are a long way from the philosophy of the I and the Other in which the only relationship between men is their immediate confrontation through the look. The truth is that Sartre's entire ontology contradicts what Merleau-Ponty said it was. According to Merleau-Ponty one would find in Sartre "the

---

* *Situations I* [Paris: Gallimard, 1947], 56.
† *Situations II*, 7.
‡ Ad, 213 [AD, 158].
§ *Saint Genet*, 542 [*Saint Genet*, 590-91].

demand of an *intuitive* philosophy which wants to see *all* significations immediately and simultaneously."[19] Such a philosophy "thinks everything in the instant," says Merleau-Ponty. "Therefore there is no longer any ordered passage from one perspective to another, no *completion* of others in me and of me in others, for this is possible only in time."*

Nonetheless, we have seen that Sartre said the experience of the other "*is completed* in my own or mine *is ended* in his."[20] But his philosophy is so far from being intuitive that he wrote in *Being and Nothingness* that "No consciousness, not even God's, can 'see the underside'—that is, grasp the totality as such."[21]

Society is for Sartre a detotalized totality which can never be reassembled for a subject; the relationships of individuals are not given to any of them in their immediacy, but imply the possibility of a dialectic and of a history unfolding in time. Merleau-Ponty's falsification tends to do nothing but deny this possibility. And now we will see how, from this rigged ontology, he interprets *The Communists and Peace* in such a way that he can find in it a negation of History, dialectic, and truth: the statement of a nothingness which would leave the field open to the pure dictate of the will.

II

In denying any interworld, any intersubjectivity, the pseudo-Sartre, obviously, denies History. For him, "History is voluntary or nothing."† "It is made of criminal intentions or virtuous intentions."‡ History is "insofar as it is intelligible, the immediate result of our wills. As for the rest, it is an impenetrable opacity."§

In fact, if "things are mute," the historical fact also must be mute. According to the pseudo-Sartre, "The fact, insofar as it is, does not carry its signification, which is of another order: signification is dependent on consciousness."**

"There is no mediation between pure fact, which has whatever meaning one wants to give it, and decision, which gives the fact only one meaning."††
This mediation must be the probable which Sartre, according to Merleau-

---

* Ad, 275 [AD, 205].
† Ad, 153 [AD, 112].
‡ Ad, 168 [AD, 124].
§ Ad, 134 [AD, 97-8].
** Ad, 155 [AD, 114].
†† Ad, 155 [AD, 114].

Ponty "does not want." There is a new paradox here: "And yet he has elsewhere said, profoundly, that the perceived world is wholly probable."*

Sartre said it and never refuted it. In the second part of *The Communists and Peace*, he reproaches the Trotskyites for playing a double game: for reconstructing bourgeois history according to necessity while reconstructing proletarian history from a probabilistic perspective. He denies *them* the right to retrospectively invoke probability when they interpret History according to a dialectic fatality. Yet Sartre himself explicitly resorts to this notion; and the identification that he established between the real and the probable caused it to intervene implicitly in all his analyses. Yet, Merleau-Ponty states, "This probability for Sartre is like nothing." In order to found this assertion, Merleau-Ponty resorts to a process which I have already mentioned: the ruse of oversignification. Sartre wrote that if one wants to judge the final goal of slogans proposed to the proletariat by the Communist Party, the bare facts explain nothing: "As always, the facts say neither yes nor no. . . . One will come to a decision on the question only after taking a position on much vaster questions."† The second part of this text clearly indicates that the first part is the simple reminder of a widely accepted methodological rule: experimental sciences, social sciences, and history are in agreement when they recognize that facts speak only if they are studied and interpreted. Merleau-Ponty, by isolating the first sentence, turns this commonplace into a privileged key of Sartrean thought. The fact, according to Sartre, would be definitely equivocal.

In the discussion in which he contrasts his own position with Lefort's, Sartre clearly says that he merely refuses "the experience-which-contains-its-own-interpretation."[22] He underscores the ambiguity of the fact: "First of all, facts are not as neat as you say: they must be reconstructed; then *each of them* is at once obscure and all too full of meaning [*sursignifiant*]. . . . All objective structures of the social world present themselves to the worker's subjectivity as an initial undifferentiation. Nothing is elucidated, nor are there guarantees: resignation and revolution simultaneously clarify the situation, but their relationship is always in flux." But immediately he adds that one can resolve the ambiguity: "Everything *will be* clear, rational, everything *is* real, beginning with that resistance to deciphering; but it simply takes time."‡

---

* Ad, 158 [AD, 116].

† Cp I, 8 [Beauvoir cites the page numbers of "Les communistes et la paix," Part 1 in *Les temps modernes* 81 (July 1952); We have inserted the page references for the reprinted essay in *Situations VI*, followed by the page references for the English translation: Cp, 90-91; CP, 11].

‡ RL, 1588 [RCL, 33; ARCL, 253].

Merleau-Ponty acknowledges that for Marx, too, "any situation is ambiguous." And even, he says, "nothing is more Marxist than the mixing of act and signification." Then why does he claim that Sartre is condemned to negate the historical reality which is recognized by Marx? It is because, he answers, "Marxism does not mix them in an equivocation but in a genesis of truth."[23] Interpreting with bad faith the lines from Sartre that I have just quoted, Merleau-Ponty retains, "the facts are obscure and all too full of meaning [sursignification]." But Sartre was saying that *each fact* in itself is equivocal, not that it is impossible to explain facts by means of other facts. One finds a specific example of this process of elucidation in the passage from *Henri Martin* where Sartre questions the meaning of the tracts posted by Martin: "Considered in its objective reality, the act informs us *up to a certain point.* . . . Beyond that, there is total indetermination and one would not be able to judge it without relating it to the universe."*

Yet, we have seen that Sartre concluded that "Everything will be rational." The time needed for deciphering is not infinite, as Merleau-Ponty suggests; if it were, it would in practice eliminate any criterion. The time needed for deciphering is the time required by experience. Elsewhere Sartre says, "The difficulties which we have already encountered bring us back to the usual idea of experience: an obscure ensemble of 'consequences without premises' which require a number of men to decipher."[24]

If we keep these lines in mind, we will find the dialogue Merleau-Ponty has with the pseudo-Sartre highly comical: "What is this dubious relationship?" demands the pseudo-Sartre enamoured with Cartesian clarity. "Is or is not the meaning of the present given in it?"[25]

And Merleau-Ponty, who knows existential ambiguity, answers, "It is neither given in it nor created out of nothing. It is elicited from the present, and such is the function of a congress."†

The real Sartre had spoken clearly about a deciphering which requires time and several hands. He adheres to the Marxist idea of a genesis of truth since he writes that "everything *will be* clear." This having-become truth [vérité devenue] has nothing to do with the pseudo-Sartre's willed truth [vérité voulue] of which Merleau-Ponty says, "it authorizes one to go ahead against all appearances; in itself it is madness."[26] One has the right to ask whether Sartre's paradoxes and madness could not, in fact, be explained by his commentator's lack of comprehension.

---

* *Henri Martin*, 185.
† Ad, 157 [AD, 115].

As a matter of fact, untruths keep cropping up. Having wrongly asserted that for Sartre "realization [*la prise de conscience*] gives meaning,"[27] Merleau-Ponty adds, "And in the case of an event, the meaning it gives is *irrevocable*."* Relying on Marx, he reminds Sartre that, "Realization . . . is in itself a fact; it has its place in history,"† and that, "I give meaning to history only because I occupy a certain stopping point in it."‡

Yet, Sartre had written in *Being and Nothingness*, "There is only the point of view of *engaged* knowledge. This amounts to saying that knowledge and action are only two abstract aspects of an original, concrete relation."§ Sartre applies this idea to History. The main theme of his *Reply to Albert Camus* is that under no circumstances can consciousness withdraw from History, since any realization is a historical fact: "If I thought that History is a pool of filth and blood . . . I would look twice before diving in. But suppose that I am in it already, suppose that, from my point of view, even your sulking is the proof of your historicity."** [28]

The meaning, reached by the historically situated consciousness, is so far from being *irrevocable* that Sartre wrote, "Thus, human history would have to be finished before a particular event, for example the taking of the Bastille, could receive a *definitive* meaning. . . . He who would like to decide the question today forgets that the historian is himself historical; that is that he historicizes himself by illuminating history in the light of his projects and those of his society. . . . Thus it is necessary to say that the meaning of the past is perpetually *in suspense*."[29]

The text just quoted utterly refutes Merleau-Ponty's assertion that "For Marx there was, and for Sartre there is not, a becoming of meaning in institutions."†† For neither the meaning of institutions nor that of events is, according to Sartre, irrevocable; it is historicized in the context of praxis: and this brings us back, against the *folie* of a willed truth, to the idea of a having-become truth. Meaning is given neither *ex nihilo* nor irrevocably: it emerges from the facts and is critiqued through its contact with History.

However, this History according to the pseudo-Sartre is only a history of persons; since, according to him, there exist only men and things, he is forced to carry out "the reduction of History to personal actions."‡‡ Such an

---

* Ad, 156 [AD, 115].
† Ad, 157 [AD, 115].
‡ Ad, 269 [AD, 199].
§ EN, 370 [BN, 284].
** *Les temps modernes* 82, 353.
†† Ad, 167 [168; AD, 124].
‡‡ Ad, 134 [196; AD, 146].

assertion is surprising, since for Sartre, the person can truly be understood only through History: it is this view which emerges in *What Is Literature?* among other texts, and also in *Saint Genet* where Sartre writes, "In order for a man to have a history, he must evolve; the course of the world must change him in changing itself, and he must change in changing the world. His life must depend on everything and on himself alone; he must discover in it, at the moment of death, a vulgar product of the age and the singular work of his will."* In *The Communists and Peace* he is even more decisive. The complete text that Merleau-Ponty truncated is, as a matter of fact, as follows: "There are men, animals, and objects. And men are real and singular beings who are part of historical wholes."† Elsewhere Sartre clarifies that "The historical whole determines our powers at any given moment, it prescribes their limits in our field of action and our *real* future; it conditions our attitude toward the possible and the impossible, the real and the imaginary, being and what ought to be, time and space. From there on, we in turn determine our relationships with others, that is to say, the meaning of our life and the value of our death: it is within this framework that our *Me* finally makes its appearance. It is History which shows some the exits and makes others cool their heels before closed doors."‡

Thus, the Me and the acts of the person depend upon the historic circumstance [*conjoncture*]. One must also not forget that for Sartre the act is something quite different from the intention which animates it; by falling into a world which is alienated from us, our wills escape us: "The event transforms our best intentions into criminal desires not only in history but even in family life."§ The meaning of the event, far from always reflecting a conscious intention, possesses an *objective meaning*. "It matters little then whether strikers or demonstrators have or do not have the *will* to make revolution: *objectively*, every mass demonstration is revolutionary,"** writes Sartre. And he shows in *The Communists and Peace* how the action of skilled workers objectively takes a reformist meaning which no will has subjectively chosen to give it.

Since History is a history of persons according to the pseudo-Sartre, History is also nothing more than a "history of projects" where the past plays no

---

* *Saint Genet*, 288-89 [*Saint Genet*, 310].

† Cp II, 725 ["Les communistes et la paix," Part 2, *Les temps modernes* 84–85 (October-November 1952); Cp (*Situations VI*), 197; CP, 89].

‡ Cp II, 717 [Cp, 184; CP, 80].

§ *Saint Genet*, 548 [*Saint Genet*, 597].

** Cp III, 1801 ["Les communistes et la paix," Part 3, *Les temps modernes* 101 (April 1954); Cp (*Situations VI*), 356; CP, 210].

role.[30] We have already seen how false this thesis is regarding the history of literature. In *The Communists and Peace* Sartre continually reminds us, against the Trotskyites and against Lefort: "This *confused* history, so full of delays and lost chances, in which the working class seems to exhaust itself in making up for an earlier delay, whose path is often disturbed by exterior violence, wars, etc."* He emphasizes—and we shall revisit this point—the singular characteristics the French proletariat owes to its singular history, to this *confused* past which is neither the immediate result of personal wills nor an impenetrable opacity. And he radically condemns sociological interpretations which flout history. "For having begun by eliminating history, the anti-communist is constrained to reintroduce it at the end in its most absurd form."†

* * *

At any rate, Merleau-Ponty says, this History is discontinuous; it does not envelop the becoming of a truth, since, "An intuitive philosophy posits everything in the instant."[31] The result must be that Sartre envisions political action as a pure present: "Political time is atomized for him into a series of decisions taken in the presence of death."[32] "Political questions can and should be resolved in the instant, without looking back or starting over."‡

We could object to Merleau-Ponty that for Sartre no reality is instantaneous, and that the theory of temporality, elaborated at length in *Being and Nothingness*, inextricably solders different moments of time, with the present perpetually recapturing the past in fleeing toward the future; it is nothing other than this double ek-stasis. Merleau-Ponty would probably retort with the ruse of the paradox: in politics, Sartre disowns his previous work. We could then remind him that in *The Communists and Peace*, Sartre speaks of a "true time of the dialectic," and that he writes about the masses: "In point of fact, their most elementary desire is separated from its object by the universe, and can be satisfied only by *long and exacting labor*."[33] Merleau-Ponty will answer that, as a matter of fact, in the last part of *The Communists and Peace*, Sartre "has given up the point of view of the instant."[34] Merleau-Ponty will nonetheless continue to interpret the whole of Sartre's essay from this point of view. Then, we are justified in asking Merleau-Ponty whether he fears that the incoherence he notices in Sartre might indicate a defect in the method he uses. Sartre's last essay would contradict his entire work, and each part of this essay would contradict each one of the others.

---

* RL, 1606 [RCL, 59-60; ARCL, 272].
† Cp III, 1732 [Cp, 256; CP, 134].
‡ Ad, 144 [AD, 105].

Would it not be the commentator's role to restore the unity of the work and situate the elements in the whole instead of interpreting each of them separately and against all the rest? Perhaps then he would notice that Sartre did not have to give up the point of view of the instant, given that, faithful to his earlier thought, he had never adopted it.

What are Merleau-Ponty's bases for claiming the contrary? Is it because Sartre in *The Communists and Peace* proposed to study a specific moment in History? Therefore, according to him, moments can be isolated! says the deeply shocked Merleau-Ponty. Let us look at his proof more closely.

Sartre has written, "Leaving eternal France at grips with the proletariat-in-itself, I am undertaking to explain events rigorously defined in time and space by the singular structure of our economy, and the latter in turn by certain events of our local history."*

This attitude, which is that of historians in general, also the very one often adopted by Marx himself and Lenin, appears to Merleau-Ponty as being singularly Sartrean: "But it is this reference to the present as such which is theory. There is theory precisely in this manner of treating the event as ineffaceable (?), as a decisive test of our intentions (?), and an instantaneous choice of the whole future and of ourselves (?)."†

The process used here by Merleau-Ponty is what one can call "the ruse of gratuitous affirmations." I have emphasized each one with a question mark. The quote is even more stupefying since Sartre wrote *The Communists and Peace* in opposition to those anti-communists who sought to treat the events of May 28th and those of June 4th as ineffaceable, to judge them as the decisive test of the proletarians' intentions and the expression of an instantaneous choice.[35] Sartre, on the contrary, maintains that they were only a "negative sign" and as such "decipherable with difficulty." It is impossible, says Sartre, if one limits oneself to the present, to know if the masses have disavowed something, or what they have disavowed. "We are dealing with *local* and *day-to-day* history, opaque, in part contingent, and the connection between the terms is not so tight that we cannot vary some of them within certain limits without modifying all the others."‡ Hence he considers that a reference to the pure present can never suffice to clarify the event.

---

* What makes Merleau-Ponty's bad faith even more blatant is that Sartre wrote these lines in the last part of his essay, where, according to Merleau-Ponty himself, he does not adopt the point of view of immediacy. See Cp III, 1735 [Cp, 259 and following; CP, 137 and following].

† Ad, 144 [AD, 105].

‡ Cp II, 751 [Cp, 234; CP, 118].

Merleau-Ponty pursues his indictment by using a new process: "the ruse of dichotomy." He traps his adversary in a false alternative: "Not to speak of the proletarian, of the class in itself, or of the eternal Party, is here to make a theory of the proletariat and of the Party as continued creations, that is to say, as the dead reprieved from death."*

Merleau-Ponty is a professor of philosophy at the College de France; how does he dare to propose the dilemma: Idea or continued creation? Doesn't he know of systems—phenomenology, for example—which, going beyond Plato and Descartes, endow existents with a temporal dimension without immobilizing them in eternity? Does he really ignore the fact that one can negate the *idea in itself* while believing in History, dialectic, and time?

Nonetheless, Merleau-Ponty does not bring forth any additional weightier arguments to support his assertions regarding Sartre's treatment of the dialectic. In the name of the intuitive philosophy which he attributes to Sartre, Merleau-Ponty calmly writes, "Today Sartre says that the dialectic is twaddle."† "He provides an admission of the failure of the dialectic."‡ "One *feels* that for Sartre the dialectic has always been an illusion."§

No text by Sartre authorizes these assertions. Sartre did call the finalist optimism which usually hides behind dialectics "twaddle," but not the dialectic itself. He does not think that History can be informed by some sort of Idea-Force, foreign to the men who make it, a Force which would drive History with a sure fatality toward a happy ending. Nor did Marx accept this idea. He wrote, "History is only the activity of man pursuing his own ends." Sartre adopts these words as his own;** according to him the dialectic is the product of our activities, which, falling into a world where they are thingified, escape according to the dimension of the for-others, and immediately motivate new activities. The historical dialectic is so remote from being "twaddle" because it is correlative to the dialectic originally implied in temporality and to the dialectic implied in the relationship of the for-itself with the for-others. Sartre is so far from negating it, that he describes—as we have seen—the history of literature in a dialectical form. And he writes, "The process of capital is dialectical."††

---

* Ad, 144 [AD, 105].

† Ad, 312 [AD, 232].

‡ Ad, 133 [AD, 97].

§ Ad, 135 [AD, 98].

** RC, *Le temps modernes* 82, 352 [RAC, 123; ARAC, 102].

†† RL, 1596 [RCL, 44; ARCL, 261].

"Hegel's panlogicism is coupled with a pantragicism, and in Marxism likewise, there is the process of capital and the drama of man: two inseparable aspects of the same dialectic."*

"But how could you even conceive of what Trotsky called 'the dialectic of the heads of the Party and the masses'?"† "Marxist dialectic is not the spontaneous movement of the Spirit, but the hard work of man to fit into a world which rejects him."‡ "Marx has allowed us to recover true dialectical time."§ How can Merleau-Ponty *feel* that Sartre negates the dialectic when Sartre writes down in black and white, "In truth, there are dialectics and they reside in facts; it is for us to discover them there, not put them there."**

Merleau-Ponty goes as far as to claim that "An action which is a disclosure, a disclosure which is an action—in short, a dialectic—this is what Sartre does not want to consider,"†† while Sartre keeps on saying that any action is a disclosure, any disclosure is an action. I have already quoted the text where Sartre says, "Knowledge and action are nothing but two abstract sides of an original and concrete relation." This is one of the theses developed in *Being and Nothingness* and found at the source of *What Is Literature?*

"The engaged writer knows that the word is action: he knows that to disclose is to change and one cannot disclose without projecting to change." The *act* of disclosure is strange because of the type of redoubling it implies: it *posits* as an *end* one of its immediate dimensions. But, according to Sartre, all the conditions for a dialectic are brought together in the relation of consciousness to the act, as well as in the relationship of the me and the other, and of the past and the future.

III

If there is no history, no truth, no temporality, no dialectic, then the meaning of events is imposed on them by decree, and action is reduced to a discontinuous series of arbitrary decisions. Such is the central theme that Merleau-Ponty used to support the building of his pseudo-Sartreanism. He announces in the introduction to his study of Sartre, that Sartre substitutes for a philosophy of History "a philosophy of absolute creation amidst the unknown."[36]

---

* RL, 1576 [RCL, 15; ARCL, 240]. The context clearly shows that this dialectic is considered as valid in this instance.

† RL, 1609 [RCL, 15; ARCL, 240].

‡ RL, 1605 [RCL, 58; ARCL, 271].

§ RL, 1606 [RCL, 59; ARCL, 272].

** Cp III, 1732 [Cp, 370; CP, 221].

†† Ad, 192 [AD, 142].

Communism then becomes "an undetermined enterprise, shielded, like duty, from any discussion, but also from any proof."* According to this conception, "the Party's action is shielded from the criteria of meaning."†

"Doing is absolute rootless initiative."‡

The militant, the Party, and the class are born out of a "will which has no basis in things."[37]

We know well enough that Sartre has never admitted that an act could be produced without motive nor that a creation could be brought about *ex nihilo*.

"The freedom of the For-itself is always *engaged*; there is no question here of a freedom which could be an undetermined power and which could pre-exist its choice."§

"The structure of the choice necessarily implies that it be a choice in this world. A choice which would be a choice *based on nothing*, a choice *against nothing*, would be a choice of nothing and would be annihilated as choice."**

"Our decisions gather into new syntheses and on new occasions the *leit-motivs* that governs our lives."††

"The act transforms the possible into the real."‡‡

"One does something *with* or *to* something."§§

There is no need to supply additional passages. Merleau-Ponty remembers quite well that for Sartre "freedom is not in the decision."*** Yet, once again he shakes off any scruples, thanks to the ruse of paradox, and reads Sartre as rebelling against his own work. "Everything takes place as if these thoughts do not arise when it is a question for Sartre of taking a position in the present: so he returns (?)††† to the ideology of choice and to futurism."

We shall restrict our comments here to Sartre's political thought and ascertain if, according to him, the revolutionary will, the class, and the Party indeed emerge "with no basis in things."

Merleau-Ponty asserts that, "Strictly speaking, the proletarian is not automatically a militant, and the fact that the revolutionary will does not arise

---

* Ad, 138 [AD, 101].
† Ad, 139 [134; AD, 98].
‡ Ad, 186, note [AD, 138].
§ EN, 558 [BN, 455].
** EN, 559 [BN, 456].
†† *Saint Genet* [397; *Saint Genet*, 428].
‡‡ *Saint Genet*, 321 [*Saint Genet*, 346].
§§ EN, 566 [BN, 461].
*** Ad, 266 [AD, 198].
††† Ad, 267 [AD, 198]. How can Sartre return to a philosophy which, according to Merleau-Ponty, was never really his?

from misery completely armed is enough for him (Sartre) to act as if it did not arise from it at all, and to see it emerge *ex nihilo.*"*

Like Orestes in *The Flies*, the militant sees freedom swoop down on him, and he becomes revolutionary by decree. Such is the meaning that Merleau-Ponty attributes to these words of Sartre: "Man is yet to be made [*à faire*]: he is *what is lacking* to man."[38] Merleau-Ponty claims that these words mean that man is a "duty-to-be [*devoir être*] and even a pure duty."[39] "It is the bite of duty or of nothingness into being, into freedom—the bite that Sartre once called 'mortal'—which constitutes the militant."† And Merleau-Ponty amusingly asks why isn't Sartre militating instead for the *Union for Moral Action*?[40]

I am afraid that Merleau-Ponty, who advises against reading Sartre with Marx's glasses, here, borrowed—God only knows for what reason—those of Lagneau.[41] Had he not done so he would have understood this passage that he so arbitrarily truncated, quite differently. As a matter of fact, Sartre wrote, "The new proletarian cannot claim the least merit. . . . Yet, *fatigue* and *misery* overwhelm it: *it must die or obtain satisfaction*. On what, then, will it base its demands? Well, precisely on nothing.‡ Or, if you prefer, on the demands themselves. The *need* creates the right. . . . This new humanism is a need itself; it is lived hollowly as the very meaning of an *inadmissible frustration* . . . for the unskilled worker, man is yet to be made, etc."§

Hence, the bite of nothingness on being is called, here, not freedom, but need. Merleau-Ponty is the only one to claim that for Sartre the revolutionary will, in order not to arise fully armed from misery, does not arise from it at all: in reality, it is born out of an *inadmissible frustration*. Sartre had already shown in the second part of his essay** that the condition of the unskilled worker does not offer any solution other than that of a revolutionary conversion: a conversion envelops whatever it surpasses; here, it arises from a total lack of everything, that is to say, precisely, from misery. As for freedom, says Sartre, in speaking of the masses: "They can't even imagine what it is."††

How does Merleau-Ponty dare to maintain that the alternative "to die or obtain satisfaction" puts the proletarian in the presence of a moral imperative in the Kantian sense of the word? How can he confuse a hungry man

---

* Ad, 145 [AD, 106].

† Ad, 146 [AD, 107].

‡ For fear that one might use the process of oversignification here, one thing must be made clear: this nothing is *nothing* only in relation with the bourgeois world of values and merit; but this absence is coupled with the very concrete presence of a need. Here, Sartre is very close to the Marxist formula: "The need of a thing is in itself a sufficient reason for its fulfillment."

§ Cp III, 1581 [Cp, 343; CP, 200].

** Cp, 756, and following [Cp, 242 and following; CP, 124 and following].

†† Cp III, 1794 [Cp, 346; CP, 203].

with the well-fed idealists who adhere to unions and moralizing leagues? The entire polemic which ensues is immediately discredited, since it is based on the confusion of a theory of need with a theory of freedom.

The reason for such a monumental error is obvious. What does not exist cannot have roots: Merleau-Ponty substitutes "the rape of freedom"[42] for the enrootedness in need because he wants Sartre to deny any existence to the proletariat. His political thought would be a duplicate of his ontology. "The party is a double of consciousness,"* asserts Merleau-Ponty. Pseudo-Sartre's ontology brings together sovereign consciousness and opaque being; his political thought leaves only "the brute will of the leaders face to face with the opaque necessity of things."† The signifying reality—here, the proletariat—would be conjured away.

"The proletariat of which Sartre is speaking is not verifiable, debatable or living. It is not a phenomenon but rather a category delegated to represent humanity in Sartre's thought."‡

The proletariat is "an idea of the leaders. It is suspended above History; it is not caught in the fabric, it cannot be explained, it is cause of itself, as are all ideas." "It is a definition and exists only in Sartre's mind."§

And Merleau-Ponty, far from being intimidated by Sartre's texts, declares, "It is not a historical reality,"** despite the fact that Sartre wrote in black and white: "The French proletariat is a historical reality."[43]

Not only did he write it but it is one of the major theses of his essay. In opposition to the Trotskyites, and in opposition to Claude Lefort, whom he accuses of treating the proletariat as an Idea, Sartre keeps on insisting on the concrete, *verifiable*, and *living* characteristics which are given to each proletariat—in this case to the French proletariat—by its singular history. The upheavals that afffect the proletariat do not express an eternal essence. When Sartre speaks of workers' struggles, he refuses to see in them nothing more than the fatal repetition of an abstract schema: "I discover the action of precise factors in these battles; and in the sleep which followed, I see the effect of defeat and Terror."††

In opposition to innumerable texts by Sartre in which he concretely describes the proletarian history and condition, Merleau-Ponty delivers one of his habitual dilemmas: the proletariat *is* or is *nothing*. To do so is to forget

---

* Ad, 143 [AD, 105].
† Ad, 227 [AD, 168].
‡ Ad, 227 [AD, 169].
§ Ad, 228-29 [AD, 169–70].
** Ad, 227 [AD, 169].
†† Cp III, 763 [Cp, 253; CP, 132].

that in phenomenology—formerly held in esteem by Merleau-Ponty—the existent cannot be enclosed in this alternative: he makes himself. Sartre, faithful to this doctrine, refuses to reify the proletariat; however, this certainly does not lead him to ignore its existence:

"If the class exists, it will be as a new proximity of each to all, as a mode of presence which is realized through and against the separative forces: it will create *the unity* of the workers. . . . I wish only to show that class unity cannot be passively received or spontaneously produced."*

"The class makes and remakes itself continuously: it is movement, action." "The *real* class unity of crowds and *historical* masses, manifests itself by an operation that can be located in time and that refers to an intention. The class is never separated from the concrete will which animates it nor from the ends it pursues. The proletariat forms itself by its day-to-day action."†

This thesis, Sartre notes, is closely akin to that of Marx who also defines class by praxis. Merleau-Ponty's bad faith consists here (knowing that for Sartre, freedom, choice, and action have never signified *decision*) in assimilating praxis, as Sartre understands it, to instantaneous and arbitrary decisions which would be motivated by nothing:

"The proletariat begins to exist only by lightning-quick decisions and against all facts."‡

To the contrary, according to Sartre, the proletariat is born out of facts: from its misery, its need, and from the system of production.

"For the worker," writes Sartre, "politics cannot be a luxury activity. . . . politics is a need."§

Without praxis, the class does not exist; however, praxis implies certain very concrete conditions: "The regime of production is the necessary condition for a class to exist. The entire historical evolution, the process of capital and the role of the worker in bourgeois society prevent the proletariat from being an arbitrary grouping."**

Merleau-Ponty will say, fine, but, nevertheless for Sartre, events take place as if the proletariat were nothing; it does not break off the abrupt encounter between consciousness and being, since the sole action it is allowed is obedience to the Party. "It is instantaneously through obedience, and it ceases to be in an instant through disobedience."††

---

* Cp II, 725 [Cp, 197; CP, 89-90].
† Cp II, 734 [Cp, 207; CP, 97].
‡ Ad, 156 [AD, 114].
§ Cp II, 756 [Cp, 242; CP, 124].
** Cp II, 734 [Cp, 209; CP, 99].
†† Ad, 227 [AD, 169].

"There is no exchange between those who conceive and those who execute."*

The Party emerges *ex nihilo*: "If everything comes from freedom, if the workers are nothing, not even proletarians, before they created the Party, the Party rests on nothing that has been given, not even on their common history."†

Once created, the Party "exercises unjustifiable choice;"‡ it decrees undertakings "without any previous motive and against all reason."§

Is this truly the way Sartre conceived the relationship of the masses to the Party?

* * *

We have already stated it, and it will be necessary to repeat it as often as Merleau-Ponty repeats the contrary: everything comes not from *freedom* but from the situation. The living conditions of the unskilled worker, his exhaustion, the debasement of knowledge correlative to the mechanization of the work, prevent him from being able to be at once a worker and a militant; coming from the masses, the militant—as Lenin himself said—must *leave* it: "The duo of technician and unskilled worker must be balanced by that of the unskilled worker and professional militant."**

"The new functionaries are legitimized by the *need* that one has of them."††

Born from the masses, which is not *nothing*, but which is concretely defined by the singular moment of the economy which exploits it; brought to power by the need of the masses for it, the Party remains so inextricably bound to it that, without it, the Party is literally nothing. "If the masses suddenly refused to follow it, it would lose everything; as powerful as it is, it resembles Antaeus, who had strength only when he was touching the earth."‡‡

The Party is "the perspective on the basis of which the proletariat can reposition himself in society and in turn take for an object those who would make an object of him: it is both tradition and institution. But the content of these empty forms will grow through the very connections in the movement made by the masses in order to come together."[44]

---

* Ad, 202 [AD, 150].
† Ad, 147 [AD, 107-8].
‡ Ad, 230 [AD, 171].
§ Ad, 188 [AD, 140].
** Cp III, 1803 [Cp, 360; CP, 213].
†† Cp III, 1804 [Cp, 360; CP, 214].
‡‡ Cp II, 703 [Cp, 164; CP, 65].

"The Party cannot be distinguished from the masses except insofar as it is their union."*

Against the Trotskyites and Lefort, Sartre denies that the masses are endowed with a spontaneous and organized intelligence, which allows them to produce a politics without the mediation of an apparatus: here again, he concurs with Marx. But he never thought that the masses were pure inertia, an opacity devoid of meaning. He says, to the contrary, that when a great social movement is triggered, "The origin of the current remains outside of the trade unions: it is hunger, anger or terror which sets things in motion, or sometimes, as in 1936, it is a sudden bolt of hope."†[45]

"Without the trade union organism, the movements would perhaps stop ... But it is incapable of producing movements by itself; it triggers them only when it has beat them to their true cause."[46]

Therefore, it is not the masses who obey the militant: on the contrary, it is the militant who must serve them.

"The masses can be neither mobilized nor manipulated, they *themselves* decide on action in transforming themselves into an active community under the action of external circumstances."‡

The masses "indicate the goal to be attained; it is up to the militant to find the shortest path."§

Thus, we are very far from a political conception in which the leaders are exempt from the control of the masses. Merleau-Ponty claims that, according to Sartre, "any idea of controlling the leaders is out of the question."** But Sartre writes, "The masses control the militant as the sea controls the helmsman. . . . he will inspire confidence in them only if he agrees to lead them where they are going."††

"The officials steer the movement by successive approximations: a turn of the helm to the left, a turn to the right."‡‡

Merleau-Ponty claims that Sartre conceives the Party's action "as a 'technique for the masses,' which 'churns' them like an emulsion. . . . It is just the opposite of an action in which the Party and the working class jointly live the same situation and thus make the same history together."§§

---

* RL, 16–17 [RCL, 60; ARCL, 273].
† Cp III, 1807 [Cp, 365-66; CP, 217].
‡ Cp III, 1818 [Cp, 383; CP, 229].
§ Cp III, 1814 [Cp, 376; CP, 225].
** Ad, 149 [AD, 109].
†† Cp III, 1808 [Cp, 363; CP, 215-16].
‡‡ Cp III, 1867 [Cp, 370; CP, 221].
§§ Ad, 163-64 [AD, 120].

But although Sartre makes room for the *permanent agitation* by which the Party fights against the forces of dissociation exerted on the masses, he is far from reducing communist action to this technique: and to imply that he does takes quite a bit of bad faith, since Sartre wrote that the Party "is a force of mediation between men. . . . it [this mediation] is at certain times in the history of the working class, both relational and willed; this ambiguity . . . founds the possibility of a *dialectic* which sometimes *opposes* the masses to the Party and sometimes unites them. . . . Doubtless, its orders would be ineffective if they did not flow in the direction of *social currents*, but for the Party to be guided by the real tendencies of the worker's movement, such tendencies must exist, and for them to exist and for them to be concrete, a measure of integration is necessary."[47]

"Like every real relationship, the liaison of the Party and the masses is ambiguous: on the one hand, it is guided by them; on the other, it organizes them and attempts their education."*

It is entertaining to see Merleau-Ponty deny Sartre the right to resort to an ambiguous notion when Merleau-Ponty himself does not hesitate to put forward a *heavy action*, nor in every other breath oppose the simplistic assertions of the pseudo-Sartre to the complexity of the real. The same Merleau-Ponty becomes indignant when Sartre writes, "I do not think that one can explain the present situation except as an inextricable mixture of action and passion in which passion temporarily dominates."†

"But how is one to understand this mixture of fire and water?"‡ Merleau-Ponty exclaims. All Sartre's analyses seek precisely to account for this. The Party's role is, according to him, to animate passivity. "To transform misery into a factor of revolution, one must discover this misery's reason for being and its needs."§

What the Party represents in the eyes of the masses is "their aspirations, their tendencies, . . . but brought to a red heat, that is to say, to the highest degree of efficacy."**

Sartre says that the policy of the leaders and the mood of the masses are "both functions of the external circumstances. Ultimately one reacts on the other; they modify each other, adapt to each other and, finally, equilibrium

---

* Cp II, 197 [Cp, 155; CP, 58].
† RL, 1623 [RCL, 84; ARCL, 290].
‡ Ad, 232 [AD, 172].
§ RL, 1611 [RCL, 67; ARCL, 278].
** CP II, 697 [Cp, 155; CP, 58].

is established. With a reciprocal accommodation, the possibilities take off: like leaders, like masses; like masses, like leaders."*

This description, as well as many others, show us the Party and the working class living "together the same situation." We are far from the idea of an action imposed on the inert masses from the outside. However, Merleau-Ponty persists in his avowal, in spite of all these texts, that for Sartre the Party is *pure action*; so it would be contradictory to burden it with the weight of reality. Action would no longer be pure. No doubt. But when did Sartre ever take the phrase "pure action" in the meaning that Merleau-Ponty assigns it: an action without roots in the facts and without a hold on the given? Sartre used the expression only twice, and Merleau-Ponty—employing the process of oversignification—makes it one of the keys to his political thought. Opposing the party to the masses, Sartre writes, "They will ultimately change the world, but, for the moment, the world is crushing them. . . . The Party is *pure action*; it must advance or disappear."† This passage means that the Party can never slack off, fall asleep or wait: *pure action* is simply opposed here to *inaction*. A little bit further on Sartre explains that the man of the masses is hindered and burdened by individual interests: "He must be wrenched away from them. The linking organism must be *pure action*. . . . The Party is the very movement which unites the workers by carrying them along towards the taking of power."‡ Here purity is opposed to the weight of individual interests. But Sartre never assumed that the Party's action would not be *applied*. The only evidence that Merleau-Ponty gives us in support of his interpretation is the following: "Sartre's ontology requires that history as a common future be sustained by the pure action of a few, which is identical to the obedience of the others."§

What we have just seen shows us what to think of Merleau-Ponty's interpretation of Sartre's ontology. Furthermore, let us point out that the manner in which he links Sartre's political thought to his ontology is, to say the least, arbitrary. Depending on expedience, the ontology appears as either restrictive or, on the contrary, as leaving Sartre free to rebel against it. We are told here that his ontology only authorizes pure action, but I have already quoted excerpts which show that it does not admit acts which spring up *ex nihilo*; therefore it does not admit pure action. Well? Isn't it Merleau-Ponty who proceeds here by pure assertion?

---

* Cp II, 747–8 [Cp, 230; CP, 114].
† Cp II, 697 [Cp, 156; CP, 58-9].
‡ Cp II, 761 [Cp, 249; CP, 129-30].
§ Ad, 219 [AD, 163].

In light of the true Sartre, one is amused to read the dialogue that Merleau-Ponty pursues with the pseudo-Sartre. He argues: "Class does not face the militant as an object that his will molds or manipulates: it is also behind him."* "The idea is neither received from the proletariat by the Party nor given by the Party to the proletariat; it is *elaborated* in the Party."†

Yet, Sartre writes, "Since the masses cannot budge without shaking society, they are revolutionary by virtue of their *objective situation*: in order *to serve* them, the officials must *elaborate* a revolutionary policy."‡

"If active experience begins in receptivity and uncertainty . . . the deciphering *can* be achieved by a mediation. Still, a Party can only *try* its keys; it cannot *impose* them."§

Merleau-Ponty reminds us that "Lenin gave consciousness an obligation to inform itself about everything the proletariat spontaneously thinks or does."**

But Sartre says, "The essential task of the militants is to maintain contact with the masses."[48] The militant must "make conjectures about their frames of mind, the effect his speeches have produced, and the *objective possibilities of the situation*."[49]

And, "It must be able to *foresee* the workers' reactions. . . . How is it possible to decide, without gathering information, conducting surveys and consulting statistics? The masses are constantly giving signs: it's up to the militant to interpret them."††

Being situated well short of any criterion of truth "the Party cannot err," says Merleau-Ponty.

But Sartre writes regarding the militant that "The synthesis which he carries out is itself only a reconstruction whose probability, in the best cases, cannot surpass that of a scientific hypothesis before experimental verification. Naturally, it will be retested: but since the action itself takes the place of experimentation, *error is expensive*."‡‡

Merleau-Ponty criticizes Sartre for considering the relationship of the Party with the masses as a relationship of end to means or means to end, whereas there is an open relationship between them. But Sartre writes regarding the masses that "Since they represent the very forces which can real-

---

* Ad, 157 [167; AD, 123].
† Ad, 157 [AD, 116].
‡ Cp [377; CP, 226].
§ RL, 1589 [RCL, 33; ARCL, 253].
** Ad, 175 [AD, 129].
†† Cp III, 1802 [Cp, 367; CP, 218].
‡‡ Cp III, 1810 [Cp, 370; CP, 221].

ize the revolutionary enterprise, it will be said that they are the means of this politics insofar as they are its end."*

"And since it isn't a matter of changing them but of helping them to become what they are, the Party is at once their mere expression and their example."†

Merleau-Ponty reminds us that "The Party has value for the militant only through the action to which it calls him, and this action is not *completely definable in advance.*"‡

But Sartre has explained that "the class that is *already united* can surpass its leaders, *steer them farther* than they meant to go and translate into the social sphere an initial decision which was perhaps only political."§

To make a politics spring from a series of pure actions without any reference to history or truth will obviously bring about the most absurd consequences.

"The possibilities are all equally distant, in a sense at zero distance, since all there is to do is to will, in a sense, to infinity."**

Sartre explains, however, that the role of the Party is precisely to organize the possibilities grasped by the masses in the immediate as being equally distant. This is the meaning of the tactic of the "double objective": "showing the masses the remote consequences of their protest actions, and teaching them under what general conditions their particular demands will be met."††

Merleau-Ponty claims, that, according to Sartre, praxis "is thus the vertiginous freedom, the magic power that we have to do and to make ourselves whatever we want."‡‡

Sartre writes, "Praxis is sketched out in the movement of the economy."§§

But Merleau-Ponty points out that "The immediate will to change the world, resting on no historical knowledge and including neither strategy nor tactics, is, in history, the law of the heart and the vertigo of doing [*la loi du coeur et le vertige du faire*]."[50] And he wisely objects that "one cannot sanely attempt to re-create history by pure action alone, with no external strategy."[51]

However, it is certainly not Sartre who thinks that one can "restart history from zero," not the Sartre who wrote in his reply to Camus, "One must first accept many things, if you hope to change a few of them."[52]

---

* Cp III, 1815 [Cp, 377-78; CP, 266].
† Cp II, 697 [Cp, 155; CP, 58].
‡ Ad, 172 [AD, 127].
§ RL, 1609 [RCL, 64; ARCL, 275].
** Ad, 179 [AD, 132].
†† Cp III [Cp, 378; CP, 227].
‡‡ Ad, 179 [AD, 132].
§§ Cp III, 1770 [Cp, 311; CP, 176].

To tell the truth there is a certain madness in the words themselves as used by Merleau-Ponty: where is the zero point in History? Or if one situates it in the pithecanthropine age, how can one think back to that time?

"There is neither degree nor path between the given society and the revolutionary society," says Merleau-Ponty commenting on Sartre.[53] Yet, Sartre writes, "In order that they (the masses) can win one day, it is necessary to prepare for their triumph: to make alliances . . . to work out a strategy, to invent a tactic."* The Party's very role is to mediate through its politics the demands of the masses, because "need is a lack; it can found a humanism but not a strategy."[54]

We can see now that in *Adventures of the Dialectic* the misrepresentation of Sartre's political thought is as radical as the falsification of his ontology. In the face of a proletariat as opaque and mute as things, the Party would create History *ex nihilo* through instantaneous actions: the voluntarism of pure action is symmetrical to the imperialism of pure consciousness, giving its meaning to the world. They are both equally foreign to Sartre. According to him, the Party's role is, on the contrary, to isolate the truth indicated by the world of probabilities by means of experience which demands time and implies the possibility of error. It is upon this truth, based on the needs of the masses, pushed and controlled by them, that the Party is to elaborate a long term politics which would bring about the triumph of the demands of the masses.

IV

We would be tempted to think that the aberrations of pseudo-Sartreanism cut it off radically from reality. Nevertheless Merleau-Ponty admits a curious, pre-established harmony between the philosophical delirium which posits the subject as a sovereign demiurge and the madness of a politics of pure action: Sartre is thus an appropriate example of ultra-bolshevism. His sole wrongdoing is to have adopted a favorable attitude toward this most recent avatar of communism. As a matter of fact, Sartre, says Merleau-Ponty, no longer believes in the immanent truth that according to Marx guarantees praxis, i.e., the revolution. His decision is, therefore, nothing more than a moral option betraying personal obsessions. If we confine ourselves to objectivity, we will necessarily side with this agnostic non-communism which

---

* Cp III, 1801 [Cp, 357; CP, 211].

Merleau-Ponty adopted ever since the Korean War convinced him of the need to support liberty.

We are now going to examine the different steps of this demonstration.

* * *

For Sartre, revolution would no longer occur except as myth and utopia. "The revolution of which Sartre speaks is absent in the sense in which Marxism said it was present, that is to say, as the internal mechanism of the class struggle; and it is present in the sense in which Marxism believed it distant, that is to say, as the positing of ends."*

But when Sartre says that today the proletariat has lost its grip on History, he is merely stating that workers no longer feel the revolution as their daily task; there is no longer an immediate coincidence between their specific claims and their will to change the world. This does not mean that their will has died out or that capitalism has ceased to be torn by contradictions which make its breakup necessary: "Let us not go concluding that the proletariat has lost the memory of its infinite task: the truth of the matter is that the confluence of circumstances deprives it of any future by forcing it to stick to its immediate interests. . . . Never has the truth appeared so clearly: each class pursues the death of the other. . . . And in point of fact, if the crisis gets worse, it can lead to revolution, that is to the breakup of an economy sapped by its internal contradictions."†

Merleau-Ponty admits that "There is an ebb and flow of the proletariat living politically in the Party."‡ Sartre sees in this day and age a period of backward surge: the proletariat nevertheless remains revolutionary in its objective situation, and although it needs the Party for its will to be mediatized into an effective praxis, one has no right to conclude that "the Revolution itself will be the Party's doing."[55] The revolution created by the Party will not be *the same* as the one nurtured in the bosom of the proletariat; it will not be authentic, Merleau-Ponty says, for its authenticity would require the access of the proletariat to political life and management. Merleau-Ponty's entire reasoning relies on the dissociation he previously made between the apparatus and the masses. However, if the Party is distinguished from the masses only insofar as it is their union, Merleau-Ponty's objections collapse by virtue of their own contradictions.

---

* Ad, 184 [183; AD, 136].
† Cp, 1773 [315; CP, 179].
‡ Ad, 163 [AD, 120].

"For lack of warranty," he adds, "revolution is defined only by its antagonism toward the class it eliminates."[56] In fact Sartre calls revolution "surpassing the Other toward the infinite task. . . . Marx thought: surpassing the Other and itself."[57] In fact, the idea of infinite task implies for Sartre not that the revolution recedes to infinity, but that as soon as the bourgeoisie is eliminated as a class, the proletariat will necessarily have to surpass the moment of negation. Sartre refuses to describe the exact shape that society will then take because, for him as well as for Marx, revolution as a positing of ends is absent; one cannot positively imagine it without lapsing into utopia. This does not mean that the future then becomes a total obscurity: that would be the case if the Party were actually to re-create the future from the zero point by pure action; but the hypothesis is in itself mad. Incidentally, Merleau-Ponty recognizes that "one meets the Communist Party, not as pure action, but as applied action."[58] And Sartre has always described it in precisely these terms. It is a question of making a truth triumph historically, a truth which is inscribed in the structures of society; praxis is not invented *ex nihilo*; it is based on objective significations indicated by the world. From this world to a revolutionary world, there is, thus, a perfectly intelligible passage. Certainly it does not follow that the future will be entirely foreseeable—it was not for Marx or Lenin either. Merleau-Ponty is the first one to recognize that praxis, because "it agrees to commit itself to more than what it *knows* of a party and of History, allows more to be learned, and its motto could be *clarum per obscurius*."* Why, when this engagement is geared toward revolution, does he suddenly and testily conclude that "the revolutionary choice is really a haphazard choice,"[59] and that Sartre, contrary to praxis, practices the *obscurius per clarum*?

This is because Merleau-Ponty persists in reconstructing Sartre by using pure deduction, based on pseudo-Sartreanism. If Sartre denies history, dialectic, and finally the revolution, his engagement can only be founded on abstract principles. "A decisive reading into events depends, thus, upon a moral option." Merleau Ponty acknowledges that political judgment "escapes morality as well as pure science. The call to action makes for the coming and going between morality and science."† But since Sartre repudiates science, since in his philosophy "there is no truth of a society," decision is only a question of ethics. Feeling indicted by the look "of the least favored," Sartre allegedly tries to defend himself through pure action, and since he

---

* Ad, 264 [AD, 196].
† Ad, 208 [209; AD, 155].

himself cannot achieve it at every moment of his life, he delegates this task to the Communist Party with which he claims to identify through affinity. "Pure action is Sartre's response to this gaze. . . . We are in the magical or moral world."[60]

Merleau-Ponty's interpretation here seems to betray his own personal obsessions, for Sartre never spoke of *indictment* nor are the ideas of *redemption* nor the concern of being *irreproachable* in the eyes of the proletariat, to be seen anywhere in his works. Nevertheless, Merleau-Ponty makes them the ultimate motivating forces for Sartre's decisions. Feigning to reckon with the other in the highest degree, pseudo-Sartre, in reality, reckons only with himself. His attitude allegedly reveals the "madness of the *cogito* which has sworn to recapture its *image* in others."[61] Merleau-Ponty's emotional outburst makes him so distraught that he uses words side by side that clash with each other: the cogito, pure presence of the For-itself to itself, cannot have an image; the image can appear only through this transcendent object that is the Ego. Elsewhere, in a more intelligible manner, Merleau-Ponty says that Sartre seeks "to put in agreement the determinations attributed to me by the other with what I am in my own eyes."[62] Sartre has shown in *Saint Genet* that such an attempt is necessarily doomed to failure, and his book shows that there must be singular circumstances for an individual to found his life upon such an endeavor. It is clear from the way Sartre tells of Genet's experience that he does not recognize himself in it. Nothing in his life or his work authorizes us to define him through this will of recuperation. Once again, Merleau-Ponty proceeds with the use of a purely unwarranted assertion. Moreover, he should ask himself why in this detotalized totality, which is referred to by the ambiguous word "the Other," Sartre elects the look of the least favored. If he is looking for a mirror he could choose Aron's eyes, or Merleau-Ponty's, or that of the thinking elite.[63] He wishes to follow his own principles, answers Merleau-Ponty: but why are principles inscribed on this image and not on that other one? The principle is not given from the beginning. Merleau-Ponty follows his principles in renouncing the "Marxist wait-and-see attitude," since an objective revelation would have brought him to contest his previous attitude: therefore, principles depend on the manner in which we apprehend our situation, and consequently the truth of the world. The anti-communist is in line with the world and his own principles, and so is the communist. This formal explanation cannot give us an account of Sartre's concrete choice.

The fact is that it would be sufficient to read Sartre without bias; then one could grasp his objective reasons. When Sartre speaks of the look of the least favored, he in no way brings himself into play. In describing the actual condition of the unskilled worker, he explains that in order to free the masses from their sense of inferiority "it was necessary to make the masses understand that they were offering all men the chance to look at man and society *in their truth*, that is to say, with the eyes of the least favored."* For, contrary to what Merleau-Ponty claims, Sartre does recognize a truth of society, a truth which is disguised by bourgeois mystifications and which is disclosed by the man of the masses. Sartre thinks that "the only human relationship is that of the *real*, total man with the total man, and that this relationship, travestied or passed over in silence, exists permanently within the masses and exists only there."[64] Obsessed with the Sartrean theory of the look, Merleau-Ponty wants to find in Sartre only this type of relationship; however, the look appears in the text to which he refers only as the disclosure of a total relationship. Sartre also says that the existence of the masses "introduces . . . the radical demand for the human in an inhuman society."[65] Here Sartre is close to Marx who also saw the proletarian as the only one capable of denouncing the *alienation* in which the entire society lives, because he feels annihilated by it, while the bourgeois is satisfied with "the appearance of the human." Marx speaks of a categorical imperative of the revolution without Merleau-Ponty accusing him of deciphering history in the sole light of a moral option. There is in Sartre, as well as in Marx, this coming and going between truth and ethical decision which, according to Merleau-Ponty himself, characterizes political judgment.

Yet, Merleau-Ponty persists in radically subjectivizing Sartre's political attitude. Instead of questioning himself about communist action, pseudo-Sartre decided, as a demiurge, to integrate it into the "Sartrean project." "It is not so much a question of knowing where communist action is going, so as either to associate himself with it or not, as it is of finding a meaning for this action in *the* Sartrean project."† And what is *this project*? If it is a matter of "*redeeming* oneself through the future"—nothing in Sartre's work gives an echo of this expression—why then prefer this future? There are actions other than communist actions. Moreover, if it is necessary to explain Sartre through the megalomania of the subject, what was the reason for his having waited such a long time before gluttonously devouring communism?

Merleau-Ponty finds the proof of Sartre's subjectivism in the fact that the latter started his new relationship with communism because of certain

---

* Cp III, 1792 [Cp, 344; CP, 201].
† Ad, 261 [AD, 194].

historical events; he forgets that he himself chose non-communism after a specific event—the Korean War—which was also a historical event. Realization, taking place in the present, at a precise moment, can thus disclose an objective reality and provoke an engagement which is not limited to the instant: this, it seems, is a truth of common sense. Besides, Sartre explains at length in *The Communists and Peace* that it is because he has found the true meaning of communist action and its necessity that he felt obliged to associate himself with it. His attitude is clear to one who reads his essay without being blinded by pseudo-Sartreanism. He believes in certain contradictions in capitalism that, by making the situation of the exploited classes intolerable, turn the society in which we live into an inhuman society. For himself and others who are inextricably connected, he wants the abolition of that alienation that all of us bear, but whose true brunt is fully borne only by the least favored in society. He knows that only the proletariat has the necessary forces to change the world, and that it needs the Party's mediation in order to apply them efficaciously. Therefore, he decided to become allied with those who want the same thing he does and who have the means to realize it: such is the meaning of his engagement.

However, Merleau-Ponty refuses to admit that Sartrean engagement has a positive definition and leads to a true action. A pure consciousness can only keep the world at a distance; it cannot concretely project itself onto it. Hence, for pseudo-Sartre, to engage oneself will always be to disengage oneself; freedom appears only as a negation, and when Sartre claims to act, he merely contemplates. Merleau-Ponty simply forgets that in authentic Sartreanism, there is never a pure consciousness. We have said it before, and we need to repeat it again: Sartrean consciousness only *exists* in the world when it is *lost* in the world, engaged, incarnated in a body and a situation. Man makes himself be only by acting in the world through positive projects, and these projects always have a temporal thickness. Merleau-Ponty, in addition to his rejection of Sartre's theory on facticity, also dismisses his entire philosophy of time. He believes that time, for Sartre as well as for Descartes, is a continuous creation: freedom could only manifest itself through *ex nihilo* flashes, without any link between them; it could not allow any true action but only "instantaneous interventions in the world, camera shots and flashes."* In this pseudo-Sartreanism, instead of a *doing* one finds only a *fiat* whose magical dimension is similar to that of the look. And Merleau-Ponty, in a plausible way, explains to the pseudo-Sartre that an authentic action

---

* Ad, 259 [AD, 197].

bites into things, unfolds in time, implies possibilities of failure, and is founded on a choice which has roots in all aspects of our life.

Meanwhile, Sartre in *Being and Nothingness* openly states his opposition to the instantaneist concept of consciousness that one encounters in Descartes and Husserl: the three temporal ek-stases for him are indissoluble, and the cogito itself, in its upspringing, envelops both a past and a future. The choice, in particular, always retains within it the past which it surpasses: "A converted atheist is not simply a believer: he is a believer who, by himself, has denied atheism." And the choice always projects a future: "To choose is to effect the upsurge of a certain extension of concrete and continuous duration along with my engagement."[66] In such a duration, the action organizes the means in view of an end. Sartre carefully distinguishes the *fiat* of the emotional attitude which immediately posits the end in the imagination, from the *doing* which mediatizes the choice in the real thickness of the world. "To act is to modify the shape of the world; it is to arrange means in view of an end."[67] This is a long and exacting enterprise which also determines "a modification in the being of the Transcendent." By biting into a reality which is *probability* and not certainty, the enterprise obviously entails a risk of failure. Thus, we are leagues away from the pseudo-engagement of the pseudo-Sartre which Merleau-Ponty defines as negativity, as an instantaneous, magical, and imaginary intervention. Incidentally, if Sartre were to practice such an engagement, it would be as impossible for him to write a book as to act politically: he would be reduced to the radical ineffectiveness of Mr. Teste who, as a matter of fact, remained silent.[68]

Merleau-Ponty especially makes us want to smile when he sweetly asks Sartre, "How then shall I date my choices? They have innumerable precedents. . . ."* We feel compelled to smile because one of the leitmotifs found throughout Sartre's work is precisely the totalitarian character of each human life. There is a transcendent signification—a type of intelligible character— which unites all our empirical choices, each of them rooted in our entire past. Freedom is not the contingency of the clinamen: "The freedom of the For-itself is always *engaged*; there is no question here of a freedom which could be undetermined and which would pre-exist its choice. We shall never grasp ourselves except as a choice in the making."[69] Sartre considers deliberation to be pure abstraction. "When I deliberate, the chips are down."[70] According to him there is never a moment when choice begins. "I choose myself perpetually."[71] One ought to read *Baudelaire*, *Saint Genet*, and *Henri Martin* to see that

---

* Ad, 265 [AD, 197].

Sartre didn't await Merleau-Ponty to suspect that one does not become either a poet or a communist in a lightning decision, without a precedent.

Communist action does not represent a train of convulsive bids for power; and to go back to Sartre's case, neither is his adhesion to communist action reduced to a string of realizations from afar. Sartre, says Merleau-Ponty, "knows that some people want to change the world" and sympathizes with this intention, which is a way of not assuming it. Sartre, in fact, is among those who want to change the world and he chooses the means which his concrete situation offers him—that of a bourgeois writer.

On this point, Merleau-Ponty aims his most contradictory reproaches at Sartre. He claims, "For him, to be engaged is not to interpret and criticize oneself in contact with History; rather it is to re-create one's own relationship with history. . . . it is to place oneself deliberately in the imaginary."* At the time when Sartre together with other intellectuals, Merleau-Ponty included, was attempting to rally the non-communist left, such a reproach would have made sense; today, it only bewilders us. It is precisely because he has interpreted and criticized himself in contact with History that Sartre understood his powerlessness to change the world by his own force or by joining with his peers who were as powerless as him. He resolved to follow the type of action his objective situation indicated as being the only *really* valid one: an alliance with real forces capable of imposing on History the meaning he wants to give it.

Such an alliance, Merleau-Ponty argues, is only a spoken, imagined thought: it does not have the weight of an action. "There is perhaps not much sense in dealing with communism, which is an action, by means of pure thought."† But hasn't Merleau-Ponty reproached the pseudo-Sartre for falsely carving out a gulf between action and thought? What does this arbitrary opposition signify? There is no pure thought, since all disclosure is action; nor is there an action which does not imply a disclosure: one truly cannot see why "to think communism" is a contradictory enterprise. Moreover, Sartre's *intervention* does not limit itself only to that. Merleau-Ponty— mistakenly believing that he is in opposition to Sartre on this point—asserts that "all actions . . . are always symbolic actions and count as much upon the effect they will have as meaningful gesture as upon the immediate results of the event."‡ Hence, Sartre's adherence, although it has no immedi-

---

* Ad, 262 [AD, 195].
† Ad, 237 [AD, 176].
‡ Ad, 270 [AD, 200].

ate results on the event, possesses at least the not inconsiderable reality of a significative manifestation: it can be an example or an appeal. Altering his stance, Merleau-Ponty nevertheless demands immediate results; the will to help the proletariat to free itself is discredited if we do not say "how our action will free it." Neither Marx nor Lenin nor any militant has drawn up in advance such a progam of action. If Sartre were to risk doing so himself, then he would surely be labeled a utopian. But he modestly said in his *Reply to Albert Camus* that one must try to give history the meaning one sees as being the best "by not refusing our support to any concrete action which may require it."[72] This is a sensible answer to the strange alternative proposed by Merleau-Ponty: to have a plan for freeing the proletariat or to sit around doing nothing. By limiting ourselves to the accomplishment of these concrete actions, ordered by circumstances, we choose "a way of putting ourselves right with the world rather than entering into it."* But how can we *enter* into a world we are already in? What date does Merleau-Ponty give for his own entry into the world? He also reproaches Sartre for not "taking charge of the world," however, Merleau-Ponty does not indicate what this titanic operation would entail. Elsewhere, he says more sensibly that "No action assumes all that happens."[73]

Moreover, Merleau-Ponty will add that Sartre, in his desire to assume *everything*, fails to engage himself concretely in a real enterprise. Only in dreams can we attain anything we want. But once more Merleau-Ponty is misled by the erroneous idea that Sartre's philosophy is intuitive and claims to encompass everything. For Sartre, consciousness is always engaged; it is necessarily a finitude, and he intends to act only as a finite, limited, and situated individual.

"That is a solution only for someone who lives in the capitalist world," Merleau-Ponty objects again.[74] The fact is that Sartre lives in this world, and so do the communists; the struggle to change society takes place in its midst, which is where one must seek solutions. However, Sartre's solution will not be accepted by the communists, says Merleau-Ponty. "He decrees the coexistence between communism and the opposition from the outside."[75] Here one is reminded of Zeno's sophisms in which he cleverly demonstrates why Achilles will never catch up with the turtle. There is, in fact, a friendly coexistence between Sartre and the communists, and nothing authorizes Merleau-Ponty to assert that they do not *understand* him: comprehension does not imply identification but simply friendship. By associating himself with

---

* Ad, 259 [AD, 193].

the communists, Sartre proves that he understands them; and because they ratify this alliance, they show in return that they understand him. It is futile to confine in formal contradictions an attitude which proves itself by living.

Actually, in order to establish that Sartre's choice only obeys subjective motives and that in reality nothing justifies it, Merleau-Ponty would have to succeed in proving that the weight of objectivity is on the side of non-communism. Let's examine his demonstration.

* * *

The Korean War revealed to Merleau-Ponty what the Moscow trials, the German-Soviet pact, and the events in Prague had failed to make him discover, namely that revolutionary negativity is embodied in living men who exist positively.[76] The result is that "Revolutionary society has its weight, its positivity, and it is no longer the absolute Other." Hurled down from the sublime point where he had been transported in thought to await a miraculous transubstantiation, Merleau-Ponty concluded then that "revolutions are true as movements and false as regimes."[77] It is thus, as in Prévert's poem, that the scientists displeased with the results of their experiments, came to the conclusion: "It is the rabbits that are wrong."[78]

Merleau-Ponty will say no. It is not a matter of a subjective disappointment here, but a contradiction inherent in the revolutionary process. At best, the system it institutes is *relatively* justifiable: "The distinctive feature of a revolution is to believe itself absolute."[79] Indeed he says, "one does not kill for relative progress."[80] Who then would undertake to make a revolution without being convinced that he was creating a different society "because it *is the good*?"[81] The revolutionaries, of course! Merleau-Ponty, who answered the pseudo-Sartre with the statement that our intentions do not aim at closed significations, nor do our wills aim at settled objectives, seems nevertheless to assume now that the revolutionary enterprise is preceded by a deliberation where the idea of absolute good settles the decision. However, History shows Merleau-Ponty that revolutions spring up little caring if their justification is guaranteed in advance. What is found in their origins, is not the promise of a *City of the Sun*, but the most modest of demands.[82] When in 1848, the national workshops closed and the workers took their protest onto the streets; they killed and were killed not for progress, whether absolute or relative, but for work and bread. One kills from hunger, anger, and despair. One kills to live. The stakes are infinite for they are life itself with its infinity of possibilities, but they never assume the positive and utopian image of a paradisiacal society. Merleau-Ponty assumes the contrary because he ignores dire situations; neither the word nor the idea of need appear in his analyses. But an absolute of rebellion and refusal erupts from dire needs and does not allow the revolutionary the leisure to draw up a balance sheet. In the quiet of his study, Merleau-Ponty may *tell himself* that if revolution does not realize the absolute Good, then it is not worth the effort; but he is talking for himself; therefore, revolutions betray solely his dreams and not themselves.

In any case, he will say, for the one who considers it from the outside, the revolution no longer deserves a favorable judgment. The relative progress that it may accomplish could be achieved by other means. And here is when Merleau-Ponty, with surprising naivete, discovers reformism. "The question arises whether there is not *more of a future* in a regime that does not intend to remake History from the ground up but only to change it."[83] Merleau-Ponty seems to believe that revolutionaries are people who ignore the question, whereas they resolved it with the negative. Like Marx, they consider that a future freed from exploitation can only be created if one attacks exploitation at its roots: and such is the future they want. To pose the question in quantitative terms is nonsense. Here, one touches the profound defect of a thought, which feigning to believe in the class struggle, resolutely neglects to take it into account. When Merleau-Ponty decides that the concern of non-communism must be to establish balance sheets, he commits the fault he ascribes to the pseudo-Sartre: in an instant he situates himself outside of history, and claims to cast a glance from on high at the struggle between oppressed and oppressors, and to separate the combatants by setting the world into mathematical equations. But it is impossible to establish the criterion for more and less in a society which is torn apart: what is a gain in the eyes of the privileged is a loss for the oppressed, and vice-versa. The idea of the general interest is such an overused mystification that one wonders how bourgeois economists dare to serve it to us again.

While waiting for the inventory to be completed, Merleau-Ponty limits himself to proposing an assessment of the Soviet regime. He repeats the indictment of the USSR that floats around in all of Aron's books and in the columns of *L'aurore*,[84] and specifically repeats the Machiavellian slogan: revolution is nothing more than a change of elites. He concludes that "what we know of the USSR is not sufficient to prove that the proletarians' interests lie in this system."[85] But is what we know of France sufficient to prove that the proletariat's interests lie in upholding its present regime? Merleau-Ponty will say it is not a question of upholding the present regime, but of settling oneself in it in order to change it. If this is the case, then what does the USSR have to do in all of this? Let's rather compare the future of a France reshaped by the conscious action of the Elite, with the France that would be born out of a revolution. The Revolution necessarily institutes "an *impure* power,"[86] says Merleau Ponty; but is it pure to prolong without clash or violence a state of affairs which Merleau-Ponty himself qualifies as *unjustifiable*? Merleau-Ponty is suspicious of revolutionary action because "revolutionary action is secret, unverifiable."[87] Is the action he suggests verifiable?

It is here that his bad faith is so glaring. He wants to change History by working within the parliamentary regime, because the Parliament is the sole institution which guarantees a minimum of opposition and truth; he nevertheless admits that the democratic game *disadvantages* the proletariat. But he hopes to offset this contradiction by demanding that the working class, through the Communist Party, strikes, and popular movements, have the possibility of refusing the rules of the game. Thus, the new liberalism "lets even what contests it enter my universe."[88] Such a compromise is a revolting hypocrisy. It is not by chance that the parliamentary game is played to the detriment of the workers. Since Merleau-Ponty recognizes that there is a class struggle, he knows that the bourgeois democracy necessarily exerts its power *against* the proletariat; it might camouflage the injustice but it does not want to eliminate it. Therefore, the concessions of the new liberalism would be nothing but mystifications. Tolerated as a "useful menace,"[89] revolutionary movements will be stifled as soon as they appear truly dangerous. Merleau-Ponty must be quite a fool to expect that a class that is the enemy of the proletariat, if entrusted with the task of remaking history, would do so *for* the proletariat.

Why does this regime inspire Merleau-Ponty with such confidence? Because it allows the existence of an opposition. But since Merleau-Ponty confuses opposition with the form it takes in Parliament, he, in effect, cannot recognize it anywhere outside a parliamentary regime. Meanwhile, the reproaches he levels at self-criticism, as practiced by the USSR or the Communist Party, have as much impact as those that an alchemist, an astrologer, or some magus would level at scientific self-criticism. The edifice of science was built through passionate discussions and quarrels, the elimination of errors and the invention of new truths. The only restriction on the critical process, which makes up the very history of scientific knowledge, is that the process will never turn against the system as a whole. This does not signify that there were no interesting individual cases among the backward, the misled, the forerunners, the visionaries, and the illuminati who were fighting against the science of their time; but these people achieved no scientific existence. Thus in a movement or a regime which seeks to *build* society according to a universal pattern, criticism can be carried extremely far; it can lead to drawbacks, to metamorphoses of error into truth, and vice-versa; it only needs to be integrated into the positive work that is being accomplished. Whoever truly wants this construction to be successful will have to accept a rule that does not deprive him of his freedom any more than scientific discipline deprives the scientist of his. To choose a regime which is against the proletariat, hence a regime which we must disapprove on principle, under the pretext that it authorizes opposition, is to give pre-eminence to criticism over action when it should be only its guarantee. In other words, it is to place the abstract pleasure of expressing opinion ahead of the will to concretely rebuild the world. Furthermore, it is to dissociate oneself from the proletariat, whose cause one claims to espouse, knowing well that its opposition is not accepted by this Parliament which only concedes to the already privileged the right to quarrel among themselves.

In fact, the very idea of choosing *for* the proletariat implies that Merleau-Ponty, despite his statements, no longer believes in class struggle; that is to say, he has sided with the bourgeoisie. If there is a struggle, one cannot do anything *for* the proletariat without willing it *with* the proletariat. "The question is to know whether, for the proletariat, communism is worth what it costs,"[90] says Merleau-Ponty, glimpsing a surpassing of the communism-capitalism conflict. "One glimpses a generalized economy of which they are particular cases."[91] However, communism is not solely an economic system; it has a human dimension: it expresses the will of certain men who, first of all, demand to hold their lives in their own hands instead of enduring the fate imposed on them by the elites. To decide to bring them happiness in spite of themselves is to perpetuate oppression. Class struggle implies that one cannot include the will of both the exploiter and the exploited in any economy, however generalized it may be.

To be *for* the proletariat does not mean to acknowledge its misery from a distance and to carry on regardless: it is to take its demands seriously. Merleau-Ponty decisively sides with the bourgeoisie watch dogs when he no longer sees communism as a living reality, rooted in the need and rebellion of an exploited class, but instead as a figment of the imagination. For him, as for Aron and all the other bourgeois thinkers, communism becomes utopia. Therefore, the existing world, despite all the flaws that make it unjustifiable, carries with it a favorable bias. What is significant is that Merleau-Ponty repeats the charge against communism which was formerly set against Pascal's Wager: "An eternity of imaginary happiness could not counterbalance an instant of life."[92] This is to insinuate that the proletariat has to make a choice between a plenitude, perhaps minimal but real, and the emptiness of a barren dream; but for them, it is a matter of tearing themselves away, at any price, from a condition which (as Merleau-Ponty acknowledges later) does not allow them to live. Here, Merleau-Ponty, when all is said and done, rediscovers the unimaginative prudence of conservatives: "We know what we lose; we do not know what we will find." This signifies that he identifies with those who have something to lose, those for whom the *balance sheet* of this society is positive: in short, he identifies with the privileged. He has discovered, in fact, that unjustifiable societies do, nevertheless, possess a value. Or perhaps, he simply repeats here the idea of Marx and Engels, who start the *Communist Manifesto* by praising capitalism: the value of a society is defined dialectically by the possibilities of surpassing itself that are enclosed within it. Capitalist society is put forth only to be surpassed and that is the aim of communism. Or perhaps, Merleau-Ponty, together with Malraux and other champions of Western Civilization, decides that one can prefer values to men.[93] Bourgeois analytical thought confines oppression to a single sector of society and assumes that this singular wrong can come to terms with other rights [*biens*]. Marx's synthetic thought, as well as Sartre's, considers that society in its totality is corrupted by exploitation: it measures values in the light of oppression. This is what is signified for Sartre by the appeal to the look of the least favored, an appeal so poorly understood by Merleau-Ponty. For the least favored, all values carry a minus sign. They exist only insofar as they are denied to the least favored. Because the exploited are excluded, each new human conquest widens the chasm of its destitution. When one has sided with the proletariat, the values enclosed within unjustifiable societies, far from justifying these societies, only make them more unjustifiable. One feels sorry to have to remind Merleau-Ponty of these elementary truths, he who so justly wrote in *Humanism and Terror*, "The worth of a society is measured in terms of the worth attributed to the relationships of man with man." Today, he must decide whether to state with Aron that class struggle is an outdated notion; or holding out his hand to Mr. Jules Romains,[94] whether to join openly our Western thinkers and the ethics of the Elite in their contempt of the masses. But to write "a history in which the proletariat is nothing is not a human history"[95] and to adhere to a regime which reduces the proletariat to nothing, is the most shameless of masquerades.

* * *

How shall we explain the enormous inconsistencies we find in Merleau-Ponty, both on the philosophical and political planes? What emerges from *Adven-*

tures of the Dialectic is, first of all, that he fell victim to that old idealism traditional among French academics. One of them wrote about World War I that it was "Descartes' battle against Kant." And thus, Merleau-Ponty sees in the Korean War a confrontation between Marxism and Stalinism: the Koreans in this matter are not taken into account. He asks himself whether or not the proletariat is by itself the dialectic; as for the proletarians, he never pays them any heed. The revolution for him is "the criticism in power."[96] He does not attach any importance to the changes that concrete revolutions bring about in the concrete condition of men. Reverting to the pre-Kantian ages of philosophy, he fabricates antinomies of concepts that he then uses for an excuse to negate the living truth of the world. In this way, concepts of criticism and power exclude each other; thus, one must condemn revolutions as being deceptive. Or, on the contrary, he builds up ideal syntheses which he confuses with concrete solutions: if a generalized economy incorporates communism and capitalism, then communists and capitalists are reconciled! In defining a liberalism that envelops what it contests, he goes so far as to assert that the new liberals will indeed respect revolutionary movements: but it is with similar processes that Saint Anselm once proved God's existence.

It seems that this precedence given to the Idea over concrete men explains Merleau-Ponty's about-face. Revolution seduced him as long as he saw in it an already present truth whose revelation was at hand. In his book one feels the nostalgia of a golden age of revolution which is solely situated in Merleau-Ponty's inner life, not in the reality of things nor in Marxism which closely adheres to this reality. The proletariat was both "power and value;" it had a mission, in the sacred meaning of the word. Merleau-Ponty says that now it is necessary "to secularize" communism which thus signifies that he had regarded it as sacred. If communism is no longer what anticommunists claim it is—a religion—a deceived Merleau-Ponty resolves to see in it only a utopia. He who defended the rights of the probable against the pseudo-Sartre is now driven by probabilism to agnosticism. Since revolution entails a *perhaps* instead of a radiant certitude, and since it presents itself as *to be made* and not as a truth already made, Merleau-Ponty accuses those who want revolution of claiming to create it *ex nihilo* and does not see an intermediary between triumphant assertion and absolute doubt. Because he is no longer assured of an immediate apotheosis, he puts his wager on defeat. It is on this point that, politically, he is poles apart from Sartre. For Sartre, the truth of revolution is not an immediate or a distant triumph, but above all the class struggle as it exists today. This struggle aims at the future, but in the present; it is necessary right now to side with the exploited against exploitation, to refuse to let them bear the brunt of this improved capitalism that the class in power today likes to consider a universal panacea. Although the fight is difficult and doubtful, Sartre does not think that sufficient reason for throwing oneself into the opposite camp: on the contrary, it is then that one's support is most needed.

Merleau-Ponty's mood regarding communism seems, therefore, to be the reflection of a religious soul's bitterness toward a world that is all too human. This partly explains his irritation with Sartre who followed an opposite road. Merleau-Ponty's *a priori* construction of pseudo-Sartreanism remains nevertheless surprising. True, Merleau-Ponty has never understood Sartre. As early as *Phenomenology of Perception*, he coldly denied the entire Sartrean phenomenology of engaged freedom. Even if reconciling Sartre's ontology with his phenomenology raises difficulties,* one does not have the right to grab from his hands one "of the two ends of the chain," to use Merleau-Ponty's words. Such violence is even more scandalous today than ten years ago, because throughout the development of his work Sartre has insisted more and more on the *engaged* character of freedom, the facticity of the world, the embodiment of consciousness, the continuity of lived time, and the totalitarian character of each life. Yet, Merleau-Ponty does not ignore Sartre's books. When he answers the pseudo-Sartre, he usually employs Sartre's own ideas, and he uses terms which are reminiscent of those that Sartre had used himself; we have seen many examples of this. Perhaps the ideas Merleau-Ponty has in common with Sartre seem to him to be so exclusively his own that, in order to claim their originality, he is forced to invent a Sartreanism which would be a counter–Merleau-Pontyism. The method is a lazy one and not very honest. One could praise him for creating a philosophy that surpasses the difficulties of Sartreanism, but these difficulties do not permit Merleau-Ponty to multilate Sartre's philosophy. Neither is it honest to make use of the pseudo-Sartre in order to write a shallow non-communist apology without compromising himself. Instead of clearly explaining how the non-communist "enters into the world" and "takes charge of it," Merleau-Ponty suggests its flattering image to us by a negative. If conscious and deliberate action is nothing more than a dream, if, by concerning oneself with others, one is only thinking about oneself, if allying oneself

---

* Merleau-Ponty is perfectly aware that Sartre is in the process of preparing a philosophical work which attacks this question head-on.

with the proletariat is the height of narcissism, then dreaming will suffice to be a man of action, and abstention and egoism will become the most effective ways to serve men: one can understand why these insinuations fill *Le figaro* and Mr. Jacques Laurent with delight.[97]

It appears that the periods of regression children go through are beneficial to their development; perhaps they may also be beneficial in adult life: let us hope that *Adventures of the Dialectic* has no more definitive significance. Distressed for having so long mistaken Kant for Marx, Merleau-Ponty thought that he could improve things by mistaking Sartre for Kant: doubtless in the end he will give back to each the place to which he is entitled. He fears that Sartre has renounced disclosure without succeeding in acting. Nonetheless if Merleau-Ponty does not realize that pure assertion leads to the same madness as pure action, we shall have to deplore that he renounced action without succeeding in disclosure.

NOTES

This translation was first published in *International Studies in Philosophy*, vol. XXI/3 (Atlanta: Scholars Press, 1989), ed. Leon J. Goldstein, Norbert Hinske, Vittorio Mathieu, Stephen David Ross. This is a revised version of the 1989 translation, including corrections and revisions in the passages quoted from other sources.

Translator Véronique Zaytzeff wrote the following acknowledgment: "Dedicated to Dr. Carol Keene, my former Dean and friend, who suggested the translation, read the final manuscript, and made useful comments on some philosophical fine points of the manuscript. I would also like to thank Southern Illinois University at Edwardsville for granting me a sabbatical to undertake this project."

The three essays appearing in the *Privilèges* volume ("Must We Burn Sade?" "Right-Wing Thought Today," and "Merleau-Ponty and Pseudo-Sartreanism") were preceded by a foreword written by Simone de Beauvoir. This foreword, translated by Kim Allen Gleed, Marilyn Gaddis Rose, and Virginia Preston, can be found in the notes following the "Must We Burn Sade?" essay in this volume.

1. The citation in Beauvoir's footnote is from *Les communistes et la paix*, which first appeared in three parts in *Les temps modernes* 81 (July 1952), 84–85 (October-November 1952), and 101 (April 1954), and was reprinted in *Situations VI* (Paris: Gallimard, 1964), 168; hereafter referred to as Cp. Translated by Martha H. Fletcher and John R. Kleinschmidt in *"The Communists and Peace" with "Reply to Claude Lefort"* (New York: George Braziller, 1968), 681; hereafter referred to as CP. Many of Sartre's essays that origimally appeared in various periodicals were later collected and reprinted in a 10-volume series called *Situations I–X*. Many of these essays have been translated into English and published in collections under various titles.

2. Beauvoir's footnote refers to *L'être et le néant: essaie d'ontologie phenomenologique* (Paris: Gallimard, 1948); hereafter referred to as EN. Translated by Hazel E. Barnes as *Being*

and Nothingness: An Essay on Phenomenological Ontology (New York: The Citadel Press, 1965), 138; hereafter referred to as BN.

3. EN, 149; BN, 801.

4. EN, 386 and following; BN, 283.

5. EN, 396; BN, 304.

6. EN, 692; Sartre,*Existential Psychoanalysis*, 120.

7. Ad, 185; AD, 137.

8. Cp, 197; CP, 821.

9. Ad, 198; AD, 147.

10. Ad, 192; AD, 143.

11. Cp, 21-22; ARCL, 245.

12. Ad, 186; AD, 138.

13. Sartre, *Saint Genet*, 258, 276.

14. Hippolyte Adolphe Taine (1828–93), a French critic and historian, was one of the most esteemed exponents of nineteenth-century French positivism, attempting to apply the scientific method to the humanities.

15. François Mauriac (1885–1970), winner of the 1952 Nobel Prize in Literature, was a French novelist, essayist, and playwright. His 1935 novel, *La fin de la nuit* (*The End of Night*) (Paris: Bernard Grasset, 1935) was published in English translation in 1947.

16. "With a little perspective, good novels come almost to resemble natural phenomena. We forget that they have authors; we accept them as stones or trees. . . ." Jean-Paul Sartre in "William Faulkner's *Sartoris*" (1938), trans. Annette Michelson, in *Literary and Philosophical Essays* (New York: Collier, 1962), 78. This essay was reprinted in *Situations I* (Paris: Gallimard, 1947).

17. Trotskyites are followers of Leon Trotsky (1879–1940), a Marxist theorist, known for his opposition to Joseph Stalin, and leader of the Russian October Revolution.

18. Cp, 229; CP, 114.

19. Ad, 275; AD, 205.

20. RCL, 21; ARCL, 245.

21. EN, 363; BN, 278.

22. RCL, 33; ARCL, 253.

23. Ad, 156; AD, 114.

24. RCL, 33; ARCL, 254.

25. Ad, 157; AD, 115.

26. Ad, 176; AD, 130.

27. Ad, 156; AD, 115.

28. *Réponse à Albert Camus*, in *Les temps modernes* 82 (August 1952): 334–53; hereafter referred to as RC; reprinted in *Situations IV* (Paris: Gallimard, 1964), 123; hereafter referred to as RAC. Translated by Benita Eisler as *A Reply to Albert Camus* (New York: George Braziller, 1965), 102; hereafter referred to as ARAC.

29. EN, 582; BN, 477.

30. Ad, 213; AD, 158.

31. Ad, 275; AD, 205.

32. Ad, 159; AD, 117.

33. Cp, 376; CP, 225.

34. Ad, 233; AD, 173.

35. The dates, May 28 and June 4, probably refer to the failure of Communist-organized strikes and demonstrations on May 28 and June 4, 1952.

36. Ad, 138; AD, 101.

37. Ad, 144; AD, 105.

38. Cp, 256; CP, 200.

39. Ad, 146; AD, 107.

40. The *Union pour l'action morale et le spiritualisme républicain* (1892–1905), founded in 1893 by Paul Desjardins, Jules Lagneau, and others, was a circle of French intellectuals who sought "to institute the reign of Virtue and Morality" in society.

41. Jules Lagneau (1851–94) was a French philosophy professor known for his work on the psychology of perception, for his famous disciple, Émile Chartier (known as Alain), and for his cofounding of the *Union pour l'action morale et le spiritualisme républicain*.

42. Ad, 146; AD, 107.

43. Cp, 256; CP, 135.

44. RCL, 60-61; ARCL, 273.

45. In May 1936, the Popular Front, an alliance of left-wing movements, won the legislative elections in France, leading to the formation of a socialist government headed by Léon Blum and the enactment of the Matignon agreements, a cornerstone of social rights in France. The euphoria of the socialist movement was evident in the slogan, "Tout est possible!" (Everything is possible). The Popular Front fell from power in June 1937 under the economic pressures of the Great Depression.

46. Cp, 366; CP, 218.

47. RCL, 8-9; ARCL, 236.

48. Cp, 370; CP, 221.

49. Cp, 369; CP, 220.

50. Ad, 181; AD, 134.

51. Ad, 193; AD, 143.

52. RAC, 110; ARAC, 90.

53. Ad, 204; AD, 151.

54. Cp, 376; CP, 225.

55. Ad, 183; AD, 136.

56. Ad, 187; AD, 137.

57. Ad, 185; AD, 137.

58. Ad, 235; AD, 175.

59. Ad, 206; AD, 153.

60. Ad, 307; AD, 154.

61. Ad, 213; AD, 159.

62. Ad, 209; AD, 158-59.

63. Raymond Aron (1905–83) was a liberal French philosopher and journalist known for his criticism of Marxist ideology.

64. Cp, 344; CP, 201.

65. Cp, 346; CP, 203.

66. EN, 543; BN, 441.

67. EN, 508; BN, 409.

68. Monsieur Teste is a fictional character in novels by the French writer and poet, Paul Valéry (1871–1945), including *La soirée avec monsieur Teste* (The Evening with Mr. Teste) (1896) and *Monsieur Teste* (Paris: Gallimard, 1926).

69. EN, 558; BN, 455.

70. EN, 527; BN, 427.

71. EN, 560; BN, 456.

72. RAC, 125; ARAC, 104.

73. Ad, 270; AD, 200.

74. Ad, 240; AD, 178.

75. Ad, 240; AD, 178.

76. The Moscow Trials were a series of show trials in the Soviet Union during the 1930s, with predetermined verdicts and coerced confessions that were orchestrated by Joseph Stalin to eliminate political challengers to his regime; The German-Soviet Pact of August 1939, also known as the Ribbentrop-Molotov Pact after the two foreign ministers who negotiated the agreement, included an economic agreement providing that Germany would exchange manufactured goods for Soviet raw materials and a ten-year nonaggression pact in which each signatory promised not to attack the other; The events in Prague may refer to the series of political show trials held in Prague from 1949–52 in which the Communist government sought to eliminate its opposition. The Communist Party was the only judicial authority in the trials, in which 253 people were condemned to death and 178 people actually executed.

77. Ad, 298; AD, 207.

78. Jacques Prévert (1900–1977) was a surrealist French poet and screenwriter whose poems were collected and published in the following books: *Paroles* (Words) (1946), *Spectacle* (1951), *La Pluie et le beau temps* (Rain and Good Weather) (1955), *Histoires* (Stories) (1963), *Fatras* (1971) and *Choses et autres* (Things and Others) (1973). This phrase is from his poem "Les grandes inventions" (Great Inventions) in *Paroles* (Paris: Éditions du Point du Jour, 1946), which reads "si mes calculs sont justes, c'est sûrement mes lièvres qui sont faux."

79. Ad, 298; AD, 222.

80. Ad, 298; AD, 222.

81. Ad, 298; AD, 222.

82. *The City of the Sun: A Poetical Dialogue*, written in 1602 by Tommaso Campanella (1568–1639), describes a utopian society.

83. Ad, 279; AD, 207.

84. *L'aurore* was a right-wing French daily newspaper.

85. Ad, 245; AD, 182.

86. Ad, 297; AD, 221.

87. Ad, 305; AD, 227.

88. Ad, 304; AD, 226.

89. Ad, 303; AD, 226.

90. Ad, 301; AD, 224.

91. Ad, 303; AD, 225.

92. Pascal's Wager is a suggestion posed by the French philosopher, mathematician and physicist, Blaise Pascal, that a person should wager on God's existence, even though it cannot be proved, because one has everything to gain from such a bet and nothing to lose.

93. André Malraux (1901–76) was a French author and statesman.

94. Jules Romains, born Louis Henri Jean Farigoule (1885–1972), was a French poet and writer and the founder of the Unanimism literary movement, best known for a 27-volume cycle of novels called *Les hommes de bonne volonté* (*Men of Good Will*) (Paris: Flammarion, 1932–46).

95. Ad, 307; AD, 228.

96. Ad, 311; AD, 231.

97. *Le figaro* is a right-wing French daily newspaper founded in 1826 and published in Paris; Jacques Laurent (1919–2000) was a French writer, novelist, and member of the right-wing Hussards group.

5

Preface to *Djamila Boupacha*

INTRODUCTION

by Julien S. Murphy

During the final two years of the Algerian War, Simone de Beauvoir demonstrated her commitment to the Algerian rebels by advocating for Djamila Boupacha. Boupacha, a twenty-three-year-old middle-class Algerian educated in France, was a member of the Front de Libération Nationale (FLN), and was arrested on the night of February 10, 1960.[1] She was accused of having planted a bomb five months earlier in the University restaurant in Algiers, a capital offense. The bomb was diffused preventing any injury. There were no witnesses or other evidence to support her arrest. The night of her arrest, fifty police stormed her parents' house in Dely Ibrahim, assaulted her along with her father and brother-in-law and took them to the prison in El Biar where two years earlier Maurice Audin had been strangled and Henri Alleg had been tortured. At El Biar, the police attacked Djamila again. Days later she was interrogated under torture at Hussein Dey and signed a full confession which she later retracted. In the final months of the Algerian War, her trial was moved to Paris. She was spared execution largely due to the vigorous efforts of her defense attorney, Gisèle Halimi, who, from the first, sought the help of Beauvoir.

The preface to *Djamila Boupacha* represents the culmination of Beauvoir's commitment to Algerian independence.[2] This is the only book Beauvoir lent her name to as coauthor. In fact, the book was Beauvoir's idea. She suggested that the complete account of events surrounding Boupacha's trial should be published as a book or a brochure not only as a "weapon in the immediate struggle" but also as a "pledge for the future."[3] Beauvoir was a reluctant coauthor, finally agreeing in order to share responsibility with Halimi. She knew the danger of publicly supporting the FLN. Jean-Paul Sartre's flat had been bombed twice by the Organization Armée Secrète formed by French extremists, and Halimi, at one point, had been imprisoned in Algiers on false charges. On the day after the book was published, Beauvoir received a death threat.[4]

Halimi became involved in Boupacha's case at the request of her brother, Djamal, in a letter he managed to send from Camp Boussuet near Oran, another French internment camp, where he was imprisoned. At her first visit with Djamila in the Barbarossa Prison, Halimi noticed with horror the evidence of torture on Boupacha's legs as she listened to her account of rape, and her defiant proclamation, "I'm an FLN agent. I shall die for Algerian independence."[5] Unwavering in her support for Boupacha, Halimi uncovered, through a meticulous examination of Boupacha's treatment, a system of torture, lies, deception, disregard for law, and abuse of power rampant in the French army. The book is an extraordinary document of this system.

Halimi wrote the book and published it with Éditions Gallimard one month before the Evian agreement was signed and two months before Boupacha was released from prison under the Amnesty declaration in 1962. In the same year, the book was translated into English and published by Macmillan in the United States and by Weidenfeld and Nicolson in London. Juxtaposed with the book's title page is a sketch of Boupacha done by Picasso for the cover of *Jeune Afrique* (February 1962). In sixteen chapters, Halimi describes Boupacha's ordeal beginning with her imprisonment near Oran in March 1960 and ending abruptly with Boupacha's civil suit against the army in Paris in December of 1961. There are three appendixes: the text of Boupacha's civil indictment, Beauvoir's letter to *Le monde*, "In Defense of Djamila Boupacha," and the testimony of Abdelaziz Boupacha, Djamila's father, which describes his horrific treatment by French authorities. Also included after the appendixes is a Testimony section containing testimonies of twelve prominent supporters including Henri Alleg, Madame Maurice Audin, André Philip, Jules Roy, and Françoise Sagan.

In supporting the case of Djamila Boupacha, Beauvoir became a prominent force against the use of torture in the French internment camps in Algeria. She and Sartre had joined with other intellectuals on the Left to oppose French colonialism in Algeria, in part by publishing articles in *Les temps modernes* in support of the Algerian revolution.[6] Sartre had written an article for *L'express* entitled "A Victory," that became the introduction to *La question* (1958), the book documenting French torture methods as experienced by the journalist Henri Alleg. Until the Boupacha case, Beauvoir had not struck out on her own against French colonialism in Algeria.

Boupacha was not a leader in the FLN nor was her torture unusual. Other women, such as Djamila Bouhired,[7] Hassiba Ben Bouali, Zhora Drif, Elyette Loup, and Nassima Hablal, were accused of throwing grenades, and smuggling bombs and weapons, and endured torture and rape upon arrest.[8] The case of Bouhired, who was tortured in prison in 1957 and sentenced to death, had been highly publicized by her lawyer, Jacques Vergès, who was successful in stopping her execution.[9] Halimi's legal strategy, as evidenced by the book's subtitle, *The Story of the Torture of a Young Algerian Girl which Shocked Liberal French Opinion*, was also to rally public opinion and to put the government on trial for violating Article 344 of the French Penal Code. Despite the pervasive evidence, De Gaulle repeatedly denied that torture was still used in Algeria, for France had signed three international documents condemning torture.[10] Boupacha's deposition and the testimony of witnesses detailing beatings to the point of unconsciousness, electrocution, and rape, showed yet another case to the contrary. Halimi claimed that the prisons in Algeria were equipped "specifically for the purpose of torture, and operate[d] without the slightest attempt at secrecy."[11] Beauvoir allied with Halimi to use the Boupacha case to reach beyond the Left to the French middle class in order to raise awareness of the government's illegal methods in Algeria.

Halimi, who was born and educated in Tunisia, had defended other Algerian rebels and knew the tactics the government would likely use to thwart her efforts, including a rush to trial. While Halimi obtained the support of other prominent intellectuals, it was Beauvoir who led the charge of marshalling public opinion. Halimi contacted Beauvoir immediately after taking up Boupacha's case. They met in a café near the Place Denfert-Rochereau. "I had no very clear idea just how she could help us," Halimi remarked later, "but of one thing I was certain: that if her response was favorable she would stint neither time nor trouble on our behalf."[12] Quickly pledging her support, Beauvoir told Halimi that "the most scandalous aspect of the whole scandalous affair" was "the fact that people *had got used to it*."[13] Beauvoir's political writings and activities to disrupt French complacency about the war would transform her own understanding of what it meant to be French during the Algerian War.

First, Beauvoir fired off a passionate article for *Le monde*, "In Defense of Djamila Boupacha" (June 3, 1960). It was the first document added to the dossier at Boupacha's trial days later. The letter ignited international support as well as the fury of the French government. Beauvoir knew that the public had repeatedly been confronted with the evidence of the army's use of torture and yet, torture continued. Her letter demanded that readers of *Le monde* refuse to ignore the alarming reports of torture and confront the government. She begins, "The most scandalous aspect of any scandal is that one gets used to it. Yet it seems impossible that public opinion should remain indifferent to the present tragic ordeal of a twenty-three-year-old girl called Djamila Boupacha." Beauvoir reviewed Boupacha's treatment by the police, starting with the swarm of officers that stormed her house and assaulted her and two members of her family; her imprisonment in El Biar with a broken rib and other injuries; and repeated acts of torture by electrodes, body blows, cigarette burns and water boarding, including rape with a bottle that was so violent, she was unconscious for two days. Beauvoir also mentioned the nearly month-long delay between Boupacha's arrest and her charges, her thirty-three days in a prison known for torture—all without any protection from more violence—the government's rush to trial, and the use of a confession obtained under torture. She pointed out that Boupacha's family was in need of protection, that witnesses Boupacha named to testify would likely "disappear" as had happened in other cases, and that no measures had been taken against her torturers. ("Are the men who interrogated Djamila to continue their ghastly activities in peace?"[14]) She insists that "whether we choose our rulers willingly, or submit to them against our natural inclination we remain their accomplices whether we like it or not." She ends her letter calling for the public to demand justice: an end to the trial against Boupacha, a full inquiry into the matter, protection for her family and friends, and punishment for her torturers.

Le monde editors published the article but not without informing Beauvoir of some reservations. They were critical of Beauvoir's use of the word "vagina" asking her to change it to "womb" so as to not alarm young readers, as if, as Beauvoir noted, the account of torture was not unsettling. They also wanted her to paraphrase, which she refused, the sentence "Djamila was a virgin."[15] Beauvoir understood the significance of this for a young unmarried Muslim woman and held her ground.

In her memoir, Beauvoir minimized the political content and impact of her *Le monde* article. She described it as merely a transcription of Djamila's account of the facts.[16] It was actually a scathing indictment of the Army. In addition to the facts of the case, Beauvoir interrogated the notion of "French Algeria"—what did this phrase mean if the laws of France were set aside by the army? She even asked whether the government had lost control of the army in Algeria, "Such an abdication of responsibility would be a betrayal of France as a whole, of you, of me, of each and every one of us."[17] She pricked the conscience of the reader by charging every citizen of France as an accomplice to torture, "every citizen thereby becomes a member of a collectively criminal nation."[18] Beauvoir did not spare herself in these accusations. She felt an overwhelming responsibility about the war.

The government retaliated against Beauvoir's *Le monde* article by ordering all copies of the Algiers edition seized and destroyed. This was similar to their response in 1958 to Sartre's *L'express* article in behalf of Alleg, when, within hours of its publication, the police seized every newsstand copy.[19] Officials in a statement issued the same day as the *Le monde* seizure refused to name Beauvoir, "A certain evening paper had published an article describing the torture supposedly undergone by a young girl arrested and charged after a bomb-outrage committed in Algiers, in September 1959."[20] Readers were informed that an inquiry on the matter was already underway in the Military Court of Algiers and dismissed Beauvoir's account, claiming that Boupacha's confession was voluntary and that medical examiners found no evidence of torture. The silencing of Beauvoir in Algiers, compared by many to Gestapo tactics, was perhaps the single most effective weapon in quickly garnering international support for Boupacha. In the United States, her trial and its delay along with Henri Alleg's trial two days earlier, were covered by *Time* magazine under the title, "Brutalities."[21]

After the *Le monde* article, Beauvoir and Halimi formed the Djamila Boupacha Committee in France, an independent group to mobilize public opinion, that obtained the support of the Audin Committee, Sartre, and Germaine Tillon, among others.[22] Beauvoir was elected president. A main objective, in addition to freeing Boupacha, was to pressure the government to publicly punish Boupacha's torturers, an ambitious goal since corruption and abuse regarding the practices of torturing prisoners by the French was abetted at the highest levels. Beauvoir joined Halimi and others in meetings with Edmond Michelet, the Minister of Justice, and Maurice Patin, the president of the Commission for the Protection of Individual Rights and Freedoms. Beauvoir argued in one meeting with Patin that rape was a crime of war with devastating consequences for women rebels. She also presided over at least two press conferences on the Boupacha case, including the final one announcing Boupacha's civil suit against the Commander of the Army in Algeria, General Ailleret, and the Minister of Armies, Pierre Messmer.

The Boupacha Committee received widespread support from many prominent intellectuals and authors, including Sartre. The Committee's efforts delayed Boupacha's otherwise speedy trial long enough for the war to end. The Evian agreement was signed in March of 1962. However, the terms of the Amnesty declaration gave immunity to the Army ending Boupacha's civil suit. That there would be no formal action taken against Boupacha's torturers was a frustrating outcome for Beauvoir and Halimi, and one that justified publishing a book about the Boupacha case as an historical record.

The preface to *Djamila Boupacha* marks Beauvoir's most explicit act of support for decolonization in Algeria. It was her final act in behalf of Boupacha, written when the tide of public opinion had changed considerably in support of peace in Algeria. Her anger, boiling since her *Le monde* piece, is sharply focused. So much effort and risk had been taken to expose, as she writes in the preface, not isolated acts of abuse—for instance, a few army troops who used torture—but an "all-pervasive *system*" of corruption in the French army. She knew that public exposure was a more likely outcome than the punishment of key officials. Beauvoir carefully details Halimi's case against the Army, the exposure of fake documents, suppression of information, cover-ups, and the swift dismissals of any indictments of corruption. Beauvoir credits Halimi with exposing "a mechanism of lies" that operated within the French government for seven years beneath public notice. Hence, she claims, the exceptional aspect of the Boupacha case "is not the facts, but their publication," which she attributes to Halimi's persistence, the support of others, and a particularly diligent judge.

Beauvoir takes aim again at the moral conscience of France, this time with a focus on the immorality of the war itself. What has become of France, she asks, if the government resorts to barbarism in order to sustain colonialism in Algeria? Beauvoir graphically describes a reign of cruelty, maiming, and murder waged by the French army in Algeria and also extending into the streets of Paris. As Beauvoir saw it, the systematic use of torture must be cause for condemnation of the war. The war could not be won and was unjust. ("The army, for reasons which concern itself—and are completely self-serving—wants to maintain in servitude a people who are entirely resolved to die rather than to renounce their independence.") She insists that readers must act responsibly in light of these facts, by either supporting the torturers or refusing "this war that dares not speak its name." The framing of political choices in this way reflected Beauvoir's political stance on Algeria. One must accept or reject colonialism. There was no third way, as suggested by Camus, who condemned the violence of the FLN.[23]

The Boupacha case allowed Beauvoir a chance to carve out her own political response to the conflict, apart from Sartre and others, and to reconcile her moral conscience with an unjust war quietly supported by the public who had made her famous. She had emotional ties to Algeria that made her evolving opposition to French colonialism deeply personal. She and Sartre liked to vacation there in the late forties when the solace of Algeria was uncomplicated. For instance, in 1948, she wrote to the American novelist, Nelson Algren, of both the beauty of Algiers and the desperate plight of the people there. "Besides Arabians, you find a lot of French soldiers and officers; that is not better. You never saw a *colony*. You'll be indignant; colonies are a bad thing. Both are unpleasant here, masters and slaves. But the landscapes are fine, weather is sunny, nobody knows us and we know nobody; so it is a good place to breathe good air and work good work."[24] By 1956, as the uprisings intensified and the government responded with increasing force, she felt deep shame and began to vehemently reject French colonialism. Her descriptions of Algeria became filled with sadness, "The Arabs don't want us and we should go away; we did nothing for them, far from it, and they are right to hate us."[25] She predicted that France would lose control only after a war as devastating as Indochina.

Beauvoir, engaged in a long period of introspection, wrote three volumes of autobiography during the Algerian War. Her intense anger about the war filled the final chapters of the third volume, *Force of Circumstance*. She railed against the French press for lying about the war, the French majority who failed to protest even the searches and raids of Paris neighborhoods, and the docility of young French soldiers sent to Algeria. Part of her anger was fueled by the political injustices in Algeria for which neither the communists nor the Left had an adequate response, and part was self-loathing that came from her own position as a French intellectual. She called herself a "profiteer," "an accomplice of the privileged classes" and felt morally compromised by the war.[26] It dominated her thoughts and transformed her relationship to France, to her readers, and herself. Yet, in *Force of Circumstance*, she gives the Boupacha case barely a mention, referring readers to Halimi's account.

The Boupacha case figured more prominently in her life than her autobiography reveals. It seems to mark a shift in tone for her. There is a marked difference in tone in her writing after she joins with Halimi in support of Boupacha's case. In the years before meeting with Halimi, she is filled with rage and disillusionment and overwhelmed by the war atrocities. This is not to suggest that she had not taken other actions in support of the rebels. She had signed Manifesto 121 (the Déclaration sur le droit à l'insoumission dans la guerre d'Algérie) opposing compulsory military service, and given character testimony for her former student, Jacqueline Guerroudj, who was involved with the ALN (Armée de libération nationale, or National Liberation Army). After her meeting with Halimi, her *Le monde* article, and the formation of the Boupacha committee, her tone changes and it appears that she has broken through the ennui of many months. Her own activities in solidarity with Boupacha, the League of Human Rights, and the growing antiwar movement in France finally broke down the sense of isolation she had felt in fighting "from the outside" as she put it, a part of no political group. In one passage, she writes not with despair but with joy about participating in a peace march, "the crowd became infected with tremendous gaiety. And how good I felt! Solitude is a form of death, and as I felt the warmth of human contact flow through me again, I came back to life. . . . It had been a marvelous day, and one that encouraged us to hope."[27] Boupacha's trial provided Beauvoir with a way to advocate for FLN rebels with a specific focus on the treatment of women rebels.

It is interesting to speculate why the Boupacha case, in particular, resonated with Beauvoir, particularly since she never met Boupacha. She could easily have done so when Boupacha was imprisoned in France. In a sense, Halimi is right in regarding Beauvoir's support of Boupacha as rather abstract.[28] It is hard to account for this omission save for one remark Beauvoir made about her visit with Sartre to see FLN prisoners in Fresnes. It seemed that the face-to-face encounters with rebels were difficult for her to bear and made her even more ashamed to be French. "They say they like Sartre and myself," she remarked, "but in spite of that, I don't feel proud when I speak with these men. We killed *more than one million* Algerians (women, children, and so on.)"[29] By supporting Boupacha she defended her own integrity as a French citizen and her belief in France as a civilized nation. While she supported the violent tactics of the FLN, accepting, along with Sartre, the arguments of Fanon and others, she could not condone the use of torture by the French police and military.[30] Her arguments against the war were squarely aimed at the practice of torture. This was strategic for garnering public support for Boupacha. Unfortunately, it displaced other arguments Beauvoir might have made against colonialism had the government not violated its principles of justice in Algeria. Still, her arguments against torture are neither outdated nor inapplicable to the present time; one needs only to look at the dehumanizing photos from Abu Ghraib prison.[31]

Ten years after Boupacha's release from prison, Beauvoir shared her frustrations about the plight of women in Algeria. In an interview with Caroline Moorehead for the *New York Times*, she said that the ownership of the means of production was a limited understanding of socialism and went on to criticize state socialism in Algeria, saying that "the thing that really revolts me in Algeria, as in all Moslem countries, is the condition of women. I can't accept the way they oppress their women, veil them, impose forced marriages on them. Frantz Fanon[32] thought they would become emancipated after the Algerian War. On the contrary, they have been crushed."[33] Despite Beauvoir's disappointment with the slow pace of change for women in Algeria, her defense of Boupacha has inscribed Boupacha's name in the historical documents of the Algerian War.[34] Her coauthored book remains publicly available (although it is out of print); frequently cited, it has become a fundamental part of the Algerian feminist movement, a movement begun in 1943 with the Union des Femmes d'Algérie (Union of Algerian Women), and one whose history includes the author of *The Second Sex*.

NOTES

1. The *Front de libération nationale* (National Liberation Front) was the resistance organization in Algeria fighting for Algerian independence during the French occupation and colonization of that country.

2. See my essay, "Beauvoir and the Algerian War: Toward a Postcolonial Ethics," in *Feminist Interpretations of Simone de Beauvoir*, ed. Margaret A. Simons (University Park: Pennsylvania State University Press, 1995), 263–97.

3. Simone de Beauvoir and Gisèle Halimi, *Djamila Boupacha*, trans. Peter Green (New York: Macmillan Company, 1962), 170.

4. Simone de Beauvoir, *Force of Circumstance*, trans. Richard Howard (New York: G. P. Putnam's Sons, 1965), 614.

5. Beauvoir and Halimi, *Djamila Boupacha*, 28.

6. See, for instance, Martin Evans, *The Memory of Resistance: French Opposition to the Algerian War (1954–1962) (Berg French Studies)* (Oxford: Berg Publishers, First Edition, November 1, 1997), 43.

7. Like Boupacha, Bouhired was also a young woman in her early twenties when she was arrested in 1957 for planting bombs that killed many French citizens. Communist supporters Georges Arnaud and Jacques Vergès took up her case in their book, *Pour Djamila Bouhired*

(For Djamila Bouhired) (Paris: Éditions de Minuit, 1957), and she became famous. Bouhired was released from prison under the Amnesty agreement. See also, David C. Gordon, *Women of Algeria: An Essay On Change* (Cambridge: Harvard University Press, Center for Middle Eastern Studies, 1968), 53–54.

8. Gordon, *Women of Algeria*.

9. Historian Judith Surkis cites *Pour Djamila Bouhired* by Georges Arnaud and Jacques Vergès and notes the significance of Beauvoir's similar title for her *Le monde* essay in behalf of Boupacha. See Surkis, "Ethics and Violence: Simone de Beauvoir, Djamila Boupacha, and the Algerian War," *French Politics, Culture and Society*. 28:2 (Summer 2010).

10. The three agreements rejecting torture were: The Universal Declaration of Human Rights of the United Nations (1948), the Geneva Conventions (1949), and the European Convention on Human Rights (1953). Torture was also condemned much earlier in the Declaration of the Rights of Man (1789).

11. Beauvoir and Halimi, *Djamila Boupacha*, 63.

12. Ibid., 64.

13. Ibid., 65. Quoting Halimi.

14. Ibid.,196.

15. Beauvoir, *Force of Circumstance*, 501.

16. Ibid., 500.

17. Beauvoir and Halimi, *Djamila Boupacha*, 196.

18. Ibid.

19. Jean-Paul Sartre, "Une victoire" (*L'express 350*, March 6, 1958); reprinted in *Situations V* (Paris: Gallimard, 1964), 74–75. Ian Birchall describes the seizure of Sartre's article in his essay on Alleg "Algeria: Torture Last Time," *The Socialist Review* (February 2008) http://www.socialistreview.org.uk/article.php?articlenumber=10269 (accessed October 25, 2011).

20. Beauvoir and Halimi, *Djamila Boupacha*, 66.

21. "Foreign News: The Trial" (staff reporting) *Time* (June 27, 1960).

22. Halimi lists the members of the Committee as including: Jean Amrouche, Aimé Cesaire, Lucie Faure, Edouard Glissant, René Julliard, Professor Georges Lavau, Michel Leiris, Daniel Mayer, Hélène Parmelin, André Philip, André Postel-Vinay, R. P. Riquet, Jean-Paul Sartre, Laurent Schwartz, Tanguy-Prigent, Pierre Henri Teitgen, Germaine Tillon. See Beauvoir and Halimi, *Djamila Boupacha*, 70.

23. Albert Camus, "Preface to Algerian Reports," in *Resistance, Rebellion, and Death*, trans. Justin O'Brien (New York: Random House Publishers, 1960), 115.

24. Simone de Beauvoir, *A Transatlantic Love Affair: Letters to Nelson Algren*, compiled and annotated by Sylvie Le Bon de Beauvoir (New York: The New Press, 1997), 220.

25. Ibid., 522.

26. Beauvoir, *Force of Circumstance*, 653.

27. Ibid., 605.

28. Gisèle Halimi, *Milk for the Orange Tree*, trans. Dorothy S. Blair (London: Quartet Books, 1990), 294.

29. Beauvoir, *A Transatlantic Love Affair* (letter to Algren), 547. Beauvoir was writing in English.

30. Frantz Fanon (1925–61) was a psychiatrist, philosopher, and writer whose works have been very influential in anticolonial liberation movements. He was an active member of the

FLN and defended the right of colonized people to use violence in their struggle for independence; See Sartre's preface to Fanon's *Wretched of the Earth*, trans. Constance Farrington (New York: Grove Press, 1963).

31. Lawrence D. Kritzman makes this connection in his essay "Simone de Beauvoir, the Paradoxical Intellectual," *PMLA* 124:1 (January 2009): 211.

32. For a discussion of the differences between Fanon and Beauvoir on Algeria, see Annabelle Golay, "Féminisme et postcolonialisme: Beauvoir, Fanon et la guerre d'Algérie" (Feminism and Postcolonialism: Beauvoir, Fanon and the Algerian War), *International Journal of Francophone Studies* 10:3 (2007): 407–24.

33. Caroline Moorehead, "A Talk with Simone de Beauvoir," *New York Times* (June 2, 1974): 22.

34. See, for example, Zahia Smail Salhi, "The Algerian Feminist Movement between Nationalism, Patriarchy and Islamism," *Women's Studies International Forum* 33 (2010): 116.

PREFACE TO *DJAMILA BOUPACHA*

by Simone de Beauvoir

TRANSLATION AND NOTES BY MARYBETH TIMMERMANN

A twenty-three-year-old Algerian woman and liaison agent for the FLN was imprisoned, tortured, raped with a bottle by French military men, and it's considered ordinary.[1] Since 1954, in the name of suppressing rebellion, then of pacification, we are all accomplices of a genocide that has claimed over a million victims; men, women, old folks and children have been slaughtered: gunned down during search-raids, burned alive in their villages, throats slit or bellies ripped open, many tortured to death. Entire tribes have been left to starve and freeze, at the mercy of beatings and epidemics in the "relocation camps" which are in fact extermination camps—serving also as brothels to the elite soldiers—and where more than five hundred thousand Algerians currently await their death. During the course of the last few months, the press, including even the most circumspect papers, has been full of horror stories: assassinations, lynchings, violent racist attacks on Arab immigrants; manhunts in the streets of Oran; corpses by the dozen in Paris, hanging from trees in the Bois de Boulogne and along the banks of the Seine; maimed limbs and blown up heads; bloody All Saints Day in Algiers.[2] Can

"Préface," *Djamila Boupacha*, Simone de Beauvoir and Gisèle Halimi (Paris: Gallimard, 1962), 1–13, © Éditions Gallimard, 1962.

we still be moved by the blood of a young woman? After all—as Mr. Patin, President of the Commission for the Protection [of Individual Rights and Freedoms] subtly insinuated during an interview at which I was present[3]— Djamila Boupacha is alive: what she endured was therefore not so terrible.*

In telling this story, Gisèle Halimi does not claim to stir the hearts of those who remain impervious to shame if they are not already submerged in it. The major interest of her book is that it exposes, piece by piece, a mechanism of lies that fit together so perfectly that even after seven years, only a few glimpses of truth get through. How many times have I come up against this response: "But if it were really so widespread, so enormous, and so horrible, it would be common knowledge." But that's exactly it; in order to be so widespread, so enormous, and so horrible, the very fact that *it is* must be kept secret. The use of torture has been publicly advocated by General Massu, openly taught to young officers, sanctioned by a large number of clerics, applauded by the European population of Algeria, and systematically practiced in the "triage centers," prisons, military bases, and *Djebels*, so it has been easy to deny torture in each particular case, thanks to this unanimity.[4] What makes Boupacha's case exceptional is not the facts, but their publication. The stubbornness of a lawyer, the pride of the defendant, a favorable decree, and the professional courage of a judge all helped to raise the curtain of darkness that hides the daily horror of this "subversive war." Only one obstacle has held out, but at least it has become glaringly conspicuous in the process. According to General Ailleret, High Commander of the Armed Forces in Algeria (appointed by General de Gaulle), the army actively objects to the names of Djamila's torturers being made public.

Gisèle Halimi retraces, step by step, the path leading up to this last appeal. In light of her story, and considering the traps she sidestepped, the dangers she escaped, the efforts she made, and the twists and turns of luck and fate that all came together in the making of this relative success, you will come to understand why the wailing and crying and blood-curdling screams that have been emanating for so long from the land of Algeria—and that of France too—have not reached your ears, or have sounded so faint that it took but a hint of bad faith on your part to ignore them.

If a man succumbs to torture, he is killed or kills himself. And his corpse is hidden: no corpse, no crime. Sometimes a father or wife asks questions,

---

* Mr. Patin was alluding to the torture with the bottle that Djamila suffered when he said, "I had feared that she was made to *sit* upon a bottle, as they did in Indo-China with the Viets; in such cases the intestines are perforated and it is fatal. But that was not what happened here . . ." he added with a knowing smile; clearly nothing of the sort could ever happen to *him*.

but they are told that he has disappeared, and silence once again resumes. A murmur of voices became a torrent of questions regarding the case of a well-known and well-liked French professor named Audin, but they were all in vain, seeing that his assassin was never punished and even received the Legion of Honor.[5] After the spectacular "suicide" of Boumendjel, several voices were raised, and were insistent, but were also in vain.[6] However, as for all those obscure Algerians mentioned in the *Cahier vert*, and all those who are mentioned nowhere, which constitute an even greater number, their absence is met with complete indifference and has faded away; no trace remains of the torture they endured.[7]

If he survives and is found innocent and set free, then he is silenced by threats whose full meaning he is all too familiar with, and is usually placed under house arrest for more security; his jailers will guarantee his silence. If he is found guilty, it is usually too late to make an appeal. But won't the preliminary hearing provide him with the opportunity to speak? Absolutely not: he knows that if his confession is not ratified, he will be "questioned" again; sometimes the torturers are even waiting right outside the committing magistrate's door. In Algeria, the entire system rests upon the collusion of judges, doctors, and lawyers who all consider the defendant as the enemy. He must be found guilty, so the sentence is decided ahead of time and the proceedings simply aim at hiding the fact that it is arbitrary. On this point, Djamila's case is edifying. Faced with a hostile magistrate, traumatized, terrorized, her skin marked with burning souvenirs, she repeated her confession and then still managed to say, "I was tortured. I insist on being seen by a doctor." The judge did not have the interrogation redone, nor did he ask any questions; he merely had her words included in the court records. Then he called one of those doctors whose job is to cover up for the Judge when he wants to make a show of following correct procedure. A few months later, the Parisian doctors who were called in as a second expert evaluation all agreed that Djamila indeed had undergone a "traumatic defloration." In Algiers, however, it took only five minutes for doctor Lévy Leroy to declare that, having examined Djamila "completely unclothed," he had noticed "menstrual troubles of a constitutional nature." He would later—on June 14—state that Djamila had kept her underclothes on during this visit, and that he had performed no gynecological exam so as not to "humiliate her." Before such a flagrant contradiction, one is tempted to denounce an outrageous absence of professional conscience, but for the "usuals" of Algiers this notion has no meaning. They are there not to verify ill treatment, but to deny it in all cases, and they are simply performing their allotted roles. Likewise, the Algerian lawyers don't consider actually helping their clients; if this idea crossed their minds, fear would be enough to paralyze them. Maître Popie's courage cost him his life, but the immense majority of them don't even question it.[8] They ask only to collaborate with the army, the police, the courts, and the majority of the European population, in order to strike down the adversary no matter what the means. Djamila could expect no help from her Algerian defense attorney, who cheerfully told Gisèle Halimi, "It's an open and shut case; in ten minutes it will be over."

Thus, Djamila very nearly was condemned, like so many others, based on a forced confession, since no proof against her was upheld. The awful days in El Biar and Hussein Dey would have only existed in her memory.

An unexpected event changed the classic scenario: a letter sent from camp Bossuet, written by Djamila's brother, reached Gisèle Halimi. Lawyers who come from France to defend Algerians are rare, and in spite of their zeal, they can only take on a very limited number of cases. In addition everything is put into place in order to hinder their activity—you will see in detail how this works. Gisèle Halimi succeeded nevertheless in forcing a breach in the system. She spoke to Djamila and encouraged her to file a complaint. She then alerted the district attorney of Algiers, and I helped her to rouse public opinion. A committee was created to support Djamila. It caused such an uproar in France and abroad that on June 17 (the authorities having meanwhile banned Gisèle Halimi from Algiers), the court, which ordinarily would not have balked at condemning the young woman without her lawyer present, feared that such a step would provoke a serious outrage, so they decided to postpone the trial. Not long after that, they offered her a deal: a psychiatrist would declare that she was not responsible for her actions and she would be acquitted, but at the same time her accusations would lose all credit. The trial against her torturers would not take place. She refused.

Yet there was little hope that her tenacity would bear fruit. When a complaint is filed in spite of the dangers that I have indicated, the judges in Algiers are quick to dismiss the case. Not only are the lawyers generally their accomplices, but the witnesses called by the defense tend to disappear; fear keeps their mouths closed. On the other hand, military personnel and police officers deny the facts with such conviction that the judge decides to be convinced. Thus hundreds of complaints are stifled—horrible, heart-breaking stories that I have had the chance to read—and this would have been the fate of Djamila's complaint if it had stayed in the hands of Mr. Courmontagne; he was briskly on his way to dismissing the case.

Doesn't a Commission for the Protection [of Individual Rights and Freedoms] exist? Indeed it does. The trouble is that it is concerned with protecting the safety of the torturers and not that of the tortured. I knew this, but prior to the interview which a delegation from the Boupacha Committee, myself included, had with Mr. Patin—an interview described in detail by Gisèle Halimi—I nevertheless was far from understanding the depths of the President of this Commission's devotion to the army, his racism, and his fear. The Melun negotiations had just begun and Mr. Patin, like Mr. Michelet whom we had seen that morning, had high hopes, which explains the candor with which he spoke to us.[9] Mr. Michelet—to whom we had come to request that jurisdiction over this case be denied to the courts of Algiers—did not seem to doubt that Djamila and her father had in fact been tortured. As he led us to the door of his office, he said to me personally, "This canker in our midst comes from Nazism; it penetrates everywhere, corrupts everything, and we are unable to curb it. A bit of roughing up is fair enough; you can't run a police force without that. But torture is something different; it's unacceptable. I try to make them understand and tell them that there's a line that shouldn't be crossed . . ." And he shrugged his shoulders in a confession of ineffectiveness and complicity. "It's a canker in our midst," he repeated. Then he pulled himself together and concluded importantly, "Oh well, we are nearing the end!" To hear this spontaneous admission, from the very lips of the Minister of Justice, left me astounded. As for Mr. Patin, I would not have dared to credit any fictional character with the views he expressed to us. One of his gestures in particular struck me. One of us, Germaine Tillion, I think, observed that the number of massacred civilian Muslims is significantly greater than that of European victims, and that no punishment had ever been publicly ordered for their murderers. He waved his hand toward a huge pile of reports, "I know," he said, "I know." He could not have acknowledged more explicitly that, far from protecting anything, he was covering up everything.

In order to deny jurisdiction to the district attorney's office of Algiers, the Minister of Justice must agree to petition the final Court of Appeal, which then must agree to uphold the petition. No recourse exists against these sovereign authorities. They are free to stifle a complaint by leaving it in the hands of the Algerian judges. Luckily his illusions of imminent peace and the pressure of public opinion led Mr. Michelet to allow Djamila's transfer to France where she underwent a new medical exam, which concluded that she probably had been tortured like she had claimed, and at its request the Court of Appeal agreed to deny jurisdiction.

Even at that stage, the course of Justice could still have been easily thwarted. If the judge in Caen was biased or indifferent, he could rely on the lax process suggested to him from Algiers: leave the responsibility of hearing witnesses in Algeria to a local rogatory commission. It goes without saying that they would have found none in favor of Djamila, and the events that followed clearly demonstrate just that. In Algiers, terror keeps everyone silent. Zineb Laroussi, a common law prisoner whom the Algerian police kept on a tight leash, claimed on two separate occasions that Djamila, with whom she shared a cell, had not been tortured, and that besides, she seemed crazy. In Caen, however, she described Djamila in detail: unconscious, beaten black and blue, her underpants soaked with blood. Her testimony confirmed Djamila's story as well as Zakia El Mehdaoui's, to whom Zineb had reported the facts at Barberousse.[10] As for Zakia, she had written to Mr. Michelet some time previously saying that she could only speak in France. Her deposition during that final inquiry corroborated that of Zineb Laroussi and finally established the truth irrefutably. She would have never dared make that deposition when she was interned in the camp at Tefeschoun.

Luckily, Mr. Chausserie-Laprée took his duties and the truth seriously. Having gathered the pertinent reports, dossiers, and depositions, he was persuaded that Djamila had been tortured and was determined to prosecute her torturers. He then overcame one by one the obstacles that were put up before him. He made sure all the documents concerning the elder Abdelaziz Boupacha, whose complaint he was also looking into, as well as that of Abdelli Ahmed, Djamila's brother-in-law, were seized and photocopied. He arranged to bring the different members of the Boupacha family together in his office in an effort to get to the truth by hearing all sides. When Abdelli Ahmed was subpoenaed, the authorities, in keeping with a well-tested maneuver, immediately released him; it is easy to make a bothersome witness disappear as he leaves his prison or camp, either by intimidating him into hiding or by kidnapping him. But the judge sent police officers to Algiers who met Abdelli the very moment his cell was unlocked and urged him to follow them to Caen. It was thus possible for the judge to conduct the lengthy and meticulous interrogation that ended up convincing him of the plaintiffs' good faith. He was not so lucky with the two Algerian women who had heard Zineb Laroussi's story at Barberousse. Even though Nadja Hanchi and Safia Morcelli were awaiting death sentences, they were both freed, purchasing this unprecedented pardon by forgetting what Laroussi had told them. But their defection was of little importance because Zineb Laroussi herself denied her previous lies. In Caen, after having described Djamila's true state, she clearly explained the methods used by the police to obtain the false testimonies that they needed:

> *Indeed, I made statements to civilian and military examining magistrates in Algiers that were absolutely opposed to those I make now.*
>
> *Before I was called before these two magistrates, I had been called to the Génie barracks at Hussein Dey where lieutenant D . . . as well as inspectors G . . . and T . . . showed me the statements I was to make. I was supposed to say that I had seen nothing and that Djamila's side was injured even before her arrest. They also told me that I was supposed to state that Djamila had acted insane at Hussein Dey. Out of fear—I was only temporarily freed—I followed the instructions they had given me.*
>
> *On November 3, 1961, G . . . and T . . . came back and found me at my work place at the Pierre and Marie Curie Center on Battandier Avenue. When we were alone in the lobby, they asked to see my summons, and after having looked it over, they told me that I was supposed to make the same statements as I did in Algiers, and that if I felt far enough away from Algiers and spoke, I would be condemned, I would disappear and my parents would never see me again . . .*

On the other hand, it was easy to prove that Djamila had been illegally detained. In order to conceal her arbitrary imprisonment, they claimed that she had stayed at the Beni-Messous camp, but the director officially informed the judge that she had never set foot there.

The Judge accumulated charges and proofs. The report had reconstructed the crimes committed against Djamila. The only thing left was to serve the indictment and hear the accused. As early as February 1961, he made a request to the commander of Alger-Sahel for the list of police and military personnel who had been in contact with Djamila, her father, and her brother-in-law. He renewed his request on March 8, asking for "the names of all military personnel (officers, non-commissioned officers, *gendarmes* and privates) and civilian police officers who participated in the operation that took place on the night of February 10 and the early morning of February 11, 1960, at the Boupacha household, and who interrogated Djamila Boupacha at El Biar and at Hussein Dey. Also, a recent postcard-sized photograph of all such persons . . ."

He was given the identity of the soldiers and police officers who had signed the police report, i.e., those whose names he already knew. As for the others, he was met with silence, making it impossible to issue summons. He found a way—the only way—to get around this obstacle. Djamila obviously did not know the names or even the functions of her torturers, but she remembered their faces. Mr. Chausserie-Laprée again made his request, insisting on photographs of all those who had been in contact with her, so that she could identify them. All he obtained from General Ailleret was a blunt refusal:

> *I must nevertheless inform you that recent postcard-sized photographs of each of the military and police personnel who participated in the various operations during which Djamila Boupacha, Abdellaziz [sic] Boupacha, and Ahmed Abdelli [sic] were apprehended, and who interrogated these persons or even attended these interrogations in any capacity, will not be included in this next dispatch.*
>
> *Indeed, I have deemed that requesting photographs from all the military and police personnel who might have been in contact with Djamila Boupacha would likely cause undesirable side-effects on their states of mind and on the morale of the corps and services of which they are members. I made my feelings known to the Minister of Armies who kindly informed me on May 29, 1961 (letter no. 15,842/MA.CC./C.) that he completely shares my view on this matter, and intends to adhere strictly, in this affair, to the usual procedures of hearings and confrontations if necessary . . .*

The hypocrisy of this last sentence must not fool anyone: in order to fall back on the "usual" procedure of hearings, it would have been necessary for the identities of the suspects to have been disclosed "as usual." But the military authorities hid them, which, under "normal" circumstances would have incurred charges against them for the harboring of known criminals. Refusing the photos is definitively shielding those criminals from the prosecution required by law. Such a step is nothing less than a violation of the Constitution, which assures the separation of powers. Here we see the executive power—incarnated by General Ailleret and Minister Messmer[11]—deny autonomy to the judiciary power, going so far as opposing it and thwarting its efforts. In an authentic democracy, this would be considered an abuse of authority and its perpetrators would be prosecuted by the circuit court.

The reason given to justify this breach of the law should be carefully examined. No one wants to offend the army or the police, but the photos—which, incidentally, were kept on file in the corps and services of the soldiers and police officers involved so no one would have had to "request" them from the individuals themselves—were destined for a secret dossier. Innocent men would not have had to fear a public inquiry involving their names; they could have even remained uninformed. Only those whom Djamila recognized and whom the judge charged would have been "demoralized." This is the risk from which General Ailleret and the Minister of Armies intend to protect military personnel and police officers: the risk of not being able to torture without incurring punishment.

Early in 1958, General de Gaulle, called on to protest against torture, arrogantly replied that it was inherent in the "System," and that it would be eliminated with the fall of the fourth Republic. After May 28, Malraux declared to the world that torture was indeed abolished. So after two and a half years of Gaullist regime, de Gaulle's Minister of Armies and the high commander of the Armed Forces in Algeria, appointed by de Gaulle, decide to ensure impunity for their subordinates no matter what they have done, which amounts to openly granting them the right to perpetuate acts of violence as they please, with no physical or "moral" hindrances. For a long time we have piously made this distinction: torture may occur in the army, but it is not the army who tortures. General Ailleret's letter puts an end to these nuances; by protecting those who commit crimes in uniform, he takes responsibility for those crimes: it is the army who tortures.

Speaking out against these injustices would be futile [*vain*]. Protesting in the name of morality against these "excesses" or "abuses" is now an aberration that resembles complicity. There is no abuse or excess, but an entire system in place. Morality in such a war does not come into play. The army marshals such irrefutable arguments against morality that the only way to avoid its consequences is to strip the army of its power.

For the army did not need its revolts and plots to succeed in order to govern us. The man to which it lent the appearance of authority in May of 1958 was not capable of breaking its sovereignty, even with all his maneuvers, procrastinations, and equivocations. He submitted to it and would have us submit to it. The army, for reasons which concern itself—and are completely self-serving—wants to maintain in servitude a people who are entirely resolved to die rather than to renounce their independence. Against this collective and indomitable will, the army considers itself obliged to defy every law, written and unwritten; indeed, their problem allows for only one solution: extermination. "*Et ubi solitudinem faciunt, id pacem appellant* [*sic*]" [Where they create desolation, they call it peace], said Tacitus of the Romans.[12] These words apply exactly to what these military men call pacification, which can only be accomplished in regions that have first been transformed into wastelands, and it will only come to an end if all Algerians were to die or waste away behind barbed wire. No other victory is conceivable. So if it's victory we want, as the generals, colonels, paratroopers and legionnaires proclaim, then why quibble about the means? The end justifies them all in full and even surpasses them by far.

"I am but one prisoner among thousands of others," Djamila was saying to her lawyer the other day. Indeed, there are 14,000 Algerians detained in camps and prisons in France, 17,000 more in prisons located in Algeria, and hundreds of thousands packed into the camps located in Algeria. The efforts made in Djamila's case would fall short of their mark if they failed to arouse a revolt against the treatment of her brothers and of which her case represents only one very ordinary example. But this revolt will have no reality unless it takes the form of political action. There exists only one choice for you who grieve so readily and so abundantly over past tragedies, like Anne Frank or the Warsaw ghetto. You can either take sides with the torturers of those who are suffering today and passively consent to the martyrdom they endure in your name, almost under your noses—thousands of Djamilas and Ahmeds—or you can refuse not only certain practices, but the end that authorizes and demands them. You can refuse this war that dares not speak its name and the army that feeds off of this war, body and soul, as well as the government that gives in to the army. And you can put everything into place to make your refusal effective. There is no third alternative, and I hope this book will help to convince you. You are being confronted with the truth from all directions; you can no longer continue to stammer, "We didn't know . . ." And, knowing, will you be able to feign ignorance or content yourselves with a few token [*inertes*] laments?

I hope not.

NOTES

Previously translated by Peter Green (New York: Macmillan, 1962).

1. FLN stands for *Front de libération nationale* (National Liberation Front), which was the resistance organization in Algeria fighting for Algerian independence during the French occupation and colonization of that country.

2. Beauvoir is referring to the acts of violence and killings that occurred in Algiers on November 1, 1954, called *la Toussaint rouge* in French. These were the first European civilian deaths in Algeria, marking the real beginning of the war for Algerian independence.

3. The *Commission de sauvegarde des droits et libertés individuels*, which Beauvoir refers to as the "Commission de Sauvegarde," was created in 1957 by French statesman and socialist leader Guy Mollet with the official purpose of investigating the claims of torture, disappearances, and acts of violence committed by the French against the Algerians, but in reality it tried to shield the French government and army from public scandal. Maurice

Patin (1895–1962), who was then the president of the Criminal Court of Appeals, was named president of the Commission by Charles de Gaulle. See http://chs.univ-paris1.fr/cherche/seconde.pdf for more information (accessed November 3, 2011). This is not to be confused with the "Committee of Public Safety," which is how Peter Green translates it in the previous translation. The "Committee of Public Safety" (*le comité de salut public*) was the military regime in Algeria led by General Massu and formed in 1958 when the army and French Algerians seized power in reaction to France's waning support of the military operations in Algeria.

4. The *Djebels* are mountains in northern Africa.

5. Maurice Audin (1932–57), whose father was French and whose mother was Algerian of European descent, was an anticolonialism activist and professor of math at the University of Algiers until he was arrested, tortured, and killed by the French military in 1957. French historian Pierre Vidal-Naquet led a committee to investigate his death and wrote a book called *L'affaire Audin* in 1958, but not until May 2004 was there a "Place Audin" in Paris, commemorating this martyr. The main suspect in his death, a lieutenant Charbonnier, was never punished and the French authorities have still not admitted to the assassination of Audin.

6. Ali Boumendjel was a prominent Algerian attorney, whose death was made to look like a suicide. The French general Paul Aussaresses admits in his book *Special Services, Algeria 1955–1957* (Paris: Perrin, 2001), to torturing and executing scores of Algerian militants. According to this memoir, Boumendjel was thrown from a rooftop after having been tortured for forty-three days.

7. Beauvoir is most likely referring to a book entitled *Les disparus, le cahier vert* (Disappearances: The Green Notebook) (Paris: La Cité, 1959), written by Jacques Vergès, Michel Savrian, and Maurice Courrège, which lists 175 cases of suspicious "disappearances" of Algerian Muslims.

8. Pierre Popie, who was killed in 1961, was a liberal Algerian lawyer who defended torture victims and tried to publish a list of his clients who had disappeared and the French military units that had arrested them.

9. On June 25–29, 1960, Charles de Gaulle met secretly with leaders of the FLN in Melun, France, in the hopes of obtaining a cease-fire, but these negotiations failed; Edmond Michelet (1899–1970), a French politician and survivor of the Dachau concentration camp, served as Minister of Justice from 1959 to 1961.

10. Barberousse is a prison in Algiers, Algeria.

11. Pierre Messmer (1916–2007) was France's Minister of Armies.

12. Cornelius Tacitus (55–117) was a witty, insightful, and eloquent Roman historian who criticized the corruption of Rome. Some of his best known works include *Histories* and *Annals*.

6

In France Today,
Killing Goes Unpunished

INTRODUCTION

by Karen L. Shelby

In this article, published in 1971, we find themes of responsibility and solidarity that resonate throughout Simone de Beauvoir's lifetime of writing and thought. Beginning with the polemic of the title of the essay, which also stands as its final emphatic statement, she is intent on exposing an injustice that results from what she calls "bourgeois justice" and on issuing a call to knowledge and action on the part of her readers. She takes the kind of situation that all of us would regard with proper sentiments of horror when we hear of it—a factory fire in which fifty-seven people suffered severe injury or death—and asks more of her readers, as humans living in an intersubjective world in which actions and inaction can have a profound effect on the lives and freedom of others.

In this case, Beauvoir is showing that the crime involved not just the willful actions on the part of the owner, Mr. Bérion, whose negligence led to this catastrophe, but also the willed blindness of those whose complicity allowed, and allows, that negligence to persist. This involves a cultivated ignorance, one that perpetuates the injustices that confront each individual differently, depending on the individual's situation, and that must be overcome in the continual struggle to claim one's freedom. Beauvoir shows that there is a pernicious circularity to the way that incidents such as this fire are addressed and understood. A catastrophe takes place; the penalties assessed are light; and the pursuit of profit prevails when the question of the introduction, or enforcement, of protective measures for workers is raised. This is the system of business as usual that Beauvoir hopes to contest by bringing its abuses and human costs to light. When she forcefully asserts, "*They look the other way*," regarding the factory inspectors who failed to hold Mr. Bérion accountable, she is implicitly asking her readers if they too will look the other way in a case such as this, in which the penalties are light in comparison to the effects of the fire.

Beauvoir also demands that her readers act in response to their knowledge, by ensuring that regulations that are designed to protect workers are enforced, and that those who flout them are held accountable. To call the travesty of this outcome "bourgeois justice" is to invoke a long-term engagement with the philosophy of Karl Marx and support for Marxist movements in their drive to improve the living conditions of those who experience daily oppression and immiseration. After recounting the difficulties and injustices suffered by the survivors of the fire, Beauvoir calls for solidarity in a moment evocative of Marx's "Workers of the world, unite!" In this instance, she exhorts, "Fellow workers, do not let your exploiters play with your health and your life. Make them follow the safety measures. This outrage, which the tragedy of Méru sheds light upon, must stop. . . ." Against the inhumanity of this system of profit-driven complicity, Beauvoir would oppose enlightenment about the extent of the problem and (worker) solidarity. This was a pattern that she followed earlier in *The Second Sex* and in her appeal on behalf of Djamila Boupacha during the Algerian War.

For Beauvoir, it is only through our actions that we will be able to ensure the necessary conditions of our own and others' freedom. To accept a system that denies that freedom to some is to deny freedom to all. Beauvoir is, therefore, compelling her readers to turn the heartbreak behind the bitter twist of the words, "In France today, killing goes unpunished," to its opposite, an affirmation that this outrage will not be tolerated, that her readers will refuse to look the other way, and will act on behalf of those at risk: all of us.

IN FRANCE TODAY,
KILLING GOES UNPUNISHED

by Simone de Beauvoir

TRANSLATION AND NOTES BY MARYBETH TIMMERMANN

"One year suspended sentence and a 20,000 franc fine." The accused, Mr. Bérion, bursts into tears. For what is he blamed? He has very simply set fifty-seven of his female workers on fire. Three are dead; the others are mutilated or disfigured forever. Such is bourgeois justice. The court found Mr. Bérion responsible for this tragedy by finding him guilty of "gross negligence" [*faute inexcusable*]. Yet it only gave him a one year suspended sentence! What's more, Mr. Bérion benefited from an amnesty. He directs a new, prosperous business. When one speaks of Méru to him, he responds, "It was an accident."

Méru is a small town of 6,000 inhabitants, fifty-seven kilometers northwest of Paris. Artisans, shopkeepers and farmers live there. An industrial zone cropped up a few kilometers away with several large factories, very modern in appearance. One of them, all blue, is closed even though its name is still marked at the entrance of the zone: Rochel.

Built in April of 1961, this factory's purpose was the packaging of gas products for the fabrication of insecticides and beauty products. It had been classified in the category of particularly dangerous establishments because it used

"En France aujourd'hui on peut tuer impunément," *J'accuse* 2 (February 15, 1971): 475–81; in *Les écrits de Simone de Beauvoir*, ed. C. Francis and F. Gontier (Paris: Gallimard, 1979), 475–81, © Éditions Gallimard, 1979.

flammable gases: butane, propane, alcohol, kerosene, etc. It stored 27 tons of it.* Mr. Bérion, who became the CEO in 1964, employed 80 to 90 workers: some young men (fifteen or so, counting the foremen) and a majority of very young girls whom, starting at the age of 14 and contrary to the rules, he put to work at the machines. They earned between 1.7 and 2 francs per hour. Their days started at eight o'clock and ended at seven. In addition, they had long commutes to make, on foot or by bicycle. The boss fired and rehired them as he pleased, for no other factory employed girls so young. From day to day, they depended on the foremen who favored the most obliging to the detriment of the others. It was impossible for them to defend themselves because no one in the factory was in a union. They resigned themselves to their lot rather cheerfully, thanks to their youth. They were happy to earn a living. However, because the protective measures recommended by one executive, Mr. P., had been neglected after he left, sometimes the aerosol can they had just filled up would burst and the liquid would burn their faces. One of them told me that she was blinded for fifteen days.

Gas leaks that spread out along the ground often occurred because the pipes circulated in non-ventilated trenches. Also the valves of the propane and butane tanks were often poorly closed. In March and April of 1967 fire broke out several times. Marc Vivet, a young fifteen-year-old worker, was in charge of opening the factory at seven o'clock in the morning and supervising the machinery and equipment. When he arrived on May 11, 1967,[1] everything seemed normal. But at about 8:15 AM, he noticed a thick layer of gas escaping from the production machine. "We saw the gas escaping," one worker told me, "upon contact with the air, it formed into little white crystals. One fellow worker complained that it was freezing her back." Another told me, "There was a layer of gas; we saw it. It was white, or rather gray, like a fog." Marc Vivet quickly notified one of the managers, one called Vrangile, who closed the faucet and told him to start up the labeler.† "I refused. I said, 'It's going to blow.' He responded, 'Oh no, nothing will happen. Go on.' And because I hesitated, he said, 'Go on. That's an order.'" Marc Vivet obeyed. There was a spark. The gas caught on fire. Everyone fled. But the hallways were obstructed; many of the doors were blocked by piles of cardboard. The drop ceiling made of nylon caught fire and collapsed. The polyethylene coverings that the management made the workers wear burned. Horrified witnesses saw half-naked young girls coming out of the factory transformed into living torches and rolling on the ground scream-

---

* In theory, the stock should not have exceeded 15 tons.
† The machine that glues the labels onto the aerosol cans.

ing. Of the 87 workers present that morning, 57 victims were immediately transported to the hospital. Three died in the following weeks. The others underwent horribly painful treatments for months—Marc Vivet and some others for eighteen months. All remained more or less handicapped. I will come back to them.

Bérion said what all bosses say: "It's fate." In this case, like most of the time, this fate was him. All the witnesses were in agreement and formed such an overwhelming file on him that in 1969, the criminal court of Beauvais found Bérion guilty of gross negligence and sentenced him for involuntary manslaughter. Bérion claimed that there was a sudden and unpredictable "rupture in the pipes," but if it were so, the gas alone, under six kilograms of pressure, would have burst forth with such violence that it would have put all the personnel to flight. If it had caught on fire, it would have formed a sort of flame-thrower with a limited reach. Yet the whole workshop was in flames; the other side of the partition even caught fire, the layer of gas having slipped under the doors. The truth is, the leaks were habitual because of deficient machinery and equipment, and insufficient safety checks.

And why did the spark burst forth? The response is clear on this point as well. The factory had been authorized to function in 1961 on the condition that certain security measures were followed. The electric machinery and equipment were supposed to be of the "airtight" kind and the electric motors were supposed to be armed with an anti-explosion device. But in November of 1965, Bérion had deliberately ordered a classic type labeler (the one that caused the explosion) in order to save approximately 2,500 francs. The electric machinery and equipment were so defective that no local company agreed to do the few hasty repairs that Bérion asked for. In order to ensure safety, he would have had to shut down the factory for several days and redo everything. Bérion was not unaware that several short-circuits had already occurred that year. In May of 1966, after an inspection, the APAVE* had demanded numerous modifications of machines that were not equipped with the required devices. The regional office of Public Health and Safety [Sécurité Sociale] had also pointed out some problems to him.[2] In particular, he had neglected to electrically ground the portable electrical machines. He paid no attention to any of these warnings.

In addition, the workshop doors should have opened out towards the exit, yet they were sliding doors and besides, for the most part, inaccessible. The doors as well as the ceiling were made of plastic and nylon. Marc Vivet

---

* Association of Owners of Steam and Electric Machines [*Association de propriétaires d'appareils à vapeur et électriques*].

also told me that the drainage from the machines took place not outside, but inside the factory, letting toxic products into the air.

Mr. P. told me that when he reminded Mr. Bérion about the safety instructions, he had responded, "Don't be a dummy. Make them keep plugging away; that's all you are asked to do." "I was not surprised when I learned that the factory had blown up," Mr. P. added.

So how was it that the labor inspectors were not disturbed by all this?[3] "We never saw any . . . At least they never came inside," the workers told me. The Amiens Court itself denounced the "deficiency" of the Labor Inspection Authority [*Inspection du travail*]. The Rochel tragedy sheds light on a fact of extreme gravity: the inspectors who in principle are supposed to assure the safety of the workers become accomplices with the bosses who sacrifice the health and the lives of their workers for profit. *They look the other way.* They are encouraged to do so at high levels. In France, 80% of factories do not follow the safety measures required by the labor code; productivity and profits would decrease if the labor inspectors started defending the interests of the workers. They do not do it out of fear of compromising their careers. The working conditions are so dangerous that inevitably accidents happen, and this inevitability has a human face . . . The bosses use each other as alibis. "Accidents at work happen everywhere," they say. And indeed they do, because everywhere bosses deliberately risk the lives of the workers.

Another outrage in this affair is the attitude of the justice system. The trial didn't take place until two years after the catastrophe. The victims were not allowed to form a class action, according to an article in the regulations of the *Sécurité Sociale*. However, this right was granted to them a few months later by the Appellate Court of Amiens, as per an article in the Penal Code. At this, Bérion gave up trying to appeal. So the only trial was the one at Beauvais where the victims were not heard. The committing magistrate only had access to the depositions gathered by the police officers when the injured workers were lying in their hospital beds. Bérion got away with a one year suspended sentence and a fine. Vrangile, who had given the order to start up the machines, was not even bothered.

A third outrage is the measures taken by the *Sécurité Sociale*. When a person is estimated to be less than 50% disabled, he only receives half of the pension which should be his right due to that disability. Someone who is 14% disabled receives 7% of his salary. The advising doctors for the *Sécurité Sociale* embrace the interests of the *Sécurité Sociale*, not those of the victims. In Méru, most of the victims were judged to be 14% to 20% disabled and receive about 400 francs each trimester! What's more, this sum is only given to them if they start to work again; otherwise they are accused of wanting to live off the government's money!

Such is the case of Martine Baron, 19 years old, recently married. She was 15 at the time of the accident. She stayed for a month at the hospital in Lille, wavering between life and death. After seven months in Lille, she spent seven months in Berck, where she underwent an extremely painful rehabilitation treatment; attached to a board, she stayed on her back for two hours, then on her stomach for two hours. She cried from morning until evening due to the pain and loneliness. She spent a year and a half of convalescence with her parents. Seriously burned from her waist to her feet, she had a great number of skin grafts done. She has twisted feet and her kidneys and legs still hurt. All her skin appears dead. She showed me her body; her entire lower back is cracked and swollen in an awful way. However, she is only compensated at 7%, based on a 14% disability. The *Sécurité Sociale* made her work, so for nine-and-a-half hours each day she is on her feet, carrying plywood planks.

After months at the Lille hospital, Marc Vivet spent months in Berck. He was burned over his entire body, legs and arms; he suffered so much that he could not be touched. They cared for his wounds by sprinkling disinfectants onto him from afar. Because the fire reached his face, he lost his teeth—which have been replaced—and his ears; he wears his hair long to hide his scars. He has half-twisted arms and weak legs. He receives 400 francs per trimester. He has started to work again.

A young woman who has one very pretty profile, the other destroyed by the fire, is allowed no compensation.

I asked several victims why they didn't sue the *Sécurité Sociale* to get their pensions increased. "I would do it if I were a millionaire," Martine's husband told me. They do not have the money to pay for a lawyer. And if they were to lose, all the costs would be charged to them!

What is monstrous, one doctor in that region told me, is that the *Sécurité Sociale* only wanted to consider—and very insufficiently—their incapacity to work. But many other things are involved. One can not determine the exact compensation for the pain that was experienced, but one must not forget that it was atrocious and left a lasting memory. Many of these young women are morally scarred. One of them recently fell into convulsions and suffered a long nervous depression because she saw a brush fire in a field.

One little eighteen-year-old redheaded girl told me, "Now we are constantly on edge. We have changed. We have nightmares. We get scared about every little thing."

There are also aesthetic damages, the importance of which is considerable when it comes to young women. Almost all have injured legs; they must hide them; they can no longer wear bathing suits. Many are ashamed of their faces and their bodies; they do not want to be seen.

And finally, for some of them the future is worrisome. They risk having circulatory disorders during all the delicate times of a woman's life.

No effort was made to try to repair even a little of these damages.

The story of the Rochel factory is not exceptional, but dramatically typical. At this very moment in most of the factories in France the workers are in danger. To defend them against murderous bosses, they can count on neither the Labor Inspection Authority, nor the courts, nor the *Sécurité Sociale*; they can count on no one but themselves. Fellow workers, do not let your exploiters play with your health and your life. Make them follow the safety measures. This outrage, which the tragedy of Méru sheds light upon, must stop:

In France today, killing goes unpunished.

NOTES

1. The date is "1961" in the *J'accuse* article, which must be an error, given the rest of the dates in the article.

2. The French Social Security system (*Sécurité Sociale*) is much broader than its American counterpart. It is in charge of providing public heath care benefits to everyone in France, including workman's compensation and disability benefits; it also pays allowances to families with children, as well as providing unemployment and retirement benefits.

3. These labor inspectors would have been sent by the Labor Inspection Authority (*Inspection du travail*), which is a state inspection agency that is supposed to ensure the rights of workers.

7

Essays on Israel and the Holocaust

INTRODUCTION

by Susan Rubin Suleiman

These four short essays, written over a twenty-year period, are *pièces de circonstance*, each one linked to a specific occasion: the publication of a book by a young author, an op-ed piece for a daily newspaper, a symposium on Israel organized by left-wing Jewish intellectuals, the appearance of a film that would become revered around the world. Beauvoir's essays here are modest efforts, in two cases simply brief prefaces to a much longer work; but read consecutively, they offer an excellent glimpse into the evolution of French public discourse about the Holocaust and about Israel. They also show Beauvoir's own unwavering commitment to thinking about the implications and consequences of the major atrocity of the twentieth century, as well as her personal interest in the Jewish state.

The preface to *Treblinka*, published in 1966, introduces a "non-fiction novel" by a newcomer to the French literary scene.[1] Jean-François Steiner, born in 1938 to a Jewish father and a Catholic mother, had seen his father deported as a young child. *Treblinka*, which remains his only significant work, reissued several times since its publication, was one of the first attempts, in France, to give a literary representation of Jewish suffering—as well as of Jewish heroism—during the Holocaust. The first such novel was André Schwarz-Bart's *The Last of the Just*, published in 1959; but Schwarz-Bart emphasized only the victimization of his Jewish protagonist, who ends up in Auschwitz, whereas Steiner's novel builds up to a violent climax of rebellion. Both novels were best sellers, and were widely translated. Schwarz-Bart's, however, won the prestigious Prix Goncourt, and has entered the twentieth century canon in a way that Steiner's has not.

As many historians have pointed out, France after the war made no special effort to recognize the specific experience of Jewish deportees. Since many members of the French Resistance had also been deported, and since the responsibility of the Vichy government in the persecution of Jews was largely swept under the carpet, there was virtually no public discourse in France devoted to the inhumanity of "racial" deportation. Furthermore, French Jews themselves, including the few deportees who returned, were reluctant to speak about a "Jewish memory" or a specifically Jewish response to persecution. In the two decades that followed World War II, the historian Annette Wieviorka has noted, most Jews in France "put their Judaism between parentheses," preferring the anonymity of assimilation to the assertion of a specifically Jewish French identity.[2] It was only after Israel's Six-Day War, in 1967, that French Jewry as a whole moved toward a self-conscious group identification, finding (as Wieviorka puts it) a "reconciliation between their French citizenship and Jewishness."[3]

Steiner's novel, conventional in its writing style but powerful by its mere content, tells the story of the slow birth of Jewish resistance in the extermination camp at Treblinka, culminating in the armed uprising of August 1943 that put an end to the camp. Although all of the organizers of the uprising perished, several hundred inmates managed to escape into the forest; only forty survivors remained at the end of the war. Steiner, in an afterword, explains that he interviewed many of the survivors, then living in Israel and elsewhere, in order to write his book. Both the purpose and the construction of the book are suggested in its two epigraphs. The first, an excerpt from the infamous speech of October 4, 1943, by Heinrich Himmler to the assembled SS officers in Posen (Poznan), stresses that the "glorious page" of German history devoted to the extermination of the Jews must not and will not ever be written.[4] Steiner's novel obviously invalidates that prediction. The second epigraph is a short sentence identified as a "Hassidic chant": "One must descend very deep in order to find the strength to rise again." The tale Steiner tells is indeed of a "descent" and a "rising," since he portrays the organizers of the uprising as Jews who are willing to work as humiliated participants in the Nazi extermination in order to save (however temporarily) their own lives. It is out of the depth of that desperate collaboration that they eventually rise, dying a heroic death rather than the death reserved for them by the horrific system of the camp.

Beauvoir's preface begins precisely with the question of humiliation and heroism. Attributing the question to the "young sabras of Israel during the Eichmann trial," and more generally to young people everywhere, she asks, "Why did the Jews allow themselves to be led to the slaughter like sheep?" She immediately explains, citing an autobiographical novel by David Rousset (a non-Jewish *résistant* who had been deported), that in the concentration camps no real resistance was possible, even by the most politically motivated prisoners. However, she continues, that explanation was not sufficient for Steiner. He wanted to look at the situation of Jews courageously, without shrinking: were they really just passive victims? Beauvoir implies that his investigation will not be to the liking of some French Jews, who would rather not deal with certain facts; she alludes to "the embarrassment with which certain facts were evoked, the oblivion with which people tried to cover them." It is not clear whether she is referring to the humiliation of the victims or to the "collaboration" of some Jewish inmates—her statement that Steiner will surely be "accused of anti-Semitism" by those who would prefer to maintain silence allows for either interpretation.

In fact, Steiner's book did elicit a lively and sometimes bitter debate in the French press, in which Beauvoir herself participated. David Rousset, whom she cites in her preface, criticized the book at length and adamantly in two articles in the weekly paper *Le nouveau Candide*.[5] Citing some eminent Jewish scholars of anti-Semitism and of the Holocaust, Rousset attacked the book for being historically inaccurate, especially in its portrayal of Jews almost without exception as passive victims. Far from being unique, as Steiner implied, said Rousset, the Treblinka uprising was one of many heroic acts of resistance by Jews, including those caught in the most inhuman situations in extermination camps.[6] Above all, Rousset blamed Steiner for his emphasis on the Jewish specificity of the uprising—this manifested, according to him, a "Jewish racism," echoing the stereotypes of anti-Semites ("D'où sort ce beau SS," 20–21). According to Rousset, the "concentrationary universe" was the same system for Jews and non-Jews, forcing the collaboration of the inmates themselves in the running of the system ("D'où sort," 20; "Les Juifs ont combattu," 20). The Treblinka uprising was not some expression of the "Jewish soul" but a political act, similar to others in other camps, part of the fight against Nazism.

Beauvoir replied almost immediately, in a published interview in the *Nouvel observateur*, the record of her conversation with two Jewish intellectuals, Richard Marienstras and Claude Lanzmann (who at the time was known as a journalist and as Beauvoir's former lover).[7] Oddly enough, given that this was her "reply to Rousset," both Marienstras and Lanzmann voiced strong criticisms of Steiner's book! But Beauvoir put up a vigorous defense of the book, and two weeks later she and Rousset crossed swords in a direct exchange of letters in the *Nouvel observateur*.[8] Rousset repeated and defended his earlier criticisms, in particular his critique of what he had called Steiner's "racism" (we would now call it essentialism). Beauvoir, on her side, recognized that talk of a "Jewish nature" made her uncomfortable, but she nevertheless defended the specificity of the Jewish experience of deportation: "If I separate myself from Steiner when he invokes a 'Jewish nature,' I believe in the specificity of the Jewish condition, in the specificity of Treblinka, wholly populated by Polish Jews who came from communities with strong traditions, and who reacted on the basis of those roots" (3). Meanwhile, the distinguished classicist and anticolonial activist Pierre Vidal-Naquet published a balanced article in *Le monde*, commenting on the whole controversy. Vidal-Naquet, identifying himself as "a Jew, atheist, Marxist, and French" (he had lost both of his parents to deportation), came down on the same side as Beauvoir on the question of Jewish specificity: he concluded that the Treblinka uprising was not so much a part of "the anti-Nazi struggle," as Rousset had suggested, but rather a Jewish revolt against the inhuman conditions imposed by the Nazis on the victims of the extermination camps.[9]

Aside from the question of Jewish specificity and Jewish response to humiliation, Beauvoir's preface deploys an argument that owes much to her and Sartre's ideological positions of the early 1960s. She argues that Steiner's book shows the transformation of a "series"—individuals caught in a situation where every one feels alone—into a "group," in which the "serialized" individuals are melded into a single body with a collective purpose. Sartre had analyzed this phenomenon, seeing it as a hope for collective action, in his 1960 *Critique of Dialectical Reason*, the long-promised (and never quite finished) sequel to *Being and Nothingness*. Beauvoir adopts his analysis, comparing the Jewish organizers of the Treblinka uprising to workers who join together to make collective demands of their employers. The comparison strikes one today as quite odd, an indication of Beauvoir's leftist leanings and of the ongoing influence of Marxism in France during the 1960s more than anything else.

In contrast, Beauvoir's two essays concerning Israel present arguments that remain pertinent today. The first of these, "Syria and Its Prisoners," a brief op-ed piece she wrote for the daily *Le monde* in December 1973, refers to the problem of prisoner exchanges between Israel and Syria after the Yom Kippur war; the second, "Solidarity with Israel: A Critical Support," is a substantial piece that Beauvoir delivered as a speech in May 1975 at the Cercle Bernard Lazare, a left-wing Jewish group that still proclaims support of Israel as part of its platform. Her speech was subsequently published in the Cercle's journal, *Cahiers Bernard Lazare*, under the rubric "My Point of View on Israel."

Beauvoir's point of view in both of these pieces is admirably balanced. It was a courageous position for a French leftist at the time (and still is today), for by 1973 the leftist orthodoxy in France considered Israel as an oppressive "colonial" power and reserved its support and sympathy exclusively for the Palestinians. While many French people (and definitely most French Jews) had shown warm support for Israel at the outbreak of the 1967 war—Israel, after all, was the country that was threatened—the support began to be qualified, or even reversed, as soon as Israel had won the war. Beauvoir, who had visited both Israel and Egypt for the first time with Sartre in 1967, shortly before the outbreak of the war, wrote about this shift in her 1972 memoir *Tout compte fait* (*All Said and Done*). After describing the many people they had met and places they had seen on their semiofficial tour (her own interest was above all in the condition of women and young people, but together they spent many hours discussing the situation of Arabs in Israel), she describes their anguish when, after returning home, they learned about the Egyptian-Israeli crisis. Public opinion in France and in the world was, she notes, divided, with the Soviet Union and most Western European Communist Parties (as well as some conservative parties, like the Gaullists in France) supporting Egypt, while others on the Right and the Left expressed sympathy for Israel: "But [Israel's] victory transformed in a disconcerting way the classic image of the Jew as victim, and [people's] sympathies turned toward the Arabs."[10] Her own position, she says, which recognized the claims of both parties without considering either one totally blameless, was bound to alienate her from many friends, especially her friends on the Left.

By the time Beauvoir wrote her op-ed article in December 1973, the Middle East situation had deteriorated even further. Israel had fought and won another war (the Yom Kippur War), and the Left all over Europe was unanimous in its condemnation. But *Les temps modernes*, which ever since its founding by Sartre and Beauvoir in 1945 had been firmly identified with left-wing politics, published a group editorial in its November 1973 issue that reflected the balanced views of both Sartre and Beauvoir on the Middle East conflict. Titled "La guerre et la paix" (War and Peace), the editorial argued for the necessity of finding a "common solution" based on direct negotiations between Israel and its Arab neighbors.[11] This desire to recognize the rights of both sides is again reflected in Beauvoir's op-ed piece a few weeks later—in fact, the article begins with a sentence that echoes the title of the *Temps modernes* editorial: "There is war, and then there is peace, or at least a respite, a truce." Beauvoir then goes on to the specific matter of the Geneva Convention concerning prisoners of war and takes the Syrians to task because they have refused to release the names of Israeli prisoners although Israel has released the names of its Syrian prisoners. Beauvoir calls on other Arab countries, as well as on Syrian mothers whose sons are being held, to put pressure on the Syrian government.[12] Although she has harsh words for the Syrian leaders' refusal to cooperate, calling it a form of barbarism, her argument rests on her general view that both sides' rights and responsibilities must be respected.

This view was given its fullest exposition in Beauvoir's May 1975 speech to the Cercle Bernard Lazare, in which she affirmed both her firm belief that the state of Israel must continue to exist and her sympathy for the Palestinian claim to nationhood. She argued for what is now called a two-state solution, with recognition and respect for both parties' claims to sovereignty. Six months earlier, in November 1974, UNESCO had passed a resolution that Beauvoir mentions in the beginning of her talk—the resolution excluded Israel from a regional working group because it had undertaken archeological excavations in the old city of Jerusalem, supposedly altering the city's historic features.[13] A number of French intellectuals had signed a protest against the resolution, including Sartre and Beauvoir (the resolution was later rescinded). UNESCO's exclusion of Israel from its working group amounted, Beauvoir states, to a "deliberate will to symbolically do away with Israel," as if taking it off the map. It was largely in order to protest against this symbolic elimination (which, she notes, corresponds to a desire for actual annihilation), that she decided to make another trip to Israel in 1975 to accept the Jerusalem Prize, a prestigious award given each year to a writer or intellectual. Beauvoir notes that it was the only prize she had accepted over the past twenty years. During her trip, she says, she saw in person that UNESCO's accusations against Israel were false, based in part on manipulated photographs of the Jerusalem landscape. Beauvoir expresses personal indignation at what she considers a "conspiracy intended to push

Israel deeper and deeper into its isolation" and states several times that the possibility of the disappearance of the state of Israel fills her with horror.

Aside from these personal eyewitness responses, Beauvoir's essay presents a number of compelling insights and arguments. Her remarks about the negative effects of isolation and fear of insecurity on Israeli politics are as valid today as they were thirty years ago. She also notes, with acuity, that the necessary priority accorded to national security may prevent Israel from attending to social problems that demand attention: the inequality between men and women, the "second-class" status of Arab Israeli citizens, and the poverty and powerlessness of Oriental Jews in comparison to the Ashkenazi Jews. These problems continue to exist in Israel today. Finally, Beauvoir offers an extremely nuanced and still timely analysis of the issue that is closest to home. Why, she asks, is the French Left, with whom she is usually in agreement but not on this issue, so one-sided in its vehement condemnation of Israel and its unconditional sympathy for the Palestinians?

Her first reply to this question is that one cannot discount the continuing presence of anti-Semitism in France. Even though it is no longer acceptable to declare openly anti-Semitic opinions, they are not dead: "What is called anti-Zionism is often a euphemistic way of translating an anti-Semitism that one dares not admit," she notes with some irony. The second reply she proposes is, I think, even more subtle and interesting. The reason that so many leftists, especially among the young, are unconditionally for the Palestinians and against Israel is, she says, due to a romantic idealization of the former and demonization of the latter. But the only reason why the Palestinians can be idealized, or even mythologized, is that they do not yet have a country: a country that is "incarnated," like Israel, is full of imperfections, whereas one that does yet exist seems to have all the virtues. When the Palestinians will have their country—and she hopes they will have it—it too will be imperfect, with internal contradictions and conflicts, and wrongs inflicted. This clearheaded analysis shows Beauvoir at her best, trying to understand complex phenomena without opting for extreme solutions. The way to criticize Israel and influence its policies, she suggests, is not to "reject the country as a whole" but to recognize its imperfection and difficulties and to bring pressure on it regarding specific issues. Not demonization, but persuasion.

And persuasion is her own project as well: she would like to persuade her leftist friends that a "critical" solidarity with Israel, as she has outlined it in this essay, is not contradictory with the Left's historic causes and convictions. "We must try to convince," she concludes, even as she recognizes that the job will not be easy, because the "comrades I may have on the Left" are "extremely stubborn in their refusal."

The last of these essays, Beauvoir's preface to the film script of Claude Lanzmann's 1985 film *Shoah*, is one of the last texts she wrote before her death (the very last one was another preface, to the translation of an American book, *Mihloud*, about a homosexual love affair written by someone who died of AIDS).[14] *Shoah* came out at a time when "Jewish memory" was an established concept in French public discourse: only a year earlier, Klaus Barbie had been extradited to France from Bolivia, to stand trial for crimes against humanity he had committed in 1943, when he was head of German intelligence in Lyon. At his trial in 1987, dozens of Jewish witnesses would come forward to testify to his brutality, including his rounding up of forty-four children from a home in Izieu, a town near Lyon, all of whom were deported and killed in Auschwitz.[15]

Although *Shoah* does not deal specifically with French Jews (Lanzmann shot the film chiefly in Poland, Israel, and the United States), its appearance in France in 1985 was part of the intense interest in the memory of victims of the Holocaust. Lanzmann also interviewed perpetrators and bystanders, and his film was criticized by some as excessively biased in its representation of contemporary Polish anti-Semitism. Despite these and other criticisms that have appeared over the years (regarding his handling of witnesses, his "staging" of interviews, and his gender bias toward male speakers, among other things), the nine-and-a-half-hour film was immediately recognized as a major artistic achievement, and that is how Beauvoir treats it in her preface as well. "Neither fiction nor documentary," as she puts it, *Shoah* is an intricately constructed montage of "places, voices and faces," seeking to make the Holocaust *present* to its viewers. Paradoxically, this sense of immediacy is produced without any recourse to archival footage from the period of the war. Lanzmann has explained on many occasions that his film is as much about the passage of time and the vagaries of memory as about the events of the Holocaust.[16] Beauvoir discusses the film as she would a poem (she remarks on its "poetic construction" and its use of repetition as a leitmotif) or a piece of music, calling it "a funeral cantata of several voices." She notes Lanzmann's masterful use of ironic juxtaposition (without calling it that exactly), when she mentions that the facial expressions of some of the people he interviews often contradict their words. Finally, she remarks on the unexpected combination of horror and beauty in this work, which she calls a "pure masterpiece." It is not only her tribute to an old and loyal friend, but also her honest homage to a great work of art.[17]

NOTES

1. Jean-François Steiner, *Treblinka* (Paris: Fayard, 1966). I wish to thank Sara Kippur for her excellent assistance in my research for this essay, which was completed in 2004 and updated in 2010.

2. Annette Wieviorka, "Vers une communauté? Les Juifs en France depuis la guerre des Six-Jours" (Towards a Community? Jews in France since the Six-Day War), in *Les Juifs de France de la Révolution française à nos jours* (Jews in France from the French Revolution to the Present Time), ed. Jean-Jacques Becker and Annette Wieviorka (Paris: Liana Levi, 1998), 364. All translations are my own.

3. Ibid., 365.

4. Himmler's speech has often been cited and reproduced, and can be found on many Web sites, including several negationist ones that seek to deny what it means. A full transcript in German and English can be found at: http://www.holocaust-history.org/himmler-poznan/ (accessed on November 15, 2010).

5. David Rousset, "D'où sort ce beau SS, ange du mal?" (Where did this handsome SS, angel of evil, come from?) *Le nouveau Candide* 260 (April 18, 1966): 18–24; and "Les Juifs ont combattu avec les partisans. Ils se sont révoltés dans 7 camps" (The Jews Fought with the Partisans. They revolted in 7 Camps), *Le nouveau Candide* 261 (April 25, 1966): 18–22. Hereafter, page numbers will be given in parentheses in the text. For an excellent detailed discussion of the "Treblinka affair" to which Steiner's novel gave rise in French public discourse, see Samuel Moyn, *A Holocaust Controversy: The Treblinka Affair in Postwar France* (Waltham, Mass.: Brandeis University Press, 2005). Moyn attributes to this affair, which occurred a year before the Six-Day War, a major role in the shaping of French public awareness and public discourse about the specific deportation of Jews, as opposed to the more general category of deportees who had "died for France."

6. Rousset's virulent reaction was probably provoked not only by the novel but by the interview Steiner had given in an earlier issue of *Le nouveau Candide* 255 (March 14, 1966). In the interview, Steiner spoke of being part of "a people, six million of whose members allowed themselves to be led to the slaughter like sheep." This sentence was quoted in the introduction to both of Rousset's articles.

7. Richard Marienstras and Claude Lanzmann, "'Ils n'étaient pas des lâches!' Entretien avec Simone de Beauvoir" ("They Were Not Cowards!" Interview with Simone de Beauvoir), *Le nouvel observateur* 76 (April 27, 1966): 14–17.

8. David Rousset, "Steiner est un raciste juif" (Steiner is a Racist Jew), and Simone de Beauvoir, "Rousset fait preuve d'une considérable arrogance" (Rousset Exhibits Considerable Arrogance), *Le nouvel observateur* 78 (May 11, 1966): 2–3.

9. P. Vidal-Naquet, "Treblinka et l'honneur des Juifs" (Treblinka and the Honor of Jews), *Le monde* (May 2, 1966): 17.

10. Simone de Beauvoir, *Tout compte fait* (Paris: Gallimard, 1972), 447.

11. "La guerre et la paix," *Les temps modernes* 328 (November 1973): 936–39. The editorial is signed "TM," indicating that it represents the views of the editorial board, of which Beauvoir was a member.

12. Karen L. Shelby has pointed out, in an unpublished essay, that "What is particularly Beauvoirian about this text . . . is its representation of mothers and its call to Syrian mothers to demand answers and action from their government. . . . The issue is not only the release

of their children who fought in the war. For Beauvoir, women's ability to mold their own ethical existence in a defense of principles of humanity against inhumanity is also at stake."

13. The text of this resolution, along with other UN resolutions regarding Israel, can be found on the Web site of the Israeli Ministry of Foreign Relations.

14. Simone de Beauvoir, Preface, *Mihloud*, trans. Bruno Monthureux and Ghislaine Byramjee (Aix-en-Provence: Alinea, 1986); a translation of Beauvoir's "Preface to *Mihloud*" is forthcoming in her *Feminist Writings*.

15. On this episode, see Serge Klarsfeld, *Les enfants d'Izieu, une tragédie juive* (The Children of Izieu, a Jewish Tragedy) (Paris: Les Fils et Filles des Déportés Juifs de France, 1984). For a detailed discussion of the importance of the Barbie trial in French public memory, see Susan Rubin Suleiman, *Crises of Memory and the Second World War* (Cambridge, Mass.: Harvard University Press, 2006), chapters 2 and 4.

16. See, for example, his four contributions to the excellent collective volume, *Au sujet de "Shoah," le film de Claude Lanzmann* (On the Subject of "Shoah," the Claude Lanzmann Film) (Paris: Belin, 1990).

17. Lanzmann reciprocated the tribute in his recent autobiography, *Le lièvre de Patagonie* (The Patagonian Hare) (Paris: Gallimard, 2009), in which he devotes many pages to his years of love and friendship with Beauvoir.

PREFACE TO *TREBLINKA*

by Simone de Beauvoir

TRANSLATION BY MARYBETH TIMMERMANN

NOTES BY MICHAEL ARTIME AND MARYBETH TIMMERMANN

"Why did the Jews allow themselves to be led to the slaughter like sheep?" the young *sabras* of Israel asked each other indignantly at the time of the Eichmann trial.[1] In Europe also, many Jews of the younger generation, not having known Nazism, wonder about this. The fact is that, in the world of concentration camps, all peoples had the same comportment: a conditioning process carefully designed by the SS assured the submission of the condemned. In 1947, in *Les jours de notre mort* [The Days of Our Death], Rousset wrote, "The triumph of the SS requires that the tortured victim allow himself to be led to the gallows without protesting, that he denies himself and abandons himself to the point where he ceases to affirm his identity . . . There is nothing more terrible than this procession of human beings going to their death like mannequins."[2] Among the Russian prisoners, the members of the communist party and political leaders were set apart and destined to a rapid extermination. In spite of their ideological and military preparation, they put their courage into dying, but no resistance was possible for them.[3] This sort of explanation was not enough for J.-F. Steiner. His Jewish condi-

"Préface," *Treblinka*, by Jean-François Steiner (Paris: Fayard, 1966), 7–11, © Librairie Arthème Fayard, 1966.

tion made him feel uneasy. All the accounts that he had read presented the millions of Jews who died in the camps—including his father and a large part of his family—like pitiful victims: shouldn't they have rejected this role? The embarrassment with which certain facts were mentioned and the efforts made to cover them with oblivion implied that nothing could excuse them: were they really inexcusable? Steiner decided to look at them face to face: to go to the extreme of shame or to heal himself of it.[4] This courage will undoubtedly cause him to be accused of anti-Semitism by the very ones whose silence, caution, and evasiveness have aroused suspicion in people's hearts. And yet he was right to have confidence in the truth, for he has won. The story of Treblinka, pieced together from written testimonies and conversations with survivors of the camp, gave him back his pride.

A "Sonderkommando" was installed at Treblinka, originally composed of Jews from Warsaw, most of whom were massacred and replaced by newcomers.[5] Numbering about a thousand, under German orders and led by Ukrainian guards, they carried out the work of extermination and recovery for which the camp had been designed. A large number preferred to die, either by refusing to take their chances during the selection process, or by suicide. But how could the others consent to pay such a price to survive? Collusion with the Germans by notable Jews constituting the *Judenraten* is a known fact that is easily understood. In all times and all countries—with only a few exceptions—notables collaborate with the victors; it's a matter of social class. But at Treblinka, even though some Jews were less mistreated than others, the distinction of class played no role, either among the men of the Kommando or those who arrived on the train station platform to be driven directly to the gas chambers.[6] So? Must we speak of a "ghetto mentality" like they do in certain classroom books distributed to Israeli children? Or an atavism of resignation, the mystery of the Jewish soul and other nonsense? Steiner's book puts this pop psychology in its place by describing exactly how things happened.

In the curious world which is ours, aggregates of individuals who live their common condition dispersed throughout the world—Sartre calls these aggregates *series*—show behaviors which cause them to make enemies of each other and therefore enemies of themselves. In a panic, for example, people trample each other, suffocate each other, and kill each other, amplifying or even completely creating a disaster that a rational evacuation of the premises would have contained or avoided. The same goes for speculations and traffic jams. As long as workers remained isolated within their class, employers had an easy time of exploiting them. Each one saw in the other a competitor ready to accept slave wages in order to get hired, and so he tried to sell his work at an even lower price. In order for protests to become possible, it was necessary to form groups where each individual on the contrary considered the other to be the same as him. The skill of the Germans was to *serialize* the Jews and to prevent these series from becoming groups. In the ghetto of Vilna—and in all of them it was the same tactic—the SS divided the population into the pariahs and the privileged ones: only the first endured the raids, but the second category was again divided all the way to the final liquidation. All the same, there was an attempt at resistance, but easily crushed. It nourished no hopes, for even if it had won over the whole ghetto, bombardments would have put an end to it. And that also explains why only a small number of people rallied to it.

The "technicians" also elicited serial behaviors when they proceeded to the first selections. All the men who wanted to survive, considering the mass of which they were a part, said to themselves, "If I refuse, there will be others to carry out this work in my place, and so I will die for nothing." And indeed, the enormous human material at the Germans' disposal could not be made up exclusively of heroes. Predicting the submission of the others, each one resigned himself to submit like them. This trap could have been avoided only if the instructions for resistance had been given ahead of time, and if each one had been persuaded that everyone would follow them. This was not the case, for many reasons, and mainly because the situation was such a terrifying novelty that for a long time no one wanted to believe in its reality. When brutally faced with it, the Jews were plunged into a confusion analogous to that which is created by a panic, and they had no way to coordinate their behavior. Sometimes they tried, timidly. The "technicians" organized elimination tests: races on the belly or on all fours. Three quarters of the competitors would be spared: the first to arrive. The last quarter would be slaughtered. For a moment no one moved. The whips rained down upon them; the competitors knew that if they remained stubborn, they would all be massacred. As soon as a few decided to take off, they all immediately followed.

What the young *sabras* of Israel did not understand is that heroism is not given ahead of time. From their childhood on, their entire education tends to inculcate heroism in them in the form of military courage. The men of Treblinka were civilians whom nothing had prepared to confront a violent death, and most often an atrocious one. Because during the first months the teams were liquidated and replaced in a very rapid rhythm, they did not have the time to invent forms of resistance. The miracle is that some of them did all the same, and that they succeeded in rallying all the prisoners. After the tragic descent that Steiner relates, without skipping anything, in the first part of the book, he has us witness an extraordinary ascent.

The process of this ascent is exactly the opposite of abdication. A few cowards are enough for the entire series to behave cowardly, but as soon as a group appears, a few heroes are enough for people to regain confidence in each other and begin to dare. Solidarity was first marked by the efforts of some to prevent suicides. Then by the organization—in terribly dangerous conditions—of an escape network, destined less to save lives than to reveal the awful truth about Treblinka to the world. A Committee of Resistance was created, and, even though its realization appeared impossible, they formed a project for an armed revolt. Starting then, the prisoners competed with each other in dedication and courage. The *Hofjuden*, although they enjoyed some privileges, allied themselves with their less fortunate brothers and took considerable risks to help them.[7] Two men from camp number 1 chose to descend into the hell of camp number 2 in order to get the two hundred pariah who were imprisoned there involved in the revolt. For that they voluntarily committed a transgression in their work that could have just as easily been punished by torture and death as by a transfer. The impossibility of procuring arms for themselves could only be overcome at the price of much blood and suffering. Despite these failures and temptations to despair, the Committee held out. Its extraordinary courage can not be explained by the imminence of the camp's liquidation. The first attempted insurrection—which came to an abrupt end without the Germans having caught wind of it—occurred well before Himmler's visit when he condemned Treblinka to disappear without delay.[8] Moreover, the members of the Committee had already decided to sacrifice their lives; their role would be to hold up the Germans while the prisoners fled towards the forest. What they passionately wanted by massacring the German "masters" and tearing themselves from their condition of slaves, was to show the world that the Jewish people did not let themselves be led to the slaughterhouse like a flock of sheep.

Having myself gathered so many passionate testimonies about the camps in 1945, I was stupefied when I heard this reproach uttered. One must read the details of the story about the hours when the insurrection broke out and raged. Not only the Committee, but a great number of prisoners behaved with such complete abnegation, such calm heroism, that it seems aberrant to have ever blamed the Jews for a fatalistic resignation. That they were capable of such an uprising shows that their helplessness in the face of their executioners was not the expression of some secret abnormality or mysterious curse. This book brilliantly shows that it was due to the circumstances. And their helplessness is not what should amaze us, but their ultimate surpassing of it.

The author does not claim to do the work of a historian. Each detail is guaranteed by written or oral testimonies that he gathered and compared. But he did allow himself a certain amount of drama. In particular, he reconstructed the dialogues for which he obviously didn't know the exact wording, but only the content. Perhaps they will reproach him for lacking rigor, but he would have been less faithful to the truth if he had not revealed this story to us in its living movement.

The tone of the book is altogether unusual: neither pathetic nor indignant, but with a calculated coldness and sometimes even a dark humor. The horror is evoked in its everyday banality and almost as if it goes without saying. In a voice that rejects any inflection that is too human, the author describes a dehumanized world. Yet, it is about men, and the reader does not forget that. This contrast provokes an intellectual outrage within him more profound and more lasting than any emotion. However, outrage is only the means. Steiner wanted above all to understand and to make people understand. He has fully reached his goal.

NOTES

Previously translated by Helen Weaver (New York: Simon and Schuster, 1967).

1. *Sabra* is the term used to identify native-born Israelis; Otto Adolf Eichmann (1906–62) was a German Nazi and SS officer who was in charge of managing the logistics of the deportation and extermination of Jews during WW II. After the war, he fled to Argentina, but was discovered there and taken to Israel to stand trial for crimes against humanity. He was found guilty and hanged after the trial, which started on April 11, 1961, and ended on August 14, 1961.

2. (Elisee) David Rousset (1912–97), member of the French Resistance and militant Trotskyist, was a Nazi concentration camp survivor who wrote about his experiences in *L'univers concentrationnaire* (*A World Apart*) (1945) and *Les jours de notre mort*.

3. This is the end of the paragraph in the previously published translation.

4. In the previously published translation, "to go to the extreme of shame or to heal himself of it" (*d'aller jusqu'au bout de la honte ou de s'en guérir*) was omitted.

5. *Sonderkommando* is a term with two definitions in relation to World War II. First, this term can be used to describe a group of slave laborers who were given the task of working the extermination camps. These groups were often massacred and as a result there were several revolts by the *Sonderkommando* throughout the course of the war. Additionally, the term can be applied to German groups that worked with the *Einsatzgruppen* in Soviet territories to dispose of the bodies of those killed in conflict. In this text the first definition of the term is applied.

6. *Kommando* represents the units of slave laborers working within the concentration camps and operating under the umbrella of the Nazi regime during World War II. The

Sonderkommando is an example of a *Kommando* unit. Outside of the historical context the term simply implies a basic unit of measurement or command in the German language.

7. *Hofjuden* is the German translation of Court Jew, or a Jewish banker or businessman engaged in financial interactions with the Christian community. While they still faced repression and violence under the German regime they were also afforded more privileges than the average Jew of the time period because of their financial influence.

8. Heinrich Himmler (1900–1945) was a Nazi leader who oversaw the concentration and extermination camps. He visited all three Operation Reinhard extermination camps (Belzec, Sobibor, and Treblinka) in early 1943 to check on their final operations and make sure all traces of them would be eliminated. These death camps were no longer required since the Auschwitz-Birkenau death camp had increased its extermination capabilities.

SYRIA AND ITS PRISONERS

by Simone de Beauvoir

TRANSLATION BY MARYBETH TIMMERMANN

NOTE BY MICHAEL ARTIME

There is war, and then there is peace, or at least a respite, a truce. Weapons are silenced. The two sides bury their dead, care for their wounded, and the prisoners return home. Beyond the bloody confrontations, peoples reestablish a human reciprocity between themselves. This ancient tradition was established as international law by the Geneva Convention.[1] Israel immediately decided to conform to it, and, after rather long delays, Egypt consented to the exchange of prisoners, but Syria refuses to do the same. Israel gave the list of its prisoners to the Red Cross and allows the Red Cross to visit them frequently. Syria has not furnished the names of the Israelis they hold captive and authorizes no one to check on the way they are being treated.

Why this inhuman attitude? The corpses of Israeli soldiers who had been tortured have been found in the Golan Heights. As abominable as they are, these excesses of hatred can be conceptualized in the rage of combat. But how can it be understood that a government, in cold blood, subjects young, unarmed people to the anguish of a detention with no guarantee of release,

"La Syrie et les prisonniers," *Le monde* (December 18, 1973); in *Les écrits de Simone de Beauvoir*, ed. C. Francis and F. Gontier (Paris: Gallimard, 1979), 254–55, © Éditions Gallimard, 1979.

311

and condemns hundreds of families to the pangs of doubt? Syrian soldiers had received the order to render the identification of the killed Israelis impossible, or at least very difficult. The goal probably was to cause dismay among the enemy, undermining their morale, and thereby diminishing their force. But today, the war is over. If the prisoners' families in Israel stop living a nightmare, the course of history would not be changed by it.

There is nothing more painful than not knowing if a cherished being is alive or dead. The silence of Damascus seems all the more cruel since this cruelty is gratuitous. Syrian leaders hardly sympathize with the tears of Israeli mothers, but don't they care about the Syrian mothers—more than five hundred—whose sons could be returned by one simple word from the leaders? They do not share the torments of the Israeli mothers because they know their children are alive and well, yet they most likely suffer from their children's absence. Their government would rather frustrate their joy at being reunited with their children than to give up breaking Israeli hearts. Can't they make their voices be heard against this useless and harsh choice? Can't anyone in Syria or another Arab country try to persuade leaders in Damascus to modify their behavior?

It is not a matter of a political choice here. One can take Syria's side against Israel, and nonetheless require that it stop violating the Geneva Convention. At the beginning of this last war, Arabs took pains to destroy a certain negative image of themselves in order to substitute a more favorable image. In particular, the Egyptians sought to convince the world that they gave their prisoners all the care required by the prisoner's country. The vindictive stubbornness of the Syrians goes against this effort. Although they turn a deaf ear to the protestations of their enemies, maybe they would listen to their friends if they would point out what an enormous disservice they are doing themselves when it comes to public opinion. If they continue to disregard the rules recognized by all nations to limit the horrors of war, only one word can be used to describe their practices: barbarism.

NOTES

In *Les écrits*, this article is preceded by the following introduction: "This article is yet another point of reference testifying to Simone de Beauvoir's growing commitment [*engagement*] to the struggle for the rights of the individual, whether man or woman."

1. The Geneva Convention was ratified in 1949 and this compilation of four treaties was designed to address humanitarian concerns in international law. The first convention is "*for*

the Amelioration of the Condition of the Wounded and Sick in Armed Forces in the Field." The Second Geneva Convention was designed "for the Amelioration of the Condition of Wounded, Sick and Shipwrecked Members of Armed Forces at Sea." The Third Geneva Convention was "relative to the Treatment of Prisoners of War." The final portion of the Geneva Convention was "relative to the Protection of Civilian Persons in Time of War." The conventions have over 200 signatory nations and are enforced by the International Court of Justice at the Hague.

SOLIDARITY WITH ISRAEL

A Critical Support

by Simone de Beauvoir

TRANSLATION BY MARYBETH TIMMERMANN

NOTES BY MICHAEL ARTIME

The reason I am here and the reason I was in Israel has basically already been explained to you with the words exile, encirclement and solitude. I was deeply affected, outraged and even greatly distressed by the ostracism of which Israel was the victim in the latest UNESCO resolutions.[1] Several intellectuals, including Jean-Paul Sartre and myself, have signed a protest against these measures which attempt nothing less than to drive Israel from this earth, since Israel belonged to no continent, whereas Canada, for example, used to belong to Europe. Therein lies a deliberate will to symbolically do away with Israel, and a symbolic elimination is very dangerous because it implies a profound desire, conscious or subconscious, for real annihilation. That is why I have decided to go to Israel to receive the Jerusalem Prize, although until now, ever since the Goncourt Prize, I have accepted neither prizes nor any of those things that are called honors.[2]

In Israel, I was able to see with my own eyes the futility of the attacks directed against Jerusalem by UNESCO. The mayor of Jerusalem accompanied

"Solidaire d'Israël: un soutien critique," *Les Cahiers Bernard Lazare*, n. 51 (June 1975); in *Les écrits de Simone de Beauvoir*, ed. C. Francis and F. Gontier (Paris: Gallimard, 1979), 522–32, © Éditions Gallimard, 1979.

me throughout the city—I saw the ruins and archeological finds which, far from harming the Arab culture, are on the contrary very favorable to it since very important remains of the Islamic culture have been discovered in addition to remains of the Jewish culture. I saw the underground passageways that have existed for a very long time, which have only been cleaned and fixed up. And I also saw that when they claim that the new constructions built in Jerusalem take away from the beauty of the ancient city, and particularly the Arab city, we are more or less voluntary victims of a conspiracy. There is in fact a newspaper, the German newspaper "Stern," that had fun taking photographs with a telephoto lens of buildings that are 2 or 3 kilometers away from Jerusalem and, by cleverly manipulating the photo, putting them right next to the Omar mosque. I met people from UNESCO (among the highest ranking) who had seen these photos and who told me before I left, "What I deplore the most is not the excavations, but the invasion of ancient Jerusalem by modern buildings which are very ugly." But this is absolutely false. These buildings are far from the ancient city. And besides they are necessary because, of course, ancient stones and the ancient city are beautiful, but people still need a place to live; it is an absolute necessity in Jerusalem. Jews, just as much as Arabs, must have a place to live and new buildings must be constructed.

Therefore, I was able to see with my own eyes—which is, moreover, what I had predicted when I, along with the others, signed the paper against the UNESCO resolution—that it was in reality a matter of a conspiracy intended to push Israel deeper and deeper into its isolation, and intended, as I was telling you a moment ago, to symbolically deny Israel in order to pave the way for accepting that it be denied materially and in reality. But this idea of the annihilation of Israel is an idea that horrifies me. I am not Jewish, but I lived through the Nazi occupation of [19]40 to '45 and followed the horrors of the Holocaust almost daily. I followed the persecutions of which the Jews were the victims.

It is not necessary to have personal ties with someone to feel the horror of the Holocaust, but it happens that I had a rather large number of Jewish friends, and almost all of them are gone. They were deported, never to come back. I therefore lived through the occupation and the persecution of the Jews in profound horror. And yet it was a horror that was somewhat logical, because it was the enemy; it was the Nazis; it was a whole, awful world that was busy annihilating and persecuting the Jews.

What I could stand even less, if I can express myself in such a way, were the events that followed. We believed in '44–'45 that the nightmare had ended and that the Jews would be able to breathe and would, in one way or another, be able to live in freedom, with rights equal to those of other men, but what did we see? We saw the survivors of the camps, the rare survivors of the camps, thrown into other camps, where they were made to wander across the seas without anyone wanting to welcome them. And I felt that this was all the more of an outrage because the allies of yesterday, the English in particular, were the ones responsible for all of this misery and all of this suffering. We also learned what the Americans were responsible for during the Holocaust: they had refused to raise their emigration quotas, which would have allowed Jews to arrive in numbers as massive as necessary in order to escape the Nazi persecutions. What an outrage to see the complicity of all the allied countries (including France) contributing to the suffering of the Jewish people!

And so now, I have passionately followed the struggle led by Jews to be able to establish themselves on a soil that is their own, on the soil of Israel. I had friends who participated very closely in this struggle, and for me, it was almost a personal victory when finally in '48, the State of Israel was recognized by the UN.[3] At that moment I thought that everything was taken care of, especially since there were leftist powers, such as the USSR and Czechoslovakia, that had supported the creation of the State. I therefore feel very deeply attached to the existence of Israel, and the idea that Israel might not survive as a State, the idea of the annihilation of the State of Israel is unbearable to me. I know well the difficulties created by this existence.

Someone was speaking earlier about the Palestinians, and I am also familiar with the plight of the Palestinian people. I know that they are a people who also have the right to be recognized and to have a territory and a national life. It is a matter of finding a solution. What solution? I don't know. What I know is that a solution that does not simultaneously maintain the living State of Israel as such, would be a solution that would absolutely not be valid, and that I most forcefully reject. That said, and we were reminded of this just a moment ago, Israel is in danger. Danger is what I felt in the attitude of UNESCO: the danger of isolation and fear. Isolation and fear are very bad advisors.

I felt this isolation during the very short time I stayed there; it was something that was very visible. First, I was touched by the way I was welcomed, but at the same time, it was rather heartbreaking because there was such happiness to see the encirclement, exile and ostracism broken, be it by only one person. By this, I could feel how much this people suffer from the isolation and ostracism to which they are condemned. And this is something that is extremely dangerous because, like several of my friends over there told me, "If you feel completely isolated, you end up scoffing at everything.

316

You think, 'What does public opinion matter? What does justice or morality matter? There is only one thing left that counts; that is to survive. So we are all alone! Well, we are going to fight the battle all alone scoffing at what all the others might think. We are going to do whatever it takes to survive!'"

There is also in Israel a fear that is not as blatant as the feeling of isolation, but which also is very deep and very evident. Fear is a bad advisor. Politically, fear and isolation lead to a rigid attitude of refusing any measure that is not immediately a security measure. The notion of security is a notion that becomes so important in Israel that it ends up eclipsing all others. And I don't blame them for it, yet the fact is that the isolation to which Israel is condemned is what leads them to give priority to security and tightening their positions, which is probably not the most favorable attitude for a lasting peace. It is politically dangerous to feel oneself condemned to isolation and to live in fear.

There is another thing. This isolation and fear prevent the majority of Israelis from treating social problems with all the importance they deserve. Indeed, there are considerable problems, and as you were told a moment ago, it is true that I am very attached to Israel and at the same time very critical about it. There are many criticisms to make of Israel and I will not hesitate to put them forward.

First of all—and this is the essential criticism—the equality that should reign in any democracy is not found in Israel. I know well that it reigns nowhere, but that does not make the inequality less regrettable. Since we were talking a little while ago about women, I will start with this particular inequality. There is a profound inequality between women and men. Israel had a Prime Minister who was a woman, and there are women assigned to the army. However, there are only 9 women deputies, which is a pathetic number. I have spoken at length with feminists in Israel who told me about the great illusion there of the equality between men and women. In '67 I spoke at a conference at the University of Jerusalem, and I had intended to address the problem of women, but some women approached me to say, "Oh, no, don't speak about that because it's completely out of place here. We are perfectly equal to men on all planes!" I seriously doubted that this was true, but I did not want to offend them, so I spoke of something else. But this time, when I addressed the question again and said what I am in the midst of telling you now, well, even the women who had previously told me not to speak of it admitted, "Yes, we were wrong; we wanted to believe that. . . . In reality there absolutely is not equality between men and women." Naturally, since I was discussing this question in a small committee comprised of men and women, I heard the following reflection from some of the men: "But

317

why did you come to speak to us about that particular problem when Israel is in such a situation, when there are problems of much greater importance? That is secondary!" I responded, "What you say there is very amusing to me because three weeks ago I was in Portugal and had almost the same conversation. I said that the way women were treated in Portugal was shameful, and they responded with, 'But Madam, you do not understand the situation; there are much more important problems.'" In Israel security is what counts, and in Portugal it is the Revolution which is taking place. . . . In any case, women are supposed to come last. This is a very flagrant inequality.

The second inequality, which I will not stress because it is too obvious, is the inequality between the Arab Israelis and the Jewish Israelis. The Arab Israelis are second class Israelis. Of course, there are many problems; obviously they can not take up arms to go fight against other Arabs, and that fact alone implies that they are second class citizens. But there are many other inequalities. Vidal-Naquet spoke of some yesterday in an article in the *Observateur*.[4] He spoke of students, and the difficulties that an Arab student has in getting somewhere in life. At best, he will be a teacher in an Arab high school, which does not at all lead to the same positions as a Jewish high school. So there is a flagrant inequality there. The most unpleasant work is done in general by Arabs. They have worse living conditions and a much lower standard of living, without counting the expropriations of land and all the injustices of which they are victims.

Moreover, even in the Jewish community, there are considerable differences and considerable discriminations between Oriental Jews and Ashkenazi Jews in whose hands rests all the power: political power, the power of money, the power of prestige, cultural power, etc. etc. I visited a high school bearing a French name, appropriately so, since they teach French there: René Cassin High School. The principal of this high school explained to me that it is located on the border of two neighborhoods: a neighborhood of rather affluent Ashkenazi Jews and a neighborhood, on the contrary, of very poor Oriental Jews. He explained the difficulties he had in avoiding discrimination between the students, and how he tried, at the price of a few injustices on the scholarly plane, to not have too great of a percentage of Oriental Jews expelled before the end of their studies. Because apparently—and a very interesting study on this subject was done in Jerusalem actually—what a child had acquired during the first three years, or even the first two years of his existence is irreplaceable. If you take children who have lived in families that were too large, more or less in the slums, without a cultural foundation, well, these children are condemned to be culturally handicapped throughout their lives. This high school principal told me that it was rather clumsy to try to compare these children coming from Oriental and Ashkenazi families on the basis of French, because the seventeenth century—which I understand perfectly since even French high school students remain impervious to *Horace* and *Berenice*[5]—means absolutely nothing to Oriental Jewish children. Their slowness is even more marked when compared to Ashkenazi Jews because the parents of the latter group are able to introduce them to Racine and Corneille. Apparently an effort is being made now to modify the curriculum of that high school.

Of course, there are people in Israel who are dealing with these problems—that of women as well as that of Arabs within Israel and that of Oriental Jews—and even very actively. Some devote their lives to it and take it very much to heart. Incidentally, they are generally the same ones who try to have a policy of reconciliation with Arabs outside of Israel and with the Palestinians. It is basically what must well be called the *Israeli Left*. I say that it must well be called that because there are people who deny that there could be a Left in Israel, but that is not true! There is a Left in Israel which is full of goodwill, which is active, but which is tragically isolated. A leftist Israeli writer told me, "Yes, there is Israel's solitude, but also think about *our* solitude, within Israel." And this solitude of the Left within Israel results from the solitude of Israel itself, because, as I was saying in the beginning, the fact of feeling isolated, excluded, in exile, and encircled leads the ensemble of the Israeli people to have a very demanding, very hard, and rather closed attitude that is generally not very sensitive to social problems. Consequently, the Left is terribly isolated and because of that, it doesn't have the impact, power, or influence that it could have.

That brings me to something that is more personal to me. It was already mentioned earlier. It is, in fact, one of the reasons that I went to Jerusalem and that I am here tonight. This Israeli Left rightfully complains that it is not supported at all by the Western Left in general and by the French Left in particular. And it's true! This is one of the contradictions mentioned a little while ago that I assume with some difficulty. I agree with the French Left on so many points that I find it difficult to disagree on this point, but the fact is that a large number of people who belong to leftist parties are anti-Israeli. I have tried to understand just why this is the case.

Certainly, for many, there is a latent anti-Semitism. As was said a little while ago, what is called anti-Zionism is oftentimes a euphemistic way of translating an anti-Semitism that one dares not admit. No one will say that he is anti-Semitic. The Arab people, for example, say, "We are not at all anti-

Semitic; we are anti-Zionists; that's not the same thing." And I have friends in the French Left who tell me, "Anti-Semitism is awful!" Yet, having said that, they are anti-Zionist and wish for the destruction of the State of Israel. . . . I think that there is also a certain romanticism, especially among young people, that makes them *a priori* take the side of the Palestinian people, almost unconditionally, because they are a people who have no country. Since it is a country that does not exist, one can project much into it and hope much from it; one can think that it will have no defects and that it will be perfectly socialist, perfectly just and egalitarian. While in the case of Israel, well, Israel is an incarnation: the idea of the State of Israel was incarnated in the State of Israel, and any incarnation implies many defects, imperfections, hardships, and mistakes. Surely the pioneers of the State of Israel, who were mentioned just a little while ago, when they thought about what Israel would be, also thought about an absolutely perfect, pure, and just Israel, a country such as had never been seen before, a country absolutely not like the others. Well, in fact, it is a country not like the others, but also a country like many others since inequalities and injustices are found there. It is a country that is not a pure ideal as a country that does not exist can be. This is probably one of the things that come into play, particularly among young people, because they always want to create myths for themselves. There was a time when we believed in the USSR, a time when we believed in China, and there are young people now who believe in the purity of a Palestinian country. When it exists—and I hope that it will exist—it is obvious that as soon as it is incarnated, it will be in the grip of contradictions, ruptures, mistakes, etc.

That said, there are, of course, some objective reasons for which the Left is against Israel. Israel, due to the fact that its Left is not preponderant, is a State that makes a great many political mistakes. Israel has not taken the same positions as the Bernard Lazare Circle has, and in general, has not taken sides very convincingly, on the question of Vietnam, for example.[6] When I went there in '67, there was a conference on Vietnam, organized by a few members of the Israeli Left. They were against the United States and for Vietnam, but there were very few of them. I have seen numerous cases where Israel has taken positions not supporting revolutions around the world, but, on the contrary, oftentimes backing the United States or other oppressive countries. In addition, Israel is a religious state. This is obviously something that bothers the Left because, for example, marriages must take place in a synagogue, and if a Jewish man marries a woman who is not Jewish, he is not allowed to have children who are themselves Jewish. Religion is of great importance and carries great weight over there, and I understand very well that this bothers people who are on the Left and who, consequently, are for freedom of thought and action.

I understand, but that said, any country which exists and is real, has its contradictions, conflicts, and difficulties, and if one is not *a priori* prejudiced against it, one must try to put pressure on it and try to struggle with all the means one might have against what one reproaches it for, but one must not reject the country as a whole. I have brought a letter here with me, which I received the other day and which really broke my heart, precisely because it posits this problem of leftism and Israel. A young high school student, a very young Jewish high school boy wrote this to me: "The relationship I maintain with the leftist students in my high school is rather tense. It is difficult for me, as well as for my Zionist classmates, to remain open to the Left. Before any discussion, we are immediately rejected and treated to names such as fascist and racist. These insults hurt. Don't they know whom they are addressing? Many among us are those whose families have truly suffered from fascism and racism. Have they the right to use these easy and untruthful arguments, which leave us with no voice?"

The distress of this young student is certainly the distress of a great number of Jews in France, or elsewhere, who would like to get closer to leftist movements but who are rejected by the Western Left. Like I was telling you, this is also one of the reasons that made me go to Israel and come here, because I consider myself, rightfully so, I think, as someone from the Left. I have taken a stand, insofar as my means have allowed, in all the struggles of the Left. I stood by the FLN during the Algerian war;[7] consequently I can not be accused of being favorable to colonialism. (Besides, I do not consider Israel to be a "colony" since there is no mother country and the natives are not exploited and made to work, etc., etc.) I can say that I am leftist, and it is because I am leftist that I want to affirm my solidarity with Israel in general, and with the Israeli Left in particular. For me it is obvious that this country should live. Having no sense of religion, I do not found this right upon its ancient presence on that soil, nor upon the tradition about which many Jews boast—for them I know it means something very profound, and many Jews invoke it—but I personally would not found the rights of Israel upon those things. Instead, as many leftists have, and in particular Brecht in *The Caucasian Chalk Circle*, which is a very beautiful play, I would found their rights upon the fact that the "earth belongs to those who make it better!" and to those who work it.[8] The Israelis have worked that soil for a long time, and in particular since they formed their State. There is one thing that really struck me during an excursion from Jerusalem to Tel-Aviv. I crossed the Green Line, that is to say the border between the territory that used to be part of Jordan and the territory that was Israeli.[9] It is very noticeable. I don't mean to say that the Arabs are not capable of cultivating their soil—they probably have had neither the technical means nor the financial means nor the motivation necessary to work like the Jews have done—but it is very noticeable to the naked eye. You see the desert, and that is Jordan. Then, only five or ten meters away, you see plantations of orange trees, prairies, trees, and that is Israel. Maybe the Israelis had more facilities for working their soil, but whatever the case, they have taken advantage of it. They have worked it, they have put down roots there, they have founded their families there, they have lived there, they have become attached to it by their very work and by all that they have done and by all the children they have raised.

And for me, I have no need to seek other reasons. This is the fundamental reason that they have the right to live on that land and to live there, not yet again as a more or less oppressed minority, or in any case as a minority, but to live there with the feeling of being at home, on a land that belongs to them. I would like to try and share these convictions with the comrades I may have on the Left. It is very difficult because they are extremely stubborn in their refusal, and yet I think this is the work that each of us must try to do because all of us here are more or less leftist and for the existence of Israel. We must try to convince. Each one may not be able to do a lot, but still it is something. If the Left were more supportive of Israel and the Israeli Left, then they would be better equipped, stronger, and would be able to engage Israel in paths that, for the future, are certainly the paths that are more favorable to the country's happy existence.

NOTES

This article was originally the text of a presentation given by Simone de Beauvoir on May 6, 1975 at a conference organized by the Bernard Lazare Circle and chaired by André Schwartz-Bart.

1. UNESCO (United Nations Educational Scientific and Cultural Organization) had passed a resolution in November 1974 that "excluded Israel from a regional working group because it had undertaken archeological excavations in the old city of Jerusalem, supposedly altering the city's historic features" (See Susan Rubin Suleiman's introduction to this essay). The text of this resolution, along with other UN resolutions regarding Israel, can be found on the Web site of the Israeli Ministry of Foreign Relations.

2. The Jerusalem Prize for the Freedom of the Individual in Society honors authors who explore the theme of individual freedom in their work; The Goncourt Prize is one of the most

important literary prizes in France, which was awarded to Beauvoir in 1954 for her novel *Les Mandarins* (*The Mandarins*).

3. In 1947 the United Nations supported the efforts of the Zionist movement by partitioning the establishment of a Jewish state, Israel. In 1948 the State of Israel was officially created and sanctioned by the international community.

4. Pierre Vidal-Naquet (1930–2006) was a French author and historian, founding member of an organization meant to prove the existence of the Nazi gas chambers, and an outspoken critic of the revisionists who wanted to deny the reality of the Holocaust; *L'observateur* was created in 1950 as a left-wing, weekly French newsmagazine; it then changed its name to *France-observateur* in 1954, and again in 1964 to *Le nouvel observateur*.

5. *Horace* and *Berenice* are five-act tragedies written by the French seventeenth-century playwrights Pierre Corneille and Jean Racine, respectively.

6. Founded in 1954, and named after Bernard Lazare, who fought against anti-Semitism during the Dreyfus Affaire, this group of left-wing Jewish activists fight against anti-Semitism and affirm their solidarity with Israel. This text first appeared in their monthly publication, *Les cahiers Bernard Lazare* (June 1975). The Vietnam War, which officially lasted from November 1, 1955, to May 15, 1975, erupted in the wake of the end of French colonial rule in Vietnam, and became a cold war military conflict between the communist North Vietnam and the U.S.-backed South Vietnam.

7. *Front de libération nationale* (National Liberation Front) was a revolutionary movement created in 1954 in support of Algerian independence and later became one of the most important and powerful political parties of independent Algeria. The Algerian War (1954–62) was a conflict between the French government and "colons," or colonists, as well as the revolutionary FLN and the MNA (*Mouvement national Algérien*), both supporting the independence of Algeria but in competition with each other. On July 1, 1962, Algerian independence was officially recognized.

8. Bertolt Brecht (1898–1956) was a German author and playwright who was exiled from Nazi Germany. *The Caucasian Chalk Circle*, written in 1944, is a parable about a peasant girl who steals a baby but becomes a better mother than its natural parents.

9. The Green Line refers to the Israeli borders that had been established after the 1948 Arab-Israeli war. Israel later captured many of the surrounding territories in the Six-Day War in 1967.

PREFACE TO *SHOAH*

by Simone de Beauvoir

TRANSLATION BY MARYBETH TIMMERMANN

NOTES BY MICHAEL ARTIME

Remembering the Horror

Shoah is not an easy film to talk about.[1] There is magic in this film, and magic can not be explained. After the war, we read so many testimonies about the ghettos and the extermination camps, and were shaken by them. But today, when we watch this extraordinary film by Claude Lanzmann, we see that we have understood nothing.[2] In spite of all our knowledge, the awful experience remained at a distance from us. For the first time, we live it in our minds, our hearts, and our flesh. It becomes ours. Neither fiction nor documentary, *Shoah* succeeds in re-creating the past with an astonishing economy of means, using only places, voices, and faces. The great art of Claude Lanzmann is to make the places speak, to bring them to life through voices, and, beyond words, to express the indescribable through faces.

Places. One of the great concerns of the Nazis was to erase all traces, but they could not abolish all the memories, and Claude Lanzmann was able to find the horrible realities under the camouflage of young forests and new

---

"Préface," *Shoah* by Claude Lanzmann (Paris: Fayard, 1985), © Librairie Arthème Fayard, 1985.

grass. In this lush green prairie were crater-like pits where trucks unloaded the Jews who had died of asphyxiation during the trip. Into that pretty little river, they threw the ashes of incinerated corpses. Here are the peaceful farms from where the Polish peasants could hear and even see what was going on in the camps. And here are the villages with beautiful ancient houses from which the entire Jewish population had been deported.

Claude Lanzmann shows us the train stations of Treblinka, Auschwitz, and Sobibor.[3] His own feet tread upon the "ramps," covered with grass today, where hundreds of thousands of victims were driven towards the gas chamber.[4] For me, one of the most heart-rending of these images is the one that represents a heap of suitcases, some modest, others more luxurious, all with names and addresses. Mothers had carefully packed powdered milk, talcum powder, and baby food. Others had packed clothes, food, and medicine. And none had needed any of it.

Voices. They tell their stories. And during most of the film, they all say the same thing: the arrival of the trains, the corpses tumbling out of the opened train cars, the thirst, the ignorance laced with fear, the stripping of clothes, the "disinfecting," the opening of the gas chambers. But not for an instant does it seem repetitive. Mainly because of the different voices. There is the cold and objective one—with barely a few tremors of emotion at the beginning—of Franz Suchomel, the SS Unterscharführer at Treblinka.[5] He gives the most precise and detailed description of the extermination of each convoy. There are the somewhat troubled voices of certain Polish people: the conductor of the locomotive whom the Germans sustained with vodka, but who found it hard to bear the cries of thirsty children, and the stationmaster of Sobibor, worried by the silence that had suddenly fallen over the nearby camp.

But, often the voices of the peasants are indifferent or even a bit mocking. And then there are the voices of the very rare Jewish survivors. Two or three have attained an apparent serenity, but many can hardly bear to speak; their voices break, they dissolve into tears. The similarity of their stories is never tiring, on the contrary. It makes one think of the intentional repetition of a musical theme or a leitmotiv. For the subtle construction of *Shoah* does evoke a musical composition with its moment of culminating horror, its peaceful countrysides, its laments, its neutral intermissions. And the underlying rhythm is the almost unbearable roar of the trains going towards the camps.

Faces. They often say much more than words. The Polish peasants display compassion, but most seem indifferent, ironic, or even satisfied. The faces of the Jews match their words. The most curious are the German faces. That of Franz Suchomel remains impassive, except when he sings a song to the glory of Treblinka, and his eyes light up. But the embarrassed, pinched expressions of the others belie their protestations of ignorance and innocence.

One of the great talents of Claude Lanzmann was indeed to tell us the story of the Holocaust from the point of view of the victims, but also from that of the "technicians" who made it possible and who refuse any responsibility. One of the most characteristic is the bureaucrat who organized the transports. Special trains, he explains, were put at the disposition of groups who were leaving for excursions or on vacation and who were paying half-price. He does not deny that the convoys directed towards the camps were also special trains. But he claims to not have known that the camps signified extermination. He says he thought they were work camps where the weakest died. His embarrassed, evasive physiognomy contradicts his own words when he pleads his innocence. A bit later, the historian Hilberg informs us that the "transferred" Jews were given the same status as vacationers by the travel agency and that the Jews, without knowing it, financed their own deportation, since the Gestapo paid for it with the goods that it had confiscated from them.[6]

Another striking example of a face contradicting the words is that of one of the "administrators" of the Warsaw ghetto. He wanted to help the ghetto to survive and preserve it from typhoid fever, he affirms. But in response to Claude Lanzmann's questions, he stammers, his traits become distorted, he avoids eye contact, and he is visibly upset.

Claude Lanzmann's construction does not follow a chronological order. I would say—if one can employ this word for such a subject—that it is a poetic construction. A more in-depth study than this would be necessary to indicate the resonances, the symmetries, the asymmetries, and the harmonies on which it rests.[7] This explains why the Warsaw ghetto is not described until the end of the film, when we already know the implacable destiny of those behind the walls. Here again, the story is not unequivocal; it is a funeral cantata of several voices, masterfully intertwined. Karski, then a courier of the exiled Polish government, yields to the pleas of two important Jewish leaders and visits the ghetto in order to bring his testimony of it to the world (in vain, incidentally).[8] He sees only the awful inhumanity of that dying world. The rare survivors of the uprising, crushed by German bombs, speak, on the contrary, of the efforts made to preserve the humanity of this condemned community. The great historian Hilberg discusses with Lanzmann at length about the suicide of Czerniakow, who thought he could help the Jews in the ghetto and who lost all hope the day of the first deportation.[9]

The end of the film is, in my eyes, admirable. One of the rare survivors of the ghetto uprising finds himself alone in the middle of the ruins. He says that he experienced a sort of serenity then, thinking, "I am the last of the Jews and I am awaiting the Germans." And immediately we see a train roll by, bringing a new cargo towards the camps.

Like all who have seen the film, I am mingling the past and the present. I have said that the miraculous part of *Shoah* resides within that very mingling. I will add that I would have never imagined such a union of horror and beauty. Certainly, one is not used to mask the other; it is not a matter of aestheticism. On the contrary, one sheds light on the other with such invention and rigor that we are aware of contemplating a great work. A pure masterpiece.

NOTES

The text of the film *Shoah* by Claude Lanzmann was originally published in 1985 (Paris: Fayard) and more recently in the Folio collection (Paris: Gallimard, 1997), © Librairie Arthème Fayard, 1985. The first American edition was published in 1985 as *Shoah: An Oral History of the Holocaust. The Complete Text of the Film*, with the English subtitles of the film translated by A. Whitelaw and W. Byron (New York: Pantheon Books, 1985). A more recent American edition, corrected and revised by Claude Lanzmann, was published in 1995 with the title *Shoah: The Complete Text of the Acclaimed Holocaust Film* (New York: DaCapo Press). All of these publications include Beauvoir's Preface.

1. *Shoah* comes from the Hebrew word for calamity and is used to refer to the Holocaust.

2. Claude Lanzmann (1925-) is a French filmmaker and professor at European Graduate School in Saas-Fee, Switzerland. He also manages *Les temps modernes*, the magazine created by both Sartre and Beauvoir. He met Beauvoir when he joined the staff there in 1952 and had a relationship with her until 1958. Although he is best known for his work on *Shoah,* he also directed *Why Israel* (1974), *Tsahal* (1994), *A Visitor from the Living* (1997), and *Solibor/1943/4PM* (2001). In 2009, Lanzmann published his memoirs under the title *Le lièvre de Patagonie* (*The Patagonian Hare*) (Paris: Gallimard, 2009).

3. These were Nazi extermination camps whose main purpose was to exterminate Jews and other "undesirables."

4. In the previously published translation, "des centaines de milliers de victimes" was rendered as "thousands of victims."

5. SS-Unterscharführer Franz Suchomel is a critical witness to the gassings during this period. Lanzmann's interview with Suchomel is a central part of *Shoah*, and was filmed via a hidden camera. In the interview he describes the Treblinka camp, where over 800,000 lost their lives as "a primitive but efficient production line of death. Understand? Primitive, yes. But it worked well, that production line of death."

6. Raul Hilberg (1926–2007) was an acclaimed historian of the Holocaust period. His family arrived in America in 1939 after coming from Austria. He served in the United States military during World War II and then returned to the United States to finish his education.

The Destruction of the European Jews (New Haven: Yale University Press, 2003, c1961), the three-volume study of the Jewish experience during World War II, is the most noted work of his career and one of the first historical examinations to evaluate the implications of the Holocaust.

7. This sentence was omitted in the previously published translation.

8. Jan Karski (1914–2000) was a diplomat in various European countries. In 1939 Karski became a POW of the Red Army during World War II. He escaped after two months and became a pivotal leader in the Polish resistance. He disguised himself as a Nazi officer and witnessed firsthand the experience of Jews in concentration camps. He used this experience to become a vocal advocate for the Jews during World War II, including speaking to government officials in London and arguing in front of Roosevelt. His goal was to raise awareness and create an impetus for action throughout the world regarding the Holocaust. Following the war he spent 40 years as a professor at Georgetown University in the United States and continued to share his experiences by lecturing throughout the world.

9. Adam Czerniakow (1880–1942) was a member of the senate in Warsaw. In 1939, after the city officially surrendered to the Nazis, he became the leader of the *Judenrat* which was the organization with the responsibility of carrying out Nazi orders in the region. When he was given orders to send Jews to the Treblinka death camp, he desperately pleaded for exemptions. When his efforts failed he committed suicide instead of executing his orders.

8

A Walk through the Land of Old Age

INTRODUCTION

by Oliver Davis

Beauvoir is not renowned for her work with film. Aside from appearing in biopics of her and Sartre she had little active involvement in this medium.[1] In 1974, however, she collaborated extensively on a film about old age, *Promenade au pays de la vieillesse* (or *A Walk through the Land of Old Age*). This introduction explains how this forgotten work was made and received before proceeding to analyze it in the wider literary, philosophical, and political context of Beauvoir's work.[2]

Promenade was shot in France in 1974 under the direction of Marianne Ahrne, a Swedish filmmaker and writer, then near the beginning of what has proved a very distinguished career. This 70-minute color documentary was financed by Swedish Television and first broadcast in Sweden, with subtitles. Though firmly based on Beauvoir's treatise, *Old Age* (1970),[3] the film draws primarily on the sections devoted to the situation of older people in postwar France, leaving to one side the book's lengthy ethnographic, historical, and biographical analyses: the director's intention, she said, was to produce a commentary on the present. *Promenade* revisits many of the key locations of Beauvoir's treatise, in particular state-run nursing homes ostensibly devoted to the "care" of the elderly. Beauvoir not only appears throughout the film, connecting and commenting on material, but she was also involved closely in various stages of its production, including scriptwriting.

When Marianne Ahrne and her collaborator, Bertrand Hurault, approached Beauvoir about making a film based on *Old Age*, they discovered that she had already made arrangements with an American director whose budget was considerably larger. However, Beauvoir felt that Ahrne's proposal would be more faithful to the spirit of her book and so rejected the first offer. Ahrne, who later became friends with Beauvoir (and indeed collaborated with her on the script for a film adaptation of *She Came to Stay*), had first become involved with Beauvoir some years earlier while gathering material for a documentary about abortion, then illegal in France.

Promenade was shot in the autumn of 1974, after some six weeks of preparatory research and interviewing. This initial material was then presented to Beauvoir and a script was written jointly. The old people who are featured in the film were found principally from three sources: 1) large, state-run, nursing homes; 2) a religious charity working with the elderly, the "Petits Frères," featured in the film; and 3) through a trade-unionist miner, an acquaintance of Sartre's, who is also featured.

The film is centered around three large nursing homes run by the French state, in Champcueil, Ivry, and Nanterre. Although Beauvoir discusses all three in *Old Age*, it transpired that she had not been allowed access to either Ivry or Nanterre while researching her book. The first time Beauvoir actually *saw* inside Nanterre was when she viewed the rushes for *Promenade*; she accompanied the filmmakers to Champcueil, where she is shown interviewing a nurse, and to Ivry. Yet the film confirms and illustrates many of Beauvoir's suspicions, in *Old Age*, about the brutal treatment endemic in large state-run institutions intended to care for the elderly and destitute.[4] The regime at Nanterre—nursing home and containment facility in one—is particularly punitive: we see new arrivals filing in, collecting piles of folded uniforms and answering a roll call. Residents explain how the failure to take regular baths carries a mandatory penalty and those filmed in the local café, drinking, on their weekly afternoon out, complain that simply answering back or returning inebriated means they lose the right to go out for some forty-five days. *Promenade* draws attention to the myriad casual brutalities and the ordinary negligence that seem to flourish in these institutions: a man who spends hours trying to lift himself out of a bath of cold water, a male nurse who is not only drunk but speaks with some amusement, in front of his patients, about their being taken to the morgue. Nursing-home workers are revealed to be mostly young people with little training and scant understanding of the situation of those in their care. The film offers a critique of the nursing home as institution by drawing attention to the way in which "care" is bound up with repressive treatment. Around the time of Michel Foucault's *Discipline and Punish* (1975) and much well-publicized activism by left-wing French intellectuals in favor of the rights of prison inmates, Beauvoir's critique in *Old Age* and her collaboration with Ahrne in *Promenade* together constitute a less celebrated, but no less significant, attempt to expose repressive institutional power-relations in another arena.

There is more to *Promenade* than large-scale social comment. It also offers an intimate portrayal of the way in which individuals and couples confront the aging process. Married couples, in particular, are shown quarreling over their ambitions for retirement—whether they will be "free" to watch television or clean the floor—and in so doing lay bare the desperate banality of what Beauvoir then proceeds to denounce as meager pseudo-projects, all that a capitalist economy leaves to workers whom it has effectively "used up." Thus, in keeping with the staunchly Marxist perspective of *Old Age*, economic reality reaches down into the very texture of individuals' most intimate fears and aspirations.

Promenade was never shown on French television despite winning the critics' prize at the 1975 Hyères film festival. This was principally on account of an agreement with one of the three older women who talk about their experience of sex; furthermore, some of the nursing-home footage was probably too damning an indictment of state provision to be palatable to French television in the 1970s. *Promenade* was, however, screened in two Parisian cinemas, for some two weeks, in 1978. Reviewers largely divided along the lines of political orthodoxy. For *Le monde*, Claire Devarrieux complained the film showed neither grandchildren ("a reason to live") nor grandparents ("real pillars of love and wisdom") and concludes her review by implicitly rejecting Beauvoir and Ahrne's tragic vision in favor of the altogether more comforting perspective put forward by the French writer Marcel Jouhandeau.[5] Yet the picture advanced by the reviewer and Jouhandeau, of happy grandparents relaxing into an old age of serene contemplation, is precisely the sort of commonplace that Beauvoir's treatise and *Promenade* call into question: for Beauvoir was convinced that behind such reassuring images, which lend themselves to complacency, lie the socioeconomic realities of poverty and loneliness and the existential fact that aging brings alienation.

This reviewer's response is unsurprising. For these are socioeconomic and existential realities that, as Beauvoir herself suggested in *Old Age*, few are prepared to face. This tendency to avoid frank discussion of old age perhaps explains the undeserved neglect that both *Old Age* and *Promenade* have suffered over the last three decades. The plight of the film is extreme. There has, to my knowledge, been no scholarly discussion of this late collaborative project. No mention is made of it in Deirdre Bair's biography of Beauvoir and a mere paragraph alludes to it in that of Francis and Gontier, under an erroneous title.[6] The film itself is not generally available, nor is it held in any of the major French archives. The copy used to prepare this transcript was kindly provided by the director herself. The near nonavailability of this important collaborative work in a medium with which Beauvoir is seldom associated makes the publication of this transcript imperative, notwithstanding the inherent limitations of any attempt to render a filmic object into text. The transcript is not intended to be a substitute for the film.

How does *Promenade* relate to Beauvoir's other work on old age? As I have argued elsewhere, Beauvoir is invariably dissatisfied with her attempts to represent her own aging autobiographically.[7] To the singular, self-writing subject, its own aging seems elusive, indeed disarmingly inaccessible. The aging process seems curiously resistant to representation by the self-writing subject, even though it is, in an obvious sense, a basic presupposition of the work of representation. Beauvoir's move, in the mid-1960s, from mainly autobiographical to mainly biographical life-narratives can be seen as a response to this sense of impasse: *A Very Easy Death* (1964), *Promenade* (1974), and *Adieu: A Farewell to Sartre* (1981). And *Old Age* (1970), too, is packed full of biographical sketches. *All Said and Done* (1972) is, in this respect, something of an anomaly. This broad move toward the biographical—toward *the other*—should be seen in the context of the formal and representational resistance that her own aging offers to Beauvoir the autobiographer. The fact that *Promenade* was a collaborative work is, then, highly significant: having experienced the elusiveness or invisibility of her own old age as a self-writing subject, Beauvoir's involvement in a collaborative filmic project is a change of method and medium in an attempt, with an enlarged "cast," to project successfully a vision of old age, her own and other people's. That others become involved here makes sense in the context of Chapter Five of *Old Age*, where Beauvoir argues both that aging is a process in which the subject is progressively made other and one the effects of which are revealed to the subject primarily through other people. Three episodes from *Promenade* will now be examined in detail in the light of these considerations, in an attempt to explore how the film might extend and modify the state of current critical thinking about this phase of Beauvoir's work.

In the first episode (37:50–43:13), Beauvoir is filmed in the intimate sur-roundings of her impeccably tidy, split-level apartment. She descends from the balcony and puts on a record. The camera pans around the well-lit lower room, showing her many souvenirs of travel abroad and political activism at home. Looking at the camera, she says that once you cross a certain line in life, you look back on your former activities with the thought "never again." The film cuts immediately to a very different interior: a dilapidated, dark and messy single-room flat, where an old woman, Mademoiselle Desaux, lies in bed, fully clothed. She talks about how she can no longer manage the stairs to her apartment after being hit by a motorbike while crossing the road. During the remainder of the clip, we alternate between Beauvoir's apartment and that of the bed-bound old woman, a contrast with striking effect.

It has been suggested that, in *Old Age* and generally, "Beauvoir does not submit to critical reflection her attitude toward her own aging."[8] This se-quence from *Promenade* implies a rather different view, in the way that Beauvoir's living space and her narrative are intercut with those of the old, bed-bound, woman. Thus proof of Beauvoir's active and privileged life, souvenirs from her travels and her political campaigns are arranged (in a manner recalling the grave-relics of warrior-rulers) on shelves around her, whereas the old woman's flat has no such adornment. While Beauvoir ad-mits that "I am still interested in travelling" the old woman can hardly get up the stairs. The episode ends with Beauvoir taking a taxi to meet a friend; the old woman, by contrast, lives entirely alone. Throughout, Beauvoir's elegance and eloquence contrast sharply with the aphasic, repetitive, and frantically gestural utterances of the old woman, reflecting both her debili-tated physiological condition and the educational disadvantages of her class background. Beauvoir is thus exposing her own, privileged, experience of the aging process to criticism.

In addition to Beauvoir's clearly self-critical take on her experience of aging in the film, there is also a formal continuity between the confron-tation staged in this clip and Beauvoir's view of senescent subjectivity in *Old Age*. The abrupt cutting between Beauvoir and the bed-bound woman echoes the distance and incommensurability of the divide between the el-derly individual's self-image and the view of others, the breadth of the "in-surmountable contradiction" (*contradiction indépassable*), which Beauvoir suggests is characteristic of old age. A similar sense of noncommunicative juxtaposition is created in the second sequence.

Beauvoir, in this second scene (1:01:00–1:07:00), is interviewing, or at least is supposed to be interviewing, a nurse who works in the large, state-run, nursing home at Champcueil. The nurse speaks of her disillusionment and complains about the insults she is forced to endure from patients. Beauvoir becomes increasingly terse, interrupting more and more often. The body language of the nurse becomes increasingly defensive.

Much of the humor in this scene derives from the fact that Beauvoir proves unable to respect the conventions of the interview, first by failing to allow the nurse to answer her questions and eventually by failing even to ask questions. Yet it is not only the interview situation that is subverted in this scene, for Beauvoir is herself a relatively old woman and the nurse's professional role is the care of elderly. This is, then, a parodic inversion of her everyday work: an elderly woman who answers back—not, as in the case of her patients, with a barrage of insults, but rather with pointed, rational, argument, one whose hyperarticulacy smothers the nascent responses of the younger interviewee, who, like the bed-bound woman in the first clip, is reduced to mute self-expression through gesture and body language. And this body language suggests that the nurse feels the encounter is both too reminiscent of her professional life—having to deal with yet another demanding old person—and also too disconcertingly different: the power-relation has been inverted, she and the institution she represents are being called into question. It has also been argued that Beauvoir's late work serves perniciously to strengthen cultural stereotypes of old people, reinforcing "violently, cultural views about aging."[9] Yet this scene suggests otherwise: Beauvoir is challenging the stereotype of the defenseless, submissive, and silenced old woman, prey to institutional violence. Ahrne and Beauvoir together present us with a parodic inversion of those institutional forms of interaction that tend to deprive the elderly of their voice.[10]

Yet Beauvoir's articulacy, her infamous strength of voice, is also juxtaposed in this film alongside less strident, far less encouraging, examples of elderly orality. In the third and final sequence to be considered here (16:50–24:00), Marcel Jouhandeau is shown at home, surrounded by richly colored paintings of himself as a younger man. He argues that old age represents deliverance from desire: "My life is a sort of apotheosis." The film cuts to Beauvoir, who denounces this view of old age as serenity. We then return to Jouhandeau, who proceeds to sing a verse from the *Magnificat*, accompanying himself on an old harmonium. His fingers are contorted and arthritic. We continue to hear his repetitive "Magnificat, anima mea" while the camera slowly enters a nursing home from its garden walkway; by contrast with the rich colors of Jouhandeau's study, which is plastered with garish portraits of himself as a younger man, the building and its environs are an exceedingly drab grey. Nurses deliver water to patients on the wards, maneuver them into and out of beds; one old woman sings and others explain, not all that lucidly, how they ended up in this institution.

Jouhandeau's claim that old age is a time of serene contemplation is the very antithesis of Beauvoir's argument in *Old Age*. When she mentions Jouhandeau in that text, it is to dismiss him just as perfunctorily as she does in this clip with the comment: "That is completely wrong." Yet by allowing Jouhandeau to speak directly to the camera, the film inevitably accords rather greater weight to his experience of old age than Beauvoir did in her book. Indeed, Beauvoir's abrupt dismissal of Jouhandeau in the film is somewhat undermined by its very brevity: it comes across as a little too cursory. Once more this suggests a new readiness on Beauvoir's part to confront perspectives on old age that differ from her own.

Perhaps the prime interest of this particular sequence lies, however, in the use of sound, in the presentation of voices. In *Promenade*, Beauvoir talks of her ambition "to give a voice to those who are never heard" and, in her introduction to *Old Age*, she writes of the elderly that "if their voices were heard, the hearers would be forced to acknowledge that these were human voices."[11] Yet the voices that this film allows to be heard are faltering, disintegrating traces. Whether singing, as Jouhandeau and some of the inhabitants of the nursing home do, or relating how they came to be admitted, what the "grain" of these voices betray is a striking hollowness, the near-death-rattle of broken bodies, of absence or impending absence. The fading of the subject is audible in the fragmented delirium of the voice itself. And this impression can only be heightened by the contrast with Beauvoir's vocal fortitude elsewhere in the film. The film does not offer unequivocal support for Beauvoir's confident belief that, "if their voices were heard, the hearers would be forced to acknowledge that these were human voices." For many of these voices are so alien—rambling deliriously, as though from another world—that they risk undermining rather than reinforcing the recognition of a shared humanity.

Promenade reveals new facets to Beauvoir's work on the aging process: an acute awareness of her own privilege, a self-critical stance, a willingness to offer greater room to views of aging that differ from her own, and a parodic inversion of social stereotypes about the elderly. Yet it is also a bleak portrait, one which leaves the viewer with a strong sense of the limits to recognition, the suspicion that—even if particular institutions or indeed society in its entirety were radically overhauled—old age would still remain irreconcilably other.

NOTES

With many thanks to Marianne Ahrne for her most generous assistance and for granting permission to publish this transcript.

1. Beauvoir appeared in *Sartre par lui-même* (Sartre by Himself), a film directed by Alexandre Astruc and Michel Contat with the participation of Simone de Beauvoir, Jacques-Laurent Bost, Andre Gorz, and Jean Pouillon (1972), and in *Simone de Beauvoir*, a film directed by Josée Dayan and Malka Ribowska (1979).

2. See also the discussion of this film and the interview with Marianne Ahrne in my book *Age Rage and Going Gently: Stories of the Senescent Subject in Twentieth-Century French Writing* (Amsterdam: Rodopi, 2006), 164–70 and Appendix 1, 197–204.

3. This and all subsequent dates of publication are for the French originals. *La vieillesse* (Paris: Gallimard, 1970) was translated as *Old Age* by Patrick O'Brian (London: Deutsch, Weidenfeld and Nicolson, 1972) and published in the United States as *The Coming of Age* (New York: G. P. Putnam's Sons, 1972).

4. See Beauvoir, *Old Age*, ch. 4.

5. *Le monde* (June 21, 1978): 20.

6. Claude Francis and Fernande Gontier, *Simone de Beauvoir* (Paris: Perrin, 1985), 379.

7. See my *Age Rage and Going Gently*, ch. 5.

8. Penelope Deutscher, "Bodies, Lost and Found: Simone de Beauvoir from *The Second Sex* to *Old Age*," in *Radical Philosophy* 96: 6–16; 14.

9. Penelope Deutscher, "Three Touches to the Skin and One Look. Sartre and Beauvoir on Desire and Embodiment," in Ahmed and Stacey, eds., *Thinking through the Skin* (London: Routledge, 2001), 156.

10. Those familiar with the documentary of Sartre by Astruc and Contat, from 1972, will recall that Beauvoir is similarly hyperarticulate there, answering many of Sartre's questions for him; it is the context in *Promenade*, the direction, which makes this a subversion with political significance rather than a comedy turn.

11. Beauvoir, *Old Age*, 2.

A WALK THROUGH THE LAND OF OLD AGE

A Documentary Film

by Marianne Ahrne, Simone de Beauvoir, Pépo Angel,
and Bertrand Hurault. Directed by Marianne Ahrne

TRANSCRIPTION BY JUSTINE SARROT AND OLIVER DAVIS

TRANSLATION BY ALEXANDER HERTICH

[Old man tries to lift himself out of the bath. Young people run past old.]

MIDDLE-AGED MAN: Old age: couldn't you have found something more amusing?

OLD WOMAN: No, I don't like old people.

OLD MAN: Why?

OLD WOMAN: Well, because they're always talking about their problems and I don't like that.

TEENAGER: No, because each time I run into one of them, they always say "let the old folks through" . . . They're always against us kids . . .

SECOND TEENAGER: . . . "back in my day" . . .

FIRST TEENAGER: That's the first thing that comes out of their mouths.

FIRST TEENAGER: They're old fashioned, that's why. They're old fashioned. They . . . well it depends, but some of them won't accept new things,

---

Transcription of the film *Promenade au pays de la vieillesse* by Marianne Ahrne, Simone de Beauvoir, Pépo Angel, and Bertrand Hurault, directed by Marianne Ahrne (Stockholm, Sweden: 1974) for Swedish Television Ltd., © Marianne Ahrne.

young people, and, well . . . My grandfather, for example, he won't accept, uh, pop music. He won't accept it, and also American films, Americans, he doesn't like 'em.

OLD MAN: You're only old for others. Of course when I look at myself in the mirror, I see that I've got a pretty funny looking face, eh. But inside, I'm still myself, like when I was twenty.

TEENAGER: Well, I don't care anyway. I don't think I'll wait 'til I'm old to croak. I'll die before that.

* * *

[Sequence of photographs showing Simone de Beauvoir gradually getting older. Queneau's "Si tu t'imagines" sung in the background.]

SIMONE DE BEAUVOIR: There is something frightening about every meta-morphosis. I remember when I was little and I realized that one day I would become an adult: that filled me with terror. I did not see how I could be the same person when I would be twenty—which seemed very very far off to me—as I was today when I was perhaps, let's say ten. Consequently, it is not simply the act of passing from adulthood to old age that is disturbing; any passage, when understood as such, is very disturbing. The difference is that when you are young, you think there are many advantages to being a grown-up . . . because you think that you will be much freer, that you'll be able to do lots of things, and so, on the whole, you want to be a grown-up even though the prospect scares you at the same time. Yet as an adult, when you think about growing old, there are no such compensations.

PROFESSOR BOURLIÈRE: Old age, well it's the waiting room for the cemetery. It is the period of our lives when we perform at our worst, both physically and mentally, and it is especially the period in our lives when we have completely lost all ability to adapt to new situations.

SIMONE DE BEAUVOIR: When I wrote *La vieillesse* [*Old Age*], it was mainly to give a voice to all of those men and women who, in a way, had lost theirs, by virtue of having lost their place in society and their power. Old men and women—the elderly—they do not speak and we don't listen to them either; if they were to speak, we would not listen to them, and they are not, as it were, spoken of, because the subject is taboo. Or, if they are discussed, we cheat, we do not tell the truth about their condition. And that is why, essentially, I wrote this book. It is to break this sort of con-spiracy of silence that surrounds old age. Of course, there were also more personal reasons; that is, just as I wanted to understand the condition of women because I am a woman, so I also wanted to know about the condition of the elderly since I myself was entering into this age category. But in any case, the first reason is the most important, that is to give a voice to those who are never heard.

[An elderly couple waltz around a children's playground; autumn leaves lie thick on the ground. They then try, with some difficulty, to cross a busy road.]

TRUCK-DRIVER: Send the old fogies to the cemetery!

SIMONE DE BEAUVOIR: Of course, an old man, since he is not what he used to be, inspires a sort of fear in the adult and the adult has a tendency to distance himself from his life, almost to remove him from sight. However, since adults are nevertheless aware that they will become elderly, there are certain societies in which the long-term interests of the adults make them treat the elderly properly, more or less, since they will become old people themselves. Yet, in our capitalist society, these long-term interests no longer come into play because there are many other reasons, besides a sort of disgust, or fear, to keep the elderly at a distance. These are essentially economic reasons: the elderly can no longer be exploited, as the young can. Now, in the society in which we live, you see, man is viewed as human material, and when this material is no longer useful, it gets thrown away.

* * *

[The small terraced houses of a mining town in Northern France. An older couple from the town standing side by side in their kitchen.]

MAN: Yeah, I was in . . . well, it's not a question of a medal or not . . .

WOMAN: You could speak up.

MAN: . . . yeah, I sort coal . . .

WOMAN: For how long, thirty-five years?

MAN: . . . so, since the law was finally passed and you get retirement three years earlier, it's better to take it for what's left of our lives . . . and work just gets more and more hellish, as they say—well, more and more . . . difficult.

* * *

OLD WOMAN: But to see yourself like that, no longer working, you really feel like you're becoming useless, you know. I don't know if you can understand something like that. So that, that made me even more bitter, then my illness got even worse and I had a nervous breakdown because of that. And so there was this nun who used to come by pretty often to give shots to my neighbor. And I happened to be at my door a lot and she would say, "You don't feel well?" I'd say, "Yeah, I'm fine." Then one time she said, "May I come in?" and I had her come in and then she said, "Get a dog, you'll see." So I got my dog and that really changed my life. [Shown walking dog down the street.]

SIMONE DE BEAUVOIR: Man's life is not at all planned out, in such a way that when he gets to the end he still has interests and even a usefulness; this could be the case if we went about things more humanely. But this is not seen as a problem at all and once the worker has stopped to really serve, to be useful, to give the maximum return, well he's thrown out, and no one cares about how he will live after that, during the years of retirement that remain, no longer doing anything, no longer integrated in society—years that are generally very painful for him.

OLD WOMAN: I sat for entire days, then . . . I . . . well it was long. I didn't accept my retirement like many did.

* * *

[The couple in their kitchen.]

OLD MAN: Retirement, no more salary, it's not that we've got high wages, we'll live more modestly if we have to, but we'll have complete freedom, I call out for my complete freedom. To get up early . . .

OLD WOMAN: . . . then watch television until 11 o'clock.

SIMONE DE BEAUVOIR: There are many old people who long for retirement because they think that retirement will give them leisure time, and consequently freedom. Yet in fact, once they are retired, they see that they have absolutely no use for all this leisure time and that they really don't have freedom. Because, in truth, their lives have been stolen from them, and someone whose life has been stolen no longer knows what to do with the rest of his life because he finds himself with a bit of time to do what he wants.

OLD WOMAN: Staying in the house, relaxing . . .

HE: Oh yes, starting with . . . cleaning the floor, cleaning the fireplace, running errands.

SHE: Well yeah, relaxing, what else is there to do?

* * *

A RETIRED MINER'S WIFE: He worked in the mine, and he's not doing so good. Like all these workers, like all these miners, you know.

TRADE UNIONIST: Retirement age for the miner starts at fifty when his pension begins, and fifty-five for those on the surface, if they are lucky enough to make it that far. Then a whole bunch of ups and downs and worries start at fifty, because if a miner makes it to fifty, he's still got young children; sometimes he's got eight- or ten-year-old kids, school age; others are in the military. Ah, and then, to provide for his family and keep them alive, well the miner, he's there facing all of his poverty.

THE RETIRED MINER: That [indicating a finger], that was cut off at work: I fell. Smashed, and then they cut off the rest. There you have it.

A YOUNG MAN'S VOICE: And the other bit there, your little finger?

RETIRED MINER: My little finger, when I was working, well, a thing fell, and it got caught and that was that.

ANOTHER RETIRED MINER'S WIFE: Him, he never worked down in the mines; he always worked on the surface. Well, I had eleven kids, see. Eleven, madam, that ain't one, you know. I had eight boys and three girls. Pretty soon, we're going to pay the rent, and then . . . sort everything out. That there is for the rent.

HE: We're able to do it because of our little garden.

SHE: But to buy the garden was expensive.

HE: Yep, that's right, yep.

SHE: Twelve hundred francs for it. Yeah, that's hard on the old wallet.

TRADE UNIONIST: The boss, he does everything possible to take advantage of the worker. Exploited not only when he's got him under his thumb, at work, but exploited on his deathbed, at the end of his life. Until the very end, we're exploited. We've got housing, that true. It's valued at, this house of ours—now don't fall over—at about fifty-eight thousand francs per year. We don't have central heat, or a main sewer line. There's no flush toilet; we don't have a bathroom, see? [He points to the outside toilets.] And, you see how we have to . . . you see the doors, how the doors are. Well, I never changed 'em. Then, of course, you'll say, "But there are houses where, . . . there're much nicer houses! They're in better locations. There's this, there's that, there are changes!" Well, you take a look around in the area, like here, and sure you're gonna say, "There are even flowers in the front, there are flower pots, there's everything!" Bahhhh, yeah flowers, we got 'em. You can find 'em on tombstones too. But underneath the flowers, there's a rotting body, a body that was exploited here; flowers, they're no longer any use. Sure, I know well and good that you can ask me, "But why do you go on like this and your friends don't?" Some of them do. They'll tell you. But there's also, you should know, repression afterwards. You have no idea what repression is in the mines! The majority of those who work in the mines are blue-collar workers, they're miners, they're manual laborers.

343

People who've got dirty hands day in day out. They have dirty faces, that's why they're called "black faces," right? And when they finally get their pension, what happens? You find that same difference, social injustice. And this social injustice is still blatant, with this nothing of a pension that he gets, and what happens? They tell him, "Well, now if you want to fix up your house, fix it up at your own expense." And then, on the other hand, you see salaried employees who served the boss well, who were good little servants of the State, eh, who have employee subsidies, subsidized wallpaper and paint. And those engineers, they're even worse. If the wallpaper Ms. Engineer didn't put on the wall no longer pleases her, she just says the word and her husband has it taken away; people come and change it for her. It's happened. There's even one who had the wallpaper changed six times in a year. So you see, these social injustices, they're even worse than you think.

ANOTHER OLD WOMAN FROM THE MINING TOWN: You know, the area around here, it's going to be torn down, so they have these little meetings about what they're going to give to us old people. And so, this is a new life for me, I have a goal, you know. I know that, on a certain day, I have to be there, or that I've got to do something, whereas before I would let myself go. And it's a nice um . . . group of people you have around, you know. Uh . . . you know that when you go out, well, they'll never act strange, I mean, everyone gets along. It's healthy, you know? And you need that; even young people do. There are young people in among us! Well, they don't seem to reject us, and that's what's nice about it. Because the elderly . . . well, old people need young people, like they need us too, you know? And that's what's nice. This camaraderie that's all around us.

* * *

SIMONE DE BEAUVOIR: Naturally, there are cases, privileged cases, where one can retain certain reasons to live; if, for example one has projects that continue until death or even, sometimes, beyond death, as is the case for people, I don't know . . . who, um, who write, who paint, or those who are involved in a political movement that they believe in, well then they keep their interests and their values, their activities still have meaning. However, this is limited to only a small number of people.

[Cut to Marcel Jouhandeau at home, seated in front of pictures of himself from various moments in his life. The camera cuts between him and Beauvoir throughout the scene.]

MARCEL JOUHANDEAU: I knew how to live as a young man and I know how to live as an old one. I don't even know if I am old. A minute ago, I showed you a picture of me from fifteen years ago. I said, "at that time I was old, today, I'm young." I feel younger now than fifteen years ago because I have rid myself of all kinds of preoccupations and passions which, at that time, frequently . . . held me in a state of . . . of . . . of . . . expectation or of . . . of . . . suffering, of . . . I was waiting for something from someone other than myself. Whereas now, I don't expect anything except from myself, and so I have nothing to wish for. My life is a sort of . . . apotheosis!

SIMONE DE BEAUVOIR: Frequently people claim, because it is reassuring, that old age brings with it serenity, that the elderly no longer have passions and live with calm and tranquility in their hearts.

MARCEL JOUHANDEAU: I am at peace, if you wish, with . . . my fellow man. Even with those who hurt me, like Mr. Chancel, in particular, but I am ready to shake his hand.

SIMONE DE BEAUVOIR: But this is entirely mistaken. As soon as you look a bit closer, as soon as you spend time with the elderly, you realize that they're people who have kept all of the passions from their youth or from adulthood, only frequently these passionate interests have taken an extremely tragic turn precisely because they can no longer be assuaged.

MARCEL JOUHANDEAU: For me, there is only one sin, despair. It's the only unpardonable sin, you know? Uh . . . God, being for me, um, goodness itself, cannot allow us to, you know, . . . to feel sorry for ourselves; and as for me, I think that sadness is almost a trespass against God. I'm almost never sad.

[Jouhandeau plays an old harmonium, sings "Magnificat, anima mea" repeatedly. The camera lingers over his contorted, arthritic, fingers. The singing continues as the camera walks towards a state-run nursing home, through the garden. Walks through bleak corridors to the ward for women patients. One female resident sings a song.]

RESIDENT: The head nurse, she said to me, "this isn't where you belong, but we don't have any beds."

SECOND RESIDENT: I'm bored here. I'm bored.

FIRST RESIDENT: I lasted twelve months, twelve. Well, then I couldn't take it any more.

SECOND RESIDENT: Some days I would cry all the time. Especially at night.

345

FIRST RESIDENT: The patients, I won't tell you which ones, they were completely naked, they would walk around, they would come in the . . . between the two beds, they were making gestures with their hands, desperate, like someone who's not quite sane, naturally. Another time, it was an argument, another time she said "I've got a knife," she wanted to kill that nurse there in the chair. I screamed several times, so the nurse came with an orderly, they put her in a bed and then they tied her down.

ANOTHER RESIDENT: Me, I like things calm. When I'd like to eat at home and I see myself here, inside . . . it seems strange.

SINGING RESIDENT: You know, at my age, hmm, I am almost starting to count in . . . hundreds. So of course you start forgetting.

SECOND RESIDENT: I had a problem out in the street, I was out shopping with my little dog and I lost my little dog and his leash. And there was a man who found him in front of the shops, the, the restaurants on the terrace there, and then he says, "But I know you ma'am," and then I say, "Well I don't know you." "I'll take you to my clinic, it's here." He brought me here. He said, "I am your neighbor, not from the same floor but from . . . where you live. I know you, I know your husband." In Lyons, we don't know people because we don't go out there. You work and then you don't see anyone. It's the same in Paris too, you know.

ANOTHER RESIDENT: First you take a walk . . .

ANOTHER RESIDENT [ACCEPTING SOMETHING FROM A TROLLEY]: Oh, yes please.

SECOND RESIDENT [WHO MUST BE OVER EIGHTY]: They're nice, my parents. I still have both of them, and then yeah . . . but what's more is that I don't see them, they don't know that I'm here. My letters didn't reach them because there's a strike going on.

* * *

THIRD RESIDENT: So, you're going to go home ?

FOURTH RESIDENT: To where I grew up.

THIRD RESIDENT: Yes. When ?

FOURTH RESIDENT: Well, in eight days.

THIRD RESIDENT: In eight days, yes, that's changed. That's right. So, you'll see your father . . .

FOURTH RESIDENT : . . . mom . . .

THIRD RESIDENT: . . . and mom. .

* * *

346

SECOND RESIDENT: My dad's a real champ. He's still around. Then he was at the hospital because he looks after wild animals, and . . . in exactly ten days, so when he gets back with his wild animals, there's gonna be a celebration there at home with music and everything and with him in front . . .

SINGING RESIDENT: [sings another song] Oh yeah . . .

SECOND RESIDENT: The department store Printemps had the most interesting branches. I was in charge there. I had employees, the salesgirls, the lil' nurses there, they worked with me. I was their boss. Strange how you run into one another in life.

* * *

[Cut to ward for male patients.]

NURSE: Shall I prop you up again?

PATIENT: Oh, you're nice.

NURSE [TO CAMERA, SLURRING SPEECH]: Oh, it's atrocious, the patients' condition. It's a real freak-show—an awful place. To leave the sick in the state that they are in here—I sincerely find, quite honestly, is to lead them to . . . to their deaths. Oh, some, not all.

PATIENT: Not me yet, eh?

NURSE: Oh, not you, no, not you. I'm taking take care of you!

PATIENT: Let's just say I'm still too young!

NURSE [TO CAMERA]: Look at the lack of personnel we got here. The conditions that these guys are in, . . . there might only be one person here, all alone to feed a room full of 'em, of patients, uh . . . the patient can't take on . . . uh . . . one orderly can't take on the job of feeding everyone. It's not possible. If there's a line then he feeds the ones who are sick; if there isn't, well, what can he do? If they can eat by themselves, they eat. Mr. Lajolie, you can eat by yourself, can't you?

PATIENT: Oh yes. Yes, by myself, uh, by myself with my arm.

NURSE [TO CAMERA]: He's only got one hand. He's only got one hand, see?

PATIENT: This one, yeah, but I've got the other . . .

NURSE [TO CAMERA]: Luckily he has his right hand. Well if he had two paralyzed hands, if there's only one orderly tonight in the room, what can this guy do? Huh? Well, he doesn't eat. He becomes anemic and then, wham, soon he's on an IV, and then he ends up in the morgue.

* * *

[An ambulance with siren and lights going leaves Paris, heading for the state-run nursing home at Nanterre.]

RESIDENT: I left Ivry, they sent me here. It was the head nurse, Mrs. Claude, who sent me. When she punished me, she would always say, "I'm going to send you to Nanterre," saying that at Nanterre everything would be much harsher, that . . . Um, I like it better here than at Ivry, that's because at Ivry I was with the bedridden patients, you know, it's not quite the same, as far as atmosphere. It's much better here. With the cleanliness and the food. Like I told you, it's a bit harsh—that's my only complaint, that's all. Maybe it's inevitable, unavoidable; there are so many people here, right?

[New arrivals at Nanterre. They enter the room, take one of the uniform piles of folded clothes laid out on the floor. A roll call is taking place.]

RESIDENT: He just got out of the baths, just this instant and so . . . If you don't go take a bath, automatically there's a report book and at that time, it's verified afterwards, anyone who doesn't go is punished with a certain punishment, you know, evaluated by the . . . head of . . . the section.

[Pictures of residents pushing trolleys—a punishment?]

VOICEOVER: The bursar of Nanterre says . . .

THE BURSAR: They live in a closed world, one on top of the other. Government employees, too, because many of them are also housed here, lots of government employees, and you live one on top of the other, you don't have any contact with the outside world. Umm . . . if you have friends, you have to . . . Nanterre is far away from everything. You have to go for miles to uh . . . to reimmerse yourself in normal life. Here you find nothing but society's most wretched. It's not exactly fun.

VOICEOVER: The residents of Nanterre say . . .

RESIDENT: Oh, naturally, it's no picnic. Anyway, I don't even want to stay in here. For the slightest reason, you're punished, off you go. I'd rather croak outside than stay in here.

[Camera walks through refectory.]

RESIDENT: For old people like us, it's good to be with people. But there are too many of us. And so they charge us too much. I always worked, I did twenty-five years at Renault, I was a prisoner of war and everything. And they take ninety percent of our pensions.

ANOTHER RESIDENT: They're there to round up my cash. They don't give a damn about anything else. And some days, I'd like you to see what they pass off as food. Come on!

* * *

RESIDENT: I fell ill at the St. Lazare hospital and so I was sent here.

INTERVIEWER: You'll be released?

RESIDENT: No, never. I can't walk, so no way. Well, I'm happy. Everyone is nice.

ANOTHER RESIDENT: I'm all alone in the world, and that's that. There you go.

* * *

RESIDENT: I met my husband on the outside, he offered me a drink. We became acquainted and stayed together for three years without getting married and after three years we decided that we could, uh, that we really could be together, that we could get married. So that was when I decided to get married, I married here. We get fifteen thousand every three months, our food, lodging and laundry are always taken care of, so we have twenty-five hundred in pocket money every month. I take four days of vacation with him when I can, but, unfortunately, we only take three days because, with hotel rooms, it's difficult. With restaurants and everything, we can't . . . We're better off than being out on the streets like . . . I prefer to stay and come back here than be, as they say, "vagrants," you know. Unfortunately, we're separated, but what do you expect? You gotta make, as they say, sacrifices.

SAME RESIDENT: By working, you understand, he doesn't get to do what he wants either. He only gets thirty-five hundred francs a month. That helps him some to buy some little extras, you know, things you need. If you get a hotel room, what's eight thousand francs? Nothing at all. As they say . . . it's just a handful of beans. Oh, it's hard here, just for the slightest little thing . . . I can't get used to it, at night I can't say good night to him. That's right! You know, you really don't sleep at night, so he comes back at seven o'clock so that he'll be here, in what's it called, in the dormitory, and me, I'm leaving the dining hall, so we have the misfortune of seeing each other, and that's all it takes, bing, we get in trouble. So it's hard, you know. It's hard when you're married and especially since you don't ask to stay together for hours and hours, but just to say good night, to say "goodnight, see you in the morning." It's not a big de . . . and well, I get up at six in the morning, at six-thirty he brings me my coffee, but I have to hide! Ah, life in the clink is very, very hard, life's very, very, hard here, very, very. You don't dare turn right, don't dare go to the left, you're always afraid of being found out, for fear of being punished. So, anger got the best of us—we had money, see? So, rue de Flandres, when we saw that they wouldn't pay us, well, we took off, we did the same thing in Rouen, we walked back to Paris afterwards.

HER HUSBAND: She'd never been so happy. Paris - Rouen, Rouen - Paris, Paris - Rouen.

* * *

[A notice reads: "NO RESIDENTS OF THE REGIONAL NURSING HOME AL-LOWED IN THE PARK."]

MAN WHO LIVES NEAR THE NURSING HOME: Oh, there's a whole story with that park! A couple years ago there was a sign that said "No dogs and no residents of the Nanterre nursing home allowed." Well, there was quite a reaction from the residents and since then, well . . . now the sign only says "No residents"!

* * *

[In a café near the state-run nursing home. Many residents drinking large glasses of red wine, most looking and sounding inebriated.]

OLD MAN: If it hadn't been for the racetrack, I wouldn't have landed here, ya know! I used to look after horses to keep my feed bag full. Well, there's lots of players and lots of losers too. The ones who get rich at the track hit the jackpot big time and take cash from poor fools.

OLD WOMAN: I don't complain, I've been here since fifty-six. Well, you know I've never complained. I worked hard and now, naturally, I relax.

FIRST OLD MAN: I'm, well, a grandfather, a great-grandfather twice, and they're not gonna give me that for feeding horses, anyway. Oh, my wife, my wife, oh boy . . . She's remarried maybe. Me, I left, without leaving an address, so uh . . . Hey, I'll show you, you'll see . . . it's in little bits . . . she's my better half that was worth my double . . . that's why this picture . . . you know with me, you'll never get the last word, eh, 'cause I'm a smooth talkin' man . . . There, that's my wife. Unfortunately, I did some stupid things in my life, well, I left, there you have it . . . That's my son . . . a fore-man at Renault, that's my daughter who's a stripper, I don't know if you realized, that ain't honorable; ya can't make a silk purse from a sow's ear, right? Get it? If she scores a wad every night, there's the champagne cock-tails, the freebies. You see, the kids aren't the ones that are gonna feed you, anyway, I never go see them, and they don't come here. I never write . . . I have no interest in that . . .

OLD WOMAN: You know, it's monotonous. You don't always have nice roommates, so we come here to get together sometimes . . .

ANOTHER OLD WOMAN: It's the only fun we have, coming here some like this. And then to see one another like this. Oh yes, to have a little drink, eh. Because at night we have our cocoa, uh, fruit juice, so, um, have to have something solid. You comfort yourself with what you can! Back then, I went out a bit more often, since I was younger, obviously, so, well, one night I let myself come back a little late. Well the punishment—you get forty-five days, forty-five days without going out and no wine. There you go. Isn't that lovely!

ANOTHER OLD WOMAN: . . . if you stagger around, if you talk back, if you're not pleasant, that's it, doesn't take much!

OLD WOMAN [FINISHING]: . . . so we can't go out during that time and we don't have any wine! Our pitiful little glass at noon, not at night, at noon! Well, you know, it's . . . it's small, for me.

ANOTHER OLD WOMAN: And the wine, we pay for it. In our final years, we pay for the wine.

ANOTHER OLD WOMAN : We're still afraid that if by chance you go too far, unfortunately, well, when you get back, they'll take you by the shoulder real nice-like, and then, they put you in a . . . in a cell! All night! Oh yeah, whether you're old or young, it doesn't matter. Oh, but they're strict, very strict, you know; so, well, you gotta watch out! [a bitter laugh]

* * *

[Beauvoir at home in her impeccably tidy flat. She appears first on a balcony, before going downstairs to put on a record. Music. The camera pans around the room: photographs of political demonstrations, souvenirs from her many travels, the trophies of an active and successful life.]

SIMONE DE BEAUVOIR: I think that in every life there is, at one time or another, a sort of line of demarcation that one crosses; there is always a moment, where, looking back, one realizes that in certain ways things will never be the same. For me, for a number of reasons, which, moreover, are set out in *Force of Circumstance*, it was around the time that I finished *Force of Circumstance* that I became aware of this. And, moreover, I was right because, indeed, never again, let's say, would I be able to go for long hikes . . . or in any case, I no longer even have the inclination to do so . . .

I'm not talking about forty kilometers—I would certainly no longer be able to do that—but maybe even ten. I no longer do that; I get about in other ways. I go for rides in the car. So one can find other compensations, naturally, but all the same, when you really loved something, no compensation can ever be entirely adequate.

[Cut to a bed-bound old woman, Mlle Desaux, in a very untidy, even squalid, single-room flat. The flat is presumably cold: she wears her coat in bed.]

MLLE DESAUX: Oh well, back when I was doin' good, that was fine, I would walk through the stores, alone, to warm myself up, but you gotta be able to stay upright too. It's that I needed to sit down quite a lot. Oh, that happens to me in stores sometimes, that I sit down in the stairwell when I'm too tired. One time, there's a salesman, and like that he says to me, "are you tired, ma'am?" "Oh yes, I can't take it any more, that's why I'm sitting on the stairs for five minutes." And here, too, that's certainly happened to me quite a bit getting up the stairs, ya know? If I'm too tired, I sit down on the steps. Oh, and then my blood pressure, okay, okay, then my head . . . Here, now you see it's stopped for a moment, but well, uh . . . at . . . at night, if I want to sleep, there's no way that I . . . it makes my head . . .

SIMONE DE BEAUVOIR: I still want to travel, perhaps less than before, but still some, nonetheless. I still want to see my friends, I still want to read books, to reread books. I mean, I still want to do many things. And that is exactly why I seldom feel old at all, even though I know that I am.

* * *

OLD WOMAN: I was an army nurse, I cared for the . . . all of the men from . . . from every army, one after another. We were right by the front line, I'll tell you! The happiest memory of my life is when I received the Légion d'honneur from Mr. Vincent Auriol himself, in fifty-two. It was my happiest day because I knew that I deserved it. [laughing]

* * *

MLLE DESAUX: I was under state care when I was little. On farms. It was hard, that was long ago. Later, when I was twenty . . . twenty-two, I came back to Paris, I worked in restaurants. I was happy there. I was sort of . . . an assistant, I'd get taxis for clients, or, well, um, what's the . . . or tobacco, or anything, so, there was, uh, I'd get a few little tips and then, you know, all was good. Except when I got too old later, I worked in the kitchens, now that was hard, to work in the kitchens doing . . . because there wasn't any air. That's, um, y'always need air.

SIMONE DE BEAUVOIR: Hello? Ah, hello Liliane, how are you? First of all, tell me if you feel better than you did yesterday. Much better! Good. So, what is it that you are calling about?

SIMONE DE BEAUVOIR: Certainly, yes. Certainly, she will take a taxi . . . Yes, right. . . . And Gérard will come and pick her up in the morning? Good, that's perfect . . . Yes that's right, at her door . . . At six, at her door . . . Absolutely! And thank you. See you tomorrow. Goodbye.

MLLE DESAUX: It happened so fast, I didn't even have time to see it, the . . . the motorcycle. It was coming from the opposite direction. That's why . . . It was going the other way, that's why . . . it came right up on me, while I was looking for my card. Then I was thrown to the ground. Ah, I saw stars! Then I said, "but who pushed me . . . like that?" At the time, I thought it was some man but later, I decided no, to have fallen like that, that's a motorcycle! And then, as I was sprawled out on the ground, I started to hurt, obviously! I heard some guy who said "oh, but you'll be fine, you'll be fine." Ah, and I had got up . . . well it wasn't fine! I had . . . the strength to get on the bus, come home, and then go to bed. But half an hour later, I had to get up and get the neighbors so they could call for help: it wasn't fine. So, he says, "What's wrong?" Well, I said, "Call for help 'cause I've really smashed myself up." Oh, I didn't know where it was coming from, then! Just that it hurt. So the ambulance came and took me to the hospital, and then, that's where they saw that I had a . . . fractured spinal column . . . Well he says, "oh, it's not a big deal, just a little fracture." Great—that's just what I needed—a little fracture! . . . It's slow anyway! Then, at the first chance, I asked 'em—there was this case worker who came by—and I said, "I really want to leave, because I can't stand it here." So the case worker, he says, "Oh well, if she wants to go, let her go. She'll be back!" What? I told 'em, "Well, don't hold yer breath." No, as it happens, I'm here, but I don't wanna go back. And well, he'd given me uh, a . . . some prescriptions . . . Then, well, uh, there were these shots to be given in my muscles. "Oh no . . . !" I said, "No, not that, nothing doing!" I didn't have 'em filled, those prescriptions; except I still had to get a few check-ups. Two times in No . . . November. The exams, and then later, another, um . . . Well, I didn't have the time to go. Because at the exams, um, you know, they poke huge needles in your arm, there, and then the liquid runs into your arm. Oh no, not that, no thank you! No way! I've had enough of shots. Look . . . when was it that I broke my wrist—in January, I had them then, and my wrist never reset! 'Cause the cast was done wrong. It was in January that . . . that it happened. So, not only that, but then after my wrist, it's my back bone and then after that, it never ends.

SIMONE DE BEAUVOIR: There are many people, old people, who are so afraid of nursing homes, of old people's homes, or even of retirement homes, which are slightly more comfortable but where they would none-theless be uprooted from their routines, that . . . they prefer—at least the women, for it is perhaps women who are especially like this—these old women prefer to remain in extremely poor, sad, cold surroundings rather than agreeing to going into a nursing home.

MLLE DESAUX: Ahhhhh. I was down in the dumps that night, with my chest, and I go, "so what, I'm not gonna go to the hospital anyway." And last year, in October, in . . . December, I was still there, in the hospital. Do you realize, I lost my holidays, I lost, what, all of the gifts and everything— I didn't get nothing. Well, that's not gonna happen again this year, un uh! Not counting that now there ain't no more holiday parties, now that I'm not there . . . In the third arrondissement of Paris, it was . . . when I was in the third! But now, everything's different! We had some good parties, with the "Petits Frères," that was on rue . . . rue Saint-Louis-en-l'île. Oh, that was great, to be there then.

* * *

ONE OF THE "PETITS FRÈRES": Uh, the Petits Frères want to live a love-story with their old friends, with those who are poor and alone. And they want to show them this love by giving them that which is most beautiful . . . And that's how, one time, we met and visited with an elderly woman who had had a very difficult life, who had been a maid, for many years, and uh . . . she had never seen the sea. So we wanted to make her dream come true so we took her there. And for her, it was a marvelous thing to discover the sea at the age of ninety-two.

[An old woman walks on the beach, hunched with her stick, in high wind, calling to a dog.]

SIMONE DE BEAUVOIR: There are people who maintain the joy of living at eighty and even beyond, who continue to experience joy in the activities that they liked in the past, whether it be walking, fishing, hunting or riding a bicycle . . . Altogether, there are many, many things that can remain with . . . an . . . old person if he is still capable of adapting and if he has a body

354

that succeeds in adapting to the tastes that he had when he was younger. They are the happiest ones, the most fortunate.

* * *

FIRST WOMAN: How did you meet Robert exactly?

SECOND WOMAN: Well uh, I met him, uh, just like that. I was at the Luxembourg Gardens. Later, obviously, he came to see me, um . . . When we slept together, our first night, we were both apprehensive, both equally so, because we wondered how it would go, and then it went extremely well! . . . And so, now I can honestly say that I have found true love, and finally carnal love, for I must say that at sixty years old I still didn't know what carnal love was. And I've been to bed before once or twice, naturally. I had a husband, I already have a child and all that; I even had an affair, but I didn't—I certainly experienced pleasure, of course . . .

FIRST WOMAN: Yes, so you shouldn't say that you hadn't experienced carnal love . . .

SECOND WOMAN: No . . .

FIRST WOMAN: . . . because you had experienced it. . . . you had nonetheless experienced what is now called, um, what in our day we called "pleasure," right. Now, they say "orgasm."

SECOND WOMAN: Yes.

FIRST WOMAN: That's what they call it.

SECOND WOMAN: Yes.

FIRST WOMAN: So you had experienced it, anyway.

SECOND WOMAN: Um, experienced it, because I have vaginal orgasms.

FIRST WOMAN: Yes.

SECOND WOMAN: There you are.

FIRST WOMAN: Well, I have both kinds.

SECOND WOMAN: Well, having vaginal orgasms, obviously, I experienced a great deal of . . . of satisfaction, of sensual pleasure, during the act itself.

FIRST WOMAN: Yes.

SECOND WOMAN: But I didn't know anything else.

FIRST WOMAN: Right.

SECOND WOMAN: Whereas with Robert I discovered everything.

FIRST WOMAN: You were quite lucky to find Robert, like you say, because, me for example, when I think about it, if I were to meet someone . . . when you see, in life, how things are now, you see these fifty-year-old guys, um, and they want these twenty-year-old cutie-pies, or some thirty-

355

year-old. I'm seventy. So, I'm gonna land some ninety-year-old? Do you see me with a ninety-year-old man? When you imagine uh . . . love—'cause there's no problem, we'll make love . . . Now, I don't have vaginal orgasms, but I need everything else; I need everything! So you see, with a ninety-year-old man, I'd be starting on Monday and we'd still be at it on Saturday! And then, it's appalling, when you see the . . . the . . . bodies, um . . . even though they'll say, uh . . . it's age, it's age . . . a ninety-year-old man, all the same, is not good-looking! If it's a question of making love with a ninety-year-old, if I really wanted to, well that's too bad, I'd rather take care of it myself! . . . I'm not gonna explain to you how I do it . . .

SECOND WOMAN: Yes, but you, you're only thinking about physical love anyway when you say "a sixty-five year old man won't want a seventy-year-old woman." But with love, in my love with Robert, there's more than just the physical side.

FIRST WOMAN: Um, did you talk about it with your kids, about your relationship with um, Robert?

SECOND WOMAN: No, up to now I haven't spoken to them about it. First off, I'm not very close, to tell the truth, with my children and uh . . . I don't know if . . . if I would be able to tell them. Maybe yes, someday, just like that, but somehow, I'll tell them . . . I'll let them . . . well, I'll be completely evasive, because I don't want to tell them the . . . the truth. I mean, if they ask me "do you sleep with him?" I'll tell them "yes," but if they don't ask me, I'm not going to be the one to say, "yes, I sleep with him, we get along well sexually, it's altogether perfect, and so on." I'd just say, "I am very happy with Robert, he's very nice, we get along well . . . uh . . . romantic . . . no, well, yes, romantically, I mean, a great friendship, and so on and so forth." I don't know what I would say. But as far as sex is concerned, I wouldn't talk about it, unless they asked me. Now then, I . . .

FIRST WOMAN: Why wouldn't you?

SECOND WOMAN: Well uh, because I feel that, with my children, there's . . . uh . . . the line is uncrossable, you know . . . First . . . I don't know. I can't explain why exactly, but . . . no.

* * *

TEENAGER: If I saw . . . uh . . . two old people having sex together . . . let's say . . . I'd be a bit surprised, um . . . I don't think I'd be shocked, but let's say, uh . . . it would seem a bit weird to me . . . it'd be . . . I'd need to get sort of used to it . . .

356

SECOND TEENAGER: I don't know about sexual relations between . . . old people, well, it's . . . sometimes it's, it's frequently non-existent, you know . . .

THIRD TEENAGER: Yeah, but there are, like, so many problems for . . . for old people, eighty, eighty-five year olds, you know, there's a ton of problems, it's not possible . . .

* * *

[An old woman, at home, applies make-up and sets a table for two, in anticipation of her lover's arrival.]

OLD WOMAN [SINGING]: Oh oh, my dear . . . A handsome little young man . . . and when I was young, I loved a forty-year-old man—not a young man . . . Oh no! I was in love with a man who looked like a man . . . And I didn't like the young ones . . . Ti lali lala . . . I've become thin and ugly, oh, which makes, hmmm! Tra . . . lali . . . lala . . . Tra . . . lali . . . lala . . . Oh, I'm so happy to be alive! As long as I don't die! It's so good to be alive!

[It gradually becomes clear that her lover is not coming.]

SAME WOMAN [TALKING TO HER CANARY]: Oh you, you're faithful! Are you faithful my dear? Oh yes! You're a pretty little bird! . . . I wouldn't mind a little drink now . . . Yes, my dear!

* * *

[A home for retired artists. An old woman plays the piano to a room of her statue-still fellow residents. She is wearing an overcoat and carpet slippers; they are dressed very formally. One of the residents is shown dancing, somewhat ridiculously, around the gardens of the home.]

* * *

SIMONE DE BEAUVOIR: In the end, it is old age, rather than death, that should be opposed to life . . . Because it could be said of death that it changes a life into a destiny; it does not undermine what a life has been. Whereas old age is really a way of destroying life; indeed it makes a mockery of life. I believe that the condition of the elderly is the least miserable in the country, because, generally, they remain integrated in the familial community. In any case, one would be ashamed to send them to a nursing home. I remember a fifty-year-old farm woman in a little village in Alsace who said to me, "If I sent my father to a home, then everyone would stare and point at me." Whereas in cities, old folks are very

357

frequently herded into homes, and not only that, but these homes are being built further and further away from the downtown areas. And mainly because of this isolation, the old people who are there never get any visitors to speak of; the only people they see, in the end, are each other, that is other old people, and then also those who look after them, which really is an odd contradiction, I mean, an odd paradox: these caregivers, by contrast, are extremely young. And they are very young because generally these are young people without any special qualifications who come from rural areas. Many are from Brittany, for example. And so they're expecting to hit the big time when they get to the big city, and then in the end, since they're not qualified, all that they find is a position as a nurse's aide or an orderly somewhere like this. And to tell the truth, it's very thankless work, because—it's always the same situation—there aren't enough personnel. And . . . it's very destabilizing work, because, in a certain way, it forces the worker not to see these old people as human beings. Because one doesn't have enough time to see them as human, to take the time that would be necessary to speak to them, to persuade them that they need to eat, that they need to do this . . . Thus, they are treated, they are manipulated, as I said, like animals.

* * *

NURSE: Uh, at Champcueil [another state-run nursing home], at least there are some little jobs that really interest the patients, precisely because they get paid for them.

RESIDENT: Ah, ah, ah, well, not a fortune, but still! Three-fifty for every thousand.

* * *

SIMONE DE BEAUVOIR: Have you been a nurse at Champcueil for long?

NURSE: For two months.

SIMONE DE BEAUVOIR: What were your first impressions?

NURSE: Very, very bad, uh, first impressions, because I thought that I was going to work closely with the elderly a great deal, well, that the old people, that they would be happy. We'd be nice to them, they'd be nice to us . . . Then, in fact, no, that wasn't how it was at all . . . For me, in the first division, uh . . . the old people uh . . . well, we have to put up with being almost insulted . . . um . . . It was a big disappointment at first.

SIMONE DE BEAUVOIR: But don't you think that, overall, even if you're very nice to them, give them plenty of attention, don't you think that it is very difficult to be locked up in one place like this? Completely separated from the rest of society, in a type of segregation, almost?

NURSE: That's what I used to think, but, . . . um, . . . being here, . . . uh, . . . when I see certain bums who are so mean, in spite of everything that we do for them, . . . um, . . . It makes me wonder . . . me too, right now, I'm just locked up too. I'm free in the evenings, but sometimes, I don't take advantage of it. That really was my first impression, because what am I doing? Huh? . . . I eat dinner and then afterward, I collapse into bed, and the week goes by, and that's how it is for me. Consequently, there are times when I say to myself, "They're there in their beds, they're fifty, they're sixty years old; I'm only thirty," and basically, I think that me too, being in an old folks home, well, I'm kind of burying myself.

SIMONE DE BEAUVOIR: Yes, but you can always leave, you have, as they say, "your life in front of you."

NURSE: Umm . . .

SIMONE DE BEAUVOIR: While they, they don't have anything ahead of them now except the prospect of slowly, slowly wasting away and then dying here. They are abandoned by their families, they are abandoned by everyone, and then they feel that . . . in the eyes of young people—even if the young people are rather nice and devoted—they more or less disgust them, they're seen as ugly, they're seen as unpleasant. So they stay here, they are here and they are very unhappy. It can't be much fun to be here, I don't think that anyone would really choose to be here to finish his life. Perhaps it's difficult when you're young, like you are, to realize just how painful it can be to be weakened, old, cut off from the world and to no longer have a position, a role, to no longer work. . . . To no longer have, basically, anything in life but small animalistic pleasures, like eating—generally substandard—I don't know how it is here, but generally in nursing homes the food is bad—so, they don't even have that.

NURSE: Hey,. . . . uh, everything that you just said there, that's really how I thought, um really, before I got here. It's—really—but . . . um . . . When I just said all that, uh, I wasn't really talking about the whole situation, uh, just certain patients. It's a fact that when you're here . . . Personally, I know that when I come to work, I know that I'm there for certain patients and that really pleases me! That doesn't take away all that . . . all that's . . . for the patients who are bedridden, who cannot talk.

SIMONE DE BEAUVOIR: I think that the lot of the patients who are truly bedridden, who are truly sick, who are half asleep all day long is less painful because they are unaware.

NURSE: Yes, but, uh, personally, what I don't understand is that there are very few um . . . old people, chronically ill, who go to physical therapy, for example. I don't understand their passiveness. Their passiveness is a reflection of what they used to be in life. There's no question there . . .

SIMONE DE BEAUVOIR: No, I don't believe that at all. It is perhaps those who were the most active during their lives who cannot content themselves with these little "activities." Because, what is physical therapy? It's nothing in the end. When you had work that interested you, that had meaning, that gave you a salary, that gave meaning to your life . . . It meant something too because you earned a salary, you supported people. After that they tell you to have a good time. I'm not going to weave baskets! Things like that . . . you find that ridiculous, it's a kind of affront. All of the inauthentic activities that are offered to you seem ersatz; they seem pathetic. Going to the movies, listening to a concert . . . a concert, reading, unless it has a purpose and is productive in some way, for the purpose of making memories or discussing it with others . . . So, everything that is offered to old folks, basically, in nursing homes and even quite frequently outside nursing homes when one is retired, is to kill time. This precisely because society wasn't able to give them reasons to live, and reasons to live that continue through old age.

NURSE: Um, I think, uh, that, someone uh, who can go, uh, see a movie and talk about it with someone else, that will always be useful to them, and it will ease their loneliness.

SIMONE DE BEAUVOIR: It has no purpose, they are very well aware of that, and precisely, everything that is offered to them are these completely sterile activities. Because even if they talk about it a bit with their neighbor, that's not real communication, that's not enriching. Enriching for what? In order to feel enriched, you have to have projects, goals, you need to have plans; you need to still want to do something, whatever it may be.

NURSE: And that, that's on the level of . . .

SIMONE DE BEAUVOIR: It's precisely not on the level of what happens in nursing homes because they really are cut off from everything. It's certainly not by chance that half of the people who retire die within a year of their retirement.

NURSE: Oh that, well, that's terrible . . .

SIMONE DE BEAUVOIR: . . . and it happens to I don't know how many.

NURSE: Oh, well, that's terrible; but personally, if I were old and I was in a nursing home, if I could do lots of stuff, well I'd say to myself, "well, great," everything I wasn't able to do in my life . . .

SIMONE DE BEAUVOIR: . . . But that, that wouldn't happen to you if you were old. You can't understand just how much you'd be missing . . .

NURSE: . . . yes, but what am I . . .

SIMONE DE BEAUVOIR: . . . It's that, you see, you'll be unsatisfied . . .

NURSE: . . . yes, but will I ever even be old?

SIMONE DE BEAUVOIR: . . . but you don't picture yourself old in a nursing home, you see yourself, as you are now, in a house, which would offer you possibilities. And you think that you would take advantage of them. But that's not what old age is, that's exactly what I mean . . .

NURSE: But do we . . . will we ever be old? That's the question. . . .

SIMONE DE BEAUVOIR: . . . old age is to be cut off from all possibilities. This is another problem. Maybe it's not a good thing to be old.

NURSE: No, it might not be a good thing, but . . .

SIMONE DE BEAUVOIR: . . . there're cases where being young isn't all that great either.

NURSE: But at thirty, will you . . . yeah, will you make it to fifty or sixty?

SIMONE DE BEAUVOIR: You don't have the same problems and you don't have the same ways of reacting as when your future has been completely cut off from you. Particularly in nursing homes, precisely where you no longer belong to the human community; it's segregation, in any case, which is, in itself, something terrible.

* * *

DR BALIER, PSYCHIATRIST: One of the fundamental problems is obviously the problem of loneliness, which comes up again and again. But . . . loneliness is different from . . . from isolation, if you will. Isolation: well, you either have, or don't have, people around you. Loneliness: that's something more intimate, it's something that is felt from the inside and many old people complain of feeling lonely even when they have someone around them. And what plays a very important role, is that they really feel that . . . um, they need contact . . . uh, not only human warmth, but real physical contact with another body. And they can no longer have that because people . . . people don't want to uh, touch them and the old people themselves feel, um, an extreme modesty . . . um, in touching others or asking, in one way or another, for this body contact. So you can understand their extreme pleasure, a pleasure that has an enormous psychological importance, in living with younger people, with young people and in being able to interact with young people. And I believe that this is how one can also understand certain, certain joys like for example in clubs or community centers, the pleasure of dancing, for example, with young people.

[An old man feeds birds in a park. A young man kisses old people at a day center or similar. Old people shown dancing with younger and participating in organized visits. Two of those at the dance return home. They prepare for bed extremely slowly, fumbling for items of clothing; their speech is nearly unintelligible.]

SHE: What? . . . Ah . . . pajama bottoms, we need to find them.
HE: Good night, sweetie.
SHE: Good night, dear. Sleep well.
HE: Yes, sleep well.

* * *

[Many of those featured in the film give their ages and former occupations.]

— I am seventy years old and I was a cleaning lady.
— I am seventy years old and I always stayed at home.
— Tax advisor and I am ninety-one years old.
— I am sixty-two years old and I work as a coal-sorter.
— I am sixty-five years old and I made garment linings in the textile industry.
— Eighty-seven years old, writer.
— I was a school teacher in the country and I am sixty-one years old.
— I am sixty-five years old and a miner. I work on the surface.
— I am an old artist. I am eighty-three years old now. My mother and father were artists, I started at the age of five.
— I am sixty-eight, the twentieth of December this year, and my profession, I am a rope-maker and I worked in the building industry. I first started in the building industry at the age of fourteen.
— I was a seamstress; I am seventy years old.
— I am eighty-four years of age.
— I was a linen maid, I was a chambermaid, I was a governess.
— I am a pianist, a disciple of the maestro Francis Planté, who was a great friend of Liszt, with whom he gave concerts throughout Europe. Now, I am ninety-one.
— I am seventy-one years old, I was at the Post Office for twenty-two years.
— I was a dancer, I traveled widely throughout the world, I am seventy-six years old.

— I am sixty-six years old and I had one job, always standing: I made garment linings in the textile industry.

— Women's and men's hairdresser, sixty-eight-and-a-half years old. All of my teeth and not a gray hair on my head.

[Picture of Mlle Desaux, who died at the age of 84. This film is dedicated to her.]

* * *

[Beauvoir walks around a cemetery.]

SIMONE DE BEAUVOIR: My relationship with death has changed considerably over the course of my life, because when I was young, death for me was truly outrageous. I was, I wouldn't say afraid, but I was horrified by it. Perhaps because when you are young, you more or less feel, you believe yourself to be more or less immortal, and so the idea of being annihilated runs counter to everything that you feel in your consciousness, everything that you live and believe. And then, little by little, things eased, that is death is no longer as horrifying to me as it was when I was twenty or thirty. Perhaps because I know that you can only avoid death by sinking deeper—you can never really escape it, of course—but by sinking deep into old age and it's obvious that old age is not a terribly desirable state, especially, well, a state of advanced old age, and not one that I hope to perpetuate. I don't know, for example, how I will be when I am ninety years old, for example. So I don't recoil at the thought that the eighty-year-old woman that I will be will disappear from the face of the earth, whereas I couldn't bear to think that the thirty- or forty-year-old woman I was might disappear from the face of the earth. This is how my relationship with death has changed: that is, in a certain way, my disgust at old age is greater than my horror of dying.

[A black cat crosses her path, behind her, as she leaves the cemetery.]

THE END

NOTES

Alexander Hertich would like to thank Oliver Davis for his helpful suggestions for the translation.

Contributors

MICHAEL ARTIME earned a BA from McKendree University in 2003 and an MA from the University of Missouri in the field of political science in 2009. Currently, he is completing his dissertation through the Department of Political Science doctoral program at the University of Missouri–St. Louis.

SYLVIE LE BON DE BEAUVOIR, the adopted daughter of Simone de Beauvoir, is editor of several volumes by Simone de Beauvoir, including *Lettres à Sartre* (1990); *Journal de guerre* (1990); *Lettres à Nelson Algren: Un amour transatlantique* (1997); *Correspondance croisée*, with Jacques-Laurent Bost (2004); and *Cahiers de jeunesse* (2008).

DEBRA BERGOFFEN is emerita professor of philosophy at George Mason University and the Bishop Hamilton Lecturer of Philosophy at American University. She is the author of *The Philosophy of Simone de Beauvoir: Gendered Phenomenologies, Erotic Generosities*; *Contesting the Politics of Genocidal Rape: Affirming the Dignity of the Vulnerable Body*; and the coeditor of *Confronting Global Gender Justice: Human Rights, Women's Lives.*

OLIVER DAVIS, PHD, teaches in the Department of French Studies at the University of Warwick. Recent and forthcoming publications include "Eastwood Reading Beauvoir Reading Eastwood: Combative Self-Assertion in *Gran Torino* (2008) and *Old Age* (1970)," in *Existentialism and Contemporary Cinema: A Beauvoirian Perspective*, ed. Ursula Tidd and Jean-Pierre Boulé (Oxford: Berghahn, 2012), *Jacques Rane* (Polity, 2010), *Age Rage and Going Gently: Stories of the Senescent Subject in Twentieth-Century French Writing* (Rodopi, 2006), and "The Radical Pedagogies of François Bon and Jacques Rancière," *French Studies* 64 :2 (April 2010): 178–91.

KIM ALLEN GLEED is associate professor of English at Harrisburg Area Community College. She has a PhD in comparative literature with a concentration in translation studies from Binghamton University, State University of New York. She is also a freelance translator with over a dozen book-length publications.

LAUREN GUILMETTE is a graduate student in philosophy at Emory University. She graduated from Williams College in 2008, where she wrote an honors thesis on feminist interpretations of Sade and the role of the mother in *La philosophie dans le boudoir* (*Philosophy in the Bedroom*). In 2010, she presented a paper on Beauvoir's reading of Sade at the Society for Phenomenology and Existential Philosophy (SPEP), which was published in *Philosophy Today*. Lauren is currently in the early stages of a dissertation on affect theory and ethics.

ALEXANDER HERTICH is associate professor of French at Bradley University. His translation of René Belletto's novel *Dying* was published in 2010. In addition to translating he has written about Jean-Philippe Toussaint, Raymond Queneau, and other modern French novelists.

ELEANORE HOLVECK (1942–2009) was associate professor in the philosophy department at Duquesne University, where she initiated the Women's and Gender Studies Center and served, during the 1990s, as chair of the philosophy department. Her specializations were the philosophical novel and the ethics of Immanuel Kant. She authored *Simone de Beauvoir: Philosophy of Lived Experience* (2002).

SONIA KRUKS is the Danforth Professor of Politics at Oberlin College, where she teaches political theory. She is the author of numerous works on the social and political ideas of the French existentialists, including Simone de Beauvoir. Her most recent book is *Retrieving Experience: Subjectivity and Recognition in Feminist Politics*.

FREDERICK M. MORRISON (1943–2007) was associate professor of Spanish in the Department of Foreign Languages and Literature at Southern Illinois University Edwardsville. The translator and annotator, Véronique Zaytzeff, began collaborating with him in 1991. Their work includes *Musorgsky Remembered*, sections of *Shostakovich Reconsidered*, and Beauvoir's "Literature and Metaphysics" in *Philosophical Writings* (2004) and "Merleau-Ponty and Pseudo-Sartreanism" (in this volume).

JULIEN S. MURPHY is founding director of the Bioethics Project and professor of philosophy at the University of Southern Maine. She is the author of *The Constructed Body: AIDS, Reproductive Technology and Ethics* (1995), editor of *Feminist Interpretations of Jean-Paul Sartre* (1999), and coeditor of *Gender Struggles: Recent Writings in Feminist Philosophy* (2002).

VIRGINIA PRESTON is a PhD student in the Department of Drama at Stanford. She studies early modern performance and comes to theater research via contemporary dance. She holds a BA from Concordia and an MA from SUNY Binghamton in comparative literature and translation. Her research areas are spectacle, transmediality, transnationalism, dis/ability, and francophone artists.

MARILYN GADDIS ROSE, founding director of the translation program at Binghamton University, brought many women writers a larger audience by the SUNY Press Series "Women Writers in Translation."

JUSTINE SARROT, a French student of International Marketing and Management at SIUE from 2001–2, is currently working in customer relationship management and client satisfaction development with Primagaz.

KAREN L. SHELBY teaches in the Department of Political Science and International Relations at the University of San Diego. She earned her doctorate in Women and Politics from Rutgers University. Her areas of interest include gender and politics, women's political activism, and women's empowerment through creative arts.

MARGARET A. SIMONS, Distinguished Research Professor Emerita, Southern Illinois University Edwardsville, is author of *Beauvoir and The Second Sex* (1999); editor of *Feminist Interpretations of Simone de Beauvoir* (1995) and *The Philosophy of Simone de Beauvoir: Critical Essays* (2006); and coeditor of Beauvoir's *Philosophical Writings* (2004), *Diary of a Philosophy Student: 1926–27* (2006), *Wartime Diary* (2009), and *"The Useless Mouths" and Other Literary Writings* (2011).

SUSAN RUBIN SULEIMAN is the C. Douglas Dillon Professor of the Civilization of France and professor of comparative literature at Harvard University. She is the author or editor of many books, including *Crises of Memory and the Second World War* (2006) and most recently *French Global: A New Approach to Literary History* (2010), coedited with Christie McDonald. Suleiman has received many honors, including a Guggenheim Fellowship, a Rockefeller Humanities Fellowship, and several NEH Fellowships; she has been decorated by the French government, as Officer of the Order of Academic Palms.

MARYBETH TIMMERMANN is a certified French to English translator of the American Translators Association, and recently taught an online translation course for the University of Illinois at Urbana-Champaign. She was a contributing translator to Beauvoir's *Philosophical Writings* (2004) and *"The Useless Mouths" and Other Literary Writings* (2011), assistant editor of *Philosophical Writings* and *Diary of a Philosophy Student: 1926–1927* (2006), and coeditor with Margaret A. Simons of *"The Useless Mouths" and Other Literary Writings* (2011).

ANDREA VELTMAN is associate professor of philosophy at James Madison University. She is editor of *Social and Political Philosophy* (Toronto: Oxford University Press, 2008) and coeditor of *Oppression and Moral Agency* (Special Issue of *Hypatia*, 2009) and *Evil, Political Violence and Forgiveness* (Lanham, Md.: Rowman and Littlefield/Lexington, 2009). She has published articles on Simone de Beauvoir, Jean-Paul Sartre, and Hannah Arendt and is currently working on a book on meaningful work.

WILLIAM WILKERSON is professor of philosophy and chair at the University of Alabama Huntsville. He is coeditor, with Jeffrey Paris, of *New Critical Theory: Essays on Liberation* and the author of *Ambiguity and Sexuality: A Theory of Sexual Identity*. He is currently writing a book on the body and editing a collection of essays (with Shannon Mussett) on Simone de Beauvoir for SUNY Press.

VÉRONIQUE ZAYTZEFF (1937–2010) was associate professor emerita in the Department of Foreign Languages and Literature at Southern Illinois University Edwardsville. She translated from French and Russian. Her translations include *Musorgsky Remembered*, several articles in *Shostakovich Reconsidered*, and Beauvoir's "Literature and Metaphysics" and "Merleau-Ponty and Pseudo-Sartreanism." She collaborated on translations with Frederick M. Morrison until his untimely death in 2007.

Index

BOOKS IN THE BEAUVOIR SERIES

Edited by Margaret A. Simons and
Sylvie Le Bon de Beauvoir

Philosophical Writings
  Edited by Margaret A. Simons
  with Marybeth Timmermann
  and Mary Beth Mader
  and Foreword by
  Sylvie Le Bon de Beauvoir

*Diary of a Philosophy Student:
Volume 1, 1926–27*
  Edited by Barbara Klaw,
  Sylvie Le Bon de Beauvoir,
  and Margaret A. Simons,
  with Marybeth Timmermann and
  Foreword by Sylvie Le Bon de Beauvoir

Wartime Diary
  Edited by Margaret A. Simons
  and Sylvie Le Bon de Beauvoir
  Translation and Notes by
  Anne Deing Cordero and Foreword
  by Sylvie Le Bon de Beauvoir

*"The Useless Mouths" and Other
Literary Writings*
  Edited by Margaret A. Simons
  and Marybeth Timmermann and
  Foreword by Sylvie Le Bon de Beauvoir

Political Writings
  Edited by Margaret A. Simons
  and Marybeth Timmermann and
  Foreword by Sylvie Le Bon de Beauvoir

The University of Illinois Press
is a founding member of the
Association of American University Presses.

Designed by Copenhaver Cumpston
Composed in 10.25/13 Adobe Minion Pro
with FF Meta display
by Barbara Evans
at the University of Illinois Press
Manufactured by Sheridan Books, Inc.

UNIVERSITY OF ILLINOIS PRESS
1325 South Oak Street   Champaign, IL 61820-6903
www.press.uillinois.edu